MOMENTS OF TRUTH

To the best of us

Dame Margaret Clark

MOMENTS OF TRUTH

The New Zealand General Election of 2014

Edited by Jon Johansson and Stephen Levine

VICTORIA UNIVERSITY PRESS

TE WHARE WĀNANGA O TE ŪPOKO O TE IKA A MĀUI

VICTORIA
UNIVERSITY OF WELLINGTON

VICTORIA UNIVERSITY PRESS

Victoria University of Wellington

PO Box 600 Wellington

vup.victoria.ac.nz

A catalogue record for this book is available from
the National Library of New Zealand

Printed by Printstop, Wellington

CONTENTS

Media Perspectives

The 2014 Parliamentary Elections – The Campaign and the Results

Images

Figures

Tables

On 3 December 2014 it was my pleasure to welcome the Prime Minister, Members of Parliament, parliamentary staff (and interns), journalists, academics and members of the public to the Legislative Council Chamber for the Victoria University of Wellington 2014 post-election conference. This book – *Moments of Truth* – is the result of that conference.

The Legislative Council Chamber was a fitting venue for a conference on the 2014 New Zealand general election. Only six weeks earlier, on 21 October, we had gathered there to hear the speech from the throne delivered by the Governor-General; and so began the 51st Parliament, its members chosen at the 20 September election.

One of the pleasing aspects of an election campaign dominated by so-called 'dirty politics' was the increase in voter turnout after effectively 30 years of steady decline.

I remember the proponents of MMP arguing before its adoption that MMP would increase voter turnout. Since its adoption in 1996, however, the general trend has regrettably been the opposite. So it is pleasing to see a slight upturn, and it is to be hoped that academics (and others) will reflect on what can be done to ensure that more people accept their civic responsibility and take a few minutes out of their lives once every three years to cast a vote.

As a politician who has been actively involved in nine election campaigns, nothing annoys me more than meeting potential voters who say that they have no intention of voting because they cannot be bothered. Their excuse is often that their vote won't count, but it is well understood that under MMP every vote counts in determining the ultimate election result. This is something strongly recognised by both major political parties. In the recent campaign each talked about 'the missing million' voters and the crucial need to target these as potential influencers of the final result.

As Speaker, I travel overseas annually and when I recall visits to countries such as Myanmar – where I have met people who have been prepared to fight to the death for the right to be able to exercise a vote for democracy – it makes me appreciate how lucky we in New Zealand are to have free and democratic elections.

With regard to the 2014 New Zealand election, and the 77.9 per cent voter turnout, I do wonder whether the increased turnout was due to the efforts of the Electoral Commission, who led an active campaign to inform and encourage voters to cast their vote early if that was more convenient to them, and increased the number of polling places open two-and-a-half weeks prior to election day. The polarising nature of this particular campaign, and the influence of some larger-than-life characters, may actually have galvanised some more laid-back, apathetic New Zealanders to express an opinion via the ballot box.

One final point that was of interest to me on election night was the immediacy of the advance vote count after the polls had closed at 7 o'clock. As those results were available by 7:15 that evening, I was intrigued as to whether that early result was likely to closely reflect the result of votes cast on election day itself after those votes were finally tallied around 11 pm.

I recall particularly the 2005 election, which I watched with some nervousness, with the early results shifting substantially as larger polling places delivered their results and the overall outcome altered significantly. As it turned out, in this year's election the advance vote tallies closely mirrored the final result.

These are some brief thoughts and reflections from a humble sheep farmer from Banks Peninsula who happens to be privileged to be elected to Parliament and honoured to be Speaker of the House of Representatives.

It was my privilege to host and introduce the conference on which this book is based, and I commend the effort, through works such as these, to contribute to a more informed and politically engaged electorate.

Rt Hon David Carter
Speaker,
New Zealand House of Representatives

PREFACE

Jon Johansson and Stephen Levine

John Key greeted the election year, 2014, in Hawaii, seeing in the new year in the same surroundings as the US President, Barack Obama, the two of them extending the latter's remarkably numerous presidential outings to golf courses by playing a round together on the course at the US Marine Corps base at Kaneohe Bay, on Oahu. The Prime Minister became one of only a select few (outside family, friends and advisors) – including former president Bill Clinton – to be invited to golf with the President. *Time* magazine subsequently reported that 'it was the 160th round of golf of Obama's presidency, but only the 10th that included a fellow office holder' (Chris Wilson 2014).

In early January 2015 both men were back in Hawaii.

In between – from one January to the next – each had had to face challenges of one kind or another, both personal and political. These included renewed scrutiny from voters. In November's US mid-term elections – elections that the President himself, though not on the ballot, had said, perhaps unwisely, were about him and his policies – Obama's Democrats suffered sweeping defeats at every level.

In New Zealand, by contrast, parliamentary elections held on 20 September brought John Key renewed success. His National Party won its third successive general election, while its principal opponent, the Labour Party, saw its share of the vote (25.1 per cent) slump to levels not approached since 1922 (23.7 per cent). On election night – to chants of 'three more years!' – Key told an enthusiastic gathering that they had 'kept the faith' (Norquay 2014).

It was a euphoric evening for a man who has never yet lost an election. In winning a third term as prime minister, Key had once again beaten Obama – the results of their competition on the golf course are open to speculation – achieving something which a US president is politically and constitutionally unable to attain. Key's third term also put him in relatively rare company in New Zealand: he is only the eighth person to lead his party to three successive general election victories.

Political scientists sometimes consider whether taking part in an election (i.e., voting) represents a rational choice. Indeed, asking why people would choose to take time out to vote is a reasonable question. There are costs to voting, though these are moderate: the time spent in maintaining voter enrolment; in making decisions about parties, leaders and candidates; and in casting a ballot. There are also benefits to voting; although an individual may be unable to see the value of their own particular vote among the many being cast – thousands in an electorate, millions (2,405,622 valid party votes in 2014) in the country as a whole – there can be satisfactions in making the effort to meet one's civic responsibility, and in making a choice, acting on one's preferences. Yet these are to a considerable extent largely intangible, and for some they are insufficiently urgent or attractive. How to induce eligible voters to take part in an election – to actually vote – is an item on every party's agenda. Participation in an election in a country where voting is not, after all, compulsory (as indeed it very seldom is anywhere, Australia among the few exceptions) is not something politicians or political parties can in any way take for granted.

The 2014 election saw various strategies employed to attract people to the polls. There were, as ever, billboards erected all across the country, in every electorate and community of any size, put up by the supporters of parties (and sometimes vandalised by their adversaries). New Zealand's Electoral Commission made its three-yearly effort to educate voters about the moderate intricacies of the two-choice (parties and candidates) MMP system. Its advertisements exhorting young people, in particular, to register and to vote were on television and radio; in newspapers and magazines; online and in bus shelters. The popular New Zealand singer Lorde, at age 17 too young herself to vote, was induced to encourage young New Zealanders to exercise the choice presently denied to her.

The governing party's principal asset, John Key, was highlighted by National as its main attraction. His name was only on the ballot in one electorate – Helensville, northwest of Auckland, where he was his party's candidate for re-election as a Member of Parliament. He took part in one Helensville candidates' debate, on 11 August, held under strict procedural rules, being given a final warning from the chair that he would be expelled if there was any further misbehaviour (Trevett 2014b). But Key's photograph, beside that of the local electorate candidate, was on virtually every National Party billboard, and in virtually every National Party advertisement. For what the 2014 election promised – for New Zealanders as a whole as well as for National's own voters – was, in essence, more of the same: stable government, provided by an experienced group of Cabinet ministers, led by John Key. For New Zealanders happy with that prospect – or unpersuaded that any of the possible alternatives could be expected to do any better – the choice was clear: a vote for National was a vote for a government led by John Key. For New Zealanders unhappy with such an outcome there were, inevitably, a range of possibilities, none of them entirely clear-cut but all of them having Labour leader David Cunliffe as prime minister.

This book, *Moments of Truth*, tells the story of how New Zealanders came to endorse three more years of a Key-led government. In a sense each New Zealand voter experienced their own 'moment of truth' when casting their ballot. For that is, ultimately, what an election comes down to – a moment when each eligible person, weighing up the options and the consequences (for their community, their country and, for the more sensitive, their conscience), decides whether and how to vote.

When John Key, secure in the pleasure of having won a third term and an overwhelming victory over Labour, stated on election night that his supporters had 'kept the faith', it is undeniable that among those keeping the faith was the Prime Minister himself. Of course, political figures, facing an electorate, need to feel, and display, self-confidence. How else to come forward, urging others to vote for you? After six years as prime minister, Key preserved faith in himself – in his competence, his policies, his leadership. He could hardly be unmoved by opinion polls regularly attesting to his popularity and personal likeability. His rapport with world leaders, President Obama among them, and also conspicuously encompassing members of the British Royal Family, could also hardly fail to have some effect on his self esteem. Comfortable with his countrymen, seemingly unaffected by the trappings of office, Key's faith in his capacity to lead New Zealand was among the qualities that enabled him to prevail in a brief election campaign punctuated by challenges that might have unnerved, and in due course unseated, a less robust personality.

This book draws its title from one of these events, a remarkable gathering of household names – Edward Snowden and Julian Assange among them – for anyone following the news over the past several years about US government-sponsored electronic surveillance of both its own citizens and those elsewhere. Pledged to a new 'first commandment' – 'thou shalt do nothing to threaten the national security of the United States' – US intelligence agencies and operatives proceeded righteously and without inhibition to seek out and identify any individuals whose messages, conversations or behaviour might seem, to them, to be a source of potential peril. To what extent have New Zealand residents been targeted? And to what extent were New Zealand intelligence agencies (and those who, like the Prime Minister, are responsible for oversight of their conduct) involved in such activities? These were the larger questions – interwoven with more peculiar ones – with which New Zealand's 2014 election campaign became embroiled in its final week.

It is tempting, in the light of election results which saw the same parties and prime minister in power at the end as were present at the beginning, to regard the election as one in which there was, after all, no change. But there *were* changes. Can 'moments of truth' leave no impact on those who experience them? Once caught up in a web of surveillance and suspicion can a country ever entirely disentangle itself? Other campaign sensations involved allegations of 'dirty politics', as leaked emails revealed communications between ministers and bloggers that gave a less than elevated view of what takes place in Beehive offices. If the at times bizarre and unexpected features of the 2014 election campaign were akin to a bout of binge drinking, the lingering aftermath involved the blurred and fading memories of a somewhat disorienting national hangover.

***

Moments of Truth tells the story of the 2014 election from a variety of perspectives, including those of participants, political party leaders among them, but also a selection of journalists, commentators, pollsters and academic observers. Many of the authors share the view that the election was almost astonishingly peculiar: 'a most unusual campaign' (Prime Minister John Key); 'one of the most extraordinary and unpredictable campaigns of the modern era' (Andrew Little); 'a bit of a circus' (Russel Norman); 'one weird turn after another' (Nicola Kean); 'chaos and mayhem . . .' (Kate McMillan). It was an election that could have been set in the Twilight Zone, suspended somewhere between 'the pit of man's fears and the summit of his knowledge', though perhaps closer to the former than the latter.[1]

This book is the tenth in a series of publications on New Zealand's general elections, beginning with a conference held just after the 1987 election. Each book has had its beginnings with a post-election conference, held as close to the election as possible while allowing participants a degree of time to gather their thoughts and regain at least a measure of detachment.

At the same time, the 2014 election book adopts a somewhat different approach from that of its predecessors. In March, anticipating the likelihood of John Key winning a third term as prime minister – an expectation based on opinion polls that consistently found him ahead of Labour leaders (first David Shearer, then David Cunliffe) as preferred prime minister, and National far ahead of Labour in voters' preferences – he was invited to open the 2014 post-election conference, reflecting on the significance of his victory. The Prime Minister agreed, with only one condition: that, following the election, he would indeed still *be* prime minister. When that came to pass he was indeed present at the Legislative Council Chamber to give the keynote speech, and that speech, only slightly revised, is to be found as chapter 5, beginning the section on political party perspectives towards the election.

John Key launched the previous two books in this series – *Key to Victory* (on the 2008 election) and *Kicking the Tyres* (on the 2011 election). In doing so he was the first prime minister to have launched any of the books in this series. Similarly, in December 2014 his participation at the post-election conference marked the first time that a prime minister had taken part in one of these gatherings. Accordingly, John Key's chapter in this book represents the first such contribution to one of these election books from a New Zealand prime minister, and we acknowledge at the outset our gratitude for his participation, and for the support given by members of his team on the Beehive's ninth floor. It might also be said that, as editors, we have gained an author but lost a book launch speaker.

The decision to invite the Prime Minister, and his acceptance of our invitation, had consequences for the post-election conference and for this book. The pattern for these post-election conferences and books has been well established: a speaker from each party that succeeded in gaining representation in Parliament offers a perspective on their party's campaign – what worked, what didn't – and the outcome. Over the years the political party speakers have come from a variety of backgrounds: campaign organisers; parliamentary candidates; and party leaders (from the smaller political parties).

On this occasion, and with this book, having invited the Prime Minister it was decided to invite every other party leader to take part. Each agreed to do so and this book reflects those choices, though the outcome of our planning did not come without complications. David Cunliffe was originally invited to speak at the conference; his executive assistant put the invitation in his diary. Subsequently, with Labour choosing a new leader, Andrew Little was invited to participate, allowing Labour's new leader to look back at the campaign and forward towards the new Parliament and the next election. In fact, it was an invitation put in the new leader's diary even before that diary belonged to Andrew Little. Fortunately, the entry was subsequently removed from David Cunliffe's diary, sparing conference organisers the embarrassment of two Labour leaders, one past, one present, each expecting to speak.

John Key's welcome contribution to the proceedings had further consequences. With the Prime Minister offering a higher-level and more personal perspective on the campaign, it was necessary to provide for a second contribution from a speaker representing the National Party. As previously – he has contributed to the 2005, 2008 and 2011 conferences and books – National's campaign coordinator, Cabinet minister Steven Joyce, was able to provide the more detailed perspective on how National dealt with its various 2014 campaign challenges.

Mr Joyce's chapter is the first time in this election book series that we have presented two 'official' contributions for a particular party. It proved to be but the first of two to appear in this book. The replacement of David Cunliffe with Andrew Little – by the Labour Party and, less dramatically, by the organisers of this book – meant that the contribution from Labour's leader, though admittedly offering a leader's perspective, was coming from an individual not centrally involved in the party's nationwide campaign. Accordingly, Andrew Little's reflections on the campaign – and on Labour's future – are complemented by a further chapter on Labour's campaign, co-authored by the party's general secretary, former Labour MP Tim Barnett, and David Talbot, the party's campaign manager, providing information and insights about what worked, and what didn't, in the party's ill-fated 2014 effort.

The leaders of other parties elected to Parliament, invited to take part in this project, agreed to do so without comparable complication. Green Party leaders have contributed to these books in the past, beginning with former leader Rod Donald (in 1996, for the Alliance, and in 1999 for the Greens), including Russel Norman (in 2005, although as the Green Party's campaign director) and Metiria Turei (in 2011). On this occasion the Greens decided to be represented again by Russel Norman, whose contribution coincided with his decision to step down from the co-leadership. New Zealand First's leader, Winston Peters, spoke at the 2011 post-election conference and he again agreed to take part, his contribution coming several months prior to his Northland by-election victory (and his transformation from list to electorate MP). United Future's Peter Dunne had spoken at several post-election conferences – in 2005 and 2011 – and he also agreed once again to participate.

The remaining two party leaders, successful at the 2014 election, are newcomers to this series. The Māori Party's co-leader Te Ururoa Flavell – chosen as co-leader in July 2013 following the decision of Pita Sharples (and Tariana Turia) to retire – offers an overview of his party's 2014 campaign (and his successful re-election in his Waiariki electorate). His predecessor, Pita Sharples, had participated in 2005 following the Māori Party's first general election campaign

As for ACT's new leader, David Seymour, he was sworn in as a new MP on 20 October, gave his maiden speech in Parliament the following day, and – perhaps less momentously – was invited to speak at the 3 December post-election conference a day later. By participating in the conference (and in this book) he followed in the footsteps of an ACT Party president (Chris Simmons, 2011), MP (John Boscawen, 2008) and party leader (Rodney Hide, 2005).

As in previous books, these chapters appear in a recognisable, sensible sequence: the winning party (National) first, followed by the defeated major party (Labour). The smaller parties' chapters are in descending order based on their 2014 electoral performance: the Greens, 14 seats; New Zealand First, 11 seats; the Māori Party, 2 seats; ACT, 1 seat (and 0.69 per cent of the party vote); and United Future, 1 seat (and 0.22 per cent of the party vote).

Contributions from and about the media have been a further feature of this election series from the beginning. Jane Clifton's witty and informed commentaries have been published before – in 2005 and 2011 – and she provides a further chapter in this book. Her perspective is that of an experienced working journalist, a longtime observer of parliamentary shenanigans. As she emphasises right from the outset, this campaign, even to so experienced a commentator, took New Zealand electoral politics into new and far from attractive territory. This was a view shared by Nicola Kean, a producer of TV3's *The Nation*, who sums up the campaign with the word 'cray' – social media speak for 'crazy'. Her chapter – a somewhat surreal glimpse into the media's coverage of a New Zealand election –

offers a vantage point on how a weekly television news programme covers an election campaign: the choices made, of speakers and topics, and the reasons for doing so.

Kate McMillan offers the perspective of an academic experienced in teaching and writing about politics and the New Zealand media. As with other contributors to this book she emphasises the unexpected and the over-the-top – *Dirty Politics* and the 'Moment of Truth' – while drawing attention to some of the ethical and political implications arising out of these developments. The result is a rigorous critique of a media – and, to some extent, a political process – facing uncomfortable and difficult pressures and challenges.

The news media's view of public opinion polls is ambiguous and in some respects mildly schizophrenic. All media outlets – from television and radio news through newspapers and magazines and on through to the internet – regularly report opinion poll findings as 'news'. At the same time there is a latent (and somewhat indiscriminate) scepticism about 'the polls' and their ability to accurately measure public preferences. The media seldom take time to celebrate poll results which prove, in due course, to have provided a reliable pre-election snapshot of voters' subsequent behaviour. A finding that misses the mark, on the other hand, will evoke interest and the kind of amusement captured by the German word 'schadenfreude' (i.e., taking pleasure from others' misfortunes; in this case, the embarrassment of a wayward pollster).

Yet the fact is that the public is regularly polled by political parties, within the limits of their resources. Their readiness to commission polls, and to rely on their findings, reflects a respect for the usefulness and accuracy of those that have been properly conducted. This series of election books has frequently published chapters based on survey research, acknowledging, in doing so, that an election, by itself, can only disclose *how* people have voted, and not *why* they have done so. The rationale for survey research remains clear: to gain a deeper understanding of voting choices. For 2014 the editors were fortunate in securing the participation of Stephen Mills, a highly experienced survey researcher whose firm, UMR, has been providing survey-based research and advice for more than 25 years. His chapter, presented with clarity and context, and based on what New Zealanders themselves have said to UMR's pollsters, explores a range of factors critical for understanding why National did so well, and Labour so poorly, at the 20 September election.

As New Zealanders have come to realise and expect, MMP elections invariably culminate in multi-party coalition arrangements of one kind or another. This has been the case since the first such election in 1996. On several occasions, the 2014 campaign among them, there have been fleeting opportunities for one of the two major parties, National or Labour, to appear to have the prospect of governing on their own – as in what some voters, though perhaps not all that many, might consider 'the good old days'. Yet every such glimpse of a beckoning majority has always become, as a party moved ever closer to it, nothing but a mirage. Party figures thirsty for one-party government have had to put those hopes and dreams to one side, disciplining themselves for the somewhat less satisfying pleasures of multi-party partnership.

There are numerous instances of coalition government in the world of comparative politics and, as a result, there are concepts and theories intended to make such arrangements orderly and predictable. The 2014 election, like the six MMP elections before it, was also filled with the aromas of multi-party politics, as commentators, political junkies and election aficionados took turns experimenting with various coalition recipes. In some, political parties that had never been represented in Parliament, and that failed to gain representation in 2014 – Colin Craig's Conservatives, the Laila Harré-Kim Dotcom-Hone Harawira contrivance known as Internet Mana – were identified as the decisive elements, spices to right-wing and left-wing governments respectively. In addition, throughout the campaign and even (or especially) into the final week, Winston Peters was highlighted as 'kingmaker', certain to be 'the first person' to be contacted, post-election, by both Key and Cunliffe.

New Zealand's first-past-the-post elections (in the 1935–1993 era) had the virtue of simplicity, as three-yearly elections awarded political power either to one party or another. MMP elections require a bit more effort to sort out. Political consultant Stephen Church has explained the vagaries of coalition politics before (e.g., in the 1999, 2002 and 2011 election volumes). In this book he again examines coalition calculations – diverse unfolding possibilities; a final result; the coalition agreements themselves. In doing so his chapter provides an element of closure to an election campaign whose final goal, for party leaders, is to find a way of getting to a majority of parliamentary seats. By achieving that objective National was able to form a government. How this happened, and what it means in terms of comparative theory and precedent, are among the features of Church's chapter.

It is commonplace now to regard political parties, leaders and candidates as products to be sold, often to sceptical and quarrelsome individuals not so ready to make a purchase. How to sell politicians – how to win votes – is an ongoing and ever-changing business. New and steadily more sophisticated techniques are developed from one election to the next. In this book, several chapters draw attention to efforts at innovation in election campaigning.

Developments in technology have their applications to campaigning and politics more generally. Rob Salmond's chapter focuses on advances in targeting potential voters, intended to make campaign messaging more efficient. Those advances are also highlighted as positives in the two chapters on Labour's 2014 campaign, with further targeting refinements only to be expected.

This election series, over time, provides a record of evolving technology as applied to politics. The 2005 election book emphasised websites and blogs; the 2008 election book, cyberspace and YouTube; and the 2011 book included a chapter on political parties' use of social media. As political parties continue to bring additional resources to online campaigning, these efforts can be expected to have an expanding influence on voting behaviour, attracting further attention from academic commentators. In this book the developer of a social media blog, Matthew Beveridge, has contributed a chapter in which political parties' use of Facebook and Twitter are compared (using data collected for his Masters thesis). Beveridge's chapter, following on from Anthony Deos and Ashley Murchison's chapter in the 2011 election book, provides a further data-filled basis by which the efforts of candidates and parties to use social media for electoral purposes may be monitored and measured.

A further, creative look at technology in the 2014 campaign is provided by Corin Higgs, who considers five technology-related themes on display in the 2014 election. His informed and incisive chapter notes some of the many failures of the Internet Party; punctures the pretensions of TVNZ's 'Vote Compass'; elucidates some of the unplanned consequences of 'social media'; pronounces winners and losers in the 'battle of the blogs'; and, unexpectedly, discovers enduring value in the centuries-old technological marvel known as the book. How all these elements swirled about to influence a New Zealand election is something of a wonder to behold.

Political scientist Therese Arseneau has been having virtually the last word in these election books since 2005, providing chapters summing up significant developments arising out of a campaign and its outcome. In

2011 as well as in this book her assessment has been written in collaboration with experienced psephologist Nigel S. Roberts, who has never come across an election that he didn't like (to analyse, that is). Arseneau and Roberts engage in a probing analysis of the 2014 voting figures, in which the disparity between National's and Labour's electoral performance, electorate by electorate, stands out even more starkly. They also emphasise the necessity of focusing on alternative 'blocs' – right-of-centre vs left-of-centre – rather than (as in New Zealand's previous first-past-the-post experience) alternative major parties. The potential strength of smaller parties is also further highlighted in their chapter, with possible changes to the MMP system (a reduction of the threshold for representation to 4 per cent, for instance) offering further opportunities for representation and influence.

Previous books in this series have sought to highlight the distinctiveness of campaigning and political competition in Māori electorates. It is too much to say that New Zealand general elections actually consist of two distinct elections: those in the general electorates and those in the Māori seats. Even so, successive contributions to this series demonstrate that there are distinctive factors at work in the Māori seats, affecting candidate selection, political party rivalries, campaign techniques, voter turnout and voting choice. In 2011 Morgan Godfery offered a perspective highlighting fragmentation – rather than unity and consensus – in Māori politics, a contribution singled out for praise ('a fascinating chapter') in the review of *Kicking the Tyres* by Professor Jack H. Nagel (2014).

Godfery wrote that the Māori Party's leverage within the National-led government was 'reduced' and that the Mana Party was 'in an even worse position' (Godfery 2012, p. 280). It would have taken extraordinary powers of foresight for him (or, indeed, anyone) to have imagined the arrangement that Mana would enter into in 2014, with Kim Dotcom and the Internet Party, ultimately leaving its position even worse than before. Godfery's chapter thoughtfully explores the options and outcomes for Māori parties and for Māori voters, manoeuvring within the constraints of an array of challenging and peculiar choices.

Following the editors' introductory chapter – which sets the scene for the rest of the book, providing an overview of the political background, campaign highlights and the results – one of New Zealand's most experienced and respected political commentators, Colin James, provides a distinctive perspective on the election, considering New Zealand elections, past and present, within global trends and developments. The next chapter, by Jon Johansson, emphasises leadership, not merely as a significant factor in influencing voter choice (with John Key far and away the country's preferred prime minister) but as a precious opportunity, given to an individual at the helm of government, to make a difference. This is a theme further explored in the book's closing chapter, with genuine leadership seen to embrace a vision for New Zealand's future as well as a grasp of the tactics and strategies needed for winning elections.

***

This book, as noted, had its beginnings with a conference at Parliament, held only two months and two weeks following the general election – a period of time virtually identical to that between a US presidential election and inauguration. The conference could not have been held at the Legislative Council Chamber in Parliament Buildings without the support of the Speaker of the New Zealand House of Representatives, Rt Hon David Carter, whose opening remarks welcomed participants and went on to reflect on the efforts made to increase voter participation, particularly among younger voters. This was the fourth successive occasion at which the post-election conference was held at the Legislative Council Chamber, making the conference part of Parliament's post-election environment. This is, however, the first time that a book in this series has included a brief foreword from the Speaker and we are grateful to have his participation in this volume.

Few things are ever accomplished without assistance from others. At Parliament, the conference organisers were fortunate in having efficient and cheerful support from the Speaker's senior private secretary, Lisa Kinloch, for which we are most grateful. As for Roland Todd, Speaker's assistant, his role in facilitating our use of the Legislative Council Chamber (including the upstairs gallery to accommodate the numbers wishing to attend) and the Grand Hall (for refreshments), as well as the services of a photographer, Colin McDiarmid, is very much appreciated.

A major element in the success of an all-day conference has to do with the food and drink arrangements. We acknowledge services provided to us by Vikrant Singh, functions manager, and Nicola Provines, functions sales coordinator. The numbers of people attending the 2014 post-election conference increased steadily, but Epicure's ability to accommodate our evolving requirements ensured that all went well on the day.

A unique feature of the New Zealand election series, beginning in 2002, has been the inclusion of audiovisual materials as a record of the election campaign. The 2002 election book, *New Zealand Votes*, brought out at a time when DVD players were relatively rare, included a CD-ROM with the publication. The next three books – *The Baubles of Office*, *Key to Victory* and *Kicking the Tyres* – included DVDs, a vivid accompaniment to the text which allowed these publications' electoral record to be more fully appreciated and understood by those not familiar with New Zealand's politicians and political personalities. Our thanks go to Corin Higgs for assembling the DVD (as he did in 2011), and to news organisations and political parties for making access to the material publicly available.

As he has done previously, Emeritus Professor Nigel S. Roberts, an assiduous photographer, has taken the trouble to take pictures, North Island and South, of that most ephemeral of electoral elements: political party and candidate billboards. From his 2014 collection he has assembled, in logical order, a sequence of billboard photos which add further content and colour to the story of the 2014 campaign.

Pennie Gapes, the competent, cheerful and altogether invaluable manager of Victoria University of Wellington's School of History, Philosophy, Political Science and International Relations, provided enormous assistance to the conference organisers, all of it above and beyond the requirements of her job description. Nicola Yong – at the time a parliamentary intern and post-graduate student of exemplary character and ability – likewise assisted the organisers, efforts that could not have been motivated solely by a desire to register for the conference without payment. Nicola's poise and equable temperament as conference administrator proved a critical asset and is warmly appreciated. Finally, Jonette Crysell receives a brief honourable mention – as promised – for good-natured, focused efforts in dealing with a number of somewhat complicated conference-related tasks.

From the 1999 election book (*Left Turn*) onwards, Victoria University Press has been responsible for bringing out these New Zealand election publications. We value very highly our relationship with VUP and appreciate, in particular, the commitment that its publisher, Fergus Barrowman, and his team, especially our copy editor, Kyleigh Hodgson, bring to their endeavours. Many thanks, also, to Timothy Vaughan-Sanders for his meticulous efforts in putting together the index.

Our gratitude also to cartoonist Chris Slane – who prepared the brilliant cartoon imagery for the front cover and spine of *Kicking the Tyres* – for yet another vivid and entertaining cover.

Finally, as conference organisers we take the opportunity again to thank those who attended the 3 December post-election symposium. As editors we thank the conference participants for their speeches on the day, and for the more lasting contribution represented by this book.

***

At the 2014 post-election conference a foreign diplomat in attendance found it extraordinary that we had been able, in a single morning, to bring together the leaders of every single party represented in Parliament, from the Prime Minister all the way on down. Our ability to do so no doubt reflects New Zealand's political culture and circumstances, features of the country's society and politics all too easily taken for granted until an outside observer, wide-eyed, notes otherwise. Likewise, in a troubled and tumultuous world, the 2014 New Zealand election matter-of-factly continued a process, going back to the first parliamentary elections of 1853, by which New Zealanders have sought to make this country's government their own.

In his keynote address, John Key recognised the value of the endeavour represented by this book, and by the nine electoral volumes that have preceded it, when he stated that the 'discussion on the 2014 election, and the setting out of the views of participants' was to be welcomed 'so that people in 20, 50 and 100 years' time can think about what happened and why' (see chapter 5). Indeed, the editors do believe that it is important to provide a three-yearly record of New Zealand elections for future generations to study. This series of post-election conferences and publications continues to offer a valuable setting for political leaders, parliamentary candidates, journalists, commentators and academics to present their views, and to do so while impressions remain fresh, the events to which they relate not yet much faded. For the New Zealand public, students and overseas observers, these books enable a greater in-depth understanding to be gained of significant features of New Zealand's politics, elections and political leadership.

Looking towards 2017, a new round of spirited yet peaceful campaigns can be anticipated. This will surely be followed, in turn, by thoughtful, informed analysis focusing on a country whose electoral politics have become, for better or for worse, whatever else one may say of them, anything but uneventful.

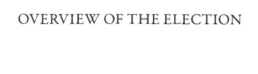

OVERVIEW OF THE ELECTION

1

MOMENTS OF TRUTH: THE 2014 NEW ZEALAND GENERAL ELECTION

Stephen Levine

> I've enjoyed a privilege afforded to only a very small group of New Zealanders, and that's to lead our country.
> *John Key, election night, 2014*

It doesn't matter that most people don't know John Key personally and can't say, based on personal experience, what he is like. The New Zealand public, overall, has a view of him. His reputation as a friendly person – an example of a nice guy who doesn't finish last, approachable, capable and engaging – precedes him as he campaigns and governs, going from one situation to the next. As 'the man who defeated Helen Clark' – a leader who had three election victories (1999, 2002 and 2005) and three National Party leaders (Jenny Shipley, Bill English and Don Brash) notched on her belt – he became a 'legend' once the 2008 election results were confirmed. With 2011 the legend deepened: now it was Clark's Minister of Foreign Affairs, Phil Goff, who was dispatched.

With 2014 the legend grew even further: two more notches on his belt – David Shearer, unseated before he could even contest an election as Labour leader, and David Cunliffe, an ambitious parliamentarian convinced that he could become a great prime minister if only given the chance. Perhaps so: but it was, after all, not to be.

A 'moment of truth' in a Hollywood western traditionally involves two gunmen walking onto a street at high noon, facing each other down, until one suddenly reaches for his gun. This is, indeed, *the* moment of truth. Only one will live out the scene, still breathing by the end of the final reel.[1]

What *is* a 'moment of truth'? It is that time when everything is at stake, the outcome now to be determined. It is a moment of unavoidable challenge – to a team, a country, a person.

In an individual's life there may be many such moments. Sometimes we don't know that a moment of truth is before us – a turning point, a decisive circumstance – until after it is past. In an election campaign with various participants there may be one 'moment of truth' – the situation when all can be won or lost – or there may be several.

This chapter considers the 2014 New Zealand election in terms of a succession of 'moments of truth', circumstances which tested parties and leaders, helping to determine their electoral fate.

Background

John Key led his National Party into the 2014 election year in a comfortable position, having the initiative in electoral matters. On 10 March he announced the 20 September election date, citing as a significant factor various international conferences taking place in November at which a New Zealand prime minister ought to be in attendance. While in New Zealand (as elsewhere) there can be said to be a 'continuous campaign', the announcement gave certainty to parties, prospective candidates, the media, voters, and agencies with electoral responsibilities, allowing campaign planning to move into a higher gear.

In other matters, too, National and its prime minister held the initiative. The party possessed a substantial lead in opinion polls over its principal major-party rival, Labour, and the Prime Minister was far and away the country's 'preferred prime minister'. The Labour Party's leader, David Cunliffe, had been selected in September 2013 under new procedures, giving the party's members and its trade union affiliates 60 per cent of the vote (40 per cent to the party, 20 per cent to the unions) on leadership selection. The outcome – a scenario easily envisaged when the new procedures were introduced – hobbled Cunliffe from the beginning. The results of the voting, released in the interests of 'transparency', put Cunliffe in a spotlight not altogether dissimilar from the headlights illuminating a deer on a dark country road. His parliamentary colleagues had voted against him: leadership was achieved through the support of the party and union membership. The numbers revealed John Key's Labour rival to be an individual lacking the confidence of his parliamentary colleagues – the 'team' that he had now been chosen to lead. This was, already, a 'moment of truth' for the upcoming contest – and it put Labour at a considerable disadvantage.

In situations such as these, in at least some Hollywood western shoot-outs, the slower gunfighter can still win if he is able to place some of his supporters on roofs overlooking the dusty street below. A bullet from up above, added to the chaos down below, could yet bring the more agile down, turning the quick into the dead. In MMP terms, Labour's leader still had ways to win if only his allies proved sufficiently resourceful.

Going into the match-up, Labour felt that it could count, as previously, on the Green Party for back-up. With Labour so far behind in the polls, it was necessary for Cunliffe to demonstrate to observers that the two parties, together, represented a safe and secure bet. Efforts were made to make their partnership appear stable. These were not entirely successful. The two parties, while indicating a willingness to form a joint government if voters gave them that opportunity, continued their rivalry, differences in outlook and over policy coinciding with ongoing 'cultural' contrasts. Making matters worse, the Labour-Green duo represented an inviting target for National, each shortcoming of the one used to tarnish the credibility of both. The stronger the partnership, the more attractive the target; the weaker the partnership, the less credible it was made to appear.

There were others whom Cunliffe thought he might be able to count on in a final showdown. None were without risks. New Zealand First's leader Winston Peters had been a consistent critic of John Key from the moment he assumed the National Party's leadership. The disdain articulated regularly by Peters in Parliament had its counterpart on the National side, with Peters ruled out as a potential coalition partner in 2008 and again in 2011. But if Peters' reputation made him an ally in anti-Key efforts, his image and outlook – as well as a prickly demeanour, sensitive to slights – made him a potentially troublesome campaign companion. How to keep Peters within reach when needed, while otherwise in the background – somewhat like a grumpy but wealthy relative, difficult to have at family functions but unwise to overlook altogether – was at the heart of things. Bringing Peters too close made the entire contrivance – Labour-Greens-New Zealand First – a target. Keeping him too far off nurtured ill feelings in a wily politician with access to the media and an openness to other options.

A further ally, delighted to snipe from rooftops as the election approached, was the newly established coalition of convenience, the Internet Mana Party. This 'party', established for MMP electoral purposes only, had a sunset clause: it was intended to come to an end once the election was held and its elected MPs took their seats in Parliament. At that point, the Mana and Internet Party MPs would be separately recognised, their formal alliance dissolved.

Such planning was premature, however. In the first instance Internet Mana needed actually to gain representation. It went into the campaign with one MP: Hone Harawira, Mana's founder, a maverick politician who had abandoned the Māori Party in 2011, when that party's alliance with National and John Key became too much for Harawira to bear. He was able to retain his Te Tai Tokerau seat, first in a by-election (25 June 2011) and then at the 2011 general election. In 2014, Harawira accepted the idea that his influence within Parliament could be increased at the helm of a larger political force – Internet Mana. In order to gain access to considerable financial resources – and to what was hoped to be a larger constituency of young, techno-savvy voters – Harawira, to the dismay of some of his followers, accepted the terms of an alliance with the Internet Party, an electoral idea developed by Kim Dotcom, a German immigrant sought by US authorities in relation to alleged copyright infringements associated with his Megaupload music sharing enterprise. Former Alliance Party leader Laila Harré (MP, 1996–2002) returned to active party politics by becoming the Internet Party's leader, standing for Parliament as the party's candidate against John Key himself, in his Helensville electorate – a move unlikely to have cost the Prime Minister a moment's lost sleep.

As a potential ally for Labour, Internet Mana represented an electoral problem of considerable magnitude. Kim Dotcom and Hone Harawira were, both separately and together, embarrassments to any party seriously campaigning for the support of the broader New Zealand public. While their potential numbers in Parliament could have been considered a further basis of support for a Labour-Greens-New Zealand First government, the idea that the New Zealand public would happily endorse the prospect of a government brought into existence through Harawira's and Dotcom's tolerant acceptance of it was far-fetched. While Cunliffe might have been able to count on their support – when the contest came down to himself or John Key – it was backing that he was unable to outwardly welcome, lest doing so further compromise Labour's weakened position going into the campaign.

None of the other participants in the election were available to Labour. The ACT and United Future parties, aligned with the Key-led government since 2008, were signed up to a further partnership with National on 28 July, when the Prime Minister signalled to National voters in the ACT and United Future leaders' electorates (Epsom and Ōhāriu) that his preference was for those voters to give National their party vote while supporting the two minor party leaders as electorate candidates (Fox and Walters 2014). Different electoral circumstances were in play with respect to the Māori Party. National's support in Māori electorates remained so slim – the party did not have an electorate candidate in any Māori seat and in 2014 its total of party votes (11,838) in the seven electorates proved to be fewer than the number gained by Labour, the Māori Party, New Zealand First (which also had no electorate candidates), the Greens and Internet Mana – that any 'signal' to National voters to support Māori Party candidates while giving their party vote to National would have had little effect beyond the comical. Nevertheless, going into the 2014 election both National and the Māori Party indicated that they would be happy, post-election, to continue a relationship that had begun when John Key first became prime minister following the November 2008 election.

While there were other minor parties and 'independents' taking part in the 2014 election, none had much significance for the campaign, let alone the result, apart from the Conservative Party. Led by a wealthy businessman, Colin Craig, the Conservatives had contested the 2011 general election, winning 2.65 per cent of the vote. Other parties with conservative views – such as the Christian Coalition (in the first MMP election, in 1996) – had tried, and failed, to win representation. With perseverance among life's virtues Craig sought, with renewed effort, to lead his party to victory in 2014: either on its own, fairly achieved, by winning an electorate seat or gaining at least 5 per cent of the party vote, or through an accommodation with National (such as achieved by ACT and United Future). In either case, the Conservatives were a party potentially available only to National. For Labour, the Conservatives represented yet another adversary – if not a particularly menacing one – rather than a possible partner to add to its far-from-coherent camp following.

The election campaign

Despite the growth in internet and social media election-related activity – well-documented elsewhere in this book – the 2014 campaign also remained visible to individuals not glued to smart phones and computer screens. Election billboards continued to add to – or detract from – the landscape. Fliers continued to pile up in letterboxes. Party political advertisements, broadcast on television and radio, opened and closed the campaigns. There were ads for parties and candidates in daily and community newspapers, and in magazines. Pollsters and party workers continued to disrupt home and family life – including meals and weekends – with uninvited door knocks and unsolicited telephone calls. And political party leaders continued their campaigns around the country, showing up at cafés, shopping malls and street corners, attracting media, onlookers and political junkies, happy to be part of 'something', whatever its larger meaning might be. Party leaders also interacted with each other in front of the television cameras as a succession of debates enlightened those watching them, offering insights into personalities and policies.

National

In May the government produced a 'bland and even boring Budget', the government having opted for 'safe' as 'its best hope' (*Dominion Post* 2014b). The main goal was to provide a surplus – any surplus, even a modest and uncertain one, would do – and that was what the Budget claimed to achieve, the Minister of Finance indicating that 'the government's main priority will be debt repayment' – hardly a commitment calculated to cause hearts to beat faster, even if it could be considered a responsible one.

The election campaign itself was founded on a formula projecting sound economic management and friendly, capable prime ministerial leadership. A publication – 'Our 2014 Priorities' – was one of many establishing message and tone. Accompanied by a smiling picture of the Prime Minister, it declared: 'National is continuing to build a stronger economy that creates more jobs, lifts incomes, and provides the essential services and support that families need'. The brochure went on to draw attention to the government's record in 'responsibly managing the government's finances', 'building a more competitive and productive economy', and 'delivering better public services', including education, welfare reform, housing, health and law-and-order, with the country's crime rate at 'a 35-year low'. Attention was also drawn to government support for Canterbury families, post-earthquakes, the efforts made at 'rebuilding our second-biggest city' described as 'the largest undertaking in New Zealand's history' – which, if so, remains something not fully apprehended by the overall public.

A more specific message from the Prime Minister – that paying off debt was the government's principal focus – allowed him to draw a contrast with Labour's allegedly irresponsible spending plans. The juxtaposition would have been more impressive if attempts to produce a budget surplus had proven more successful. Instead, there was general expectation that a government surplus, whenever it managed to eventuate, would likely be nominal – symbolic rather than substantive. The inability to run surpluses gave less credibility to suggestions that a re-elected Key government might introduce meaningful tax cuts during 2015–17, the hint of one itself seeming somewhat irresponsible.

More broadly – apart from the Prime Minister's enthusiastic initiative on behalf of a new national flag[2] – National's campaign largely lacked vision and high rhetoric, unsurprising from a party, prime minister and government emphasising stability and the status quo. Did this mean, hearkening back to the Muldoon years, that the government believed that New Zealand was already, for the most part, the way most New Zealanders wanted it?[3]

National's campaign was enlivened, if inadvertently, when the party was challenged for alleged breach of copyright in its use of US rapper Eminem's song 'Lose Yourself' in campaign advertisements. Proceedings were filed in the High Court on 16 September, only four days before the election. It was a bizarre development in an already odd campaign and remarkable, too – no doubt a further consequence of 'globalisation' – that a US-based organisation would even know about the use of a song in a New Zealand election campaign when most Americans would be unable to find New Zealand on a map.

This was not National's only hazardous campaign encounter with music. In August the Prime Minister had been the subject of a song, 'Kill the PM', depicting him as a greedy rich man taking money from the poor, deserving to die. The song, disseminated by an Auckland-based hip-hop outfit '@ peace' and described by Key as 'not worth a response',[4] led to the Electoral Commission's decision to investigate whether it breached electoral rules – as Darren Watson's satirical track 'Planet Key' had done, being banned from broadcasting as 'an election programme' (Wong 2014c).

National experienced controversy as revelations about its 'Cabinet Club' raised questions about its fundraising tactics and the possibility of donors gaining undue influence through their contributions (Davison 2014a). There were also embarrassments involving two senior National parliamentarians, Maurice Williamson and Judith Collins. The Prime Minister promptly separated himself from their respective predicaments; Williamson resigned his portfolios on 1 May (Savage 2014b) and Collins departed Cabinet on 30 August, only three weeks before the election, having survived earlier difficulties involving a 2013 trip to China.[5] A further MP, Claudette Hauiti, selected as candidate for Kelston, withdrew following controversy over misuse of a parliamentary charge card (Young 2014b).

When not coping with distractions (including allegations about 'dirty politics' and the campaign's final week 'moment of truth' event)[6] National remained focused on two main points: the government's contribution to economic security for most New Zealanders; and the dangers for the country of taking an alternative path.

For instance, a September letter to New Zealanders – 'Keep The Team That's Working' – asserted that the election was a chance to 'keep New Zealand moving in the right direction': 'By voting for National you'll be voting for strong and stable leadership, responsible economic management where we live within our means and start paying off debt, and policies that will deliver.' A series of bullet points highlighted '150,000 more jobs', 'higher wages', 'no new taxes', 'record numbers off welfare into work', 'shorter hospital waiting times', 'quality teaching in schools', 'KiwiSaver HomeStart grants', 'Keeping the Super age at 65', 'A 20 per cent reduction in crime', and 'Free doctors' visits for children under 13'. The letter also warned of the possibility 'for Labour to cobble together a government with the Greens, Doctom and others': 'With the opposition parties unable to agree on even the most basic economic issues and with Labour and the Greens' election promises adding up to a staggering $28 billion or more, economic chaos would result.'

Another National flier – 'Working for New Zealand's Environment' – saw a smiling Prime Minister highlighted against a green rural background, at the head of a government 'managing our water, oceans, air, iconic places and species while ensuring we deliver a growing economy and more jobs'. The rhetoric sought to assure New Zealanders that National was taking a 'balanced' approach, the party portraying itself as something other than environmental philistines, Key stating, 'National is showing how good environmental and economic policies can work together.'

Responding to queries about the Prime Minister's willingness to remain in office was another element of National's campaign. If John Key were the party's principal asset – the reason for voters to re-elect National – perceptions that a National win might bring about a government led, before long, by an MP other than Key were to be taken seriously. In a radio interview (Newstalk ZB, 4 February) the Prime Minister observed, when asked whether he would be committed to serving out the entire 2014–17 term if re-elected prime minister, 'I'd have to be sure I had the confidence of my ministers and all that sort of stuff, but if you're asking me "am I committed for three years?" Yes.' Key's self-appraisal was clear:

I must admit I sit there at the start of the sixth year looking at all this change and say 'the economy is getting back into surplus, debt levels are much less than they thought it would be, the country is growing, HSBC is calling us the "rock star economy", crime is at a 30-year low'. And in my heart I sit there and go 'I reckon we've done a pretty good job'. There's something energising about that.

The Prime Minister also had to cope with challenges to National's capacity to govern, post-election, given MMP mathematics. There was a possibility, after all, that the National–Māori Party–ACT–United Future group might fall short. This raised the prospect of National needing to rely on Winston Peters, as Jim Bolger had been forced to do following the first MMP election in 1996, with ultimately disastrous results. While not ruling out a relationship with Peters – as he had done at the previous two general elections – the Prime Minister indicated that there were limits to what he would be prepared to concede as the price for his cooperation. Asked whether a coalition with New Zealand First could result in an agreement to let Peters become prime minister for a portion of the term, Key observed that the idea had 'about as much chance as Amanda Knox holidaying in Italy. Zero.' (Trevett 2014c).[7]

In the campaign's final days National ran full-page newspaper advertisements with its three principal elements highlighted: *the Prime Minister* (smiling); *the message* – 'Our plans will ensure a strong, open economy that delivers more for New Zealanders and their families'; and *the overall election slogan*: 'KEEP NEW ZEALAND WORKING'. There was also a brief tutorial in MMP logic, emphasising why supporters of the Prime Minister needed to vote: 'MMP elections are always close even with the Opposition in disarray. Any vote for a minor party risks political turmoil and our economy stalling. Only a strong PARTY VOTE for National will keep New Zealand heading in the right direction.' Finally, at the bottom of the ad, there was the image of the National Party boat, rowing off with vigour and purpose.[8]

Labour

The pre-campaign period went poorly for David Cunliffe. Leaks from within Labour questioned his work ethic, with criticism of his having taken a break to go skiing with his family during the school holidays (Watkins 2014b; Kilgallon and Day 2014; Trevett 2014e). Characteristically, Cunliffe began by defending his behaviour and efforts before conceding defeat, moving on to offer regrets. It was probably something of a relief for the Labour leader when he was able to enter the campaign proper, having the Prime Minister to face rather than his own caucus colleagues.

While Labour's overall slogan was 'Vote Positive', it was difficult for officials, candidates and supporters to go through the year unmoved by grim poll numbers pointing towards a further three years in opposition. Labour caucus meetings at Parliament are held in a room with framed photographs of its past leaders on the walls. None of them had ever had to contemplate an election in which victory, at best, might involve a power-sharing arrangement with such divisive and incompatible elements. As the election neared and the poll numbers remained unforgiving, the temptation to find a scapegoat was never far from the surface. The party's leader proved an ideal choice. The prospect of a party removing yet another leader, nine months from having previously done so, was, however, a powerful deterrent; so too were Labour's leadership selection rules. Even so, stories about Cunliffe remaining under threat of removal (Vance 2014d; Bennett, Young and Trevett 2014; Armstrong 2014a) continued to add to Labour's miseries: if a leader cannot count on the support and loyalty of his colleagues, how can the public have confidence in that individual or his party's readiness to govern? Being saved by the argument that it is too late to make a change – leaving Labour's captain in charge only so that he can go down with his ship – is a poor substitute for collegial public support. Cunliffe's response, likening disloyal Labour MPs to strike breakers – 'And in the Labour movement, you know, there are some words we use for strike breakers' (Trevett 2014j) – was far from impressive from a public relations point of view.

Cunliffe's attempts to gain campaign traction were also undermined by two South Island Labour candidates whose selection raised obvious questions about the party's vetting procedures. Just putting up 'anyone' is not an acceptable procedure for choosing prospective members of Parliament.[9] In due course matters reached the point where Cunliffe indicated that he would remove Labour's Rangitata candidate Steve Gibson if he could: 'he has no future as a Labour candidate' (Newstalk ZB, 8 September). This followed Gibson's references to John Key as 'Shylock' (Radio New Zealand 2014b), and Cunliffe advising Gibson that his comments about the Prime Minister were unacceptable, a message described as the candidate's 'final warning' (Radio New Zealand 2014c). There were also problems with the party's Selwyn candidate, Gordon Dickson, over language and approach, which Cunliffe described as 'issues . . . which the party are handling'. As for Gibson, on 6 September, two weeks out from the election, the Labour leader 'refused to say whether people in Rangitata should vote for Gibson or even if he wanted them to. "People will make up their own mind. We want their party vote."' (Montgomerie and Rutherford 2014).

A party campaigns on the basis that its candidates are suitable prospects for parliamentary office. To put forward 'the best and the brightest' is the goal and to some extent a standard by which a party may be judged. In this respect Labour fell short in 2014, its difficulties harmful to the party's reputation, making something of a mockery of its 'Vote Positive' message. Notwithstanding the focus on the Prime Minister and party leaders – the 'presidentialisation' of politics – the calibre of a party's 'team' can affect overall perceptions. Having candidates attracting media attention for all the wrong reasons – erratic personal behaviour, awkward comments, retrograde views – strengthened impressions that the Labour team lacked discipline, character and competence.

The party was also not helped by long-serving MP Trevor Mallard suggesting in July that the moa be brought back to life.[10] Objections to the idea were probably based less on scientific implausibility than on the MP's priorities. The opening given to National MPs, in the wake of Cunliffe's promise that the party would be focusing on 'things that matter', allowed a range of jibes to be made about Labour's (and Cunliffe's) prospects, their chances of revival deemed gloomier than the moa's.

Labour's 'Vote Positive' slogan appeared on party fliers promoting various policies, proclaiming, for instance, that 'Labour is the party of education'. What the campaign motto meant in practice, in terms of specific programmes (as well as far-from-positive rhetoric about the Prime Minister), was less certain. In January, pre-campaign, Labour was reported to have distanced itself from policies deemed electorally unhelpful in 2011 (*One News* 2014). But Labour's plans – on taxation and on the possible repurchase of state-owned assets sold by National, among other topics – remained murky. If policy consistency and precision were sometimes absent, so too was Labour's leader – from some party billboards, for instance – and periodically he found himself forced onto the defensive, having to defend actions and statements reflecting on his character rather than on the party's plans for office. There were issues, for instance, over a trust fund used to channel anonymous donations to Cunliffe's leadership bid, Cunliffe in due course conceding that 'I don't think in hindsight that a trust structure fully represented the values that I would like to bring to this leadership' (Small 2014; Clifton 2014a).

By mid-June online readers were being asked 'which is your favourite Cunliffe gaffe?', with a choice from among seven items (Daly 2014a), among the most prominent being his attack on John Key for living in an expensive Parnell home, with Cunliffe defining his own Herne Bay residence as a 'doer-upper' despite its value. Revelations in June that Cunliffe had written a letter to immigration officials supporting a Chinese businessman's application for residence – following the Labour leader's statement that he had never met the individual or advocated on his behalf (Watkins 2014c; Savage 2014c; Trevett 2014h) – further eroded his credibility while depriving Labour of the political space needed for the party to gain momentum. The following month, Cunliffe's widely reported statement to a domestic violence symposium – 'I'm sorry for being a man' (Rutherford and Dennett 2014) – elicited further criticism.[11]

Labour's enigmatic 'Vote Positive' campaign, undermined by its own candidates and accompanied (from within the party) by attacks on Cunliffe himself, his colleagues even begrudging him a family holiday, meant that various campaign efforts made little impact. This included lucid leaders' debate performances, which availed little, Cunliffe's efforts having no appreciable effect on the polls.

One of Labour's pamphlets, 'Putting people first', children on the cover, had a smiling Labour leader declaring, 'I'm David Cunliffe, leader of the Labour Party – the party with a positive plan to unlock the potential in all people and make New Zealand the fairest, most decent place to live for all of us, not just the privileged few' – the last five words representing the less 'positive' element. Emphasising 'Your Work', 'Your Family' and 'Your Home', the flier declared that Labour had 'a positive plan for New Zealand'. If so, it was one whose details proved of little interest to much of the New Zealand electorate amid the clatter of a chaotic campaign.

Greens

The Greens continued to campaign as in past years, their election literature embellished by soft and sentimental imagery. The party's 'Love New Zealand' brochure showed children sitting beside each other, one with a sandwich and an apple, 'Love New Zealand' across the centre and 'Party Vote Green' at the bottom. The message at the back, stating 'Like you, we love New Zealand', was signed 'Metiria and Russel', the party's two co-leaders. The Greens' 2014 electoral goals were clear and unambiguous: 'We want to put 20 Green MPs into parliament this election', a standard by which campaign efforts might in due course fairly be judged.

In terms of policy, the party was portrayed as protectors of 'the New Zealand we love' – and hence, from one point of view, the true conservative party, rather than the left-wing radical fringe depicted by National. Election literature stated that 'New Zealand deserves a cleaner environment, a fairer society, and a smarter economy', the Greens claiming to 'have the policies to create' these results.

Another brochure, 'Let's look to the future', promised: 'Together we can create a smarter economy, a more compassionate society and a cleaner environment'. Policies emphasised included 'Our kids' education', with 'Schools at the Heart of our Communities'; 'Cheaper power for you', offering low-cost government loans 'to pay for solar power installation' and suggesting that 'Our NZ Power policy will cut your power bill by up to $300 a year'; and 'Smart transport solutions', including an investment of '$200 million in transport infrastructure so our kids can cycle and walk to schools safely'. The element of conservative nostalgia embedded in the Greens' outlook persisted: 'A generation ago, most kids walked or cycled. Today, only a third do.'

The desirability of restoring past values and virtues could also be seen in the Greens' promise to make the country's rivers clean enough to swim in (again, as in the past). While this vision was difficult to oppose in principle, National's Environment Minister Amy Adams did oppose it on the same basis by which the Prime Minister and other senior ministers were able to challenge other Green policies: practicality and affordability. The Minister described the policy as 'costly and impractical', an attempt to maintain 'every drainage ditch across New Zealand ... at a swimming pool standard'. The policy allegedly demonstrated that the Greens were 'anti-growth' (Kirk and Parkinson 2014), the Prime Minister declaring that 'these are people that will send New Zealand back into a significant deficit and I think New Zealanders are very worried about that' (Trevett 2014f).

On 8 September the Greens launched a public transport policy with vote-winning potential, including a 'Green card' offering 'free off-peak public transport for students & apprentices' which, if implemented, would have given those groups of voters the same benefits available to senior citizen holders of a SuperGold card. A similar combination linking policy and electoral politics was seen in the Greens' campaign to raise the minimum wage by almost \$4 an hour (from \$14.25 to \$18 an hour) by 2017.

The Greens' initial efforts to strengthen bonds with Labour, as part of an alternative government, led nowhere. The two parties did not campaign together; nor did they offer a joint programme for the New Zealand public to consider. Subsequently Labour's failure to rise in the polls led to the Greens' belated and entirely counterproductive efforts to establish greater separation from Labour through suggestions that its election promises be audited – a naïve and inherently offensive proposal from an ostensible partner, one damaging to both parties. Nor did it raise the possibility of any sort of partnership with National: far too late for that, given the Greens' sustained attacks on the Prime Minister and other members of his government over the 2011–14 parliamentary term. A relationship with a senior partner viewed as an unenlightened enemy could hardly be contemplated mid-campaign, even against a backdrop of dismal Labour Party polling.

New Zealand First

Winston Peters' campaign, as ever, retained its capacity to fascinate. On 18 September he was still being hailed as 'the likely kingmaker', the Prime Minister indicating that he wouldn't rule him out as a possible deputy prime minister (O'Brien 2014d). Peters' preferred prime minister rankings, three days before the election, reached a three-year high (9.1 per cent) in the *3News*/Reid Research poll (*National Business Review* 2014).

The campaign's final week had Peters attacking the Greens for 'extremist policies' while urging voters to consider a Labour–New Zealand First government as an alternative, not only to the Key-led government but also to the idea of a Labour–Greens administration. Ten days before the election Peters highlighted the need for parties going into coalition negotiations – as he expected to do – to address 'public concerns', listing these as export growth, savings, foreign ownership of housing and land, immigration levels, poverty and employment (Rutherford and Small 2014; Young 2014a).

Although his statements were often ambiguous – attracting something of the same puzzled scrutiny given in Cold War days to mystifying Kremlin pronouncements – as the election loomed Peters, his star ascendant, a return to executive power beckoning, laid down a number of apparently firm stands. He ruled out working with Internet Mana on the basis that it was a 'race-based party', excluding it from involvement with any Labour–Green–New Zealand First arrangement. The same could be said for the

Māori Party (Rutherford 2014a), denying that party a place in a National-led government if Peters were 'kingmaker'.

Peters had other bottom lines. The release of *Dirty Politics* (in his view) required the appointment of a wide-ranging royal commission into the book's allegations (Trevett 2014d), as New Zealand First did not wish to be 'tainted by association' in any future coalition government. Peters also identified several policies as essential to any possible coalition agreement: buying back energy companies partially privatised under National; keeping foreign fishing crews from New Zealand waters; and opposition to Labour plans to lift the superannuation entitlement age.

Not all of Peters' campaigning went his way. The Race Relations Commissioner Dame Susan Devoy described the New Zealand First leader's comment, 'two Wongs don't make a white', made at the party's campaign launch (10 August), as 'outdated rhetoric', 'disappointing and shameful' (O'Brien 2014e). Several days later a dispute with a heckler at a public rally in Hamilton found the New Zealand First leader using his forearm to keep the man away from the microphone (Smallman and Gulliver 2014). There were also difficulties at the outset when two of New Zealand First's incumbent MPs, Andrew Williams and Asenati Lole-Taylor, found themselves demoted on the party's list, Williams being removed altogether after publicly complaining over his low ranking (having dropped from third to thirteenth on the party list).[12]

Although raising the possibility of not joining any government – an option he labelled 'sitting on the cross benches' – Peters displayed confidence in his campaign fortunes, declaring at New Zealand First's 21st birthday celebrations in July, 'We are going to be stronger after 2014 than we ever were: stand back and watch.' Among his policies was an offer of $1,000 to all babies, the money going into KiwiSaver accounts opened at birth, intended to encourage children to develop a savings mentality (Armstrong 2014b).[13] How well the party's policies meshed with its overall election slogan – 'It's common sense' – was for voters to consider.

Conservatives

Colin Craig's well-funded campaign emphasised the party's rivalry with New Zealand First for what might be described as the 'populist' vote. For instance, a Conservatives pamphlet (dealing with drugs and alcohol) explicitly asked: 'How are the Conservatives different from Winston Peters?'[14] Another party publication had on its back page the heading

'Conservatives or Peters', inviting voters to consider the differences between them. On one side was a picture of Craig, 'Leader of the party voted cleanest in NZ Politics'; on the other was one of Peters holding up a 'No' sign, the flier declaring, 'Saying "No" when the truth was "Yes"' – a reference to Peters' difficulties in 2008 in relation to election campaign donations. The brochure, indicative of a campaign against Peters and New Zealand First rather than the government, paraded a page of policy contrasts over issues ranging from the country's anti-smacking law to the policies of the Reserve Bank (Conservative Party 2014c).

A further example of the Conservatives' competition with New Zealand First was seen in a similar stance taken on Māori issues, typefied by a full page ad, 'One Law To Rule Us All and other crazy thinking', which began: 'The fact that in this day and age Māori are treated as 2nd class citizens and victims drives us nuts', and ended with: 'Let's change a broken system. Nothing loony about that' (*Dominion Post* 2014c).

Peters' response to Craig's efforts was at times playful ('imitation is the most sincere form of flattery', Cheng 2014d), at other times less so:

> Mr Craig claims he is taking votes off New Zealand First. None of the New Zealand First voters think that vapour trails are poisoning the people or that the Americans didn't put a man on the moon, or that alleged promiscuity is all the fault of women. In short, none of the New Zealand First voters are bigoted wackos (*Stuff* 2014).[15]

While in no way decisive, it was probably not helpful that Craig's press secretary, Rachel MacGregor, resigned her position two days before the election, describing the Conservatives' leader as 'a manipulative man'. Craig's response to a radio interviewer (Newstalk ZB) – that he was surprised, believing that she was having the day off and hoping that she would 'unresign' – did little to improve matters.

On 19 September, the day before the election, the Conservative Party ran a full-page advertisement in newspapers – 'Party Vote Conservative: People and Policies you can Trust' – reproducing the front covers of five brochures distributed by the party; voters were invited to read them at the party's website. Six issues were highlighted: binding citizens-initiated referendums 'to hold politicians accountable and to prevent them dictating laws against the wish of the people'; 'tougher law and order'; 'one law for all New Zealanders', 'the original vision of the Treaty of Waitangi'; 'a smaller more efficient government'; 'time to stop selling out to [foreign business interests]'; and 'say no to drugs' (*Dominion Post* 2014d).

On 11 September, pondering the prospect of victory following a *3News* Reid Research poll giving the Conservatives 4.7 per cent, edging towards the 5 per cent threshold needed to gain representation, Craig stated that he would not immediately want a ministerial position if elected to Parliament: 'It's never been a condition of mine and I certainly wouldn't want that straight away anyway' (Radio New Zealand 2014d). That he would actually have the opportunity to ponder ministerial options was a matter still to be determined.

ACT

The 2014 election represented the latest attempt at determining whether the ACT Party's approach to government – perhaps best encapsulated by US President Ronald Reagan's observation that 'the nine most terrifying words in the English language are "I'm from the government and I'm here to help"'[16] – resonates amongst a public accustomed to seeing government support as natural and appropriate, and its absence as a sign of incompetence or indifference.

For ACT, a new election campaign represented yet another effort to make a fresh start. Its 2012–14 leader, John Banks, a recruit from the National Party, had been lured out of retirement into a political career which, in the end, came undone.[17] The result of the Banks experiment was to leave ACT in an even weaker position than it had been under Don Brash (who led the National Party from 2003 to 2006 and ACT in 2011, expressing hopes at the time of winning 15 per cent of the vote, but actually acquiring only 1.07 per cent). Making a new start in 2014 meant rejecting the leadership ambitions of former ACT MP John Boscawen (2008–11), notwithstanding his steadfast political and financial support for the party. Instead, ACT chose to launch its campaign with two new faces: Jamie Whyte, elected party leader in February (and selected as candidate for Pakuranga), and David Seymour, the individual with the good fortune to have a clear path to the Epsom seat previously held by ACT's Rodney Hide (2005–11) and by John Banks.

ACT launched its election campaign in Auckland on 7 September. While Jamie Whyte's campaign opening failed to electrify the country, another of his speeches did have an explosive effect, at least on one of the party's would-be MPs, its Dunedin North candidate Guy McCallum, who resigned not only as a candidate but also from the party's board (Bennett and Rees 2014). The speech was Whyte's attempt at channelling Don Brash (and his famous January 2004 Orewa speech), a 'one law for all' address in which Whyte claimed that Māori were legally privileged 'just as the aristocracy were legally privileged in pre-revolutionary France' (Bennett 2014f). Regrettably, the briefly glimpsed possibility of New Zealanders being diverted and enlightened through a debate about the French Revolution failed to eventuate.

This was not the only instance of remarks from ACT's leader having unintended consequences. Shortly after becoming party leader, Whyte – not surprisingly – became an individual about whom more needed to be known. The media became interested. He was interviewed. In February, responding to a question, he indicated that he believed that incestuous relationships should not be illegal. Subsequently Whyte went on to defend his comment, saying that it would be 'intellectually corrupt' of him not to be honest when asked questions (Bennett 2014). The following day he offered a somewhat different view, not, however, extending to his outlook on the 'issue': 'I regret the comments, mainly because I feel I let the party down' (Bennett 2014a). Indeed, no doubt Whyte neglected to point out his support for the legalisation of incest between consenting adults when seeking the ACT leadership.

The result, however, was that a New Zealand election campaign reached the point where a party leader actually felt it necessary to say that he was, in fact, personally 'very opposed' to incest: 'I find it very distasteful. I don't know why anybody would do it but it's a question of principle about whether or not people ought to interfere with actions that do no harm to third parties just because they personally wouldn't do it' (Bennett 2014a). The brief focus on Whyte's views represented one answer to the opinion that ACT needed to come up 'with fresher ideas than flat tax' (*New Zealand Herald* 2014c) – though probably not quite in the way that was expected.

John Key's observation about Whyte's comments – that they were 'stupid' – represented, no doubt, the broadest multi-party consensus position of the entire campaign: 'There's no place for incest. It's a ridiculous kind of statement.' His advice to Whyte – that 'the New Zealand public are interested in hearing about the issues that matter', incest not being among them (Bennett 2014b) – would have come too late to rescue a campaign undercut at the outset by the party's own leadership.

Nor was incest the only matter on which ACT unhappily stood alone. In August, ACT's leader, proceeding further with philosophical argument, suggested that the numbers of New Zealanders cycling could be doubled: 'We need only abolish the law that makes wearing a cycle helmet compulsory' (*3News* 2014d). In foreign affairs, too, ACT marched to the beat of a different drummer, urging New Zealand to abandon its bipartisan bid to win a seat on the UN Security Council – achieved in October on the first ballot – because the UN was an organisation that allowed 'terrorist states' to tell New Zealand what to do, and Security Council membership would bring New Zealand enemies due to the votes and decisions the government would have to take (Collins 2014).

A *Dominion Post* (2014a) editorial, summing matters up well before the campaign got under way, described ACT as 'a joke party', stating that 'under normal circumstances' it would 'expire' at the election were it not kept alive by its Epsom deal with National.

United Future

Peter Dunne's United Future campaign had little nationwide visibility, its inability to figure in opinion polls giving it little credibility and minimal access to media. Such attention as it did receive was no doubt counterproductive, highlighting the party's poor showing in the polls as well as Dunne's difficulties during the 2011–14 term, when he briefly lost his ministerial position due to an unwillingness to cooperate fully with an inquiry into a leak of materials, and when his party was briefly deregistered by the Electoral Commission for failing to maintain the required 500 paid-up members (*One News* 2013). Even with the Prime Minister's 'signal' to National voters in Ōhāriu, Dunne's own position was under threat, his majority having declined over the years, with electors failing to appreciate his 'common sense' positions supporting Labour, then National, all the while retaining his own presence in government. The campaign was not helped by Dunne's statement during a televised minor party leaders' debate, noting why he had gone into politics – 'We've never set out to be spectacular' – as it succeeded only in attracting Colin Craig's best interjection of the campaign: 'you've succeeded' (*One News* 2014b; Bennett 2014c).

Māori Party

The Māori Party's co-leader, Te Ururoa Flavell – MP for Waiariki since 2005 – made it clear from the beginning that the party would support National again if it won more votes than Labour. The highly personal origins of the Māori Party's outlook were articulated yet again by the party's departing founder, Tariana Turia, a former Labour MP who left the party and her ministerial position in 2004 over the Clark government's foreshore and seabed legislation. The estrangement between Labour and the

Māori Party – which was dismissively described by Helen Clark in 2005, when considering coalition possibilities, as 'the last cab off the rank' – has continued from that moment. In April, Turia stated of Labour,

> I don't believe they deserve our vote. I don't believe they deserve the vote of the Pasifika people.' Her critique went further: 'I think that our people have to ask themselves that for all the years that Labour were in government, the nine years of plenty, what is it that changed in their lives? What is it that Labour did that made them feel that things had changed for them, and have made a difference? And I want to say that when I look at kohanga reo, kura kaupapa, all the health services, all the social services, did any one of these things come out of the Labour Party? And the answer's no (*New Zealand Herald* 2014b).

In July, Flavell described the Māori Party as the latest attempt by Māori to consolidate a place in New Zealand's national politics, saying that the party, no longer 'political novices', were 'serious contenders for a piece of political pie with very healthy appetites'. Arguing once more in favour of the relationship with National, Flavell stated: 'We pushed the door of government wide open', arguing that 'it's about being in the right position to at least try to make a difference' (Cheng 2014e).

Internet Mana

For Internet Mana the 2014 campaign was a high-stakes struggle. On one side there was an opportunity for Kim Dotcom to oust a political leadership believed to be willing to see him removed from the country. As for Mana, there was a chance to suddenly and dramatically expand its parliamentary numbers and political influence over the government and the country.

A succession of extraordinarily inept events during the campaign made these dreams impossible to achieve. There is no doubt there was little appetite in New Zealand for a party happy to orchestrate expletive-laden chants directed at the Prime Minister (or anyone else).[18] Abusive language directed at the media also fell somewhat short of the mark.[19] Differences of opinion over marijuana legalisation also bedeviled the Internet Mana 'joint campaign'. Harawira and Harré espoused different views, leading, in due course, to an 'expletive-laden email', leaked to the media, highlighting their divisions, with Harré observing that Harawira 'needs to take responsibility for his own language' (*One News* 2014c).

John Key's views of Internet Mana were dismissive from the outset. He observed in January: 'I put him in that grouping of a whole bunch of sort of random, minnow kind of people' (perhaps the only time the rather substantial Dotcom had ever been compared to a minnow) 'whether it's Bill and Ben or McGillicuddy Serious or a bunch of other people, he's in that grouping' (Bennett 2014e).

Other parties' attitudes to Internet Mana were articulated as the party's personality and approach became more apparent. The Māori Party ruled out discussions with the Internet Party and Dotcom, the party president Naida Glavish saying on 25 March, 'There is no benefit for te iwi Māori in aligning with sideline splinter parties' (Small 2014a). While the Greens had been willing to talk with Mana, co-leader Metiria Turei indicated that an arrangement with Kim Dotcom would change things: 'Mana would be a different kind of political organisation if they do the deal with Kim Dotcom; we'd have to consider what that might mean for us' (Fox 2014c). In June, David Cunliffe indicated that he was open to a deal with Internet Mana (*New Zealand Herald* 2014f). By August he was giving assurances that Internet Mana would not be part of any Labour coalition (Vance 2014e), but there were sufficient elements of ambiguity in place to leave Labour vulnerable to suspicions that it would be prepared, if necessary, to work with Internet Mana in order to form a government.

Internet Mana's greatest gamble – what could have been viewed as something of a 'coup' – took place in the final week of the campaign: its suspense-filled media extravaganza, the 'Moment of Truth'. It is difficult to imagine ways in which this event – intended to indict and convict the Prime Minister and his government in a single evening, based on testimony from celebrated 'leakers', joined by a US journalist and Kim Dotcom himself – could have been any more disastrous. As it was, Internet Mana emerged, for those willing to consider it, less as a party than as a New Zealand version of 'the gang that couldn't shoot straight'.[20] As for Mana's sole MP, Hone Harawira, it would soon be clear that the agreement to form an alliance with Kim Dotcom and the Internet Party was nothing less than a political suicide pact.

Civilian Party

As in the past – dating back at least to the McGillicuddy Serious Party, which 'thrived' over six elections (1984–1999), taking part in election campaigns through televised advertisements and the allocation of broadcast air time – the 2014 campaign featured deliberate forays into semi-elaborate silliness, aspects of the country's political culture reflected in an inclination not to take politics and politicians all that seriously. In this election, however, with its myriad zany and offbeat elements, openly satirical and deliberately perverse campaign ploys were more difficult to notice, given the competition.

Nevertheless the miniscule Civilian Party launched its first television ad with a policy to build a wall around Hamilton. The 'great wall' of this city, south of Auckland, might well, if constructed, have evolved into a major tourist attraction and perhaps a tempting target for a politician driven to urge, someday, that it be torn down. The party's proposal for Hamilton to be made independent of the rest of the country noted that if every New Zealand household used energy efficient light bulbs the amount of energy saved would be the same as that used annually by Hamilton – much simpler, therefore, simply to be rid of it. Other attractive party policies included a llama for every poor child and free ice cream (Nelson 2014).[21]

The election results

All party leaders viewed election night results – the 'moment of truth' delivered by the voters – from North Island locations.[22] From whatever location the story was the same: a further term in office for National.[23] As Table 1.1 indicates, National's electoral strength remained remarkably stable. For the second election in a row the party won more than one million party votes, the only political party yet to do so. Its share of the party vote, at 47 per cent, remained virtually unchanged from 2011 – an enviable endorsement for any democratic government seeking a third successive term in office. Labour continued to slide in support, while the Greens proved unable to improve on 2011. The only parties able to do better in 2014 than three years earlier were 'populist' – New Zealand First and the Conservatives, each, in their own way, seeking to speak for individuals unhappy with elements of economic, demographic and cultural change. Other parties – ACT, United Future and the Māori Party – ended up essentially on life support, artificially propped up in one way or another, lacking broad public support for their policies and perspectives. In 2014, political party competition narrowed down to a contest in which National remained dominant, as Labour, the Greens, New Zealand First and the Conservatives searched for ways to catch up.

At the electorate level – in constituency races that matter greatly to many voters, irrespective of their virtual irrelevance to the overall composition of Parliament and the executive – the first-past-the-post system remained firmly in place. In these, too, National continued to hold a commanding lead: 41 seats to Labour's 27. For that matter, the result left Labour so enfeebled as to become virtually a first-past-the-post parliamentary party, with only five list members to accompany its 27 electorate MPs.[24] National more completely embodied the MMP idea, with nearly a third of its MPs – 19 out of 60 – coming from the party list. With those 60 MPs, National managed to achieve the largest parliamentary caucus of any party since the introduction of the MMP system.

For the Prime Minister, election night was another glorious experience: 'I'm very, very happy. It's a huge night for us' (*Dominion Post* 2014f). The media's immediate response was equally clear. The ten-page election special from the *Sunday Star Times* (21 September) featured, across two-thirds of the front page, a photograph of a smiling Prime Minister, wife and son waving beside him, at the National Party's election night victory party – and the one-word headline: 'Landslide'. Another story provided a comparable summing-up: 'Nothing stuck to Teflon John' (Duff 2014). The overall tone of the 2014 election was captured in yet another *Sunday Star Times* headline: 'Ugly campaign turns into a beautiful night for National'.

The media were united in giving Key credit for National's victory. With the Prime Minister's smiling face across the top of its front page, the *Dominion Post* had as its headline 'Key the poll slayer', with ticked boxes labelled '2008', '2011', and '2014'. The paper's editorial declared:

> National has won a resounding victory, with the best result of any party in the MMP era. That it has done so at the start of its third term, when voters usually start to tire of their leaders, is astonishing. The result is a testament to the prodigious political talents of Prime Minister John Key. Despite a torrid campaign, he banked on a simple assumption: that voters like him, and that they want, as he has often put it, 'strong, stable government'. He was right.

It concluded, of Key: 'He has won one of the most convincing election victories in our history' (*Dominion Post* 2014e).

The *Herald on Sunday* agreed: 'Last night the country spoke. It has given John Key a resounding endorsement. . . . After so much mud was flung, last night was Key's moment of truth, a moment he deserves to savour' (*Herald on Sunday* 2014).

For Key's counterpart the front page message was equally clear: 'Knives out for Cunliffe' (Vance 2014f). Other immediate post-mortems were

Table 1.1: The results of the 2014 New Zealand general election

Party	Number of party votes	Percentage of party votes	Percentage difference from 2011 to 2014	Total number of seats won	Percentage of seats won	Number of electorate votes	Percentage of electorate votes	Percentage difference from 2011 to 2014	Electorate seats	List seats
National	1,131,501	47.0	-0.3	60	49.6	1,081,787	46.1	-1.2	41	19
Labour	604,535	25.1	-2.4	32	26.4	801,287	34.1	-1.0	27	5
Green	257,359	10.7	-0.4	14	11.6	165,718	7.1	-0.1	0	14
ACT	16,689	0.7	-0.4	1	0.8	27,778	1.2	-0.2	1	0
Māori	31,849	1.3	-0.1	2	1.7	42,108	1.8	0.0	1	1
IM	34,094	1.4	+0.3	0	0.0	37,181*	1.6*	+0.2	0	0
United	5,286	0.2	-0.4	1	0.8	14,722	0.6	-0.3	1	0
NZF	208,300	8.7	+2.1	11	9.1	73,384	3.1	+1.3	0	11
Conserv.	95,598	4.0**	+1.3	0	0.0	81,075	3.5	+1.1	0	0
Others	20,411	0.9	-0.4	0	0.0	22,567	0.9	+0.2	0	0
Total	2,405,622	100.0		121	100.0	2,347,607	100.0		71	50

Turnout: 77.9%

Notes: IM=Internet Mana; United=United Future; NZF=New Zealand First; Conserv.=Conservative Party. The total given at the bottom of the Table – for the numbers of party votes and of electorate votes – excludes 'informal' votes (i.e., votes cast but not counted for any party or candidate).

* The Internet Party and Mana Movement had separate electorate candidates; the totals – 4,848 votes and 0.21 per cent for 15 Internet Party candidates; and 32,333 votes and 1.38 per cent for 18 Mana Movement candidates – have been combined. The percentage difference columns represent the difference between Internet Mana's 2014 vote totals (combined, in the party vote; campaigning separately, in the electorate vote) and Mana's 2011 vote totals.

** The Conservatives' party vote – 3.97 per cent – has been rounded up in the table. Thus, even if the threshold had been lowered to 4.0 per cent the party would not have gained representation.

Source: Electoral Commission, http://www.electionresults.govt.nz/electionresults_2014/

equally concise, capturing the post-election moment: 'Greens searching for answers' (Vance 2014g). For Winston Peters and his hopes the verdict was similarly unambiguous: 'More MPs but kingmaker job redundant' (Rutherford 2014c).

Apart from choosing the government, every election brings changes to the membership of Parliament.[25] In 2014, some of the most significant changes took place in the governing National Party. Although not always thought of as the party of youth, following the 2014 election it was National's caucus, with new MP Todd Barclay, 24, which had the youngest MP. Of the 60 National MPs elected on 20 September, 14 were in Parliament for the first time, the party able to make changes to its parliamentary caucus without destabilising its leadership. This required considerable leadership and organisational skill and was in sharp contrast with Labour's inability (under Helen Clark) to do the same when Labour won *its* third term.[26] Of course, not all of National's newly elected caucus represented renewal and rejuvenation. Deposed ministers Judith Collins and Maurice Williamson were back, their majorities somewhat reduced: Williamson held a 12,867 vote majority in Pakuranga against the Labour candidate (the margin was 13,846 in 2011); Collins's vote in Papakura dropped from 18,096 in 2011 to 15,588 in 2014, reducing her majority from 9,890 votes to 5,119. The Prime Minister, acknowledging Collins' desire to return to Cabinet, had indicated in August 2014, when she resigned, that she would not immediately get her wish: 'there's been one or two slips in recent times' (*Otago Daily Times* 2014). Post-election there were further reminders from the Prime Minister that for Collins it would be a long road back; as for Williamson, the way back was obviously so winding, and so arduous, as not to require comment.

Of the other 61 MPs, only ten were newcomers: Labour, three; Greens, one; New Zealand First, four; Māori Party, one; and ACT, one. To these were added a few 'returning' MPs. For New Zealand First there were two: Pita Paraone (2002–08) and Ron Mark (1996–2008). For Labour there were three, each of them an MP from 2008 to 2011. Carmel Sepuloni won the new Kelston electorate established by the Representation Commission following the 2013 census; Stuart Nash was successful in Napier, aided by the Conservatives' candidate Garth McVicar (well known as founder and former chief executive of the Sensible Sentencing Trust), who took enough votes from National's candidate Wayne Walford (incumbent National MP Chris Tremain having chosen to retire) to give Nash the seat – the only electorate seat to change from National to Labour. Kelvin Davis won Te Tai Tokerau, receiving a significant boost from Winston Peters' endorsement only two days before the election (Cheng 2014b).

These were rare moments of satisfaction for the Labour Party. Even in seats retained by Labour MPs, most voters gave National their party vote, as in New Lynn, where Cunliffe held his seat while National won the party vote (13,136 votes to Labour's 12,085), and in Wellington Central, retained by Grant Robertson but with both National and the Greens outpolling Labour in the party vote. In New Plymouth, Labour's Andrew Little (11,788 votes) was soundly trounced by incumbent National MP Jonathan Young (21,566 votes), with National winning the party vote in the electorate by an even larger margin (National, 20,969; Labour, 7,947). In the Māori seats voters aligned with Labour, the Māori Party's campaign to win all seven seats failing by a considerable margin. Overall, however, Labour's weak party vote left four of Labour's list MPs out of Parliament, three of them women (Carol Beaumont, Moana Mackey and Maryan Street, as well as Raymond Huo), leaving Labour's 12 remaining women MPs constituting just 37.5 per cent of its caucus,[27] no progress having been made towards the party's goal of 45 per cent in 2014.[28]

Several electorate races had particular points of interest. Two of Labour's more dysfunctional South Island candidates, Gibson and Dickson, achieved great things at the polls, although unfortunately not for their own party. National's Jo Goodhew more than doubled her majority in Rangitata, rising from 6,537 in 2011 to 14,107 against Gibson; in Selwyn, National's Amy Adams managed to increase her 19,451 majority in 2011 to 20,790 against Dickson (who brought Labour a third-place electorate race finish behind National and the Greens).[29] As for veteran MP Trevor Mallard, victory in his Hutt South electorate was accompanied by reminders of the moa, a link likely to follow him right through to retirement; his 709-vote win over National's Chris Bishop (elected on the party list) was headlined, 'Moa-hunting Mallard hangs on in Hutt [South]' (Stewart and Fensome 2014).

The performance of some high-profile minor party candidates gave some indication of their true standing within their electorates. Colin Craig won 4,923 votes in East Coast Bays, demonstrating convincingly what happens when John Key does *not* give a signal to National voters to abandon the party's electorate candidate (in this case, Minister of Foreign Affairs Murray McCully, whose 19,957 votes gave him a 15,034 vote majority over the Conservative Party leader). Another party leader, Laila Harré, received 1,315 votes against John Key (22,720 votes) in Helensville, sufficient for a fourth-place finish (Internet Mana winning 338 party votes in the electorate). Internet Mana's Georgina Beyer, a former Labour MP (1999–2007), ended her political career a second time with an overwhelming defeat, receiving 1,996 votes as Mana's candidate in Te Tai Tonga and finishing fourth behind Labour, Māori and Green Party candidates.[30] In Te Tai Tokerau, Hone Harawira became the only electorate MP to lose his seat at the 2014 election – his political fate, arising out of his own choice to enter into an alliance with Kim Dotcom and Internet Mana, foreshadowed long ago in Scripture: 'He that diggeth a pit [for others] shall fall into it.'[31]

'Moments of truth'

There were, of course, multiple 'moments of truth' in the campaign, situations in which decisive steps were taken, some of them politically fatal.

ACT

ACT's 'moment of truth' came when its new leader mused publicly about the absence of philosophical objections to the legalisation of incest, hardly an 'issue' or 'problem' on voters' minds. This was, in more than one way, Jamie Whyte's 'moment of truth', and it set an upper limit, right at the outset, to what ACT could hope to achieve in 2014. From this statement there was no hope of recovery. The opportunity for ACT to make a new start as a credible party with an alternative message, slim as it already was, disappeared at that point. In politics, as in relationships, first impressions matter. In this case, following this debacle, ACT was unable to get a second look from voters.

The party's other (and more positive) 'moment of truth', of course, came when John Key decided to renew the arrangement by which Epsom's National voters would be encouraged to cast their electorate vote for ACT's candidate rather than for National's. The lifeline tossed to David Seymour – ACT's 31-year-old candidate – meant that ACT would continue to be represented in Parliament. John Key had options – most obviously, allowing matters to take their own course, almost certainly leading to National's Paul Goldsmith becoming Epsom's MP – but, risk-averse and committed to 'stability', the Prime Minister opted to continue, with Seymour, the arrangement that had been in place for his predecessors.

Jamie Whyte's pre-election remarks, given in a speech on 14 September, had optimistically envisaged ACT holding 'the balance of power' following the election, based on its winning a fairly modest 1.2 per cent of the vote, and Whyte joining Seymour as an MP (Whyte 2014). In all this he was fated to be disappointed. Whyte himself brought in just 2,030 votes in Pakuranga, allowing him to finish fourth among four candidates, 18,358 votes behind the winner, National's less-than-charismatic Maurice Williamson.

United Future

United Future's 'moment of truth' came at the same time as David Seymour's. Separated by more than 29 years – Seymour was not quite 13 months old when Peter Dunne was first elected, aged 30, to Parliament in 1984 – the two men, one seeking his first term, the other his 11th, had their political fates decided at the same moment, 28 July, and by the same person: John Key. It would have been possible for the Prime Minister to have brought the United Future experiment – the ostensibly moderate self-described centrist party, committed to balancing the 'extremes' of both left (Labour) and right (National) – to an end. He chose not to do so, persevering with an arrangement that allowed Dunne to retain his Ōhāriu seat, extending United Future's existence for at least a further three years, Dunne's share of the vote (36.9 per cent) sufficient to retain the seat against Labour, Green and National challengers.[32]

Another 'moment of truth' is described by American writer Ernest Hemingway in *Death in the Afternoon*: 'The whole end of the bullfight was the final sword thrust, the actual encounter between the man and the animal, what the Spanish call the moment of truth' (Hemingway 1932).[33] This 'moment of truth' observes a matador in a ring, alert, steadfast against a charging bull. In 2014, with ACT and United Future, John Key faced two entities that were anything but fierce. Possessing the power to annihilate each of them – a step which, had it been taken, would have won the cheers of the multitude – Key chose to spare them both. Each party subsequently faced a further, less compassionate 'moment of truth' – a judgement delivered by an unsympathetic electorate on election day that saw two parties, each launched years ago with conviction and commitment, face to face with the facts of electoral humiliation, their combined share of the vote less than 1 per cent (0.91 per cent).

Conservatives

When it came to the Conservatives – a potentially more lethal adversary than either ACT or United Future – the Prime Minister acted more boldly, delivering a third 'moment of truth' on 28 July when announcing that the party would be receiving no electoral accommodation. While the implications of such a deal for National's own party vote cannot be known – the party might well have been punished by some of its supporters had it aligned itself with the Conservatives – the consequences for the Conservatives can be noted with some confidence. Given National's success with its Epsom and Ōhāriu arrangements, a similar gesture in an otherwise safe National seat might well have brought a Conservative candidate into Parliament. Indeed, with a Conservative MP likely to be elected, its already strong party vote – even without any arrangement the party won nearly 4 per cent – would almost certainly have grown, its vote no longer 'wasted'. A successful Conservative Party candidate could have been expected to lead a small team of newcomers, a band in sufficient numbers to have had an impact on a third Key-led government. The absence of an electoral accommodation, however, made the Conservatives' campaign fruitless, its hopes of power and influence unfulfilled.

Colin Craig's other 'moment of truth' – the turning point of his campaign – had nothing whatever to do with his party's policies, outlook or campaign messages. Indeed, when attention returned to those matters, in part through a well-funded and energetic campaign, the party's target constituency – conservative New Zealanders – proved at least somewhat receptive.

Craig's 'moment of truth' preceded the campaign, arising out of his uncertainty as to whether human beings had ever actually managed to land on the moon. As the moon landings are among the most well-documented events in human history, Craig's ambiguous assimilation of their veracity raised questions about his outlook and judgement. At least several ministerial appointments – higher education; science and innovation – already appeared off limits. Craig's campaign was regularly punctuated – via cartoons, headlines and commentary – by references to the moon landings, as in union leader Helen Kelly's televised remarks on TV3, on 7 September, that he had a better chance of being made head of the Neil Armstrong fan club than of being elected to Parliament.[34]

On 12 September (*Dominion Post*, p. A8) a cartoon under the editorial found Craig in an astronaut's suit, standing on the moon, the earth in the background, looking at a small flagpole with a newspaper headline (rather than a flag) stating 'Conservatives close in on 5%', with Craig thinking, 'Wow, I'm over the Moon! Wait . . . Do I believe it? Is it a conspiracy?'

As with Jamie Whyte's comments about incest, Colin Craig's musings about the moon were an entirely unforced error. It is one thing for a political leader to come unstuck because of views and policy preferences relating to issues and problems on voters' minds. That is the very essence of democratic politics, with voters making choices among alternatives on matters of relevance. For a leader to raise a question that is completely outside what voters are concerned about – and to do so in a way that calls into question that leader's grasp of reality – is to violate what is as much a political leader's first maxim as it is a physician's: 'first do no harm'.

Labour

The Labour Party's 2014 campaign was accompanied by so many self-inflicted wounds that there was hardly much need for Key to inflict any of his own. In retrospect Labour's first 'moment of truth' came when the party abandoned David Shearer without giving him the opportunity to face the Prime Minister in a general election. It was an impressive display of division and disloyalty, one which in due course paid huge dividends – for the National Party.

A further 'moment of truth' came with Labour's adoption and implementation of new leadership selection rules – the party's own choice. Its new approach to leadership selection brought with it the obvious possibility that a new leader could be selected without the support of the parliamentary caucus, and this is precisely what happened. The media loves nothing more than political embarrassment, and in its procedures, leading to the election of David Cunliffe, Labour gave it to them. In any case, the change of leadership achieved little for Labour's parliamentary performance or its level of public support, making the entire selection process an exercise in futility.

For David Cunliffe, a final 'moment of truth' came with the admittedly painful realisation that his colleagues did not want him as leader, and that the country did not want him as prime minister.

Greens

For the Greens, the 'moment of truth' came with the party's inability to forge a credible working arrangement with Labour. While the two parties had appeared to commit themselves to forming a coalition (if in a position to do so), their failure to develop a genuine working relationship – a common programme; a coordinated campaign strategy; a coherent approach to post-election coalition leadership – turned a potential asset into an electoral liability. The coup de grâce for the Labour–Greens partnership came near the end of the campaign, when the Greens called for a financial audit of Labour's campaign promises. While this might seem a serious and sensible way to analyse policy initiatives, the idea could not have any effect other than to undermine their partnership and the Greens' effort at appearing to be a politically mature prospect for government participation.

Internet Mana

For the originator of the 2014 'moment of truth' turn of phrase – Internet Mana – the decisive moment came not with the bizarre gathering of fugitives Edward Snowden, Julian Assange and Kim Dotcom, but with the decision by the Mana Party to enter into the arrangement with Kim Dotcom in the first place. The destiny of Mana and its MP, Hone Harawira, was foreordained from the moment they chose to link themselves with Kim Dotcom. For the overall New Zealand public, the combination of these two parties managed to achieve an even lower level of political credibility than the almost negligible amount each had possessed on its own.

Māori Party

The Māori Party's 'moment of truth' could be said to have occurred, of course, with its decision in 2008 to defy its own voters by forming a partnership with National. It may well be, as successive Māori Party leaders have argued, that Māori voters gain advantages by having the Māori Party 'at the table', its alliance with National permitting policy gains to be made. If this were clearly the case, of course, the Māori Party would never have lost the momentum associated with its establishment (see Sharples 2007). Instead, from 2008 onwards, the Māori Party has continued its decline, its credibility compromised seemingly beyond repair, in the process ending National's dream of a reliable and electorally potent Māori partner. For the Māori Party, of course, a further 'moment of truth' can be said to have come in 2005, in allowing Hone Harawira to be selected as a Māori Party candidate in the first place, setting in motion processes that were to weaken and divide a fledgling movement.

Given its links to National, it was only a matter of time before the Māori Party was going to lose its support in Māori electorates. With the departure of its founder (Tariana Turia) and its co-leader (Pita Sharples) that time – in

2014 – had arrived. A party can defy its own constituency only for so long; eventually, in a democratic society, the people make their own decisions. In 2014, the Māori Party came face to face with its own 'moment of truth', spurned by voters in six of the seven Māori electorates.

New Zealand First

For Winston Peters, the awful truth on election night was that it was possible to be both winner and loser at the same time. On the one hand, there were now eleven New Zealand First MPs, up from eight in 2011. More important, however, was the bitter truth that the phone was not going to ring; that he was 'kingmaker' only in determining which individuals were going into Parliament on New Zealand First's party list; and that he was going to spend the next three years in querulous opposition.

How had this happened, when it seemed that he was on the brink of renewed influence, once again at the centre of things? Added to other factors identified by the New Zealand First leader (see chapter 10) was the failure of New Zealand's elderly – voters over 65 years of age, receiving superannuation and in possession of a SuperGold card – to recognise and appreciate Peters' role in their well-being and vote accordingly. This, too, was a 'moment of truth', the perception of ingratitude. As Peters observed, 'when people say that New Zealand First is backed by old people they're wrong. If all – or most – or even 15 per cent – of all the people on super, and with Gold cards, had voted for us, the result of this election would have been very different.'[35]

National

As for National, in a sense its 'moment of truth' was in its capacity to retain its composure in the face of an extraordinary series of challenges, from 'dirty politics' through to the 'Moment of Truth' at the Auckland Town Hall. It benefited from the accumulation of errors and mishaps perpetrated by each of its opponents. ACT, initiated in 1993–94 as a challenge to National, was now in so weakened a state that it was only through National's effort that the party retained a presence in Parliament. United Future, likewise, had no leverage available to 'balance' National. The Māori Party, too, launched with great expectations, now lived on through a single electorate victory. National's principal adversary, Labour, was deeply divided, disoriented by factionalism, lacking confidence in its own leadership. The Greens retained a devoted following, but were not a serious threat to National's hold on power. As for New Zealand First, its leader, who turned 70 in April 2015, remained the only member of his party with the necessary flair and 'star' power to allow it to retain its tenuous foothold in Parliament.

The old saying – that oppositions don't win elections, governments lose them – also describes National's re-election triumph. In 2014 the Key government avoided losing, its record and its leadership unrejected by the electorate.[36]

For John Key, the challenge – easier to perceive than to overcome – had been to maintain his balance, avoid mistakes, and close matters out with a clear, focused, good-humoured appeal for support. This he proved able to do, on 17 September, during the final leaders' debate on TVNZ, breaking unexpected new ground in New Zealand campaign rhetoric by declaring, 'It's as simple as this. If you want to have steak for dinner tonight, go into the supermarket or your butcher and buy steak. Don't buy a lamb chop. Go in there and buy steak. If you want National to be the government, give your party vote to National.'[37]

Electoral aftermath

National

John Key quickly entered into post-election confidence and supply agreements with his three pre-election partners: ACT, United Future and the Māori Party. Ministerial portfolios were allocated to United Future leader Peter Dunne and to Māori Party leader Te Ururoa Flavell, while ACT's leader, David Seymour, as a new MP, was given a parliamentary under-secretary position on the fringes of the executive.[38]

In the post-election aftermath the sudden departure of one of National's re-elected MPs, Mike Sabin, on 30 January gave opposition parties a chance to weaken National's parliamentary position and image of electoral invincibility. It was an opportunity taken up by Winston Peters, who chose to stand in the Northland electorate where he had long-standing ties, winning the seat on 28 March with an assist from Andrew Little, whose eventual nod to Labour voters to give Peters their support contributed to the victory.

Labour

The post-election period opened with prevarication and excuses, Cunliffe arguing, 'I honestly don't think it was a candidate or a leader problem. I think we need to reflect on all of our systems and processes' (*Sunday Star*

Times 2014). From his perspective as a newly returned MP, Stuart Nash observed that 'there will be a whole lot of soul-searching going on. When 75 per cent of the electorate say they don't want Labour, you have to do something different' (Kilgallon 2014).

Cunliffe's resolve to stay on as leader was evident on election night in his speech to supporters acknowledging the results, and in a letter, declaring, 'I will be seeking a new mandate from the party, the affiliates and the caucus by the end of the year' (*New Zealand Herald* 2014d). Resigning a week later, Cunliffe again indicated that he was ready to lead the party at the next general election: 'I am announcing today that I will nominate for a primary contest, which will be held across the caucus, the party membership and the affiliates as the party constitution requires' (*New Zealand Herald* 2014e). On television he observed, 'We've had three leaders in three years. I've learned on the job. I'm match fit, I'm tough now, and I'm ready to run' (*Breakfast*, TV One, 30 September). Among his arguments was the notion that while Labour had lost support in 2014, its decline – from 27.48 per cent in 2011 to 25.13 in 2014 – was less than it had been in 2011 (from 2008, when it had won 33.99 per cent), suggesting, in his view, a degree of progress: 'This is the third election in a row the Labour Party vote has gone down. Fortunately it hasn't gone down as much this time as the two previous ones; you could argue that we're starting to turn that around' (*Campbell Live*, TV3, 29 September); 2014 reinterpreted, not so much a further defeat as an improved performance. This was, however, probably not quite what the party had had in mind when removing David Shearer from the leadership.

Equally uncompelling was Cunliffe's suggestion that the Prime Minister preferred that the Labour leader resign, not wishing to have to come up against him again in 2017. This came about when Key, asked what he would have done had National lost the election, simply reiterated the position that he'd articulated previously – namely, that if defeated he would resign the leadership. In response, Cunliffe observed that Key 'would say that, wouldn't he', adding, 'Perhaps he doesn't want to go up against me again and so he's doing what he can to ensure that's not what happens' (*Campbell Live*, TV3, 29 September; Bennett 2014d). This was, in reality, another decisive 'moment of truth', in this case for Cunliffe, the idea that a victorious John Key didn't want Cunliffe to remain leader out of fear of facing him again in 2017 probably the very definition of delusional.

With Cunliffe describing himself as a 'battle-hardened leader' (RadioLive, 21 September), seeking a new mandate for the good of the party, not himself, he again envisaged seeking the leadership even without the backing of his own (now somewhat reduced) parliamentary caucus. Cunliffe also argued that previous Labour leaders had lost and been permitted to stay on to fight again, with examples including Norman Kirk (unsuccessful as party leader in 1966 and 1969 but successful in 1972) and, less happily, Bill Rowling (who led Labour to three election defeats in a row – 1975, 1978 and 1981 – and was removed, against his will, in February 1983, allowing David Lange to assume the leadership and bring the party back to power in 1984).

In the end, Cunliffe wisely chose not to compete in what became a four-way competition for the leadership, one that was, yet again, decided by the votes cast by the party and union membership, as the choice of the parliamentary caucus – Wellington Central MP Grant Robertson – was narrowly defeated by list MP Andrew Little (50.52 per cent to 49.48 per cent). The possibility that Robertson's sexual orientation might have been a factor in the vote also did little to embellish Labour's image as a progressive and tolerant political force. What the election further revealed were failures within Labour to learn lessons from its 2014 defeat, as personal egos and factionalism retained their important place in the competition.[39] It also showed, ironically, how much Labour owed to MMP, as without the system its new leader would not be in Parliament, his precarious presence made possible only by being the last of the five Labour MPs able to be elected via the party list.

Greens

With Labour weak and Internet Mana discredited, the Greens might have been expected to achieve a better result than they did. Nevertheless, characteristically, there were no public rumblings against the party's leadership or its campaign, MP Gareth Hughes saying, 'They've run a spectacular campaign' (Easton 2014).

Post-election the Greens found themselves caught up in several unexpected scenarios. A Green MP, Steffan Browning, did lasting harm to his own reputation, if not that of his party, by suggesting in late October that the World Health Organization make headway against the virulent ebola virus by treating patients with homeopathic remedies. The image of a 'flaky' Green Party – midway between hippie 'new age' and far-left Marxist philosophies – was at least temporarily revived, even as the Greens' parliamentary team did their best to quickly squelch this line of thinking by removing Browning from his natural health products portfolio.

On 30 January 2015 the Greens' co-leader, Russel Norman, announced his intention to resign from his co-leadership position. While opening up the opportunity for new leadership to emerge and a new 'image' to be developed, the loss of a senior figure, owing to disappointment over the election results, could hardly be viewed as an entirely positive outcome. Subsequently the Greens held elections for a new male co-leader, as four candidates – MPs Kevin Hague, Gareth Hughes and the newly elected James Shaw, as well as Vernon Tava (the Greens' Auckland province co-convenor) – competed for the position (Green Party 2015). The contest revealed divisions within the party, over personality as well as policy, with Shaw seen as the more centrist figure. The leadership vote, won by Shaw on 31 May, meant that post-election the Greens would be challenged to unify behind a new co-leader while contemplating policies and strategies intended to expand the party's support.

New Zealand First

Winston Peters' post-election response applauded New Zealand First's increased support while lamenting that it had fallen just short: 'We did just fail by 1 per cent to achieve that. Near enough is not good enough' (Rutherford 2014d). Prior to the election the media envisaged a very different election night for the veteran politician: 'John Key and David Cunliffe could be in a race to pick up the phone to Winston Peters tomorrow night' (Watkins 2014d). A scenario involving three more years in opposition, leading his far-from-stellar caucus at Parliament, could not have been other than a depressing prospect. What soon followed, however, was unexpected: another campaign, in Northland, and the New Zealand First leader, long ago content (in his own words) simply to be 'the member for Tauranga', now had a new electorate to represent. With the victory came new energy and momentum, the three-year term at Parliament no longer a sentence so much as a platform from which to conjure up fresh dreams of power and influence.

Conservatives

For Colin Craig, election night brought its own unavoidable 'moment of truth': the discovery that for all his efforts, and all his electoral expenditure, he was not, after all, going to be spending the 2014–17 years as a member of the New Zealand Parliament. This should have been no surprise to him, though it may well have been.

Looking to the future, the party's Epsom candidate (1,725 votes, in fifth place) and chief executive, former Families Commission member Christine Rankin, promised, 'We will be back', describing the Conservatives as 'a force to be reckoned with' (Wall 2014). In the meantime, however, the Conservatives were 'away', out of Parliament, once again in the position of having limited access to the media and the attention of the voting public – limited, that is, until the time bomb set ticking by the resignation of Craig's press secretary, Rachel MacGregor, two days before the election finally exploded in June 2015, leading to Craig's resignation (as leader), as well as that of Rankin and other members of the Conservatives' board. Whatever the 'truth' may be about MacGregor's departure, the Conservatives' 'moment' as a potential parliamentary player would seem to have come and gone, yet the latest example of a party based on traditional values foundering amid farcical and somewhat fantastic confusion.

ACT

On 3 October Jamie Whyte resigned as ACT's leader, describing the party's brand as 'tarnished' and the result as a 'terrible disappointment': 'I'm the leader of the party, the failure is my responsibility.' He went on to say that ACT was 'still a powerful brand': 'I don't think we need to re-brand, I think maybe what we need to do is – oddly enough, sometimes what you need to do is stick to your knitting – if we just keep doing what we believe in, I think we can earn the respect of the population' (Manning 2014). He added: 'I think that if we just keep true to our principles, our election fortunes will rise again' – a philosophical position with no evidence to support it.

ACT's survivor (and leader), new MP David Seymour, needed the electoral aftermath to recover from his wounds, having campaigned so vigorously that he injured his hand knocking on Epsom electors' doors: 'I really do have tissue damage on my hand, there are a lot of doorbells and intercoms in Epsom but you do knock on a few doors. You do get a few raps on your knuckles' (Dastgheib 2014). Seymour had already described himself in his pre-election meet-the-candidate video, available on YouTube, as probably 'the first candidate in New Zealand political history to be sunburnt from campaigning' (Seymour 2014). Whether treatment for such occupation-related mishaps would be covered by accident compensation – and whether an ACT MP would be entirely comfortable in accepting it – were matters left to be explored.

The day after the election Seymour talked about the need to be 'disciplined and collegial', claiming that 'at this point everyone's happy where we are', while stating that 'we acknowledge that over the three years to come we have to find a way to get more than 0.7 per cent of New Zealanders interested in voting for us. How exactly that strategy goes is obviously not something we've figured out entirely this morning' (Manning 2014). The post-election environment for the ACT Party was perhaps more 'balanced' than the party's campaign. With an outcome lending itself neither to euphoria nor depression, ACT survived to go on competing for votes and seats. In David Seymour the party had a fresh mandate from Epsom's voters and a new MP whose attributes include the many things that he is not (when contrasted with previous ACT leaders): he is free from scandal; lacks prior political baggage; and cannot become caught up in divisive quarrels with parliamentary colleagues (not, in fact, having any).

United Future

Post-election, United Future's leader and sole MP, Peter Dunne, described the result as 'embarrassing', attributing the outcome to an inadequate 'resource base in terms of candidates or finances'. He also candidly referred to another, more fundamental element: 'I think that also frankly we didn't give people sufficient reason to vote for us.' He observed that voters, in his view, 'quite like our policies [and] they quite liked what we stood for', but did not consider what United Future was offering sufficient to give the party their vote (Radio New Zealand 2014f). As a result, Dunne stated that the party would need to go back to basics (whatever that may mean) and focus on the party's core principles (whatever those may be) so as to regain voters' trust and support. In the meantime, as MP (for the eleventh straight term) and as United Future party leader, Dunne was in a position to sign a further confidence and supply agreement with John Key and retain his ministerial position outside Cabinet.

Māori Party

On 1 November the Māori Party completed its transition to new leadership with the confirmation of new MP Marama Fox – the party's first ever list MP – as the party's female co-leader. Post-election discussions at the party's 1 November Annual General Meeting found Flavell again defending the Māori Party's association with the National Party, stating: 'One issue that comes up as criticism of the Māori Party is that we have given up on our people, have turned our backs on our people. How on earth can people come to that conclusion?' (Trevett 2014g). Whatever Māori Party leaders themselves may feel – and irrespective of how many Treaty settlements National governments are able to negotiate and implement – it is evident that voters on the Māori rolls remain to be persuaded that National is their 'friend', rather than an historic and implacable adversary. Nevertheless, after the election National and the Māori Party signed their third successive confidence and supply agreement, with Flavell becoming Minister for Māori Development and Minister for Whānau Ora, arguably achieving 'the right position to at least try to make a difference' (Cheng 2014e).

Internet Mana

Hone Harawira's response to his election night defeat had been to ring Labour candidate Kelvin Davis to say that he was not going to concede. According to Davis, 'He started off [saying] I've never conceded anything to anyone and I'm not going to concede tonight' (Fox 2014d). The ability to concede defeat graciously thus became another of the political conventions unappreciated by the departing MP, the requested recount in due course leaving him four votes worse off than on election night.

Reflecting on his defeat, Harawira saw the result as an example of negative voting: 'This isn't love for Kelvin [Davis], it's a hatred of me and a hatred of Mana.' He also reinterpreted the broad multi-party desire for his defeat as an example of 'our success that four other parties backed one candidate' (Nippert 2014d), rather than a measure of failure, taking a defiant pride in having evoked such hostility that so many otherwise incompatible political movements looked forward to his departure from Parliament.

In Harawira's view the deal he had made with Kim Dotcom had been 'a risk worth taking' so as to get other MPs into Parliament (Rutherford 2014b). It was, nevertheless, an arrangement in which he had something to lose – his seat in Parliament. Those with less at stake also looked back with little apparent remorse. On 13 December Mana's co-vice president, John Minto, said, 'we knew it was a big risk, but it was a risk we were prepared to take' (Radio New Zealand 2014g). As noted, it was a risk with no real consequences for him; as candidate for Mt Roskill – he received 300 votes against incumbent Labour MP Phil Goff's 18,637 – he had no chance of getting into Parliament on his own. It was an alliance with the Internet Party, and with Kim Dotcom, that gave him that prospect; if unsuccessful he had nothing to lose. Apart from Harawira the same could be said of all of the other individuals on the joint Internet Mana party list.

Kim Dotcom's election night response to Internet Mana's performance was admirably candid: 'I take full responsibility for this loss tonight because the brand Kim Dotcom is poisoned' (Nippert 2014d). So too, it seemed, was the Internet Mana partnership. With no MPs, the two parties agreed to stop working together, formally dissolving their alliance on 13 December (Radio New Zealand 2014g). Those complicit in the Internet Mana fiasco began to move on. Laila Harré officially resigned as Internet Party leader (and party member) on 15 December (Wong 2014d). The Internet Mana alliance – an expedient arrangement which proved inexpedient for those entering into it – came to an end officially when, on 19 December, New Zealand's Electoral Commission cancelled the party's registration, removing it from its register of parties. This followed a letter from Harawira, in his capacity as Mana Party leader, advising that Mana had formally split from the Internet Party.

In the end, the slight rise and precipitous fall of Internet Mana took less than five months to accomplish: registered on 24 July, terminated on 19 December.

Last words

Aspirations for change – bringing new perspectives, renewed energy – were evident, as ever, in the maiden speeches made by new MPs.[40] Green MP James Shaw – while describing himself as 'a member of our country's loyal opposition', his role 'to challenge and to speak truth to power' – rejected 'partisanship for its own sake', identifying 'political tribalism' as 'the single greatest barrier to creating enduring solutions to the great challenges of our time'. Admitting 'I do not know what the answers are', he observed, hearkening back to elements of the impulse behind the move to MMP in the first place, that 'the first step in finding the answers is to work together'.

ACT leader David Seymour celebrated 'the creative power of a free society', including 'the power to try new things and find what works', before reaffirming the core ACT outlook towards the individual and government, looking towards the day 'when the role of government is not "whatever the government defines it to be", as one former Prime Minister put it, but clearly defined to maximise individual freedom'.

New National MP Sarah Dowie was similarly eloquent:

On winning the seat of Invercargill I was told by a friend to 'dream big'. In response I defer to one of the most powerful symbols of triumph over adversity, someone who achieved and inspired despite the odds. Helen Keller said: 'One can never consent to creep when one feels an impulse to soar.' I promise to listen, to learn, to work, to dream and to do my best to soar.

The last word on the 2014 election belongs, however, to the person who won it – the prime minister, John Key.

On election night, in celebration, he declared that it was 'a victory for those who kept the faith', 'a victory for those who refused to be distracted'. In some measure he could be said to have been speaking of himself, having remained focused amid the sound and the fury of an astonishingly peculiar campaign.

No doubt the new term would bring its own hazards and opportunities, new choices to be made, potential 'moments of truth' of one kind or another. Knowing how quickly everything can go wrong, the Prime Minister was already cautioning about dangers associated with a third-term victory: 'One of the worst things you can do is let this sort of thing go to your head', emphasising to himself as well as to his newly elected colleagues 'not to be out of touch or be seen as arrogant'. Such sentiments are consistent with a perspective attributed to Abraham Lincoln: 'Nearly all men can stand adversity, but if you want to test a man's character, give him power.'[41]

Having power (and responsibility) yet again, the Prime Minister took time out to laud the country and people he had just been given a mandate to lead: 'I've never stopped marvelling at the creativity, the ingenuity, the compassion, the generosity and kindness of New Zealanders. We are the finest little nation on the planet, and I truly believe that.'

The 2014 election saw New Zealand's voters give John Key a renewed vote of confidence. With those words, the Prime Minister returned the favour.

2

ELECTION IN A BUBBLE

Colin James

The 2014 election came 30 years after the 1984 election which triggered a tectonic shift in policy, ideology and our understanding of ourselves. There was no tectonic wrench in 2014, though the Labour Party could be forgiven for thinking the ground was liquefying under its ageing edifice. But pressure had been building up in the political, ideological and social plates and seismic analysis is appropriate in addition to the usual microscopic and telescopic inquiry.

In the 20 years leading up to 1984 the tectonic tension comprised two main elements.

One was the rise of a generation born late in or after the Second World War, which began to reach its twenties from the mid-1960s. This was a generation born into security and plenty and was the first to go to university in large numbers. Security and plenty gave it the confidence and brashness to demand and live out personal freedoms its parents had suppressed in pursuit of security after a severe economic depression and a world war. Security and plenty also allowed the new generation scope for idealism, to demand a society of equal opportunity – access to education, health care, decent jobs and wages, as well as gender and racial equality. This idealism extended into international affairs, in opposition to nuclear weapons and apartheid and cold war imperialism, as in the United States' intervention in Vietnam.

This new-generation phenomenon was widespread in various forms and to various degrees among this rising generation in other rich countries – even, behind the veil, in the Soviet Union and its satellites (Riga Theatre 2010). In New Zealand there was an additional dimension: the confidence to separate from Empire and express a distinct culture and way of life, evident first in the arts, then business, then political radicalism, then revisionist history. The 1980s were New Zealand's independence revolution, a tectonic shift of mentality.

That mentality shift applied also to our demography, specifically to accepting the value of our indigenous culture as equal in status to the culture bequeathed from Empire. That invention of biculturalism and its formalisation in the power structure through legislation and practice, endorsed in court decisions, was another tectonic shift.

There was also pressure – one might say a tsunami – from outside: a combination of a changing global economy and a challenge to the Keynesian orthodoxy of the post-1930s-Depression decades.

The post-1945 job-and-wage-rich rebuilding of North Atlantic economies – known in France as the 'trente glorieuses', the '30 glorious years' – stalled when the Organisation of Petroleum Exporting Countries quadrupled the price of oil in late 1973. Inflation, which had risen through the 1950s to 1970s, turned to 'stagflation' as GDP growth stalled. In addition, the rapidly industrialising countries on the east Asian periphery challenged the North Atlantic's dominance.

A new cohort of market-liberal economists blamed stagflation on the state's substantial role in taxation, social spending, business and resources regulation and ownership of major companies and utilities, the Keynesian mixed economy. They argued that this fuelled inflation, veiled price signals, added to transaction costs of doing business, discouraged innovation and investment and undermined productivity and profits. This market-liberal critique and resultant policy prescription, which I call 'Friedmanism' after its highest-profile exponent, Milton Friedman, urged strict control of the money supply to contain inflation and a smaller role for the state in taxation, regulation and ownership of business assets.[1]

In New Zealand the Treasury adopted the analysis and prescription and argued for it behind the scenes, including to Labour's finance spokesperson, Roger Douglas. A dissident National backbench advocated 'more market' policies from 1979, which some senior Labour members of Parliament echoed mildly in speeches. The direction of policy change was clear, though it was unclear when and how vigorously and extensively it would be adopted and implemented.

The 'when' turned out to be the period after the 1984 election. The rising postwar generation was prominent in the new Labour cabinet. Its valuing of freedom predisposed it to market liberalism. Removal of protection, deregulation, privatisation and tax reform followed in fast order in a series of rolling waves that added up to a policy revolution. The result was an upward transfer of income and wealth which greatly increased inequality and insecurity of employment and income – in effect ending the near-guarantee established by the 1935–49 Labour government of employment and of an income from that employment that ensured a reasonable standard of living. On the other hand, in keeping with the rising generation's idealistic dimension, the post-1984 Labour government actually increased social assistance (health care, education, housing, benefits, assistance to Māori) as a percentage of GDP. It also continued to support collective workplace bargaining.[2] The National government that replaced the Labour government in 1990 carried on the policy revolution, deregulating the labour 'market' and cutting social security payments.

Broadly, this Friedmanite orthodoxy has held since then, modestly qualified with some 'third way' modifications by the 1999–2008 Labour government and some re-regulation by the fourth National government since 2008 to fix serious failures of light regulation, notably in the non-bank finance sector, building rules and workplace safety.

A fresh challenge to orthodox thinking

But now the Friedmanite orthodoxy is under sustained scrutiny, debate and attack. That has developed over the past six years in the wake of a convulsion of financial capitalism, the 'global financial crisis' (GFC) precipitated by the bursting of the 'derivatives' bubble in 2007–08. The GFC was a disjunctive shock, of the sort from which there can be no return to business as usual. We are commemorating a similar shock – the First World War – right now.

The challenge has come from many angles, including from those who want to secure market capitalism and those who think it needs considerable modification or replacement (Wolf 2014[3]). The most influential challenge so far has come from the French economist, Thomas Piketty, who in 2013 published a detailed analysis of the relativity between capital-income and labour-income which finds a major shift in favour of capital during the Friedmanite period (Piketty 2013–14).

There is as yet no replacement orthodoxy. But whatever it turns out to be, it cannot be a simple revival of Keynesian economics with modifications. The world has changed and is continuing this decade to change rapidly, disturbing social order, reshaping and relocating global value chains and markets and redefining the nature and location of work and income.

Drivers of change

There are two main drivers, which intersect and interact.

One is the rebalancing of the global economy and, with that, global politics.

This is well known and has been rapidly and deeply relocating production and work. It has lifted hundreds of millions of people out of poverty, has created global companies owing allegiance to no country, and has changed supply chains into global value chains which make tariff protection less effective or counterproductive and potentially obsolete. China, India and other 'emerging economy' nations are demanding a bigger role in the rules, conduct and leading positions of international forums and organisations, and those rules may change in ways that are sub-optimal for New Zealand. These countries also assert different forms of government and political organisation to compete with liberal democracy and different forms of economic organisation to compete with liberal market-capitalism They will also generate new science and other innovations (for example, in surgical and other healthcare procedures). Half a millennium of North Atlantic – 'western' – dominance of ideas is coming to an end. There is a contest now.

At the same time global security structures are being reframed, reworked and remade. In place of global order – four decades when the United States and the Soviet Union kept an uneasy but mutually self-interested 'peace' followed by two decades in which the United States assumed unipolar dominance – there is global disorder (Haass 2014). China and Russia are asserting the reconstitution of their past empires. The Arab world has gone tribal and sectarian in Iraq, Syria, Lebanon, Palestine, Yemen and Libya, with serious implications for the stability of Saudi Arabia and the Gulf States. Egypt has reverted to authoritarian rule. Turkey is increasingly authoritarian. Others, including non-Arab Shiite Iran, may be drawn into the turmoil, with unpredictable results. New types of conflict both localise and globalise insecurity. Identifying the 'enemy' is not simple, as the 'western' forces found in Afghanistan and as others are finding in Iraq and Syria.

Moreover, in addition to the well-known globalisation – or hyper-globalisation (Rodrik 2011) – of capital, finance and production there is a globalisation of people. Some 300 million live outside the borders of the countries they were born in. This is changing and in some cases destabilising the societies they have moved to; once homogeneous societies are becoming multicultural. At the same time the GFC and consequent economic contraction or disruption have generated considerable economic and social stress, spawning populist movements with substantial followings in Europe and the United States, which can destabilise politics and policies in non-rational and unpredictable ways.

The second major driver of global change is a disruptive technology, digital technology, which has been developing since the 1940s but has come of age in this decade. It is turning the hyperglobalised world into one which is hyperconnected (both between and among individuals and between individuals and organisations ranging from terror groups to firms and state authorities). It is also hyperdatamined, stripping privacy from individuals as their identities, shopping habits and other activities become the property of firms, other organisations and state authorities.

Digital technology is rapidly and radically transforming how goods and services – no longer distinct categories – are designed, funded, produced and marketed and how 'factories' are organised, operated and located. It is robotising production and processing lines. With 'additive manufacturing' (3D printing), in ten years much 'trade' may be in raw materials and software and 'production' may be at the point of sale or consumption. Digital technology is changing how children are educated and how adults add to their skills and it is changing the nature of skills, not just the specific technical skills, that workers need. It is changing how illness and disability can be diagnosed, offset and treated, for example with nerve interference and gene manipulation. It is changing the definition of scale, enabling niche operators to find collaborators, backers and buyers. It is redefining national, corporate and individual 'security'.

The social impact is profound, deep and fast – and global. Called by some the third industrial revolution and by others the fourth, it is akin to the first industrial revolution, but multiple times faster – within a cohort, not across generations. Coming on top of the relocation of jobs in the 1980s' and 1990s' globalisation, which changed the *location* of work, it is changing the *nature* of work and income.

The coming changes in politics and policy

This social change will in turn drive big, possibly wrenching, changes in our politics and policy imperatives. We are only beginning to get an inkling of the extent and complexity of the privacy, trust, ethical and intellectual property issues, let alone write laws for them or develop social customs to manage them, and the laws that are written go quickly out of date.

In addition, global life-sustaining ecosystems are being destabilised and other resources put under increasing strain. Water is scarce in many places. Climate change is coming. There is serious pollution in many 'emerging economy' countries. Food security is a worry for at least one billion people and the global population is projected to increase by another two billion by 2060. That opens opportunities for resource-rich New Zealand but also the risk that the world becomes a much more hostile place or that big, strong nations muscle in here. A tiny indicator of that possibility was the pre-election controversy over the sale of farms and houses to Chinese.

Add all this up. We are in a very different world from 20 years ago and probably a very different one from 20 years hence. The 2014 election came in the middle of a decade of tectonic change, which might slide through smoothly but may be painfully disruptive.

Deep, fast, disorienting, exciting and scary change was the context for the 2014 election: one presaging a shift in political-economy thinking, at least on the Keynes-to-Friedman level and possibly at the more fundamental level of the Enlightenment and the decades that followed.

An election in a bubble

But within New Zealand as the election campaign wended through August and September there was no general-public sense of impending or actual tectonic change, either at home or abroad. So to examine the election we need to put aside the seismic instruments and reach for the GPS locator and the microscope.

New Zealand was in a little bubble of fortuitous economic growth. Rapidly expanding demand and high prices for dairy, and to some extent other primary products, was one factor. The rebuilding of Christchurch, by early 2014 fully in gear, was another. They generated economic numbers that built very strong business confidence. The commentary was optimistic.

This fed into improved household finances, which are the marker for how the economy plays in elections. There had been modest gains in income and jobs and there was cautious to modest confidence the improvement would continue. Consumer confidence was strong through 2014, though it peaked mid-year.

A tight government

The government projected confidence and competence. At its apex was a tight trio. John Key was the presenter. Bill English was the fiscal manager and policy wonk who at the ministerial level was associated with most reforms, including the public service ('more with less', then a set of quantified 'results' stretching out several years and in some cases crossing portfolio boundaries), tax, water policy (using the 'collaborative governance' technique involving all interest groups to generate a consensus), education and social assistance (welfare). For welfare English imported from ACC the actuarial-investment approach which may be the National-led government's most important policy change. Steven Joyce was the project manager, focused on short-term measures designed to lift GDP growth (a way of thinking akin to business quarterly reporting) and quick to heavy those who got in his way, overshadowing the ministers in related economic development portfolios such as energy and ensuring other initiatives didn't get in the way of GDP growth.

These three formed a strategic inner cabinet with Gerry Brownlee, who brought the 'ordinary' person's perspective, and Murray McCully, billed as a political strategist though actually more of a shadowy tactician. Paula Bennett and Simon Bridges occasionally looked in.

Down the cabinet Tony Ryall squeezed more from hospitals and kept the pips from squeaking too much, Chris Finlayson set a cracking pace in Treaty of Waitangi settlements, and Tim Groser managed trade relations with aplomb, but was hampered in climate change by conceptual and Joycean difficulties.

Failures and lapses of oversight management by weaker or blinkered ministers didn't detract significantly from public confidence (though they did raise questions about Key's management). Likewise, growing agitation about 'inequality' didn't translate into a shift in support for opposition parties riding that issue. And when something went badly wrong, as in the collapse of the badly managed Pike River coalmine in 2010, the response was remedial legislation.

Moreover, Key proved remarkably adept at getting underperforming or ageing ministers and MPs to contemplate life after politics. By election time 2014, 15 of those elected in 2011 had moved on, with zero fuss. No such regeneration of a major party has been done in 'peacetime' (that is, while in power) before.

And a macro-personality

Key himself was the third main factor working for the government. He is likeable, blokey and jokey and at home with radio 'shock jocks', good with his family, an easy mixer, moderately pleasant-looking and plausible. He was trusted to get things more or less right, even if some things he did were not entirely in accord with proper process.[4]

Key, in short, is a macro-personality. A macro-personality personifies the party and attracts votes to him/herself, including of many who would not otherwise vote for the party (Anderson 2014).

Voters are prepared to give such macro-personalities the benefit of the doubt – as they did in Key's case over the revelations by the self-regarding Nicky Hager in his book of emails detailing grubby behind-the-scenes National Party machinations, launched on 13 August (Hager 2014). This benefit of the doubt was despite Key's evasive responses to the book's charges and his implausible labelling of the controversy it caused as a 'left-wing conspiracy'; and despite, or because of, his firing of Judith Collins on 30 August when a right-wing blogger publicised claims (not upheld in the subsequent government inquiry) that she had helped undermine a senior public servant. Voters told focus group pollsters they didn't understand the implications of the Hager assertions and their relevance to the election and few deserted National on that score. (The actual relevance was that rules-observing conduct and process – that is, a well-functioning democracy – is *the* issue in an election (James 2014a). But that would likely play a decisive part in people's decisions as to how to vote only if it stripped trust off a party or leader.)

The improved economy and household finances, the picture of government competence and Key's macro-personality added up to very strong positive readings in the UMR and Morgan polls that the country was on the right track/going in the right direction. Such a high reading normally points to re-election of an incumbent government in some form.

And no visible alternative government

There was a fourth factor: the lack of a clearly visible alternative government.

Through 2013 the combined polling by Labour and the Greens headed National's polling by 0.5 per cent. This suggested that there was a genuine choice between a Labour–Green-led government and a National-led one.

It also suggested, given reasonable polling for New Zealand First, that the outcome could very well depend on the choice Winston Peters made after the election.

By April or May – and certainly by July – Peters was looking more likely to go with National. This was even though he harboured a deep resentment at Key's treatment of him in 2008 over his (Peters') acceptance of business donations, which probably contributed to the New Zealand First Party's exit from Parliament at that election. The likely choice of National was also despite New Zealand First's manifesto being much closer to Labour's policy line than to National's, its conference-delegate-level rank and file also being nearer Labour than National and some serious sticking points with National, including over immigration and inward foreign investment.

Labour could at best offer Peters only third in a Labour-led lineup after the Greens, and even then it might need Internet Mana votes for a majority. With National, New Zealand First would have been second biggest, far ahead of National's three supporting micro-parties.

Moreover, by April-May Labour's support was sliding. There is a range of reasons for that but one is that David Cunliffe as leader fluffed his lines on several high-profile occasions, was exposed as having a secret trust to fund his campaign for the Labour leadership in 2013, accused Key of having a house in a leafy suburb when he did too and said different things to different audiences. Cunliffe, though personable – a competent former minister, a capable debater against Key on television and an orator with presence – was no macro-personality. If anything, he was, for Labour, a negative factor.

In addition, Cunliffe had drawn back from the cooperative relationship with the Greens that had been developing in 2013 under previous leader David Shearer. When the Greens tried to resuscitate the cooperation in May, proposing that the two parties campaign as a coalition, Cunliffe rejected that – but then did not fill the void with a formulation that would have given a clear voting option to those looking for an alternative government to vote for.

That turned away those looking for an alternative government and set a spiral. Labour slid in the polls, and the more it slid the less attractive it looked and the more it slid.

Populism and poison

And as Labour slid, some voters wanting a brake on National shifted to New Zealand First, which climbed from a poll average of 4.9 per cent at mid-August to 8.7 per cent in the election. There may also have been an element of brake-seeking in the Conservatives' 3.97 per cent: while the Conservatives were to the right of National on moral and social issues, they were not market-liberals: they were against open foreign investment and asset sales and wanted binding referendums as a restraint on governments.

There was also probably an element of populist response in the rise in these two parties' votes: populism is a channel for voting 'against' policies and people, especially the elites, or in protest at financial and other stress.

But compared with the populist waves in Europe and the United States, in 2014 New Zealand it was very mild – unless, that is, Key's macro-personalisation of National could be interpreted as a brand of populism.

Might the Hager exposures have generated a quasi-populist surge to Labour away from National? If anything, polling suggested Labour was damaged as much as National. Voters seemed to read the phrase 'dirty politics' as a tautology: all politicians do it, so what? Key rode it out, even though initially handling it ineptly.[5]

In addition, Kim Dotcom administered what he himself on election night called 'poison'. The more Labour slid in the polls, the more it looked to voters as if Labour would need Dotcom's Faustian Internet Mana concoction: Dotcom's lavish funding of a joint campaign in return for leveraging some seats on the back of Hone Harawira's Te Tai Tokerau seat. The poison killed Harawira's hold on his seat. It attracted few of the young freedom-and-idealism voters whom Internet leader Laila Harré (ex-Alliance, ex-Green) discerned as potential recruits (as the Pirate Party had briefly managed in Germany). Those it did attract were mainly in the 'university' seats where the Greens do best. At one of the rock-concert parties Dotcom put on to attract young people he got them chanting 'Fuck John Key'. His trumpeted king hit on Key on 15 September featuring United States spy leaker Edward Snowden, Snowden write-up journalist Glenn Greenwald and Wikileaks' founder Julian Assange, detailing spy cooperation with the United States, fell flat. An alleged 2010 Warner Brothers email of a secret plan involving Key in Dotcom's extradition appeared to be a fake.

Dotcom's achievement, apart from destroying Mana and tainting Labour, appears (from discussions with National activists) to have been to add weight to National's campaign to persuade National-leaning potential non-voters to vote. That, plus dumping Mana's support into the wasted vote, was likely the difference between National forming a government with its three lapdog support parties and needing New Zealand First.

Targeting the vote

After the 2011 election there was much talk, especially on the Labour side, of the 'enrolled non-vote' and of declining overall voter turnout. On 29 May 2014 the Electoral Commission sponsored a one-day conference to discuss this and promote, especially to young people, the value of voting.

In the run-up to the 2014 election National worried that its supporters might become complacent and deprive it of the votes needed to form a stable government post-2014. At the party's annual conference on 28–29 June, John Key and campaign manager Steven Joyce hammered home the need to activate every possible National vote. That message was repeated at the launch on 24 August. According to party officials, twice as many phone calls were made to actual and potential supporters as in 2011. By using electorate demographic data from the election study and coupling that with the party's own extensive canvassing data, National was better able to target its calls, as well as the content and vehicle of its messages and its follow-up contact.

Labour drew on United States techniques (Issenberg 2012, 2012a) to run an even more targeted campaign than National, trialled successfully in the Ikaroa-Rāwhiti and Christchurch East by-election campaigns in 2013 and drawing on meshblock-level data (as described in detail elsewhere in this book by Rob Salmond). The voters targeted were those who had not voted in 2008 and/or 2011 who had characteristics likely to tip them into the Labour camp if they voted. Labour officials say that around four times the number of calls were made than in 2011.

Logically, if the two main parties were equally effective in getting sympathetic non-voters to vote, Labour should have added more votes to its total than National. That is because past experience indicated more Labour-leaning people were likely not to vote than National-leaning voters. One argument is that those in lower socioeconomic and minority ethnic groups perceive less of a stake in the system than those in higher socioeconomic strata and those of mainstream ethnicity, as evidenced, for example, in the low turnout in successive elections in Māori electorates and in general electorates with a high proportion of Māori and Pasifika.

But the broad results suggest that National was more effective than Labour: the biggest swing to National in a bloc of seats was in its strong seats on the Auckland isthmus. Labour could not counter the strong tide running for National and against itself.

The Greens also did far more canvassing, in keeping with their status as the third largest party and their growing political professionalism.

National's small parties – and the going home of the Māori vote

In the 2014 election voters did serious damage to National's three small support parties.

ACT, which early in 2014 had grandiose visions of nine MPs (ACT 2014), finished with only the Epsom seat, by grace of National indicating to its supporters that they should cast their electorate vote for ACT's David Seymour. ACT's party vote was 0.69 per cent, down from 1.07 per cent in 2011. United Future got Peter Dunne's Ōhāriu seat, also by grace of National's nudging its supporters Dunne's way. But Dunne won only narrowly and United Future won only 0.22 per cent of the party vote, so low that Dunne's is an 'overhang' seat. ACT might well survive and even possibly grow a bit in 2017. But United Future is close to extinction, which was in effect acknowledged by Dunne himself in an address to the United Future board on 15 November in which he said that the party needs to go back to basics and focus afresh on core principles – though Dunne also said in that address that membership had grown (Dunne 2014).

For the Māori Party the election spelt near-asphyxiation: a total of two MPs and down to only one electorate seat from a high point of five of the seven Māori electorate seats in 2008. The Labour Party is in control with six of the seven – or is it?

From a Māori perspective the logic is that a Māori party or grouping holds the Māori electorates. This has been the case three times in the past 100 years: after 1935 when the Rātana movement progressively won all four seats (the total at the time); in 1996 when New Zealand First's 'tight five' held all five seats (the total at that time) in a party led by a Māori, Winston Peters, who was endorsed by Tūwharetoa paramount chief Sir Hepi te Heuheu; and in 2005 and 2008 when the Māori Party won four, then five, of the seven seats.

In each case the Māori grouping lost its independence. Labour over time absorbed the Rātana movement and the seats became Labour seats that happened to be Māori, not Māori seats that happened to be Labour-aligned. Labour lost one of the seats in the 1993 election, then all five in 1996. Four of the 'tight five' split from New Zealand First when it left its coalition with National in 1998 and all five lost their seats in 1999. The Māori Party, which entered National's governing coalition in 2008, split in 2010 when Hone Harawira formed Mana, then lost support.

The bulk of voters in Māori electorates, if pushed to a choice between Labour and National, choose Labour, as the party votes since 1996 reflect. In effect, New Zealand First's 'tight five' and the Māori Party delivered Labour-side votes to National.

The Māori Party's decision to formally support the National-led governments of 2008 and 2011 was logical. It gave the Māori Party some influence with the government and it used that to advance specifically

Māori cultural or self-management ambitions. Among the gains were: the Whānau Ora Māori-run social services programmes; New Zealand's signature to the United Nations Declaration on the Rights of Indigenous Peoples; and a rewrite of the 2004 Labour-led government's legislation which overrode a Supreme Court decision that iwi and hapū could argue traditional ownership of stretches of foreshore and seabed – the trigger for then Labour MP Tariana Turia's defection to form the Māori Party.

Despite the cost to its support, the same logic continued to apply even after the 2014 election – principally to preserve and develop Whānau Ora, out of respect for Turia whose policy it was and for fear that if the Māori Party were absent from the ruling coalition National would let Whānau Ora atrophy. Yet there was a strong view within the party, expressed vigorously at the post-election annual general meeting on 1 November, that the National link was toxic, and that the Māori Party was seen as in effect an arm of a National-led government which had not operated in the interests of lower socioeconomic strata where the bulk of Māori electorate voters were. That only 55 per cent of Māori opted for the Māori electorate rolls after the 2013 census compared with 58 per cent in 2006 (from 55 per cent in 2001 and 54 per cent in 1997) may reflect disenchantment with the Māori Party; the percentage had been expected to rise, not fall; the eighth seat hoped for did not eventuate.

In 2017 it is possible that the Māori Party's vote might lift a bit if some of Mana's voters return. More likely, it will either stay at two seats or contract on to Te Ururoa Flavell's Waiariki electorate; it might even lose that seat if Labour continues to pick up votes there and if Mana's Annette Sykes is not a contestant. If Flavell were to hold his seat and join a Labour-led government, that would de facto deliver that seat to Labour.

But that is not to say that Labour has the Māori seats back for good. There will be more Māori movements. To develop a durable hold on the seats, Labour will have to learn to treat those it holds as Māori seats that happen to be Labour.

What does National do now?

Unusually for a third-term government, National has strategic policy aims which break new or expand existing territory: natural resources (initially freshwater management and waterway pollution, where the government fears coming adrift from public opinion); a shift in education focus to lifting teachers' professional status and performance; reducing regulatory complexity and making legislation and regulation fit for purpose; and widening the application of the 'investment approach' to other services. These are in addition to continuing the policy line of the first two terms: principally fiscal consolidation and associated public service reform (including devolution of some activities to private, not-for-profit and local government agencies) and policies aimed at boosting GDP growth, including infrastructure investment, business-friendly regulatory reform, oil and minerals exploration and trade deals. And they are in addition to burying issues as they arise or become politically embarrassing, notably 'at-risk' children, (un)affordable housing, security threats and foreigners' purchases of land.

National will face the usual third-term erosion of public trust and confidence. This will be compounded by slowing GDP growth as the Christchurch rebuild peaks then slows and as commodity prices settle on a more sustainable path, which will slow or reverse the lift in household finances and reduce consumer confidence. The hospital system will at some point need release from the straitjacket Tony Ryall applied to it, at some fiscal cost. The inequality/poverty and (un)affordable housing noises are likely to get louder and start to bother moderate conservatives who like an ordered, cohesive society, not a fractious one.

John Key lost some personal authority as a result of his and his office's dealings with *Whale Oil* blogger Cameron Slater and his evasion of responsibility, which he repeated in late November when the Inspector-General of Intelligence Services tabled her report on the Security Intelligence Service's part in those dealings. That did not affect the election result but may affect his prospects in 2017.

Key has said he will serve the whole 2014–17 term. That accords with his practice of doing the bigger and riskier currency trades early in his past occupation. Whether Bill English will be alongside him is unclear: on one hand English is driving the strategic policies and is constantly looking for new ideas; on the other, he went on the list, which could be taken as signalling retirement. Tim Groser is set to depart in 2017 (or earlier) and Murray McCully's 2015 New Year Honour (Companion of the New Zealand Order of Merit) 'for services to foreign policy' suggests he will go, too.

National will also need new support parties. That means starting to cultivate New Zealand First – which, however, may not survive the 2017 election if, as many in the party think, Winston Peters is now in his last term – and maybe setting up an arrangement with the Conservatives, which would require skilful and assiduous nurturing.

There is a deeper issue: whether National in 2017 will be seen as in tune with those now under 45 who will be a majority of voters by 2017, especially if it sticks with market-liberal Friedmanism, even in modified form. In its employment and business policies, it has been the most business-friendly – right-leaning – government since the end of the radical reforms of 1984–92. As Friedmanism is increasingly questioned, challenged and debated through these next three years, National risks coming to sound outdated, despite its acquisition of five new MPs under 46 in the 2014 intake to add to its existing three.

Labour's opportunity

That is both the challenge and opportunity for Labour as it rebuilds from its 25.1 per cent party vote. Can it recover the lead in policy thinking and reform that it had in the late 1930s and the late 1980s?

Labour went into the 2014 election still in the long shadow of Helen Clark's 'third-way' modification of market liberalism (though it did add some substantial modifications reminiscent of the 1940s–70s mixed economy) and was still stamped with the Clark-era image as the party representing disparate minorities – gays, feminists, ethnic groups and the disabled – and the poor (and unions) and so not as a party of the majority. Grant Robertson, a gay man and also a former rugby front-row prop, summed up the party's dislocation from the majority in a *Nine to Noon* Radio New Zealand interview on 22 September when he said Labour had to be 'part of the communities we live in', implying that it wasn't. Many MPs are well-ensconced in their communities, as evidenced in Labour's 34.1 per cent of the electorate vote (down only 1.1 per cent on 2011). But the party generally is not a strong, visible presence, especially in the provinces and mortgage-belt suburbs. Its membership is much smaller than National's and so the networks which tie a party into the public are less pervasive and visible. For most voters Labour appears to speak for others, not them. If Labour is to 'swim among the people', as Mao Zedong put it, it needs multiples of its present membership.

And in policy the party has often sounded 'as if we talk from the head and not from the heart', as British Labour MP Simon Danczuk put it in the wake of a poor by-election result on 9 October (Lowe 2014). Some of Labour's 2014 policies, for example to control the electricity market or adjust monetary policy, had a 'geeky' feel.

New leader Andrew Little brings from his union background a blunt, direct way of speaking which may reconnect with some lost voters. The commission he has set up under Grant Robertson to refashion economic policy is predicated on a very different notion of 'work' from that of the Clark generation. Robertson has international contacts on whom to draw. He understands the need to apply Labour first principles to modern realities.

And at 43 Robertson is of the under-45 generation. His number two in economic development is David Clark, 41. His running-mate in the post-election leadership contest was Jacinda Ardern, 34, who might possibly be deputy leader a year from now. With Chris Hipkins, 36, in the crucial education portfolio, Megan Woods, 41, in environment and climate change, and Carmel Sepuloni, 37, in social development, Labour has a claim to be the party of the 'new generation' despite the fact that Little is 49.

That gives Labour the opportunity to present itself as a party focused on aspiration, not problems. It was not in 2014.

Then there is the Green factor

And, for Labour to be competitive in 2017, it needs to re-forge a working relationship with the Greens so that there is a visible alternative government.

The Greens have become well established, with close to 11 per cent of the party vote in both 2011 and 2014. They have become a respectable option for disillusioned Labour supporters or environmentally conscious National supporters. In 2011 they decided they did want to be part of a government, with all the risks of attrition for smaller partners in coalitions. In 2014 they proposed to Labour that the two parties run as a coalition.

Labour rejected that. But Labour also knows it is unlikely to be the government in 2017 without the Greens alongside. Ideally, it would like the Greens under 11 per cent but not so far under as to drag the combined vote down short of a majority. The Greens in 2014 wanted a higher vote and talked of getting 15 per cent but recognised privately that too high a vote would reduce Labour's vote and could cause the combined vote to fall short of a majority.

In fact, the Greens' vote went down slightly, by 0.4 per cent, not up. This may have been in part because some potential young voters went to the Internet part of Internet Mana, which did best in the same general electorates as the Greens did; in part because other potential voters concluded there was not going to be a Labour–Green government; and in part because the Greens were stereotyped as well to the left of Labour on social and economic issues – and too sympathetic to 'poisonous' Kim Dotcom on spying matters – which may have discouraged environmentally conscious centrist or National-leaning voters.

The static vote has triggered a debate within the party. Kennedy Graham, in a post-election opinion piece in *The New Zealand Herald*, argued that the Greens need to reposition themselves on a 'vertical sustainability axis' as distinct from a left–right axis, which he said consigns sustainability to secondary status when it is the primary issue – 'whether we shall live, tomorrow'. He noted that one of the Greens' charter's four principles is 'social responsibility', a centrist notion flowing from sustainability and implying individual obligation, and not 'social justice' (a left–right term, which is one of the Global Greens' six principles). 'The vertical axis of sustainability allows us to move more freely along the left–right axis in analysis and prescription,' Graham wrote, implying Greens could (in theory) be open to coalition with National as well as Labour (Graham 2014).

With new MP James Shaw, a business consultant (elected co-leader on 30 May 2015), Graham also shares an understanding that the economy (as well as the environment) is global and that policy has to reflect that reality – which poses difficult policy questions similar to those Labour faces.

So which party will define the new way of thinking?

This brings us back to the rapid and deep changes in the 2010s in geopolitics, in the geo-economy, in geo-demography, in technology and in political-economy thinking. The 2014 election was in a bubble, sealed off from all that. That bubble is likely to become permeable by 2017, so more of the outside world is likely to seep through, as in the elections leading up to 1984.

Traditionally, of the two main parties, Labour has been the progenitor of major policy change and its younger-generation policy commission may promote more innovative rethinking. True to its moderate liberal/moderate conservative core, National has been incremental in its policy reforms. And John Key and Bill English explicitly adopted an incremental approach in 2008 – making some change each term and carrying public opinion along.

But notably it is English who has applied the 'investment' approach, though so far only cautiously to some aspects of welfare reform, with a fiscal focus, and, in a small way, to intervening to help 'at risk' children in their very early years (James 2014b). Only recently has Labour begun to come round to seeing application of the 'investment' concept as a way to legitimise the welfare state. A logical next step for Labour, which English is unlikely to take, could be to join the Greens in applying the investment approach to environment and climate change policy.

Also notably, the Treasury has been evolving. In 2011 it adopted a 'living standards' framework and in its 2014 post-election briefing (Treasury 2014) to English it set 'prosperity' inside 'inclusiveness' and both within 'sustainability'. Treasury Secretary Gabriel Makhlouf took this further post-election (Makhlouf 2014) when he quoted long-dead economists' descriptions of economics as a psychological science or a study of human behaviour, then noted the rise in his time of a 'dominant hypothesis' composed of 'models of economies with complete and efficient markets across space and time, populated by super-rational individuals with perfect foresight'. From those models 'we learn a lot' but the global financial crisis showed their limitation. 'The days when social achievement was measured exclusively by GDP are on their way out.' Economists must work with experts in other disciplines. 'We [The Treasury] are at the frontier of economic thought.'

The Treasury, in other words, is edging beyond or away from Friedmanism. This should not be over-interpreted but it underlines that the debate is open and that it is not a foregone conclusion that the next orthodoxy – if there is one – will be Labour–Green-generated.

You wouldn't have thought so just watching the 2014 election, sequestered inside its bubble from seismic forces. But beneath a placid surface deep pressures can be building.

3

LEADERSHIP IN A VACUUM:
CAMPAIGN '14 AND THE LIMITS OF 'FOLLOWERSHIP'

Jon Johansson

Campaign context: the contours of a vacuum

An old rule of thumb in election campaigns says that in status quo elections the actual election campaign merely serves to mobilise voters to the equilibrium position they already held before it started. New Zealand's 2014 election campaign strongly conformed to this logic. For the six months before polling day every poll showed a centre-right majority, a result confirmed on election night. For all of the political energy expended around 'Dirty Politics' and the 'Moment of Truth' – the respective and effective bookends of the pre-campaign and campaign periods – National's winning position was never threatened.[1] Despite three years of frenetic political activity since the 2011 election, with millions of dollars spent on polling, impression management and other marketing ploys by both National and its opponents, as well as proxies on both sides, in and outside of Parliament, the election, in its simplest form, saw approximately 2 per cent of voters move from the New Zealand Labour Party to New Zealand First.

Everything else stayed basically as it was before New Zealanders voted. John Key's National Party substantially replicated its 2011 result, and then did the same when signing confidence and supply agreements with its client parties, ACT and United Future, as well as one with an electorally decimated but surviving Māori Party, again without National actually needing the Māori Party to achieve a minimum winning coalition. In the absence of winning an electorate seat Colin Craig's Conservatives again failed to reach the necessary electoral threshold of 5 per cent of the party vote, a casualty of National's declining to act on the recommendation to lower the threshold to 4 per cent, following the 2011 referendum on MMP and subsequent review by the Electoral Commission. Labour and the Greens remained firmly entrenched in opposition, having collectively gone backwards during the term. Alongside Winston Peters, their strategic challenge post-2014 – how to present themselves as a credible alternative government – is identical to where they had begun three years earlier. Even voter turnout – at 77.9 per cent, up 3.7 per cent from the nadir of 74.2 per cent in 2011 – reveals an electoral flatline of sorts, with National now having won three of the four lowest turnout elections since the 20th century's first election some 112 years ago (Electoral Commission 2014a).

There are good reasons for the evident electoral stability that was witnessed in 2014, the 30th anniversary of a prolonged consolidation phase of our post-Rogernomics politics (Johansson 2009; James 2014a). The National government's incrementalist approach and fidelity to the ongoing consolidation of its policy inheritance – the partial privatisations of state-owned energy companies and further labour market deregulation representing the significant domestic policy thrust of its second term – kept it close to public opinion. The deep cognitive tracks driving voter behaviour also included strongly positive perceptions of National for having managed an improving economy out of the depths of the global financial crisis; high public confidence in John Key's leadership; and the complete absence of a credible alternative government to challenge the Prime Minister or his government. These factors combined to almost guarantee Key's chance to match the achievement of each of his National Party predecessors in office: namely, winning a third term. In early April 2014 an entreaty by the Green Party for the Labour Party to collaborate with it, so as to offer voters an alternative government, was rebuffed. From that moment, some six months before polling day, the election was over as an effective contest.

Leadership during an election campaign – persuading and mobilising voters to choose the leader's party, reinforcing voter expectations, and helping the citizenry better understand their future choices – is a microcosm of wider leadership phenomena, but conducted under the intense pressure of four short weeks of campaigning. Policies are developed for the campaign to respond to adaptive challenges facing the country as well as attract voters to support the direction articulated by respective party leaders. Leadership should also, at its very best, provide, in the words of Scottish writer Thomas Carlyle, a 'deliberate illumination of the whole matter' (1841, p. 136). This is the educative function of leadership, whereby the public is taken into the leader's confidence as complex trade-offs and policy choices are explained. During a campaign, the various levels of leadership on offer operate in a bi-directional fashion, with voters feeding back to their leaders via opinion polling and other forms of feedback how well their policies and personnel are being received. Leadership during a campaign dynamic can be viewed conceptually, as in Figure 3.1:

Figure 3.1. Leadership dynamic during election campaign

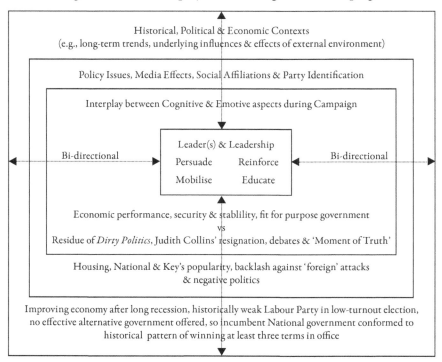

The 2014 campaign strongly demonstrated the one-sided nature of the political dynamic, as shown above. Aside from housing policy, or, rather, some level of debate around housing affordability issues, pollster Stephen Mills has shown in chapter 20 that the only policy-oriented news story from the campaign to compete with the many distractions involving political sideshows was the sale in August 2014 of a 14,000 hectare farm, Lochinver, to Chinese buyers. Policy did not get much attention. Even had it done so, perceptions favoured National on the key policy indicator of economic management and as safe custodians of the nation's health and education systems, two perennial policy areas of high voter expectation. Neither did the televised leaders'

debates move voters away from their pre-campaign preferences. Labour leader David Cunliffe outperformed John Key – unequivocally so in the first debate, and by smaller margins in subsequent ones – but it made no difference to the polls or to the result, another sign that the campaign mattered little, as most New Zealanders had long since made up their minds about both Cunliffe as an alternative prime minister and Labour's ability to govern themselves, let alone the country, in cooperation with other parties.

Yet, three years earlier, on election night 2011, the actual narrow margin between left and right blocs made my stock analysis that while National would struggle to win the 2014 election, the opposition parties would probably conspire to lose it. The political prediction market, iPredict, reflected this logic immediately after the 2011 election, installing Labour as slight favourites to win in 2014. Pointedly, iPredict did not do so after the 2014 result, looking towards 2017.[2] National's campaign advert, the best by any measure, contrasted its hegemony over the hopeless rabble of their opponents: National's finely tuned oarsmen and women planed through the water, purposefully rowing as one, while their Labour/Green/Internet Mana opponents were moribund, rowing in different directions. Voters agreed with the message's sentiment. Labour – largely through its own choices, freely made – did not offer the electorate competence, unity, or an alternative leadership choice. Labour's last term in opposition surely competes with its disastrous 1987–90 implosion while in government, or its long years in the wilderness under former leader Bill Rowling (1974–83), for the self-inflicted quality of demolishing its own electoral viability.

It was once written about Quaker Joseph Paine (father of the great 18th-century revolutionary Thomas Paine), Paine Sr having opted for a bitter-tongued, nit-picking spouse, that 'every man should provide his own purgatory' (Woodward 1945, pp. 18–19). So it proved with the Labour Party. It chose its own poison. For instance, in the name of democratising leadership selection, shifting power away from the caucus to its party affiliates and membership, Labour provided itself with a set of rules that have twice codified for the New Zealand public the precise levels of disagreement that exist between its various selectorates – caucus, party members and union affiliates – over who should lead the party and the direction it should take. Moreover, its leadership selection rules grossly violate the idea of 'one person, one vote', as the affiliate unions have disproportionate influence when compared to either caucus or ordinary party members. This had a non-trivial impact on Labour's last leadership contest.[3] Having three different classes of voters with three disproportionately valued votes is not a recipe for stability.

Six years of public disunity and the associated undermining of successive leaders Phil Goff, David Shearer and David Cunliffe by a variously interchanging set of caucus and party malcontents and/or factions, exacerbated by an ageing caucus badly in need of rejuvenation to match National's energetic and continual renewal – one of Key's standout leadership legacies – resulted in Labour losing even further support from its previous low of 27.48 per cent of the party vote in 2011. The tide was still going out on Labour in 2014 and its leadership instability did nothing to assist its comeback efforts. The average length of tenure for the Labour leadership, from its foundation leader, Harry Holland (1919–33), through to the recently vanquished David Cunliffe, is six years, six months. David Cunliffe was in the position for one year; David Shearer, for one year and nine months; Phil Goff, for three years and a month. Like National during Helen Clark's nine-year dominance, Labour is finding opposition enormously challenging. As in the 1999–2004 period, this leaves the New Zealand public deprived of necessary political competition.

Nowhere, however, has Labour's strategic performance been found more wanting than in how it presented itself to the public as an alternative government. Given that Labour began the last term nearly 20 points behind National, how Labour expected to explain itself to the New Zealand public in terms of its legitimacy to govern was never made clear. When leader David Cunliffe did attempt to do so, during the campaign, it was far too late. The challenge for Labour, by necessity, required it to explain to a culture still socialised largely by the concept of winner-take-all – a culture steeped, after all, in All Blacks success – how second and third favoured parties could legitimately form a government over the single most popular party. By fearing the worst (i.e., voter disapproval of any association with the Greens) or through misplaced pride, typified by former Labour MP Shane Jones' call for 40 per cent of the party vote,[4] Labour eschewed cooperation with the Greens in any tangible fashion that would help elect it, instead choosing to project confusion and indecision about what an alternative government might look like, which parties would comprise it, and with what significant policies. The public were therefore left with only one effective choice for leadership of the country, which they exercised decisively in National's favour.

For the Green Party, pride in solidifying a new plateau of support over 10 per cent competed with disappointment that co-leader Russel Norman's call for 15 per cent of the party vote went unanswered. Entering the last week of the campaign at 12–13 per cent in the polls, the 'Moment of Truth' wrecked the last few days of the Green campaign, its messaging crowded out as voters supported their prime minister against 'foreign' attack, with some also returning to prop up Labour in order to prevent a complete hollowing out of its vote.[5] In late January 2015, Russel Norman's decision to retire from Parliament represented a bittersweet moment in political time. Stepping into the co-leadership in tragic circumstances, after the unfortunate death of Rod Donald in 2005, Norman helped during the next nine years to transition the Greens from the party of its founders, and bare parliamentary survival, to stable third party status.

Norman became the elder of the Green co-leadership team after Metiria Turei replaced the party's other founding co-leader, Jeanette Fitzsimons, in 2009. As economic spokesperson he repositioned the Greens as a serious voice in economic debate. His solid performance as unofficial 'leader' of the opposition, when Labour's spiral into leadership instability and caucus disunity hampered its ability to competently perform that role, was further testament to his political and leadership skills. Beyond these qualities, Norman proved a very adept organisational leader, with party infrastructure keeping pace with its voter growth. Co-leader for nine years, during which the Greens doubled its party vote, it was not Norman's fate to serve as a New Zealand Cabinet Minister, although he, like Donald and Fitzsimons, possessed the necessary skills – intelligence, passion for policy, an eye for detail, and the right temperament – to have been a very good one. Like his predecessors, Norman enhanced the Green co-leadership during his nine years, strengthening its mana, its political capital. That is a significant legacy.

The Māori Party, too, suffered an incalculable leadership loss after the founder of the party, Tariana Turia, retired from politics at the 2014 election. Turia had gained wide respect for her advocacy on behalf of Māori. Whānau Ora is her policy legacy and she may prove irreplaceable as an effective agent for her supporters. She exhibited courage when she left the Labour Party in 2004 to form a new party. It must be difficult to have achieved so much but see her party's parliamentary representation reduced, with Māori voters overwhelmingly returning to a familiar Labour Party. The party's other co-leader, Pita Sharples, also retiring at the 2014 election, was likewise a popular and highly effective communicator, who alongside Turia forged a mutually beneficial relationship with John Key and his senior colleagues. The challenge for their legacy will be to see if this 'mana enhancing' relationship survives National's next turn in opposition, whenever that may come. Paradoxically, with new leader Te Ururoa Flavell having effected a quality transition to the co-leadership, there may now be more opportunity post-Turia to gain leverage in a future Labour-led government, although the difficulty of his primary challenge, rebuilding the party's electoral strength, cannot be understated.

Despite the lack of contest, a week from election day the dynamic appeared to be leading the strategic voter down the path of binding John Key to New Zealand First as his third term partner – an ironic consequence given Key's previously inviolate dismissal of Winston Peters and his party, as a matter of democratic principle.[6] However, a political stunt which must rank as the most stupid yet conceived in New Zealand's domestic setting, Kim Dotcom's infamous 'Moment of Truth', instead delivered some wavering voters back to Key, depriving New Zealand First of its momentum and Peters of his rare chance at the ultimate act of redemption (or revenge): a return to a National-led Cabinet.

An American Kiwi friend occasionally explains the latest maladaptive happening in his former homeland by saying, 'you can't legislate against stupidity'. Election campaign laws, likewise, could not prevent a tiny collection of individuals, drawn from across several continents – Glenn Greenwald from North America, Edward Snowden from Russia, and Julian Assange from Equatorial Knightsbridge, and Kim Dotcom, New Zealand's most infamous resident of German origin – from deluding themselves that the New Zealand public would give them a fair hearing while they ridiculed and trashed the character of the country's leading citizen six days out from an election. That these overseas-born critics of the Prime Minister, along with the Internet Mana Party – or at least the part of the party that was controlled by internet entrepreneur Kim Dotcom, and the bit of it that was Laila Harré – failed in their goals should guarantee, in a properly functioning electoral market, that none of the political actors associated with such strategic incompetence, from decision-makers through to fringe advisors, would ever be welcomed back into party politics.

National's strength during the last week of the campaign was demonstrated in its decision to abandon Colin Craig and his Conservative Party. Key adroitly played his position, leaving open almost to the end the idea that National could work with Craig, when he thought he might need him, casting him adrift after the 'Moment of Truth' kickstarted National's final days of campaigning. The Conservatives, accordingly, contributed nearly 4 per cent of what would prove an MMP high of 6.25 per cent wasted vote, materially lowering National's threshold for securing a majority, which it fell short of by only a single parliamentary seat. National's strategic position, however, is significantly improved from what it faced immediately after the 2011 election, with there being a greater gap between centre-left and centre-right blocs, and with opposition parties still in various stages of transition, and, at the time of writing, public disfavour.

Key's campaign had been a poor one up until the 'Moment of Truth'. When the official campaign openings began, three weeks earlier, Key was still under siege from questions raised in Nicky Hager's *Dirty Politics* (2014), most notably about the then Director of the Security Intelligence Service, Warren Tucker, providing information to the Prime Minister's political staff, which was redirected to a blogger so as to embarrass then Labour leader Phil Goff prior to the 2011 election (Gwyn 2014, pp. 7–8). Key and his strategists decided to stonewall the media, day after day, for over two weeks, which meant that the issue dogged Key for longer than it should have, on into the campaign period proper. National had made the calculation that the public would weary of the scandal. As a result, if only for the briefest of moments, Key became a champion for policy-focused elections. That strategy never worked, either, and it was not until the resignation of Cabinet Minister Judith Collins, accused of allegedly interfering in a Serious Fraud Office investigation in collusion with bloggers and other proxies in public relations, that the dirty politics boil was lanced, allowing Key to finally break free of the furore.

The fact that Hager's book generated two official inquiries and indirectly led to the resignation of Key's most ambitious potential successor, former Minister of Justice Judith 'Crusher' Collins, suggests that the substance of the *Dirty Politics* allegations, and the ongoing fallout from (and response to) them, will attach themselves to Key's legacy. Add to this about a dozen resignations or sackings during its first two terms, by National MPs or their support partners (ACT and United Future) – from ministerial portfolios, from Cabinet or from Parliament altogether – and the Key government is easily maintaining pace with the Clark government, which was once described by Don Brash, John Key's immediate predecessor as National Party leader, as the most corrupt in New Zealand history.[7]

The historic weakness of the Labour Party and the poor quality of the 2014 election campaign – one in which political activists drawn from outside the political parties had extraordinary effects on the campaign's beginning (and its end), to the extent that the efforts of party leaders to persuade and mobilise citizens, and to offer leadership, was badly disrupted and undermined – meant that a leadership vacuum was created. Additionally, the 2014 election was not one where the choice was felt to be undeniably vital, as evidenced by the low voter turnout. In such a situational void, New Zealanders stayed with what they knew and still felt comfortable with: the incumbent and his party.

John Key has now won three consecutive elections, putting himself in the conversation with his peer group of National Party prime ministers as to which one of them is *primus inter pares*. Key also has the best prospect for securing a fourth term of any recent prime minister in memory. It wasn't even close, in 2008, for Labour's Helen Clark. Jim Bolger was deprived of the chance of a fourth contest by his colleagues, an opportunity which his successor, Jenny Shipley, subsequently squandered. Robert Muldoon was effectively finished by 1981; even though he won a third term he was demolished three years later in an ill-judged and unedifying bid for a fourth. Keith Holyoake, after comfortably winning his third term in 1966, probably had lower expectations for a fourth win than those held by Key as his third term got under way. If Key were to win a fourth term in 2017 he would be regarded, certainly to begin with, as National's most successful prime minister, most especially because Key would have achieved his success in the much more complex MMP environment.

John Key is also our first celebrity leader, famous for being prime minister. This phenomenon is a surface manifestation of the greater personalisation of the modern prime ministership, as well as its centralisation (see Strangio, t'Hart and Walter 2013). In this respect Key is to the information age what Muldoon was to the television age: the first to truly master a new medium and become its focal point. In a self-revealing interview, given in the *Financial Times*, Key told interviewer Tim Montgomerie his calculus for 'selfie' penetration during his election campaign: 20,000 'selfies' multiplied by the 100 shares each one typically generates (Montgomerie 2015). While that number is likely inflated, when combined with Facebook, YouTube and Twitter, John Key has been able to directly reach well over a million New Zealanders over the course of each year with his preferred set of messages and images, unmediated by any media filter. Through these (and other) instruments of social media, Key is seen to be very much 'one of us'.

His personal popularity, and that of his government, is significantly better than that of his Labour predecessor and her government at a comparable stage, five months after a third election win. Any ambivalence about staying on as prime minister has been replaced by a new, publicly expressed desire to win a fourth term. Key admitted to 'kicking the tyres' on his future resolve to hagiographer John Roughan (2014, pp. 212–213), after a difficult year in 2012, but the Prime Minister is likely buoyed by his still strong personal support, and, given the position of his political opponents, his better-than-even odds of further electoral success in 2017.

Followership: staying close to the people

In the realm of leadership studies the concept of 'followership' is under-pinned by the belief that over the long haul, if not always the short, leaders act as 'agents' of their followers (Burns 1978). Media consultant Brian Edwards described Helen Clark in this way in his portrait of her, as a servant-leader to the people, as someone devoid of personal ambition, motivated by goals larger than herself (Edwards 2001, pp. 8–9). A cynic, however, could be forgiven for seeing this type of leadership posture – developed, refined and perfected during the 1990s by President Bill Clinton and Prime Minister Tony Blair – as camouflage for a median voter-chasing strategy and poll-driven managerialism: a form of sophisticated followership while policy change is slowly massaged through public opinion, its motivation as politically self-serving as it is altruistic.

The reality of leader-follower relations, therefore, is more ambiguous because there are also a number of questions to contemplate about a leader's followers and their motivations. Who precisely are the followers for whom a leader is acting as agent? Are they his Cabinet and caucus colleagues, party members, the party's financial donors? Are they ideologically aligned interest groups; those who voted for the leader's party; all voters? The answer is that it is all of these groups, but they do receive different levels of return from their relationship(s) to the leader, and their party, in the form of policy and political trinkets. There is further ambiguity in leader-follower relations because each leader has their own motivations for doing what they do (see Renshon 1996; Greenstein 2000; Winter 2003; and Johansson 2005). Some are driven primarily to achieve policy goals; others have more partisan political objectives; others, again, act for personal goals and needs; some even reluctantly serve out of a sense of duty. It is, therefore, by no means straightforward disentangling a leader's purposes or their motivations, and frequently the manner of a leader's exit is needed to confirm what these were. As with followers, the supporters of a prime minister and their government remain so for as long as they feel they are sharing in any success. Many will stay supportive because of personal characteristics of the leader. Supporters may also stay loyal out of necessity, because they do not see an alternative or fear the one(s) they do see.

John Key's leader-follower relations can be appreciated by considering his overarching policy inheritance (e.g., keeping Labour's Working for Families and interest-free student loans initiatives) and the policy changes his government has made. Key has been content mostly to respond to events, following public opinion. Here Key conforms to the idea of trying to disappoint his followers at a rate they can tolerate. Like Helen Clark, he understands that you have to take voters with you, and keep them with you, if you wish to be a long-term leader. Over time, according to the strategy, policy and political achievements will accrue. It is the principal lesson that each took from the 1984–90 Fourth Labour Government's revolution: Clark as a participant-observer, and Key as a keen student of leadership. In Key's initial inner circle, forged in opposition when he took over the leadership from the hapless Dr Brash, its significant actors – Key, Steven Joyce, Bill English, Simon Power and Gerry Brownlee among them – understood that gradualist means would be needed to achieve their future ends. In doing so the crucial element to their future success – their accurate discernment of their historical context and the opportunities and, crucially, constraints it offered – was established at the very beginning of Key's leadership (see Hargrove 1998, pp. 25–38). Key's leadership style has therefore replicated that of one of his National Party lodestars, Keith Holyoake (see Key 2006). The approach was also a natural fit for Key, as events drove his first term – notably the global financial crisis and the devastating Canterbury earthquakes – and their ongoing consequences dominated his second term as well.

Helen Clark's leadership brings out another interesting facet of the modern leadership challenge. As with every prime minister since David Lange – their terms accompanying the growth of qualitative and quanti-tative research capability – Clark relied upon polling data as an essential leadership instrument, from both operational and strategic standpoints. Clark also began the practice, replicated by Key, of skipping Parliamentary Question Time on Thursdays to instead travel around New Zealand, the public functioning as part of a personal focus group (i.e., qualitative research), although neither prime minister would describe it thus. While the prestige of a prime ministerial visit leaves lasting impressions on those who receive it, for a prime minister there is, apart obviously from the joy of being away from Wellington's politics and, instead, being amongst the public, the opportunity to listen first hand to how people are feeling about their lives. In their myriad personal encounters, especially in an intimate society such as ours, prime ministers get to continually test their polling reality against the feedback of real New Zealanders talking in their familiar settings. Over time this becomes a powerful source of market intelligence. In John Key's case, during the election campaign, the 'selfie' action in suburban malls, and the phone calls of support coming into his office during the day or two after the 'Moment of Truth' fiasco, reinforced the daily tracking polling data he was being fed. Key knew then that he was going to win.

When analysing how Key's leadership has evolved, after three election wins it is becoming more obvious that as prime minister Key is a product of his earlier professional socialisation, first as a highly successful currency trader, and then as a senior manager at Merrill Lynch. The Prime Minister takes 'positions', whether policy or political. These positions are mostly transitory and they are overwhelmingly not fixed by ideology, nor, generally speaking, made rigid by his personality. There are exceptions – his foundation promise not to raise the age of superannuation eligibility, Key's regressive embrace of monarchy, or whenever he feels his virtue to have been threatened – but over most policy and its associated politics Key's positions are, instead, flexible; they are also thoroughly tested, measured, and constantly monitored by Key and through extensive market research. His positions are then adapted as demands, situations and expectations dictate. His flexibility and market intelligence help make him the formidable politician that he is, as does his usually cheerful demeanour and pleasant persona. A more partisan Key is also emerging as time marches, to rival the partisan combativeness he has always displayed in Parliament. Nevertheless his likeability remains high, and his popularity and celebrity are unprecedented for a New Zealand prime minister.

According to leadership scholar Erwin Hargrove (1998, pp. 172–181), the master skill of discernment, or insight, is mediated by a leader's character. One character-related weakness (and a less pleasant aspect of Key's personality) has been on display whenever he 'doubles down' – that is, when he increases his risks or commitments – maintaining his need to be right by defending a previous position with his virtue attached to it. Three corrections to the parliamentary record, in the Dotcom and related cases – alongside his frequent date-shifting to match new political information, his 'brain fades' (as with his prior relationship with successful SIS Director candidate Ian Fletcher), and the times when he has self-servingly chosen a different hat to wear so as to avoid accountability – all suggest otherwise. All the serious 'errors of judgment' that occurred in the SIS–Prime Minister's Office–blogger nexus took place in the executive branch of our government, led by John Key (Gwyn 2014, p. 7). If John Key is not responsible for the conduct of his office, and refuses to accept that he is accountable for aberrant behaviours taking place within it, then it draws attention to the lack of any constitutional instrument available to rebuke a prime minister who will see or hear or speak no evil. A prime minister is not a king. John Key's imprudent (but self-confessed) relationship with a not-altogether-stable blogger is surely ended, even though it was reckless to establish one in the first place. If his self-professed humility for winning a third term fails to translate from words into actions, Key's probability curve for winning a fourth will fall.

There have been occasional flashes of leadership, as opposed to 'followership' – in this past term his government's partial privatisation of 49 per cent of three energy companies is the primary one – but even here Key made certain to signal his intention to pursue this policy before the 2011 election. He and his government therefore had a solid claim to a mandate for implementing their self-styled 'mixed ownership' model, with arguments about the propriety of the subsequent referendum – one initiated by opposition political parties as well as the Council of Trade Unions and Grey Power – degenerating into whether an electoral mandate means total capitulation by the opposition or not.

The referendum debate exhibited much that is wrong about New Zealand's contemporary political discourse. It was hyperpartisan, misleading, and, at times, shrill. Prime Minister Key was not able to rise above the partisan noise, nor did he particularly attempt to, with the government's rationale for its policy frequently changing. The battle ultimately raged over whether the government's mandate to pursue the partial sell-offs was valid or not, and whether its mandate was being downgraded by opposition parties in their (successful) campaign to force a referendum on National's self-styled 'mixed ownership' policy. Given that National received 47.31 per cent of the party vote in 2011 and that polls revealed, conservatively, that at least 60 per cent of New Zealanders were against the partial privatisations, the referendum was arguably the best use of that constitutional instrument so far; certainly better than using it to decide an industrial dispute or to resolve matters best left for individuals and their own common sense to decide.[8]

Mediocre public leadership on the partial asset sales policy rationale further supported a (re)testing of the policy. For instance, the lack of economic benefit to be gained by transferring partial ownership of the companies, and their steady stream of dividends, from public to private hands was confirmed by The Treasury, no less. Just as National was entitled to implement its policy by virtue of its mandate, the known public opposition to the policy and the dubious benefits of policy implementation meant that the citizenry, through their representatives, were entitled to test the contours and strength of that mandate. In the end, following the referendum – which saw 67.3 per cent reject the government's sell-off, but on a low turnout of 45.07 per cent (Electoral Commission 2013) – nothing changed. National implemented its policy. The opposition parties worked together in a rare collaboration, but National won again at the 2014 general election because negative perceptions about this one policy did not undermine voters' other reasons for preferring it over an amalgam of Labour, the Greens and New Zealand First.

One standout achievement of the Key government is the progress it has made in trying to complete the historic Treaty of Waitangi claims process. Even if discussion is momentarily diverted by a debate around the country's national flag and the Prime Minister's nostalgic form of nationalism, it is nevertheless going to be an important national milestone when the last historic Treaty claim is settled. If enough New Zealanders of good heart and tolerance agree, the country can then shift its gaze forward, less weighed down by history. The other significant achievement of the Key government, an effort extending over more than six years to bring the budget back into surplus, now delayed but poised somewhat precariously to happen in 2016, has helped fuel and maintain perceptions of its competence as a prudent economic manager, which, alongside Key's personal popularity, has carried the government so far. Again, however, the legacy test for the Key government's fiscal management will be the extent to which promised surpluses are used to pay down public debt, extensive borrowing having materially helped underwrite the government's economic strategy.

These twin successes, alongside the ongoing reconstruction of Christchurch, have dominated the government's domestic agenda and constitute the main signposts of a nascent legacy. The government would also see itself as having achieved significant foreign policy goals during its terms in office: the winning of a UN Security Council seat; getting around the 'rock in the road' in the relationship with the Americans; being embraced, once more, by the old Anglosphere countries; and reaping the benefits, at least so far, of good political and economic relations with China. Although hyperactive on the trade front, the results have been less spectacular, with the multilateral Trans Pacific Partnership Agreement seemingly forever trapped in larger scale politics beyond New Zealand's capacity to control or affect.

Key is clearly at ease overseas, again a product of his professional socialisation, facilitated by an easy manner and his social intelligence. Support for his government's foreign and defence policies were certainly not tested during the election campaign, but the selling of them by the Prime Minister has been helped from a perceptual point of view by having President Barack Obama in the White House. An aspect of Key's cultural leadership that might not outlive his government, however, is an out-of-step nostalgic conservatism. Under his leadership the nation has returned ever closer to its mother's bosom, with the acceptance of every new military or royal invite from its traditional allies, abetted by Key having close conservative colleagues – and, in British prime minister David Cameron's case, a personal friend – currently serving as leaders of the United Kingdom, Canada and Australia. The question of how real, in substance, our so-called 'independence' is has come into stark relief after six years of the Key government, and a reassertion of that independence is more likely to occur once his government is no longer in office and the current configuration of Anglosphere leadership changes. His promotion of a referendum to change the flag, when viewed in this context, suggests Key is attempting to lock in New Zealand as a constitutional monarchy rather than loosen the constitutional bonds with the old country.

The limits of followership

As time proceeds, the ongoing imperative for short-term popularity comes into direct competition with the need to effect a legacy that will outlive a leader's tenure in office. It is, however, also exceedingly difficult for any government to shift gears from the methods that have proven successful during its time in office. That crossover point is approaching for the Key government, whether it wins a fourth term or not. And given his gradualist commitment to reform, like Keith Holyoake's governments during the 1960s, as Key's leadership matures, and then ends, he will face some of the same questions asked about the Holyoake years: have the Key years similarly been ones of lost opportunity? How effective has been our local response to an increasingly information-based global economy? After six years of tinkering, is our education system – from pre-school right through to continuing education – any better suited as an incubator for future economic and social progress? How can New Zealand better protect its natural environment against the demands being placed upon land and waterways from a narrow, still largely protein-based economy? Can New Zealand more effectively marry ideas around sustainability and the market economy? How can the economy provide more equitable opportunities for an ever greater number of New Zealanders? How do New Zealanders relate to one another in making the transition from our bicultural foundation and history to the undeniably rich multicultural society of the present and future?

These first principle questions were being asked in 2008, when John Key was elected Prime Minister, and they remain with us today. Governments, political parties and political leaders strive to provide answers to fundamental questions about our future economic and social wellbeing. Political leadership, in its highest form, transcends partisanship and petty politics to offer a 'deliberate illumination of the whole matter'. Alas, the leadership on display at the election campaign of 2014 never rose to this quality. Relief at winning a third term may have been palpable for John Key and his party and their supporters, but the absence of competition, the bizarre campaign distractions, and the low turnout make 2014 a forgettable election. As party leaders continue transitioning through generational renewal, and as our concerted cycle of consolidation grinds on, we remain mired in a present where political leadership is operating in a vacuum, one where Prime Minister John Key is as good as it gets.

4

IN OTHER NEWS: FORMING A GOVERNMENT IN 2014

Stephen Church

The weeks following the 2014 general election were dominated by the sorts of images we have come to expect since the introduction of MMP: the press gallery camping outside meeting rooms; stand-up media conferences to throngs of microphones; and rumour and speculation about the outcome. Unlike previous elections, however, the subject of this intense interest was not who would lead the government, but who would lead the opposition.

It is not surprising that this was what captured our attention. Any suspense about who would sit on the Treasury benches dissipated on election night. Even when National's election night majority soon ebbed from 61 seats to 60 with the final results, it raised barely a ripple compared to the choppy waters of Labour's leadership strait. We already knew that, regardless of its strong position, National would continue to work with ACT (one seat), United Future (one seat) and the Māori Party (two seats). These were the same parties that had worked together in government for the previous two terms, under more or less the same type of 'enhanced confidence and supply' agreements.

It would be tempting to end this chapter right here, but there are a few features of government formation in 2014 that are worth noting. As clear cut as the result seems in retrospect, it is easy to forget the uncertainty of the months leading up to the election. Although there was a prevailing expectation that National would win the most votes, the matter of which *combination* of parties would win sufficient seats to govern was still an open question.

From a constitutional perspective, there is nothing to prevent the formation of a government which excludes the largest party. There are even precedents for this under first-past-the-post, in 1928 and 1911. Accordingly, the stance adopted by parties such as New Zealand First and United Future – to give the largest party the first opportunity to form a government – was a political judgement rather than a constitutional necessity.

A government can also be formed with the support of fewer than half of the MPs in the House, if a party chooses to abstain on confidence matters. As the current Governor-General has stated (Mateparae 2013), if a party chooses to abstain on a confidence vote it 'is constitutionally significant, because it reduces the number of votes another party or grouping of parties will need to win confidence votes and command the confidence of the House'. This opens the way for the types of pre-election stance adopted by New Zealand First, which once again raised the possibility of 'sitting on the crossbenches' (without specifying exactly how this would work in practice). Such subtleties might be lost on the wider voting public, but the fundamental question of who would work with whom was not.

Under MMP the likelihood that parties will need to cooperate in government, after competing for votes, has meant the question of who will work with whom has become a central issue of election campaigns. The 'horse race' media coverage of the contest between two parties under first-past-the-post has since been extended to the race between competing party blocs, complemented by speculation about the rank outsiders. In 2014 an entire TVNZ leaders' debate between the major party leaders was devoted to the subject of potential coalition partners. Some might decry this emphasis on the race between clusters of parties, rather than focusing on matters of policy. Yet there is also a fairly clear public interest in knowing how a party vote will translate into a potential government, a relationship that was arguably more direct under the old electoral system, where single party majority governments were the norm.[1]

Pre-election possibilities

Uncertainty about who could put together a winning combination was also reflected in the pre-election stances of parties. In 2008 and 2011, National calculated it could safely exclude New Zealand First from consideration. By 2014 the electoral arithmetic had changed, as polling for National's existing partners – ACT, United Future, and the Māori Party – suggested that they would struggle to provide a sufficient buffer of support.

Political scientists have argued that these types of decisions involve trade-offs between the three goals of policy, office and votes (Müller and Strøm 2000).[2] Casting the net wider for coalition partners could increase the chances of winning office, but it could also mean sharing more of the spoils in terms of policy and posts. It can also cost a party votes if the prospective partners are unpopular with their own supporters. As a consequence,

National's mitigation strategy was to present New Zealand First and the Conservatives as secondary options behind its existing relationships.

Labour, on the other hand, may have lost support for failing to rule out working with Internet Mana, even though it would probably have needed their support if it was in a position to form a government. By August 2014 Labour leader David Cunliffe had attempted to maintain an equivocal approach by ruling out Hone Harawira or Laila Harré as ministers in a Labour-led government, while leaving the door open for Internet Mana to support Labour on confidence and supply.[3] In the final weeks of the campaign, Labour adopted a similar approach towards the Māori Party (*Stuff* 2014a).

Although it was widely anticipated that Labour and the Greens would work together in government if the election results allowed, campaign competition prevailed over cooperation. In April 2014 Cunliffe appeared to reveal, and at the same time reject, a Green proposal to present a united front to voters prior to the election (Young 2014d). It is not clear what this arrangement would have entailed (e.g., whether it was simply a stated intention to work together or involved the development of a common platform), but the resulting disagreement had the opposite of the intended effect.[4] Labour was no doubt conscious that it was also likely to require the support of New Zealand First, which had made the exclusion of the Greens from Cabinet the price of its support for a Labour-led government in 2005.[5] Thus an advantage that National already appeared to have over Labour were partners which did not seem to mind there being parallel arrangements with other parties.

In the final week of the campaign, as Labour's vote looked unlikely to recover, the Greens themselves sensed an opportunity and raised the prospect of seeking a policy-based memorandum of understanding with National, similar to that agreed in 2008 (Vance 2014h). Winston Peters drew on this suggestion, alongside Russel Norman's call for Labour's alternative budget to be audited, to accuse the Greens of an 'assault' on Labour (ironically, just as he had in April when the Greens' approach to work more closely with Labour was exposed). Peters used the opportunity to promote New Zealand First and Labour – rather than Labour and the Greens – as the nucleus of an alternative government.[6] This seemed an unusual step for a party which had taken great pains, over a number of elections, to maintain an ambiguous approach to its preferred coalition partner. At the very least this episode undermined Cunliffe's claim that he could put together a three-party coalition involving both the Greens and New Zealand First, and reflected a shift in party tactics from support to survival.

Unlike in previous elections, the major party leaders avoided public displays of affection with their prospective partners. Perhaps it was the sour aftertaste from the last 'cup of tea'[7] that led John Key to make a stand-alone announcement at his post-Cabinet press conference on 21 January 2014 of National's coalition preferences. It remains to be seen whether this clear-cut declaratory approach will be repeated ahead of future elections.

As with every MMP election to date, coalition preferences were also signalled by accommodations in strategic electorates.[8] In 2014 National's decision to campaign only for the party vote in Epsom and Ōhāriu, but (ultimately) not do so elsewhere in a seat which could assist the Conservatives, underlined its first choices. The manner in which major party leaders telegraph these accommodations under MMP has certainly evolved. An early approach was to comment, part-way through the campaign, that the minor party candidate has the best chance of winning an electorate, thereby spiking their own candidate in the process.[9] In 2014 National used the release of its party-list ranking in late July to confirm its preferred partners, as announced by Key in January, and to finally quash speculation of an accommodation with the Conservatives. In compensation, National's Ōhāriu candidate Brett Hudson received the highest list spot (39) for a non-MP – above several sitting MPs, and high enough that he was elected in September – and Epsom candidate Paul Goldsmith was ranked 30th, nine places higher than Hudson.

As it eventuated, the impact of the accommodations on the government which was formed following the 2014 elections was marginal. If National had won both seats, denying United Future and ACT representation, it would have held 61 seats in a House of 120. Alternatively, considering another scenario, if Labour had made an accommodation in Te Tai Tokerau (allowing Harawira to retain his seat), Internet Mana would have had two seats, but National would still have had 59 seats and been able to govern with its current partners.

Building a surplus majority

If National had not lost its election night majority the process of government formation could have been as perfunctory as it had been under first-past-the-post. Although single party majority government is certainly a novelty under MMP, it has always been a possibility, particularly where the tally of wasted votes helps to manufacture a majority of seats. National actually had a slightly higher vote share in 2011, but there were half as many wasted votes as in 2014.

That National immediately sought to construct a government with ACT, United Future and the Māori Party, when it could have governed alone, might seem counterintuitive. After all, game theory predicts that the government which is most likely to form is a 'minimum winning coalition', comprising only as many parties as are necessary to win, and no more, so as not to dilute the benefits of office. In comparative terms, it is rare for a single party majority government to form a coalition: only 13 of 424 Cabinets formed in Western Europe in the postwar period were of this type (de Winter and Dumont 2008).

National Party leader John Key may have been mindful of the reasons why MMP was introduced by referendum, and endorsed again in 2011, when he pledged on election night to continue working with other parties, even though National had a parliamentary majority in its own right. History suggests that, notwithstanding her popularity, Helen Clark's clear bid for a single party majority in 2002 was ultimately rejected by voters in favour of votes for centrist parties such as New Zealand First and United Future, in an effort to provide a check on the next Labour-led government. Key labelled the prospect of National relying on its bare majority, rather than attempting to build wider support for legislation, as the 'lazy option' which he was sure would 'make the top of the bulletin' (Rutherford 2014e).

Of greater significance is the fact that, although this was the first single party majority government under MMP (at least on election night), a consistent thread running through all governments since 2002 is the reliance on more parties than strictly necessary to govern. Overseas experience suggests such 'surplus' or 'oversized' coalitions reflect unique political conditions that override the costs of sharing office, such as the presence of extremist parties, the need to bridge ideological gaps, or the existence of an upper chamber (Volden and Carrubba 2004; Mitchell and Nyblade 2008).

In New Zealand the rationale has been more pragmatic. Both major parties have realised that expanding the range of partners yields a number of benefits. First, it inoculates against erosion of the government's majority in the short term. In 2008 and 2011 National entered into negotiations with the ACT, United Future and Māori parties when the provisional results suggested it wasn't necessary to talk to two of them to secure a majority, let alone three.

Yet on each occasion National lost a seat on the final results, and so it proved to be again in 2014. Looking beyond the election results, governments are also vulnerable to events throughout the term that could reduce its majority, such as by-elections or defections (of which there has been at least one each term since 1987).[10] This insurance policy may also be a legacy of the first two MMP governments. Tensions within both the National–New Zealand First and Labour–Alliance coalitions manifested themselves in the splintering of the junior party, leaving the major party looking for other options to survive. More recently, splits within the ACT Party prior to the 2011 election also made it difficult to govern in the final months of that parliamentary term.

A second advantage of a surplus arrangement is that it provides major parties with more options for building *future* governing majorities. This is particularly relevant considering that almost all minor parties that have participated in government under MMP have lost support at the subsequent election (see Figure 4.1 below). From 2002, Labour encouraged a range of cooperation agreements with the Greens that were not strictly necessary for it to govern, but enabled it to groom a potential government partner. Similarly, in securing New Zealand First's support for the Foreshore and Seabed Act in 2004 (when neither United Future nor the Greens would support it), Labour began a relationship that subsequently led to a governing arrangement with that party in 2005. During negotiations with ACT, United Future and the Māori Party in 2014, Prime Minister Key also indicated a desire to build a stronger relationship with New Zealand First over the coming term (Young 2014f).

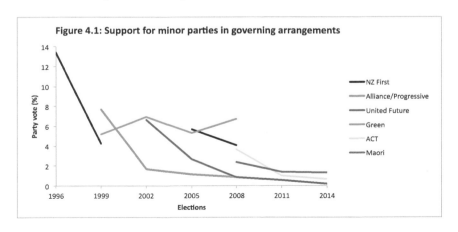

Figure 4.1: Support for minor parties in governing arrangements

A third reason for a surplus arrangement is to enable the major party to build alternative legislative coalitions to progress its policy platform, without having to rely on the same partner for every issue. This oscillation can contribute to the ability of a government to maintain broad appeal to voters. Before National lost its election night majority, Key's rationale for reaching out to the three support parties was that it 'makes a stronger and I believe a better government'.[11] The presence of an alternative policy partner has enabled National, and the Labour-led government before it, not to be beholden to the parties on its wings and risk alienating voters in the centre.

Maintaining a pre-existing partnership when it is not strictly necessary also recognises the 'sunk costs' that make it easier to continue the relationship rather than break it, a form of 'path dependency' (see Bale et al. 2005). Finally, if a major party has more partners than strictly necessary, no single partner is indispensable to the government's majority. Any threat to withdraw will therefore lack potency if the party issuing the ultimatum is expendable.

The agreements

The governing arrangements following the 2014 election also continue the pattern since 2005 of 'enhanced confidence and supply' agreements, surviving the change from Labour to National. At first criticised (including by National) – and characterised as a one-off response to unique circumstances in 2005 (Boston 2007)[12] – an enhanced confidence and supply agreement was the preferred option for minor parties in 2008, even though full coalition membership was on the table (Arseneau 2010).

Once again, this adaptation can be viewed as a reaction to the first governments formed under MMP. The highly prescriptive National–New Zealand First coalition agreement demanded a level of discipline, through collective Cabinet responsibility, which proved too restrictive. The much looser Labour–Alliance coalition agreement that followed provided mechanisms for differentiation, but they were not exercised, perhaps due to the culture of collective decision-making that came with full Cabinet membership.

As a hybrid between full coalitions and standard confidence and supply agreements, enhanced confidence and supply agreements enable junior partners to differentiate themselves, while retaining ministerial posts outside Cabinet and the ability to initiate policy in those portfolios. Collective responsibility only applies to decisions made in their particular portfolios, or where they have fully participated in the development of policy that has led to an agreed position.

Notwithstanding differences in policy, over four elections and across different parties the enhanced confidence and supply agreements have remained remarkably similar to the first MMP agreements of this type signed between Labour and New Zealand First/United Future in 2005 – and even contain similarities to the confidence and supply agreement between Labour and United Future in 2002 (Church 2012). Differences in process between the Labour- and National-led agreements – such as greater flexibility for minor party ministers to attend Cabinet committees, or to undertake their own consultation – have reflected different leadership styles.

Unsurprisingly, National's minor partners have continued to seek portfolio responsibilities which reflect their particular policy priorities (e.g., Conservation for United Future, given its interest in outdoor recreation, Education for ACT, to match its focus on charter schools, and Māori Development in the case of the Māori Party). This conforms to the theory that, if coalitions are formed by policy-seeking parties which are 'connected' (or adjacent) on the ideological spectrum, then the allocation of portfolios is how they oversee the implementation of their policy agreements (Lipsmeyer and Pierce 2011).

However, the 2014 agreements do differ in some respects, due to the weaker bargaining positions of the junior partners following the initial election results. For example, ACT's Cabinet post has been downgraded, at least in the interim, to undersecretary, ostensibly due to the fact that David Seymour is a new MP.[13] In addition, where National had previously committed to 'adopt and implement' selected policies of its partners in 2008 and 2011, there is now only an agreement to work in 'good faith' to 'progress' the junior partner's policies. Further, on a quantitative basis alone, the number of policy priorities to which even this reduced commitment applies has decreased across all of the minor parties, to four priorities for United Future (down from 16 in 2011), three for ACT (down from 11), and four for the Māori Party (down from 26).

On the other hand, unlike their previous agreements, United Future and ACT no longer pledge to support all legislation required to give effect to National's 'Post-election Action Plan'. Rather, all of National's partners have agreed only to consider its proposals on a case-by-case basis. All three agreements also clarify that, on issues outside the portfolios held by the minor parties (i.e., where collective responsibility does not apply), they may speak independently as the leaders of their respective parties or as local MPs. New sections in all of the agreements also state that National may consider reallocating its parliamentary questions or speaking slots on debates to the junior partner.[14]

It is not clear why ACT and United Future agreed to conclude agreements with National before the return of the writs (i.e., before the 2014 results had been finalised). There was a reasonable chance, given the final outcome of previous elections, that National would lose its election night majority, strengthening the hand of those whose votes might be required to support it. At the time, United Future leader Peter Dunne noted that the agreement provided an overarching framework, but that 'If the numbers change I guess that the weight to be added to those issues increases.'[15] Although the Māori Party's enhanced confidence and supply agreement was signed after National had lost its majority, its previous agreements had also been 'by invitation', coming once National had already secured the support of ACT and United Future.[16] It could be argued, however, that implementation of the Māori Party's policies has been accorded a higher degree of commitment from National, as under its agreement these priorities will guide the work of Te Puni Kōkiri and be reflected in its Statement of Intent.

The costs of coalition

Writing after the 2011 election, I suggested that the persistent pattern of these surplus coalitions, based on enhanced confidence and supply agreements, might reflect an emerging New Zealand approach to multiparty government (Church 2012). The government formed after the 2014 election appears to support the theory that this may indeed be an enduring adaptation. The initial impulse to build exclusive coalitions, with their own disciplined majorities, following the first two MMP elections, has since been replaced by another characteristic of the first-past-the-post governments of old: namely, an arrangement that retains the dominance of the major party.

But there is at least one caveat to this approach. European research shows that almost two-thirds of parties suffer at the polls from participating in government (Müller and Strøm 2000a). At the same time, more often than not, coalition partners see their respective electoral support moving in different directions, leading to vote exchange within the coalition but only minor aggregate changes in support for the coalition as a whole (Narud and Valen 2008). As Figure 4.2 shows, although loss of support for major parties in governments was associated with changes of government in New Zealand in 1999 and 2008, their votes hold up reasonably well in the interim (i.e., prior to eventual defeat).

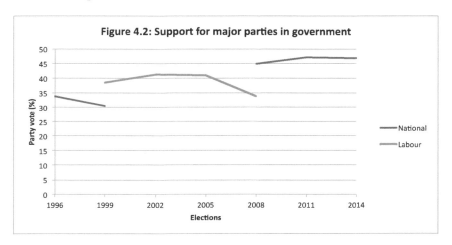

Figure 4.2: Support for major parties in government

By contrast, Figure 4.1 suggests that minor parties have almost always suffered by association. The type of governing arrangements adopted since 2005 may have stemmed the loss of support for minor parties participating in government, but the decline is still continuous to 2014 (even in the context of the highest vote share for minor parties since 2002). Any slowing may also be due to the fact that the vote for these support parties has now reached negligible levels.

Notwithstanding the greater flexibility offered by enhanced confidence and supply agreements for minor parties to disagree on government policy while maintaining office, minor parties appear to have lost electoral support because their influence over government policy is diluted by the major party or its other partners. To date, these tensions have manifested themselves less in terms of conflict between partners, and more frequently as intra-party division within the minor party (e.g., New Zealand First 1998, Alliance 2001–02, United Future 2005–07, ACT 2009–11, Māori Party 2009–11).

It is possible that the advantages offered by the current arrangements are not being fully exploited by the minor partners. The relative freedom to differentiate has yet to be really tested, and while minor parties continue to accept a bilateral relationship with the major party they may fail to monopolise their attention. Alternatively, there may be something about participation in government that is fundamentally debilitating for minor parties, a weakening process which the form of governing arrangement can only temporarily forestall. Perhaps this pattern of decline is something of interest that all parties, both within and outside the current arrangements, can draw from the story of government formation in 2014.

POLITICAL PARTY PERSPECTIVES

5

NATIONAL: THE PRIME MINISTER'S PERSPECTIVE

John Key

I would like to begin by thanking Professor Stephen Levine and Dr Jon Johansson for their work in organising the 2014 post-election conference and the book that has emerged from that event. I also acknowledge the Speaker, Rt Hon David Carter, not only for opening the conference proceedings but also for his tolerance and patience in refereeing 'Question Time' each parliamentary sitting day. I also want to acknowledge other Members of Parliament from across the House, and all others who have chosen to take time out from busy lives to reflect on September's general election.

There have been nine previous books arising from these post-election conferences. These conferences – and the books that arise from them – can only be considered a good thing. The immediacy of the modern news cycle, together with social media, creates a focus on instant reporting and judgement, but it is also important to reflect in a more considered way on important events like elections. Academic scrutiny of elections, politicians and political parties is an important function of democracy; it is also something that strengthens it.

As Prime Minister, I am privileged to represent New Zealand at international meetings around the world. On these occasions, I often see first-hand the steps that emerging democracies take. And they are not always steps forward. In November I took over from former Australian prime minister John Howard as Chairman of the International Democrat Union (IDU), a grouping of some 50 or so centre-right parties from around the world. At its most recent meeting in Korea, where I was represented by my Cabinet colleague Hekia Parata, the IDU admitted a number of new members. These included political parties from Lebanon and Montenegro – countries where there are challenges and where people do not enjoy all of the privileges of our democracy. In contrast, New Zealand can boast of an unbroken parliamentary democracy stretching back to the 1850s, and universal suffrage from 1893. Few countries can match our record of democracy, or our openness, stability and focus on the rule of law. So I welcome this book's discussion on the 2014 election, and the setting out of the views of participants, so that people in 20, 50 and 100 years' time can think about what happened and why.

Steven Joyce, who was National's campaign chair, is going to go through the 2014 National campaign in a bit more detail. I want to put the election, and its result, into the context of the last six years – 2008 to 2014 – and then look forward to the future.

I want to start by putting on record what a privilege it was to win a third term. I can speak for all my National Party colleagues in saying that we are conscious every day of the trust that voters have placed in us. We are determined to repay that trust. Achieving 47 per cent of the party vote highlighted the support the modern National Party has. Periodically I say to my caucus colleagues, 'When you walk down the street, look at the people you pass by and think about how we need to reflect the hopes and aspirations of one in every two of them.' That requires a very broad appeal, built on a strong understanding of our communities – women and men; Māori and Pākehā; Pasifika and New Zealanders from other ethnic communities; the old and the young. This is at the heart of the National Party. While we were formed by a mix of farmers and small business owners more than 70 years ago, today we are a much broader church and long may that remain.

What's more, I never take our support for granted. When I look at the current fragmentation of the political left, I recall 2002. The year I first became an MP was also National's worst election result. We learned a lot about ourselves in the years that followed 2002. One lesson is that voters look forward as well as back. Even being a major political party will not insulate you from punishment if the voters consider you to be irrelevant to their world and to their hopes and aspirations.

Looking back at the 2014 election, I want to start at the beginning of the year. In the interests of transparency and predictability, I thought it was important to explain to the public who we could or couldn't work with in a prospective government. That's what we did in February.

My stated preference was to continue working with the three parties we had enjoyed confidence and supply agreements with since 2008 – ACT, United Future and the Māori Party. Over six years, notwithstanding a few ups and downs, we worked constructively with these parties to provide New Zealand with the stable government people want. This is an appropriate point for me to acknowledge and thank United Future's Peter Dunne; Tariana Turia, Pita Sharples and Te Ururoa Flavell from the Māori Party; and from ACT, their leaders going back to Rodney Hide and more recently John Banks and now David Seymour.

We also said we could work with the Conservative Party. Ultimately, however, we took the view that there should be no electoral accommodation with that party. Ōhāriu and Epsom were the limit. Even so, Colin Craig did very well – 4 per cent is a lot of votes. In fact, the word we were getting from our candidates across the country was that in the last week or two, National voters were seriously considering voting Conservative in an effort to 'help' us. We wanted to tell people that taking a vote off National to vote Conservative didn't actually help us. Hence our strong advertising along the lines of 'if you want a National-led government, vote for it'.

Perhaps the strongest call early in the year was to leave open the possibility of working with New Zealand First and Winston Peters. A lot of time, and two elections, had passed since 2008. New Zealand First, with Winston Peters as leader, had been returned to Parliament in 2011, so the electorate had – in an important sense – made their judgement about the party. So it was timely to look forward, not back. As it turned out we didn't need New Zealand First, and we have formed the third-straight government with ACT, United Future and the Māori Party.

In March I named the election date as 20 September. As in 2011, it was my view that naming the election day many months in advance was the right thing to do. It assisted business confidence, and gave all political parties and agencies involved in the election time to properly plan. A key reason for choosing 20 September was to enable a new government to be formed so that the Prime Minister – whoever it was – could attend the important multilateral meetings taking place at the end of the year. I believe that the benefit New Zealand has gained from these meetings – APEC, the East Asia Summit and G20, and of course the visits to New Zealand of President Xi Jinping, Chancellor Angela Merkel and Prime Minister Stephen Harper – demonstrates that the right decision was made. I hope that future prime ministers will continue both the practise of announcing the election date some months early, and scheduling elections to allow attendance at these important meetings. Looking ahead to 2017, that is certainly my intention.

Perhaps the one downside of naming an election day some months in advance is that the parliamentary press gallery gets impatient to move straight into the campaign – and even into post-election negotiations – well before the election. That is all very premature, and we were more concerned with bedding-in a strong fiscal situation and making more progress on reforms across a range of areas.

We also took the opportunity at this election to rejuvenate the National Party caucus. With 14 retirements last term, National has been able to bring in a large and talented new backbench that augurs well for the party's future. I have also made changes to the Cabinet, refreshing both people and portfolio allocation to give us a strong sense of energy as we start our third term. In my view, the failure of the Clark government to refresh both the Cabinet and the Labour caucus contributed to its defeat in 2008, and has continued to dog Labour since. By the time of our annual National Party conference in Wellington at the end of June, candidate selection was largely complete.

That conference opened at a time of high polling numbers for National. As an example, the TV3 poll on 26 June had National on 49.7 per cent and Labour on 27.3 per cent. As a result, a key theme for Party President Peter Goodfellow, Steven Joyce and I was the absolute imperative of avoiding complacency. I recalled the 2011 election, where despite all of the polls National only won narrowly. While Labour was constantly talking about 'the missing million', what was clear was that many of the people who didn't vote in 2011 were National supporters. In particular, a number probably believed the talk in the media that we would win easily so didn't bother to vote. That, and the inevitable closing of the gap that occurs in campaigns, meant a very tight contest in 2011. I was concerned that could happen again in 2014. The campaign team, led by Steven Joyce and Jo de Joux, was certainly taking nothing for granted, and a very strong 'get out the vote' campaign was well underway by the time of the annual conference.

We also wanted to point out to New Zealanders the chaotic relationships between our opponents, and the impact this would have on any alternative government. In the end this led to our effective 'rowing boat' ads, which reinforced what was clearly already a concern held by many voters. The strong advertising campaign reflected the strength of the broader campaign, and the contribution of National Party members and supporters, from the President down. Experience and genuine enthusiasm make a real difference.

It is fair to say, though, that events out of our control meant that for much of the campaign, policy issues were not top of minds, for the media at least. When the Hager book came out it became clear that much of the campaign would be about so-called 'dirty politics', even though the voters wanted it to be about policy and the future of our country. Throw in the made-for-TV personality Kim Dotcom and the recipe for a most unusual campaign was complete.

My views on the Hager book are well known and there is no need to repeat them here. During the campaign it became clear that New Zealanders were frustrated with the attention given to the whole saga. That was the impression I got very strongly on the campaign trail, where there was a lot of support for National and general bemusement that a couple of issues they didn't care about were taking over the whole campaign. On the positive side, the risk of complacency was well and truly over. Polls also highlighted just how close the election between the centre-right and left-wing blocs could be.

Just a few days out from election day came the so-called Dotcom 'Moment of Truth'. And so it came to be, but not in the way that he and his supporters intended. The level of anger was palpable. The next day my office received a large number of calls from ordinary voters outraged at what was going on. I have sometimes wondered how many additional votes National may have won as a result of this whole exercise. There is of course no way of knowing. But I do know from feedback we received at the time that the combination of Hager and Dotcom galvanised National voters to get out to the polling booths in big numbers. One of the most pleasing things to come out of the 2014 election was that it reinforced the notion that New Zealanders make up their own minds and won't be dictated to.

Achieving 60 seats in Parliament under MMP was a superb result and shows National's widespread appeal. I put this result down to five key factors. First, New Zealanders understood the strength of the economy and that this flowed directly through to more jobs, and better paying jobs, for them and their families. Second, voters saw that National had a plan for the future that was consistent with their hopes and aspirations. We were talking about the things that really mattered to people's futures. Third, over six years in government we had won the trust of voters. We had always been very careful to get a mandate for reform – including the mixed ownership model – and we kept our promises. Our approach has been to undertake incremental, sustainable reform, and to take the electorate with us, as opposed to what might be described as the 'big bang theory' of politics. Fourth, we had the strongest team. Put simply, many New Zealanders were not listening to Mr Cunliffe. Finally, we ran the best campaign. It really did make a difference.

At the end of it all, I said on election night that I was determined to govern for all New Zealanders. I feel that just as strongly today as when I said it on the evening of 20 September. There will be challenges over the next three years. New Zealand is a small country that makes its way in the world by trading with others, and we do feel the impact of events that take place far from home. But throughout it all I remain optimistic for our future as a country. There is so much we have going for us.

At the core of my government is a clear focus on the economy. I have said before, and want to repeat here in this chapter, how fortunate New Zealand is to have Bill English as Minister of Finance. It was fitting that, after a little persuasion, he joined me on stage on election night. He deserves a lot of the credit for the success of our government.

I also want to take the opportunity in this chapter – as I did in speaking at the post-election conference – to place on record my appreciation to my wife Bronagh. Everyone involved in politics understands the pressure it puts on family life. Throughout my time in politics Bronagh has been supportive of me following my dream – with all the ups and downs that entails. My children Max and Stephie have also been supportive, and it's not always easy having a father who is in politics.

As for me, I am just as excited to be Prime Minister as I was on the day my first government was sworn in back in November 2008. It is a great privilege and one I never forget.

6

THE 2014 CAMPAIGN: WORKING FOR NEW ZEALAND

Steven Joyce

The 2014 election campaign was my fourth political campaign and my fourth as chair of the National Party campaign operation. During this period the National Party has probably had its most settled campaign team since the 1970s. We have different individuals coming into and out of the team at each election but we have been lucky enough to have consistent organisational 'scaffolding' in place for each campaign. As a result we have a reasonably well-oiled organisational plan, which saves a lot of time when preparing for a campaign.

Even so, the team spends months preparing for the last six weeks or so prior to the election. We spend time developing, tuning and refining campaign messages. We spend time on volunteer training and diary planning and so on. A particular focus this election was in lifting our 'get out the vote' capability, as we knew we'd need a strong performance in that area of the campaign to keep our party vote as high as possible.

In my experience it is only when you have a strong clear plan that you have the clarity and flexibility to move from that as required. That may sound a little counter-intuitive but when your blueprint is clear, it is easy to then adjust it when the heat goes on, and the heat always does go on during a campaign.

It is also important not to confuse a settled organisational plan with a settled political environment. Every election is different and fought on different grounds and on different issues. Across the party we regularly remind ourselves of the need to look to the future and not fight the last war. They are all different. And so it proved again in 2014.

Campaign strategy

The strategy for our campaigns is driven firstly by our assessment of where the voting public is at in regard to the electoral cycle, and their view of the state of New Zealand politics. Our analysis is informed primarily by our research and the direct feedback we receive from voters and party members.

It is interesting exactly how often those three sources are in sync.

Our strategy is never set at a point in time, but continues to evolve in response to events. In this election it was centred on three things. The first was that the New Zealand economy was strengthening in a way that was quite unique in its recent history, and in a way that compared well with other developed countries across the OECD. People generally wanted that trend to continue, and wanted to see us continue with the same plan. The second point was that we had a record as a competent government that was managing issues well, and that appeared to be acknowledged by voters. And thirdly, we had a strong plan for the future.

One area of divergence between the views of some of our party faithful and the voting public was how much we should focus on what New Zealand had achieved over the past six years. There is an understandable desire amongst insiders to remind people how far the country had come in the party's period of government. And indeed that is a useful context for an election campaign. However, voters more generally are not interested so much in the road the country has already travelled and what you as a government have achieved. They are more interested in what you plan to achieve next. And that is where laying out the plan for the future is very important.

Of course, as always in any election campaign, no strategy is laid out in isolation. Each election is a story of competing visions and competing policy directions, and the contrast between them. The contrast in 2014 was stark. What was proposed by the opposition parties was a quite radical shift in economic direction. These included fundamental changes to monetary policy, significant plans for government to move into sectors of the economy which it had previously not been involved in, such as house building, and significant moves away from orthodox economic policy. They also proposed quite big increases in government spending, not perhaps as big as in 2005 or 2008, but big in the context of where New Zealand and the world are at today. They also proposed significant changes in tax policy. We were not unhappy with this contrast in approach, because we did not believe the public would see the need for a big change in direction just as the New Zealand economy was gaining speed and doing reasonably well in the world context.

In order for the Opposition to sell their need for radical change, they had to start from a position of denying what was actually happening and what New Zealanders were actually experiencing. They had to concoct a view of the country and its prospects which was much darker than the public mood. The Opposition's declared view was 'oh, things are terrible, everything's hopeless and these guys have done an appalling job' while at the same time the public could see quite a bit of progress. Nobody was arguing that things were perfect but it was clear that as a country we had been having a much stronger period since the Global Financial Crisis than most other countries. Unfortunately for Labour and the Greens, that disconnect with the public created problems for them right through until election day.

Campaign advertising

Advertising and marketing are important components of any election campaign, and in my view they are becoming even more important as the news media gets more and more wrapped up in the 'game' of politics or, if you like, the description of the horse race. People looking for a reason to vote a particular way are less and less likely to find it on their newspaper website or as part of television or radio news. That is not a criticism so much as a description of what is happening, and political parties need to adapt to that reality. Parties need to set out a clear plan in their advertising and marketing, because the traditional media is no longer going to help to do it for them.

We settled on the rowing crew metaphor for summarising our plans and New Zealand's progress quite early on in the election cycle. In fact, unusually early. I've been involved in campaigns where you have a number of options and settle on one quite late in the piece, but this one presented itself months ahead of the campaign launch. We wanted a symbol that showed how New Zealand was a team that was working together and really starting to get somewhere. New Zealand's success in rowing as a sport would also assist to engender pride in what the country was starting to achieve.

And then we added the 'Laboureens' boat to that, to symbolise the confusion and loss of momentum that would ensue if there was a change of government. The 'Laboureens' boat was a two-ended boat with people dressed in green and red on it, arguing with each other. At least that is how it was when the ads were filmed. Then Kim Dotcom came along with the Internet Mana Party, so we thought in order to be authentic we had to get them in the boat as well. However, we did not have the time or money to record the ads again, so a very patient colour key person coloured in one of the people on the boat as wearing purple.

The 'Laboureens' boat ended up being used in our advertising much more than we intended, as the Opposition campaign steadily appeared more and more like that boat. There was the debate about the Greens wanting Labour's fiscal numbers checked, there was no coordination on policy announcements, there was no agreement on key portfolios, and no consistent answer from Labour about whether they could work with Kim Dotcom or not. It truly became a case of life imitating art. The 'Laboureens' boat and the 'Laboureens' campaign became steadily more in sync, so we steadily lifted its weight in the campaign.

Other key elements of our campaign advertising were the 'Working for New Zealand' caption and the use of Prime Minister John Key front and centre once again. I have stopped being surprised at the number of pundits that are critical about the regular use of John Key as the face of the national campaign. They studiously ignore that in the modern age, a time-poor public puts more and more emphasis on the leader of each team. Modern political campaigns simply reflect that reality. Our prime minister is a great asset for our campaign. The only recent campaigns I have seen anywhere that didn't place emphasis on the team leader were the New Zealand Labour Party campaigns of 2011 and 2014.

Once again we adopted a consistent brand style and approach across all media. This is more important than ever in a fragmented media environment. We have also stepped up our engagement in social media, which can be a superb tool for laying out policy information and campaign information for different people seeking different levels of engagement. However, it does also demand a higher level of discipline from every member of the team. For the first time we aggregated our social media into one hub or channel. That channel harvested Facebook, policy announcements, Twitter feeds and so on, and people could download an app which brought the campaign to them in real time. The app was helpful for both partisans and people who have a high level of curiosity and wanted to make a more informed decision.

So far so good, and then of course the election campaign ended up being about a whole lot of other things besides what we had planned.

Dirty politics

One of them was the book from Mr Nicky Hager: *Dirty Politics*. I do not think there is any doubt that Mr Hager's book was designed to influence the outcome of the election. In my view it suffered from what I would call Mr Hager's Achilles heel, which is that the material he obtains comes always from nefarious sources, and is never checked for accuracy or context. That modus operandi creates at least two ironies in the publishing of this particular book that Mr Hager seems determined to be oblivious to.

The first irony was him writing a book called *Dirty Politics*, which was horrified about what he calls 'dirty politics' but was in fact based on material gained by what can only be called 'dirty politics'. The second irony was his approach of selectively using information to make his case, and not checking with the people who are the subject of the information, so they are not given the opportunity to present their perspective or fill out the facts. He instead put a very negative spin on the information and published it. That sounds like 'dirty politics' to me.

However, Mr Hager seems completely unable to see that he is as guilty of the so-called dark arts of politics as the people he sought to accuse. The net result was a highly partisan book that simply served to reinforce a lot of people's impressions of Mr Hager. Either they believe him or they do not believe him. He is either a saint for the left-wing cause or an out and out conspiracy theorist. Either way he certainly is not an investigative journalist. Whatever your perspective on the book, there was no doubt from the moment it was released that it was going to be the sort of thing the media loved, and would take up a lot of air time in the election campaign.

In terms of handling these sorts of issues when they are thrown at you in the middle of a campaign, it is ultimately about how you respond. Initially I stepped up, as campaign chair, on behalf of the campaign. Our first job was to put the book and its author into context. And then the approach had to be to answer all the questions on the book in the coming weeks. We had to accept that Mr Hager's book was going to have quite an influence on the media agenda and not get frustrated and upset about it cutting across the real issues of the election. The Prime Minister was just going to answer the questions and then as much as possible focus on the election campaign.

Interestingly, the feedback we had suggested that approach did come across for most New Zealanders. Our research showed many people were impressed with how focused the Prime Minister had remained on the election campaign despite what was a pretty aggressive attack. For many people that reinforced their positive views of him.

The politics of personal attack

Which brings me to this whole concept of personal attacks, and how little they generally work.

The left-wing parties continually run what I will paraphrase as the 'John Key is a devil beast' campaigns. This goes along the lines that 'the John Key you know is not John Key at all, there's some sort of secret nasty John Key who comes out of a crypt each night and does awful things to New Zealand while you're not watching'. The trouble with that approach is that the public have got to know the Prime Minister over the past eight years: two years in opposition and six years as prime minister. He is on their television most nights and on the radio and in print all the time. They know him better than any other public figure. And they believe that on the whole he is a pretty good guy making good decisions for their country. The evidence, as against the hype, is good. Not perfect, but good.

And yet the 'devil beast' approach has dominated Opposition strategies against John Key for three elections now. And each time the public has received that information from the Opposition, processed it, and still voted for him and the National Party. In 2008 they voted for him. In 2011 they were told that they were wrong and that they shouldn't have voted for him, and they voted for him again. Then in the lead-up to the 2014 election they were told 'no, no, you are still wrong, you shouldn't have voted for him in 2008, you shouldn't have voted for him in 2011, you'd be mad to vote for him in 2014'.

Political attacks are of course legitimate. Anybody can do what they like. But surely there is a point where you would start to say to yourself, 'we are trying to sell the public the concept that they have made a grave misjudgement on someone, not once, not twice, but three times'. And every time the tools and techniques are more colourful, the lines used are more exotic, more of the campaign is devoted to the strategy. And every time it has failed because the public have the temerity to make their own decisions.

I cannot think who the master political strategist was who thought of that approach in 2014 but that is for others to be concerned about. The good news is the approach seems to be continuing, so I say I am keen to see more of it and if the Left want to continue down that path until 2017, they should knock themselves out.

Support partners

One of the major challenges for us, and for any major party under MMP, is the whole issue of identifying support partners and campaigning on the subject of support partners. It is a fraught process because you are trying your best to say that your supporters should vote for you, but then on the other hand say that you can work with others, so it is okay to vote for them. That can get to be quite an interesting and confusing message.

The Prime Minister and our leadership team had a number of discussions towards the end of 2013 and early in 2014 about how to handle this issue in the 2014 election. It was decided that we would make it clear at the start of the year which parties we could work with, and then by the end of July we would announce in which electorates we would encourage our supporters to vote for another party's candidate. Part of the plan was to deal with the issue early so it did not take up too much of the campaign oxygen, and voters would be clear about who we could work with so they could park that and start assessing who they wanted to vote for. We successfully executed our plan and maintained the same position all the way to election day. However, there was no way of knowing ahead of time whether it would be a successful approach. That would depend on how big a vote we looked like getting and, of course, the size of the vote we actually received.

Both of the major parties, National and Labour, prefer to have more than one option of partner or partners to obtain a majority in Parliament following an election. If you have only one option to be your support partner then that party has a lot of leverage, and the big party is going to end up looking a lot like the smaller party in terms of the decisions it makes. That often frustrates the public ('we voted for the big partner not the small partner'). It is a particularly likely outcome for third-term governments and can lead to fraying stability and a greater appetite for change at the next election.

As well as working out who we could work with we also needed to set a party vote target which signalled internally and externally what we needed to achieve. We knew of course that our most reliable support partners were likely to have quite small numbers in Parliament. We realised that we actually had to target 47 per cent of the vote, which if we could achieve it would be a phenomenal result – equalling what we achieved in 2011, which was in itself the highest vote in New Zealand MMP elections ever.

So that was our challenge, and we were constantly measuring ourselves against it as we moved through the campaign. The scary part was that quite regularly the polls were showing that we weren't going to make 47 per cent. The same polls showed that the only smaller party on the centre right that would have sufficient numbers to get us over the line was New Zealand First.

Given the notorious pre-election unreliability of New Zealand First and their historic tendency to damage third-term governments, pressure was bound to come on to find other partners, to ensure we did have a choice if our numbers turned out to be insufficient to take us to 51 per cent with the help of our traditional small partners, ACT, United Future and the Māori Party. 'Other partners' could only really mean dealing with Colin Craig and the Conservatives. And the difficulty with that option was that any late-stage signal to support the Conservative Party would mean some of our voters would shift their vote to the Conservatives to 'help', while others might move to New Zealand First or even Labour to help in a different way because they didn't like the idea of National forming a coalition with the Conservatives.

In short, we would be giving a license to some of our loyal supporters to use their vote to go and design a coalition. And many were looking for that license. We were getting regular feedback from our own supporters, saying 'oh maybe we could help you by doing this', or 'how can we vote strategically' and of course that would have been very risky. There was potential for any signal to lead to a breaking of the dam, with our party vote support dropping four or five points overnight.

Helen Clark was confronted with a similar quandary back in 2002 and she gave the nod to voters to support their preferred partner for Labour. That sent a whole lot of voters off in all directions, and while National's vote collapsed, Labour also lost votes through the campaign and finished in a weaker position than when they started. We could not afford a similar outcome in 2014, and in our view, neither could the country. So there was no additional nod to the Conservatives or anyone else. We would stay staunch on securing the maximum party vote for National in order to provide strong and stable government, and go flat out to achieve the necessary 47 per cent. As a result, our final week vote message was much stronger and more direct than it had been in any previous campaign. We spelt out that any vote for a small party would likely lead to political instability, and that only a vote for National would ensure the continuation of strong and stable government. The only problem was that at the beginning of the last week, our public and private polling numbers were indicating more like a 44 per cent result than a 47 per cent one.

The moment of strewth

So we come to the last week, and the 'Moment of Truth', where the 'great and the good' got together at the Auckland Town Hall on the Monday night to tell New Zealanders what was 'really happening'. We were of course concerned about the impact it might have. Despite *Dirty Politics* not achieving what its protagonists had sought in terms of influence over the campaign, it had provided a wearing effect on our poll numbers as the weeks went by. Voters were understandably frustrated that so much airtime was being given to 'the game' of politics rather than issues important to them, and they were frustrated we could not 'get above it'. We were too. We knew if we had the opportunity to campaign on issues like the economy and public services we would be able to lift our numbers, but that opportunity rarely arose outside the paid advertising.

The whole idea of the 'Moment of Truth' was fascinating. I was in Hawke's Bay and watched a bit of it at my hotel. However, I had not been watching for long when it dawned on me that this was going to go down badly with the New Zealand public. What we had on screen was a group of people, mostly from overseas, brought in and beamed in to tell New Zealanders how they should vote in just five days' time. They were there to reveal to New Zealanders they had apparently been duped by the governing party, and they needed to remove the scales from their eyes if they knew what was good for them. It had overtones of the dumb locals being lectured by international types who knew best. And the ringmaster was a German immigrant trying to avoid extradition, supported by a group of obvious left-wingers who had signed on because they could not win an election any other way.

And if you are still reading this and thinking what is wrong with that, can we consider an alternative scenario? Imagine if a couple of centre-right think tanks had turned up in New Zealand four or five days before an election, held a televised public meeting and said 'if you know what's good for you, you will vote National'. How would that go down? Very badly, and rightly so.

The 'Moment of Truth' was the straw that broke the camel's back for dirty politics. All the weeks of frustration about what had been a soap opera of a campaign boiled over and a whole lot of New Zealanders suddenly decided they had had enough and they wanted their election campaign back. It was like they had been mostly happy with the country's direction, had suddenly found themselves in this whirlwind of an election campaign which was about a lot of stuff they didn't care much about, and then they were pushed too far and decided that they wanted it to stop, and to resume normal business. Overnight the mood for National became a lot stronger.

And over the next few days, we picked up the mood change, as the

Prime Minister said at the time, very strongly. Our voters were energised and determined to vote. I have never seen in four elections such a strong attitude.

Still, it was late, and too late to pick up much of a shift in the polls. We were trying to get as close to 47 per cent as possible, and the polling still suggested we were going to get more like 44 to 44.5, and we tend to end up one or two points below what the numbers say. Running counter to that was this very strong groundswell of people telling our candidates and volunteers that they were going to vote and how they intended to vote for us. It felt really good. So the question for a worried campaign chair at that stage becomes, how much am I kidding myself? I'm meeting all these people, many of them National partisans who are excited to win, and yet the polls say it's not going to be enough.

On the night the Prime Minister mentioned that I had been more nervous than usual on election day and that was indeed true. However, when I walked in the door of our election night party and the first numbers were up on the screen at 49 per cent, I knew that although the numbers would come back a bit from there, we were probably going to do okay.

Looking back

Every election has a period of 'coming down' afterwards for the members of a campaign team, from the frenetic activity of the previous few weeks, where you wonder how much of what you experienced in the campaign really happened. This one was no exception.

However, I think in 2014 the sense of waking from a dream was true for many New Zealanders. The general sense prior to the election campaign was that New Zealand was doing better and going along okay, and then suddenly this election campaign happened which was a frenetic eight-week campaign of some pretty weird stuff that bore no relation to what had come before. My barber described it best to me when I dropped in a few weeks after the election. Her opening line was something like 'Gosh, what a fantastic election campaign.' I said 'What? Why?' 'Oh it was the most amazing soap opera. Every day was different, it was so entertaining. I nearly voted Kim Dotcom just to keep it going.'

Entertaining or not, at the end of the campaign the question many people were asking was how do I vote for stability? How do I vote for a continuation of what we had before? The job of our campaign team was to help them make that decision. And on that score, it was a success.

Like all campaigns, the 2014 election campaign was entirely different to how we anticipated it playing out. I have never yet been the one at the end saying 'yeah that's pretty much how we expected it'. They just don't happen that way. But they are amazing and exciting to be involved in and it is always a privilege to have the opportunity to participate in the democratic process.

The 2014 election also highlighted what I believe is the biggest current change in the New Zealand election landscape – the move to wholesale advance voting. In 2014, more than 700,000 voters cast their vote in the two weeks prior to election day, which was more than double that at the previous election. This illustrates a massive shift that political parties, the Electoral Commission and Parliament are still coming to grips with. Advance voting has impacts on things like the timing of advertising, policy announcements, and the relevance of election day rules around election activity. It is likely that the number of people who vote early will keep growing, and parties will need to think much more about what the phenomenon means for traditional campaigning.

I want to place on record my appreciation to all our party members and our MPs for their hard work and strong discipline in the 2014 campaign. Once again we had the absolute minimum of self-generated distractions. It is that hard work and discipline which provides the platform on which a campaign can operate. I particularly want to acknowledge Jo de Joux, who managed our campaign operations for the fourth time, Greg Hamilton, who looks after the National Party machinery, and our President Peter Goodfellow, along with everyone who works for them. Given my other responsibilities, my role has tended to become more one of simply conducting the orchestra. That orchestra performed well in 2014.

7

LABOUR 2014: LESSONS FROM THE CAMPAIGN

Andrew Little

When asked to provide a chapter reflecting on the experience of the 2014 campaign, I find myself in the interesting position of writing about a campaign in which I wasn't the Labour Leader, or even on the front bench. However, this is a great opportunity to reflect on the 2014 election, which will surely go down as one of the most extraordinary and unpredictable campaigns of the modern era. New Zealand sent Labour a pretty clear message in 2014, and that gives us, as a party, a great deal to think about. In the Labour Party, we've been doing quite a lot of reflecting on the campaign already.

The election result was nowhere close to what we wanted. With just 25 per cent of the party vote, we have some real soul-searching to do. In this chapter, I want to reflect on the core lessons I think we need to learn from the campaign and I also want to highlight some areas where I think we did do well, and will be looking to build on in the future.

Let's start with the unavoidable and the obvious. This was the fourth election in a row in which our party vote has declined, and the second consecutive loss where our party vote has been below 30 per cent. To score below 30 per cent in back-to-back elections is a clear message from the electorate that Labour isn't connecting and that we weren't seen as a credible alternative government. And the fact that this happened even when the government spent much of the campaign embroiled in the 'dirty politics' scandal shows that our approach really does need to change.

In my opinion, this result is down to four main issues. First, the public saw Labour as divided and ill-disciplined, focused more on our internal struggles than on their lives. Second, the public had real concerns about elements of our policy platform, especially our capital gains tax and plans to raise the retirement age. Our policy platform tended to be cluttered and many of our policies were complicated, which made it harder for the public to digest. This led to a real feeling amongst the electorate that they didn't know what Labour stood for, what our real priorities were, or whose interests we would champion in government. Third, voters were deeply uncomfortable with the prospect of a coalition with Kim Dotcom, who, rightly, they regarded as toxic. Labour should have been clearer right from the outset about our intentions when it came to coalition partners. And finally, our campaign planning and organisation was hampered by a late start due to the party's 2013 leadership change. In terms of the effect on the campaign, these first three issues meant that people simply did not regard us as a safe pair of hands, and the fourth issue robbed us of the opportunity to change the voters' minds.

What all of these factors have in common is that they are not just the result of decisions made during the 2014 campaign, but point to larger issues of performance over the past ten years. Bluntly, when a party loses the trust of the country and is sent into opposition, New Zealanders expect that party to sort itself out and rebuild that trust. It seems obvious now that we haven't done a good enough job of that.

These long-standing issues of performance had to be addressed, but when formulating our strategy, message and themes for 2014, our campaign team was trying to overcome the fact that Labour was seen as negative, fractured and distracted. It was this thinking, and the need to refresh our party brand, that underpinned our 'Vote Positive' messages and themes. 'Vote Positive' was about responding to the fact that not only was the public pretty cynical about Labour, they were becoming cynical about politics in general. What the campaign team found from the market research was that New Zealanders were increasingly tired of 'politics as usual'. They didn't believe politicians were focused on the things that really mattered in their lives. And unfortunately for us, this was especially true of Labour.

The campaign themes selected centred on things which would make the biggest impact on the daily lives of ordinary voters: their work, their homes and their families. In these core areas the approach was to try to focus as much as possible on practical, positive solutions to make their lives better. Now there are some theories out there, on blogs close to the Prime Minister, that the 'Vote Positive' brand was the result of a large-scale conspiracy led by 'master hacker' Matt McCarten. This is the same Matt McCarten who, it should be noted, has managed to lock himself out of his parliamentary email more than once. The fact is that 'Vote Positive' and the campaign themes we ran on in 2014 were about trying to reconnect New Zealanders to a political system that has largely been turning them off for years. They were also about trying to show New Zealanders that Labour was focused on improving their daily lives, rather than on sideshow issues that we had been perceived to be too heavily focused on in previous years. It's worth noting that we did actually have some success with this. Despite the election result, internal polling reported positive feedback when voters saw us as focused on issues relating directly to their lives.

However, it was here that the long-term issue with ill-discipline really became a problem. It is unhelpful when politicians go 'off message', and even more so in an election campaign. In any other year, campaign trail gaffes and distractions, of which we had more than our fair share, would have been bad enough. But in 2014, when the whole strategy rested on changing New Zealand's perceptions that we were consumed by internal divisions and distractions, they were even more damaging. New Zealanders wanted to see a united, effective opposition that held the government to account while providing concrete, practical ideas for moving their country forward. In campaign 2014 that's not what they saw from Labour, and much of my work as Leader over the next few months and years will be reconnecting with New Zealanders and regaining their trust.

As we look forward to this period of reconnecting, it is worth highlighting some areas of our campaign that did go well and can provide us a base from which to rebuild.

The first of these is our strong performance in the Māori seats. Ten years after the foreshore and seabed legislation seriously shook Labour's relationship with Māori, the hard work of our Māori caucus and campaigners has returned a result where Labour once again enjoys significant support from the tangata whenua. This is a huge achievement, and a big responsibility which we are determined to live up to.

The second area where we performed strongly was in the large strides we made in on-the-ground organisation, especially when it came to direct contact. Thanks to the hard work of our volunteers, in this election Labour was able to vastly increase the number of direct person-to-person conversations we were able to have with voters. In fact, in this election we were able to add more canvassing data to our system than in all the previous elections. Part of the reason for our greater success in getting our volunteers out on the ground was the adoption of a hub-based organising model. Our hubs are groups of electorates which pool resources and strategy. They were formed because we recognised that Labour has not always done the best job campaigning in an MMP environment, with too much of our organisational strength based around our urban centres. Our rural and regional hubs allowed us to make better use of our resources and target likely Labour voters in non-Labour seats. In the MMP environment, Labour needs to do a better job of reaching out to voters all across the country.

This is an area we want to continue to build on in future. As anyone who followed the Australian Labor Party victories in the 2014 state elections could see, the power of individual volunteers having personal conversations with their friends, neighbours and co-workers is a huge tool for parties like ours. In a world where voters are becoming increasingly cynical about politics, a personal conversation with a volunteer who believes in our cause is going to be far more convincing than a television ad or snippets on the television news.

The other area in which our campaign made great strides was our engagement in the digital space, with more money raised, and more volunteers recruited, through our online channels.

Finally, we can take some solace in the fact that even though National ran a classically tight, negative, third term election campaign, complete with slick negative advertising and a tightly choreographed roll out of policies, they once again saw their popularity drop over the course of the campaign.

Despite these bright spots, however, we remain deeply disappointed in the 2014 election result, and our party now begins the hard work of making sure we never see a result like it again. New Zealand sent us a clear message, and we intend to take it on board, to change, and to regain trust. For me, as Leader, this starts with being very clear about who Labour is and what we stand for. It means simplifying our policies so that people can clearly see the difference we can make for them. It means reaching out beyond our traditional support base, to show all New Zealanders that we can fight and deliver for them.

As I said in a speech in Auckland last year, I believe that if Labour wants to be the party of working people, we need to update our definition of working people to match a world where the very nature of work is changing. That is why we will speak to people who are feeling forgotten, who feel that Labour doesn't speak for them. We will reach out to small business owners, to people working under contracts or trying to get an idea off the ground. We will deliver a clear, credible alternative to a government that I believe is becoming arrogant and deceitful. I am confident we can do this. So, in three years, I'd like to be in the position to write a very different chapter for the next book.

8

THE 2014 LABOUR CAMPAIGN: A PARTY PERSPECTIVE

Tim Barnett and David Talbot

Context

Labour entered the 2014 election in a complex position. We had experienced three leaders in less than three years, having to handle the changes which accompany leaders coming and going. We had also won two potentially awkward by-elections – Ikaroa-Rāwhiti, won by Meka Whaitiri on 29 June 2013 following the death of Labour MP Parekura Horomia; and Christchurch East, won by Poto Williams on 30 November 2013 following the resignation of Labour MP Lianne Dalziel. Our membership was on the rise and new campaign methods were engaging members as never before. Our new policy platform was complete and – as ever – we had developed a comprehensive (i.e., lengthy) and strong manifesto. Yet we had experienced a major defeat in 2011, and National looked strong, if not impregnable.

Valence

The word 'valence' was used more than a little in the course of Labour's election planning and implementation, and seemed to be a new word to all but a few, even if the concept was pretty central to the political game. In our vocabulary it meant 'all that we offer apart from policy' – in essence, the strands of Labour in 2014 which generated the gut feelings which voters had about the state of our party and caucus, and our readiness for government. The reason we kept using the word was that valence was a recurrent challenge for us in the campaign, as evidenced by polling, media comment and coverage, and many of the conversations we had with voters.

Polling

The messages from Labour's internal polling, and those from the regular public polls, were all very similar. Despite Labour's record of strong economic management in government, negative perceptions around our economic credibility were a particular weakness, as was the public impression of internal tensions within Labour, and disarray on the centre-left of politics in general. Political 'macro' environmental factors appeared to favour the incumbent, with indicators such as economic confidence and standard of living expectations being strong. The Prime Minister appeared to have largely recovered from a rocky patch in terms of his personal approval ratings in the second half of 2013. Against this background Labour's campaign 'tone' was always going to have to be well-calibrated. The factors outlined above played a significant role in the selection of the campaign theme and slogan discussed later.

Despite all of this, through much of 2013 a post-election centre-left government looked possible, though over the course of 2014 the position worsened significantly. While there were undoubtedly a large number of factors in play, there were perhaps a couple of forces of particular importance.

The first was a 'pull' towards National driven by stability and competence. An important factor in consolidating this was the government's success in stabilising a ship that for many months appeared to be listing dangerously. Controversies in education and over the Government Communications Security Bureau (GCSB) had destabilised them. Tightening up their political management while presenting a Budget that signalled a return to surplus, albeit narrowly, combined with expansion of (Labour-initiated) social initiatives like paid parental leave and free doctor visits for children, didn't leave much space for the centre-left. The government's economic and social credentials were both reinforced, as was Key's brand as a strong leader.

The second relevant force was a 'push' away from Labour. This appears in retrospect to have been all but decisive, driven by the increasing public perception that the centre-left was in disarray. This was compounded by the uncertain look and shape of an alternative government led by Labour. From Labour's low polling position, an agreement between three or more parties would inevitably have been required for government, a prospect challenging for many voters when the alternative was a National-dominated arrangement. The launch of the Internet Mana Party, and the worries that then crystallised in the minds of voters, may well have been the straw that broke the camel's back. Kim Dotcom was an increasingly politically poisonous figure and, to some extent, was perhaps lumped together in people's thinking with the 'dirty politics' affair, and with opposition politics more generally.

Branding and messaging – 'Vote Positive'

Labour's branding approach was in stark contrast to that of National, and indeed the Greens – and different to much of what had been used in previous elections. Billboards, printed materials and much of our media interaction was themed around 'Vote Positive'. The rationale was that, faced with a government and prime minister high in the polls, as well as the threat of a lower voter turnout fed in part by antipathy to polarised and negative politics, an aspirational people-centred campaign embedded in the strength of Labour policy was most likely to succeed.

And the reality? The internal reaction was mixed, in part because external developments during the campaign (such as the publication of *Dirty Politics*) were difficult to respond to with entirely positive sentiments, and in part because the 'Vote Positive' concept was intended as a catalyst for a significant culture change, a hard thing to achieve in the limited time available, especially in the intense heat of an election campaign.

Early on in the campaign a decision was made to segregate policy communications into three broad areas: Home, Work and Family. It was anticipated that underneath the 'Vote Positive' banner these three 'lenses' would help remedy a historic Labour messaging weakness and lend focus to what could often seem a complex suite of rather disparate policies. These three themes underpinned all of the public-facing central communications material: separate TV advertisements, radio spots and a range of photographic hoardings with imagery employed to reference them.

Thought was also given to prioritising a clearer articulation of the 'why' of Labour policy. The proposition settled on was 'People matter most'. Visual imagery throughout the campaign was designed to reinforce the priority of people and communities. In our opening and closing broadcasts, for example, the comparison with National could hardly have been more stark: Labour with a working bee in a neighbourhood community centre, John Key alone in a studio.

Despite the extra attention on messaging, things didn't really work as planned. The general noise of the campaign, heightened by *Dirty Politics*, made conveying *any* message a challenge. A big-spending National Party articulating a negative Labour policy frame prominently throughout its own advertising, combined with a number of well-orchestrated tactical disruptions – for example, the Prime Minister's focus on capital gains tax in the *Christchurch Press* debate – made things tougher still.

The lack of a general election pledge card – or something like it –

remains a weakness for Labour. Controversy surrounding the use of the pledge card in 2005 meant that what had become a feature of Labour campaigns throughout the Clark years was not used subsequently. Labour must run a clear, alternative, policy-backed narrative and needs every tool available to do so effectively. That being said, lack of memorable or attractive policy appears not to have been the main driver in terms of the end result in 2014.

In relation to delivery of branding and messaging, 2014 was a transitional election for Labour. There was a distinct shift from an untargeted to a targeted approach, as well as a substantial move from traditional media to online and new media. Overall, Labour has rightly been subject to both internal and external criticism in the past for lack of clarity and specificity around its messaging. Despite the fact that much more effort went into this campaign element in 2014, there still appears to be a way to go.

Policy

Labour ran a typically rigorous policy-making process, stretching over two and a half years and involving virtually all caucus members and around 200 party members. A long-term impact of MMP, combined with historic factors, has been to reduce (and more sharply focus) fundamental disagreements in policy. This was reflected in the calm way in which a major new initiative – the Policy Platform, a high-level statement of Labour's positioning in relation to all the major issues, which could only be amended by the Party Conference – was introduced and passed in 2013.

This sense of broad policy consensus flowed through into the manifesto development process. Certainly there was internal debate on some of the tougher and more complex policy areas, but that was often more around presentation than fundamental content.

Leader

Even under MMP it is still all but certain that only one of two people will end up as prime minister after an election. The personality, skills and presentation of Labour's leader is consequently of crucial importance, in what is becoming an increasingly presidential approach to elections.

Labour leader David Cunliffe ran an energised election, and came out as the overall points winner of the three leadership debates. But that was not enough when the valence was running the wrong way, and when a misspoken comment or two was propelled into such sharp relief in the campaign.

Candidates

Labour put significant effort into improving the processes around both electorate and list candidate selection between 2011 and 2014. This included more intensive candidate training and support. We were rewarded with an historically exceptional team of candidates (with, as always happens in these processes, the odd exception); that made the reality of our party vote, and the reduced number of list MPs, even more disappointing.

Party vote

Over the seven Parliaments now elected under MMP both major parties have gone through the cycle of learning – and apparently at times unlearning – the skills required to run a party-vote focused campaign. The gap between party vote and electorate vote at this election was, for Labour, wider than ever – Labour received 25.1 per cent of the nationwide party vote as against 34.1 per cent of the vote for the party's electorate candidates – in spite of a clear focus on party vote messages and a powerful uniformity of brand nationwide.

Some would see this gap as an inevitable element in a predictable cycle (as National experienced in 2002). Others would see it as saying something more fundamental about the attractiveness of the Labour Party 'brand' in comparison to the image and popularity of sitting Labour electorate MPs.

Our distinct Māori campaign ran a 'two ticks' message, whereas our general electorate campaign ran a party vote focus. The strategising, balance and communication of this party vote message will continue to be an area of intense interest for Labour.

Māori electorates

An obvious spark of light in a hard campaign was Labour winning three additional Māori electorates: two previously held by the Māori Party, and one by Mana (Te Tai Tokerau, held by Hone Harawira). The factors behind those wins included two incumbent retirements (Pita Sharples in Tāmaki Makaurau; Tariana Turia in Te Tai Hauāuru), the pact between Mana and the Internet Party, a divided opposition and the strength of the Labour candidates. For the first time Labour formulated a distinct Māori campaign, including TV and radio advertisements. As previously, the hoardings followed the general branding approach with appropriate whakanikoniko [Māori design/ornamentation].

Voter turnout

One of Labour's strengths as a party is diversity. At elections this is reflected in concentrated activity within specific communities. In 2014 our Pasifika focus and our affiliate (trade union) activity was especially high profile, the former driven by strong candidates (two of whom, Jenny Salesa and Carmel Sepuloni, were elected to Parliament) and the latter centred around the 'Get out the Vote' movement, which was a significant player in a veritable flood of similar initiatives by non-governmental organisations. In what may well be a precursor of things to come, a wide range of nationwide and local organisations encouraged political engagement, and the fact that turnout increased – albeit modestly – will surely encourage this approach to become more intense in future elections. Various issues around the too-limited mandate of the Electoral Commission and the declining real size and outdated scope of the Broadcasting Allocation, again intimately linked to voter turnout, were also brought into ever-sharper relief in this campaign.

Direct voter contact

In what some have termed a 'back to the future' approach, cutting-edge political campaigning globally is combining traditional techniques of doorstep conversations, phone calls and targeted mail with the opportunities offered by new technology to be better informed about voters and their characteristics. Labour made changes in its internal approaches to structured conversations with voters, based on overseas research, and there was a greater focus on holding conversations over the telephone, in addition to door-based direct voter contact.

Observations from overseas campaigns illustrated the impact in close political races of personalised engagement with individual voters, relating the party's values and policies with the voter more precisely. Labour is fast taking on these approaches, and in 2014 we achieved a three-fold increase in completed voter contacts compared to 2011.

Of course such a transition involves challenges, but it does allow more cost-effective use of resources. It also places intriguing conundrums in front of local electorate campaign machines – for example, thinking through who the local Labour voters and potential voters really are, and evaluating whether spending on, say, a billboard or an equivalent value of targeted mail or phone calls is likely to be of greater impact. The approach, more people-focused and less reliant on volunteers being established party members, also offers those who are new to organised politics a real chance to quickly reach the front line of the campaign.

Targeting and data

In 2014 Labour worked much harder to get relevant messages directly to those voters liable to respond best to them. As noted, this work was underpinned by a much larger commitment to data collection than in previous campaigns. Targeting allowed efficiencies in the production of campaign material and often meant more frequent contact with a smaller number of target voters.

Data is ever more integral to political campaigning. One of Labour's key performance measures through this campaign was the number of voters about or from whom we had generated data (involving things like policy interests and communications preferences). The analytic technology related to this is ever-changing, combining publicly available demographic data with internally collected data from 'real-world' engagements with voters. This effort assists the decision-making process, but the greatest challenge lies in how best to put the data to use with the limits of time and money available to any political campaign. The process of reviewing and analysing the efficacy of the approaches made is still ongoing, but the results will feed into Labour's planning for 2017.

Digital

The emergence of digital platforms like Facebook and Twitter presents both an opportunity and a challenge. Digital promotion of the campaign further complicates the task of dedicating limited campaign resources appropriately across many campaign elements. Labour's digital and social media campaign was nevertheless a highlight of the election campaign, with a heavy focus on Facebook, Twitter and email engagement.

Despite a relatively small paid content programme, figures suggest that Labour performed well on Facebook, reaching millions of people and engaging hundreds of thousands of voters. Labour's Facebook 'likes' (though just one measure of success) grew rapidly throughout the campaign, matching the well-funded National Party until election day. This success appeared to be driven by a focus on producing engaging content with a high 'virality', combined with an enthusiastic and active supporter base. Labour also made forays into new areas on social media, using a Facebook app to more directly engage voters by showing them how Labour policy could impact on the issues they cared about.

Twitter was also used extensively, especially around the leaders' debates. It proved a particularly important tool for engaging with the commentariat and journalists, and as a quick response channel for counteracting National Party attacks. For the first time, candidates were all encouraged to engage with voters on Twitter using the #AskLabour hashtag, printed on nearly all campaign hoardings. Many had great success.

Labour made limited use of website and YouTube advertising. This was helpful in getting messages to a larger (and potentially different) audience, though we could not match our opponents' spending, which saw full-page ads on major news sites and extensive digital advertising. We continued our practice of posting all relevant video content online, this time with a stronger commitment to closed captioning, as well as producing, for the first time, YouTube ads encouraging people to enrol and vote early.

Email campaigning, particularly around the debates and fundraising, played a larger role in Labour's campaign than previously. During the last weeks of the campaign, Labour emailed supporters multiple times per week, encouraging them to take various actions, including supporting efforts on social media, volunteering, and donating for on-the-ground support. The ties between Labour's digital effort and its on-the-ground campaign were stronger than ever, and included initiatives like custom Facebook apps and online chats (and a leaders' question competition) during televised leaders' debates.

Funding

Contemporary Labour is not blessed with a surfeit of funding. Even so, overall spending for Labour's election campaign in 2014 was very similar to that in 2011. The fundraising environment in 2014 was different to previous campaigns – indeed, it is one of the fast changing factors in election planning and execution – and this may well have had the effect of somewhat constraining what could be raised. Controversies around Donghua Liu[1] and National's cash-for-access 'Cabinet Club' initiative[2] are examples of factors influencing (and perhaps inhibiting) preparedness to donate.

The highlight for Labour was the significant increase in (often modest) donations given electronically, often around specific campaign initiatives or events. There is surely scope to refine and enhance this fundraising channel. Labour will remain constantly vigilant in terms of maximising the cost-effectiveness of what is spent.

Planning and support

The Campaign Committee met for the last eight months of the campaign, following two years of strategy preparations. Governance and strategy was divided from management and operationalisation. The campaign manager (David Talbot) and the party's general secretary (Tim Barnett) were responsible for the latter, co-opting party staff and resources as required.

On the ground, Labour remains strong, though resources are far from evenly spread nationwide. The recent move from an 'electorate-based' to a 'hub-based' campaign organising model shows great promise, but there is still a way to go.

New Zealand politics works through cycles of two- or three-term governments centred on one or other of the major parties. Only once in a few decades does a government last either for only one term or for as many as four. While the Key-led National government remains a formidable campaigning opponent, in Labour's defeat in 2014 the sparks of a win in 2017 shine through. Only time and a lot of work will reveal whether the sparks brighten into a victory.

9

STABLE IN THE STORM: THE GREEN CAMPAIGN

Russel Norman

As it turns out, the 2014 election campaign was my last as co-leader of the Green Party. It was a tumultuous campaign, with *Dirty Politics*, Kim Dotcom and the Labour leadership issues occupying a lot of airtime. In the end we held our vote steady at around 11 per cent of the party vote, but failed to reach our own internal goal of 15 per cent.

With restricted access to mainstream media coverage we relied heavily on the channels we have grown over the last decade: email database, social media channels, paid advertising, doorknocking, phone calling, and leaflets in letterboxes. We held onto most of the voters we won in 2011 but we didn't expand.

For me, this election saw two of the things I've worked hardest on – policy and organisational strength – come together to deliver a strong and positive campaign for the Green Party that saw us hold our vote in the context of a strange and tough election.

Policy platform

We went into this election campaign with the goal of putting forward a comprehensive policy platform within our three priority areas. We released a series of policy initiatives to achieve our vision for a better New Zealand, focusing on a *cleaner* environment, a *fairer* society, and a *smarter* economy. These priorities built on our 2011 campaign priorities of 'kids, rivers, and jobs', and the issues that we'd been championing within Parliament over the previous term.

What we produced was a blueprint for a progressive green government.

We released full fiscal costings and revenues for our election priorities, which were analysed by independent economic consultants Infometrics. It was the first time the Green Party had produced an independently audited budget. Not only did it show that we would be able to run bigger surpluses than National, it showed that we could do this while taking significant steps to advance our election priorities of reducing child poverty, making rivers and lakes safe enough to swim in again, and creating a smarter, more innovative economy.

I was most involved with our economics package – a set of policies for a smarter economy. The centrepiece was a big increase in research and development spending, as part of a move to add value in New Zealand while simultaneously reducing our environmental footprint. It included a plan for cleaner, cheaper, and smarter power through a target of 100 per cent renewable electricity generation by 2030, reducing families' power bills, and enabling homes and schools to invest in solar panels. We also put forward transport plans for Wellington and Auckland, as well as nationwide policies to make it safer for kids to walk and bike to school, and cheaper for students to take public transport.

We proposed the Green Investment Bank, a government-owned, for-profit bank that would partner with the private sector to fund new projects to accelerate New Zealand's transition to a greener economy. These all sat alongside an additional $1 billion of government investment in research and development to kick-start a transformational shift in how our economy creates wealth. Arguably most important was our climate protection plan – a set of policies to ensure New Zealand shows leadership on the biggest issue of our time, climate change. At the core of this climate protection plan was a fiscally neutral carbon tax, with the revenue being used to introduce a tax-free band into the income tax system and a cut in the company tax rate.

Co-leader Metiria Turei took the lead on our social package with the priority of achieving a fairer society. At the heart of that package was a $1 billion a year plan to reduce child poverty. With one in four New Zealand children living below the poverty line, ensuring that every child in New Zealand has enough to thrive is one of the biggest moral and economic challenges of our time. Greater investment in children's health and education will reduce the harm caused by poverty, which is why we targeted funding in these areas. Our policies included extending free healthcare to age 18; giving a welcome package to every newborn; creating school hubs to cluster health, welfare and other support services at low-decile schools; and ensuring a healthy home for every child by improving rental housing. We also put forward policies to provide greater support for workers and New Zealanders living with a disability to help build a fairer society.

Our environmental package focused on two key issues – rivers clean enough to swim in and beaches safe from oil spills. To achieve our vision for rivers where families can head down to their local swimming hole and jump in without worrying about getting sick, we put forward a plan to establish a protected rivers network to permanently safeguard our most precious rivers; proposed robust water quality standards; and promised to keep our wild rivers wild by not building any new dams on them. Our plan to protect beaches included prohibiting deep sea oil drilling, and building up Maritime New Zealand's oil spill response capability. We also couldn't ignore the plight of Maui's dolphins, which are at serious risk of extinction, so we developed a plan to save them.

The rebuild in Christchurch was also identified as an issue that we needed to focus on. The entire Green Party caucus, as well as our Christchurch candidates, were in Christchurch for the launch of our plan for a fairer, smarter and more democratic rebuild, with smart transport solutions, a plan to insulate Canterbury homes and a pledge to restore local democracy.

Every policy we announced during the election campaign was coupled with an event or a photo opportunity to try and ensure media coverage. It meant that over the campaign I got to visit schools where installing solar panels has had a really positive impact on their budgets and on their kids. I visited innovative businesses using smart technologies, drove in an electric car and tried out a 3D printer. I played with freshwater crayfish at a smart, green farm, visited Lake Karapiro (the site of National's attack ad) to highlight how polluted it is, and paddled the Mohaka river.

Despite our best efforts, the inevitable happened and the focus of the campaign became the day-to-day dramas and distractions. Even before *Dirty Politics*, there was plenty of fodder to take attention away from the real issues. Questions about Labour's leadership, Kim Dotcom, the Internet Mana Party, Colin Craig and Winston Peters were already proving distracting. And then the *Dirty Politics* storm hit, followed by the fiasco of the 'Moment of Truth'. It was reminiscent of the Corngate saga of 2002 and the Exclusive Brethren in 2005, but on a whole other scale.

As the campaign turned into a bit of a circus, we made a conscious decision to stay above it. We didn't chase the issues of the day. For us, it was about chasing a better future for everyone instead. That's not to say that the issues raised in *Dirty Politics* weren't important. Our assessment early on was that what was exposed in that book raised some serious questions about democracy in this country. We laid complaints with the Police Commissioner, the Privacy Commissioner, Parliamentary Service, and the Inspector-General of Intelligence and Security on the allegations in the book because of concerns that National had eroded New Zealand's clean and transparent political system. Our complaint to the Inspector-General of Intelligence and Security on the book's claims that Security Intelligence Service (SIS) documents were declassified for political purposes was investigated and found to be true by the Inspector-General (in fact she found it was worse than the book had exposed). But in the context of the election, our campaign plan was to focus on positive policy. And we stuck to that plan.

We also made a conscious decision to limit our relationship with Internet Mana. I regretted that I wasn't able to convince Kim Dotcom to not go ahead with the Internet Party. A united opposition could have more effectively countered National. Internet Mana, on top of Labour's decision to reject our proposal to form a united opposition early in the campaign, made it difficult.

Amidst the chaos, we had to be smart to ensure our message was heard. As mainstream media coverage was constrained, we became relatively more dependent on our digital and on-the-ground campaigns, relying on the strength of our party organisation. We made the decision to fight positively amidst a negative campaign.

Strength of organisation

Our success in the election was significantly due to the strength of our organisation. Our supporters and volunteers were amazing. Over 6,000 volunteers gave their time and energy to the campaign. We doorknocked and phoned 60,000 New Zealanders to talk about our policies and our vision for New Zealand. We put up 6,500 billboards, delivered 1.8 million leaflets and attended hundreds of community events. And 8,800 New Zealanders made a donation to our campaign fund.

All of that is a far cry from the campaign I managed in 2005 where our ground and digital campaigns were much weaker.

During the 2011–14 parliamentary term, our work on achieving a Citizens Initiated Referendum on asset sales (22 November–13 December 2013) helped to pave the way for 2014 to be our largest campaign yet. The CIR forced us to go onto the streets and reach out to people face to face. The ground campaign methods and tools that the party utilised during the asset sales campaign prepared us for fighting this election.

Our party organisation has improved by leaps and bounds.

We also really focused on the strength of our digital work, especially social media. Social media is an area that we've worked on for years, cultivating a strong and consistent presence with a growing following, and I feel it really blossomed this election. Our strong social media presence acted as a direct channel to communicate our campaign messages and activate supporters and volunteers. An example of this is our presence on Facebook, which gave us a considerable head start compared to other parties. At the start of April 2014 the Green Party had 38,000 Facebook likes, compared with Labour's 11,400 and National's 8,372. By the end of the campaign, our Facebook likes had grown to 65,328. The reach of our most popular Facebook posts now peak at over one million likes.

What's important about this – other than the huge number of people we can communicate directly with – is that these are Green Party likes, not individualised for our leadership. When the popularity of John Key's Facebook page is compared with that of the National Party's, it really emphasises the personality politics at play. We won't suddenly lose our Facebook following when we have a new leader. The same can't be said for National.

We also continued with some of the innovative tools we'd used in previous elections. We again held a 'Green Room' – an alternative debate livestreamed during the first Key vs Cunliffe leaders' debate that we were shut out of. This time we decided to be a companion to the TV debate rather than a competitor, choosing to run the livestream during the debate's ad breaks. It gave Metiria Turei and me the chance to give our perspective on the topics discussed as well as talk about the issues that weren't being covered in the leaders' debate. The livestream itself was a relative success, streaming to approximately 10,000 devices (some with multiple people viewing). The social media noise generated was significant, with the #GreenRoomNZ hashtag proving popular, outranking both the #TeamKey and #forabetternz hashtags during the debate.

Retaining 14 MPs in such a tumultuous election was a positive result. I'm confident that this was in part because of our ability to communicate outside of the mainstream media. We were told by some in the parliamentary press gallery that they wouldn't cover our policy launches. There were some exceptions, but in general what we saw was the de-politicisation of the election. Not covering policy and instead focusing coverage on scandals is not what our country needs. Electing a government should be about the issues. We tried, but in the face of a campaign that focused on personalities and dramas, we were left to do it on our own.

We grew our number of votes and held our percentage. More than one in ten voters voted for us. We largely did it on our own. Our campaign infrastructure held our base in a messy battle when it was a challenge to get into the mainstream media. And I'm personally pretty proud of that.

10

LOSING AN 'UNLOSEABLE' ELECTION

Winston Peters

In early 2014 National called an early election for September 20th. Their excuse or pretext was that an election at the normal time would conflict with APEC meetings. In short, National argued, there was a need to calibrate a critical date in our constitutional democracy with an international conference. Despite APEC's leading economy, the USA, having a president caught with home affairs on Super Tuesday in November every four years, or mid-term elections every two years, the National government's manipulation of the electoral timetable barely received a comment from the media.

The National Party's excuse for an early election was therefore extremely weak, particularly when the real reason was the government's fear of emerging evidence of serious economic doubt over the promised surplus, which would have been seen with greater clarity had there been an October election.

Notwithstanding the foregoing, the potential opposition parties lost 'the unloseable election':

- National picked up 72,000 votes;
- the Greens picked up 10,000 votes;
- New Zealand First picked up 61,000 votes;
- Labour's party vote fell by 2.4 per cent;
- the Māori Party declined;
- ACT's nationwide party vote was 0.69 per cent;
- United Future's nationwide party vote was 0.22 per cent;
- Internet Mana lost representation;
- the Conservatives, despite massive spending, gained only 3.9 per cent of the vote and have gone to oblivion.

National won 47.05 per cent of the vote but were the greater beneficiaries of over 8 per cent of wasted votes. The other relevant parties – Labour and the Greens, if the Māori and New Zealand First party votes were added – got 45.81 per cent of the vote.

Those two total vote percentages are extremely close. Suffice to say that the second group lost 'the unloseable election' for reasons that were within their collective powers to avoid. They lost for five principal reasons:

First, the timing and the manner of the release of Nicky Hager's book *Dirty Politics* was a strategic disaster. The book was released too close to the election, and it contained a blitzkrieg of information that was too much to take in all at one time. In short, the political fan was given an overload and the commentariat choked on it. That was totally foreseeable and it defies logic why the information was not drip-fed in palatable amounts which, given the information in the book, no government could have coped with.

Dirty Politics was, after all, a book the National Party wrote, so credible deniability on its part should have been impossible. It made no sense to release all the information at once in the book, thereby giving opponents days and weeks to prepare their defence. When the defence did come it was predictably not as to the substance of the book but as to the character of the book's author and his supporters. Instead of reacting and re-reacting to each day's emerging news on new information, the government escaped rightful and constant pressure because it knew the full scope of the allegations.

Whatever Nicky Hager thought he was doing, he should have taken some sound advice because if he had done so the election would have been dramatically different. Instead of people getting sick of 'dirty politics' they would have been hungering after every day's new disclosure. This is not to doubt in anyway the seriousness or integrity of Mr Hager. After all, every subject in his book was a revelation of the inner workings of the National Party and some of those in the bureaucracy.

Second, the Labour–Greens alternative government was never a mathematical possibility, which, nevertheless, the commentariat blithely or blindly refused to see. Whether it was arrogance or ignorance it did not matter. National was able to go on the negative at their opponents and on the positive for themselves.

National benefited from what can only be described as anti-Green paranoia, which damaged Labour. That aversion was strengthened when the Greens demanded the Finance portfolio and two deputy prime ministerships, and then shocked Labour and other political parties with a demand for an independent audit of Labour's alternative Budget. That demand clearly implied that they did not trust the integrity of the Labour Party Finance spokesperson, Hon. David Parker. Whether or not the latter has shortcomings, a lack of integrity and scholarship are certainly not among them.

Third, Labour was in trouble for the second campaign in a row over its capital gains tax and its proposed age increase to 67 years for Superannuation entitlements. Labour failed to grasp, despite numerous warnings, that the near-65s were not hearing the timeframe for these two changes. Voters are busy people. New Zealanders work the second longest hours in the OECD. And so their snapshot grasp of these two policies was that they would be enacted 'tomorrow', a deeply unappealing prospect.

Fourth, Mana was being destroyed by the Internet Party's toxicity. Paid for and hired audiences do not a campaign make. Again the commentariat misread and grossly overrated the Internet Party's potential. The Internet Party's intervention in the election, led by a foreigner, was even too much for the voters in Te Tai Tokerau to stomach, but all the hype enabled National to paint the alarming prospect of the Internet Party somehow being in control. When the Internet Party, preceded by chaotic meetings, failed to deliver on the 'Moment of Truth', around 4 per cent of the National vote which was contemplating shifting camps decided to stay home.

Fifth, the campaign spending by the various political parties demonstrates the prodigality of some and the frugality of others. Clearly the New Zealand First Party suffered from a lack of financial resources and would have had to go into serious debt to do better.

Fundraising frequently owes much to the perceived potential position of a political party. If the polls in the pre-election build-up have a record of constantly underrating a political party's chances, there is an adverse effect on its fundraising. That is why the New Zealand First Party has been so opposed to the polling methodology persisted with by pollsters in this country. In the critical period when rising poll support generates financial support – i.e., the period immediately before the campaign proper – the polls have invariably, election after election, grossly underestimated New Zealand First, at great cost to the party's fundraising machine. It begs the question – how does the polling industry explain not being within 300 per cent of getting New Zealand First's final poll on election night aligned with their pre-campaign predictions? It is New Zealand First's view that the polls in this country are a disgrace, seriously misrepresentative, and would in any other commercial sense be blocked out of the market. Throwing in the odd comment 'you can never rule out New Zealand First' in no way exonerates a key element in the political marketplace, the pollsters, interminably getting it wrong where New Zealand First is concerned.

As an aside, the preoccupation of the media with the Conservatives was mystifying. Despite massive amounts of money, this party was unelectable. The National Party knew what a highly dangerous risk they were. When their leader, Craig, sought an accommodation with National in East Coast Bays, New Zealand First also said it would contest that seat. The threat worked and the Conservatives were gone.

In any election there are circumstances that a party cannot control but must nevertheless seek to influence. New Zealand First underestimated the media penchant to write up the Labour–Greens coalition. We did not on sufficient occasions point out how mathematically impossible that was. And again while we did react to the Greens' attack on their so-called Labour partner we should have done it within the first few hours of it occurring. As it was we did it on the Monday out from the election, but of course that was all lost in the 'Moment of Truth' which was to happen that night.

In the 2014 election New Zealand First increased its vote by 33 per cent, or 61,000 votes. The party knew that it could have and should have done better. In short, so many elements of this campaign could have been better controlled despite how difficult that might appear.

Postscript: the Northland by-election, 28 March 2015

New Zealand First nominated for the Northland by-election on 27 February. While national campaigns are largely determined by the size of one's war chest, in by-elections the parties are on a more level playing field. In Northland, New Zealand First demonstrated how strong a campaigning force it is, and what an effect it could have at general elections if it were as well-resourced as the major parties.

Northland showed that people have become jaded by the same old talk, from the same old parties, with the same old lack of results. This time, people turned to a new option – New Zealand First. Northland showed that New Zealand First is in an excellent position to rapidly expand its voting base, given the preoccupation of 'beltway politics' with Auckland. It showed that people who have only ever voted one way in their life are prepared to change that habit. This should be a real concern to the status quo and a relief to those in the long forgotten corners of this country.

The campaign was a complete campaign – from grassroots volunteers waving signs and knocking on doors, to the down home, intimate style of campaigning that only New Zealand First can do, to the high tech, with a well-run social media presence. The viral 'nail fail' video shows just how dangerous it can be for an inexperienced political leader when he doesn't have the trappings of big money in American-style politics.[1]

The campaign showed that National is not the great unbeatable machine that many, including National, thought it was. It is beatable.[2]

It showed that when the media closely examine National and don't fall for its tricks, that National panics and actually personifies not the strong, disciplined rowing crew from its general election ads, but rather the 'old dunger of a row boat', with nothing to be seen but oars splashing, out of unison, and the panicked waving of blue arms. In short, a sorry shambles.

11

TU MĀORI MAI: THE MĀORI PARTY CAMPAIGN

Te Ururoa Flavell

On 23 January 1946, the streets of Wellington welcomed home from World War Two some 2,000 servicemen and women, and another 800 veterans of the 28th Māori Battalion. The troops were to march from Pipitea Marae to the entrance to Aotea Quay where a traditional reception would be held.

At the reception, Lieutenant Colonel James Henare made an impressive and impassioned rally call to the troops which would be remembered for decades to come:

> Hoki atu ki ō tātau iwi, hoki atu ki ō tātau maunga, hoki atu ki ō tātau marae. Engari kia mau ki tēnei kōrero – tū Māori mai, tū Māori mai, tū Māori mai.
>
> Go back to our people, go back to our mountains, go back to our marae. But cling to this command – stand as Māori, stand as Māori, stand as Māori. (28th Māori Battalion (NZ) Association, 2012)

When Tariana Turia crossed the floor in 2004 and formed the Māori Party, she echoed these sentiments to honour our right to stand as Māori. I heard her call. In turn, I rallied the troops within my tribal rohe of Te Arawa, and when we reached the hikoi of 5 May 2004 Hone Harawira asked me to be the master of ceremonies for the day. It was an invitation I was proud to accept, to do my bit to ensure we stand as Māori – tu Māori mai.[1]

In 2014, I took up the challenge of my fourth election campaign, this time as co-leader. The same story of resilience and revival as in 1946 would be repeated many times as our election campaign mantra.

The 'Tu Māori mai' tagline resonated among our membership. It reflected our commitment to stand as Māori in Parliament for the past nine years, and our devout belief that we will never deviate from that call. We have always said we would defend Māori interests while advancing our kaupapa in the best interests of the nation.

Through that commitment, over 100 major policy initiatives have been set up, and in the 2014 budget, we secured $90 million for free doctors' visits and prescriptions for under-13-year-olds, $15 million to support Whānau Ora Navigator's work with whānau, $10 million for Māori sporting and cultural activities ('Moving the Māori Nation') and $20 million additional funding to expand the free sore-throat clinics for tamariki at risk of rheumatic fever.

We could not have gained so much had we not been at the table. We are unapologetic about our position to sit alongside the governing party, whoever that is. We know that it doesn't matter who is on the other side: they are all the same. What is important is our belief in ourselves to carve out our own future.

We have always been clear, however, that we would never win the confidence of the people unless we gave as much attention to the spirit of inspiration as we did to the nuts and bolts of an election strategy. I am always very focused on the tin tacks of any campaigns, but for 2014 in particular we were realistic that tactics would only be effective if coupled with a 'hearts and minds' strategy.

The significance of my re-election as Member for Waiariki was a major driver in our 2014 campaign, right from the onset. As a party we knew that retaining this seat was crucial to our survival, and while oversight of the national landscape was critical we needed a sharp-edged strategy at the local level. This chapter reflects on that strategy as pivotal to our campaign. Ultimately it was the success within the Waiariki rohe that led to us retaining not only the seat, but also the bargaining chip to negotiate an ongoing role in a Relationship Accord with Government for the 51st term of Parliament.

#TuMāoriMai

The hashtag #TuMāoriMai had particular appeal for my campaign as it enacted a play of words on my name, Te Ururoa (T.U.). In previous campaigns we had used the concept of 'tu' (to stand) to draw the attention of voters to a 'two-tick' strategy at the ballot box – 'e TU tika ana Te Ururoa': two ticks for Te Ururoa and the Māori Party!

Māori love the magic of metaphor. I am always reminded of the whakatauakī, 'kaua e mate wheke mate ururoa' – literally, 'don't die like an octopus, die like a hammerhead shark'. Octopuses are renowned for their lack of resistance when being captured, while a hammerhead shark will fight bitterly to the end. The message is clear: don't give up, no matter how hard the struggle.

And so it was, in 2014, that the election pledge 'Tu Māori Mai' became a vigorous call for unity across the membership and particularly in Waiariki. Our most fundamental campaign collateral has always been our people power, and this election I was truly blessed with a winning combination: a strategy team that never gave up and a compelling plan to believe in. The key members of my strategy team were campaign novices but they made up for it with forceful enthusiasm and intellect. The people responsible for implementing the strategy and conducting our campaign activities were the loyal membership of the electorate. The campaign manager maintained contact with the branch coordinators via teleconferences, electorate meetings, email and phone correspondence.

Our approach – melding the new strategists with the cause champions who have driven my campaigns over the last decade – gave our team a fresh edge to a tried and true formula for success. Campaigning in the Māori electorates is a hard slog. The most effective methods have always been old-fashioned electioneering: knocking on every door, distributing fliers, hosting cosy 'cottage-style' meetings at homes and larger hui at marae or runanga offices. 'Kanohi ki te kanohi' is the key – a face-to-face meeting in which political contenders get the chance to be seen up close. It is a formidable recipe for getting to know the voting constituency, but it is also time-intensive, requiring amazing commitment from the small team at the core of a campaign. After ten years of relentless dedication I know that my loyal warriors who have stood by me through it all were grateful for the new energy of the 2014 cohort. With a finite pool of resources it was important that we were discerning in our approach.

In 2014 we faced the additional pressure of competing for airspace against two political juggernauts who were also vying for the Māori vote.

One was a desperate Labour Party, destined to achieve one of its most humiliating defeats, its worst result at the polls since 1922, with just 25 per cent of the vote. As mainstream New Zealand deserted them, the Labour Party machine knew it had to channel considerable resource into targeting the Māori seats as a rescue strategy from political oblivion.

The other was the larger-than-life Megaupload maestro who brokered an audacious alliance between the Mana Party and the newcomer Internet Party. For their unlikely marriage, Mana and Internet were rewarded with a fighting fund of about $4 million donated by their 'party visionary', Kim Dotcom.

As history would eventually reveal, the extravagance of the Internet Mana campaign would ironically lead to its demise. The ultimate 'Moment of Truth' for their unusual alliance reflected their founder's view, expressed when the election results were in, that 'the brand Dotcom was poison', but unfortunately the damage extended beyond their own membership. The polarising impact of Dotcom's campaign became a disincentive to wider Māori political engagement. We knew we had a lot of work to do to mobilise interest amongst the whānau, hapū and iwi of Waiariki and further afield.

Our campaign strategy was underpinned by research and analysis of previous election results and the demographics of our rohe. From the analysis we identified the areas across our electorate that had a high population density. We looked at the booths that had yielded success for us in previous campaigns. We examined the 'swing voters', geographic slices of the electorate profile in which potential voters had indicated an openness to a range of political options.

We endeavoured to capitalise on the strengths of the 'incumbent' in our messaging. The strategy team concentrated on five central planks to our platform:

1. *Integrity:* Te Ururoa Flavell walks the talk;
2. *Kanohi kitea ('the face that is seen'):* Te Ururoa is seen at every hui;
3. *Tino pukumahi ('very busy'):* the 'hammerhead' is a relentlessly tireless worker;
4. *He rangatira ia ('a leader'):* Te Ururoa is already a leader;
5. Te Ururoa is committed to whānau.

Once those messages were in place, the rest became easy. We needed to know how to create the sense of inspiration and motivation that stirs the senses, moves the emotions. Those messages helped us to do that.

Advertising and coverage

Despite our best efforts, the Māori Party failed to entice the scale of corporate sponsorship that we saw become an important campaign resource for other parties. Nevertheless we appreciated the generosity of the many smaller scale donors, leading us to our largest campaign fund ever, with just over $58,000.

We have always identified the billboard hoardings as a key component of our election expenditure. In 2014, 31 per cent of our income was allocated in this way. The messaging was pivotal to designing billboards that captured core attributes. We honed our approach to three concepts: whānau, rangatira and kanohi kitea.

We then charged each of our branches with the responsibility of identifying prime locations that might respond best to targeted messaging. For example, the whānau/mokopuna messaging might be effective when placed around marae locations, while the rangatira design might be better placed on the open roads.

Our electorate campaign was also strengthened through the national billboard campaign, which focused on two 'local' personalities with nationwide notoriety. Named 'New Zealander of the Year' in February 2014, Dr Lance O'Sullivan was very familiar to the people of Waiariki following his time as a GP in Rotorua. And charismatic personality and Māori Party list candidate (ranked seventh), Tame Iti, championed all the messages that were so pivotal in our approach:

> The Māori Party has got credibility. They've established themselves as an independent Māori movement that walks the talk. I also support them sitting at the decision-making table of Government, it's the only way Māori can bring about change. It's no good moaning on the outside.
>
> I support Te Ururoa [as] 'kanohi kitea', people who are seen in their communities (Māori Party 2014).

Another core component of our electoral spending (approximately 18 per cent) was radio and newspaper advertising. We identified the major newspapers within the electorate and focused our schedule on the fortnight before election day. Our assumption was that undecided voters are more likely to change their minds closer to the day. For 'brand recognition' we used the same photographs in our newspaper advertising as on the billboards, pamphlets and fliers.

In hindsight we now believe that our advertising strategy should have begun far earlier. The total number of New Zealanders who took to advance voting in 2014 (717, 579) far exceeded the combined total of the last two previous elections (334,558 in 2011 and 270,427 in 2008).

Our radio campaign was targeted around more popular appeal. We utilised humour with the backtrack sounds of the Māori Party waiata. Te reo Māori was also a foundation to our approach. The advertisements featured on the most four most prominent iwi stations within the Waiariki electorate and we also targeted a mainstream station with a younger listening audience. The financial outlay was minimal and well worth the expenditure.

Tama Tu Tama Ora!

One of the most exciting initiatives in our 2014 campaign was the 'Tama Tu Tama Ora' concept. Every Saturday morning and Tuesday lunchtime a 'Tama Tu Tama Ora' run would set off around the Rotorua central business district.

Once again, the success of this strategy had its underpinnings in our own cultural capital: the magic of metaphor. The concept evolves out of the proverb, 'Tama Tu Tama Ora, Tama Noho, Tama Mate' – 'an active person will remain healthy while a lazy one will become sick'. Like the hammerhead shark message, the implication is that to stand is to live – to lie down is to die.

It is a powerful message that I have taken to heart not just in our policy approach ('Moving the Māori Nation') but in my personal commitment to fitness. Two months after the elections I competed in my third Iron Māori event requiring a 2km swim, a 90km bike ride and a 21km run. It took me seven hours and 27 minutes to cross the line, but I gave it all I had – and that was pretty much the message of our election approach as well.

The purpose of our runs was to raise the profile of the party and the candidate, while at the same time demonstrating the value of keeping whānau healthy. This is about walking the talk of Whānau Ora – we had young dads running with babies in pushchairs, nannies on a mission with their power-walking routine, and our tamariki trying to overtake us all.

Another feature of 'Tama Tu Tama Ora' was its capacity to entice those of our whānau who may not typically be interested in politics to run alongside us, and to understand our intentions. 'Tinana ora, wairua ora, whānau ora' – 'physical, spiritual and social health and wellbeing' – is an important investment plan.

A fabulous reinforcement of this message came through the parallel campaign initiated by Tame Iti, who led a cycle relay from Ruatoki in the Bay of Plenty to Tāmaki Makaurau (Auckland). The 280km 'Tame Tu Tame Ora' cycle tour took Tame through three electorates: Waiariki, Hauraki Waikato and Tāmaki Makaurau. The aim of the relay was to motivate people to literally get on their bikes and think seriously about the message of the Māori Party as a party where health and wellness count.

It was an incredible spectacle biking alongside a solid core of supporters as we pedalled through Rotorua, Tirau, Cambridge, Hamilton, Ngāruawāhia, Pukekohe and Papakura, ending at Manurewa Marae.

In Whanganui, meanwhile, #TeamNancy, a team supporting Nancy Tuaine in her bid for the general seat, took to the streets for a bit of line dancing, while Tāmaki Makaurau candidate Rangi McLean shimmied along the catwalk in the Miromoda showcase at New Zealand Fashion Week. The underlying message of the catwalk campaign – consistent with the effort to advance the quality and status of Māori fashion design, a purpose of the Indigenous Māori Fashion Apparel Board (Miromoda) – was to promote the possibility of te reo rangatira as 'being back in vogue'. It appeared the fitness phenomenon was catching!

Tweeting, liking, boosting and blogging

For many of our stalwart supporters, the 2014 campaign introduced another new language to our repertoire. Encouraged by its effectiveness at reaching voters, our team eagerly started posting on Instagram, indulging in Snapchat, and making good use of the wonders of Voxer, Messenger, and Twitter.

To assist the novices amongst us, we established a closed Facebook group which shared interpretations about activities within the wider political landscape. It turned out to be an invaluable resource, not just within our electorate but also at Parliament and at the wider strategic level. It became a confidential forum to vent, to upload media alerts, to share possible responses and create robust solutions to events as they arose.

I also had a private Facebook team, 'Team Tu', responsible for promoting messages and ensuring they were distributed extensively at the local level. The material posted included articles, photos, infographics and updates on campaign activities.

A new initiative we piloted was posting photographs of supporters with small billboards saying 'My Whānau supports Te Ururoa Flavell'. Earlier in the year, we had seen US First Lady Michelle Obama and Pakistani Nobel Prize laureate Malala Yousafzai create a social media sensation through use of the trending hashtag #bringbackourgirls. Their campaign involved celebrities posting their support for political intervention to rescue the schoolgirls kidnapped from their school in northeast Nigeria on 14 April 2014 by Boko Haram.

Impressed by the impact of that campaign, our strategy team encouraged members to take photographs of themselves and their whānau with the billboards. The concept was to 'photo-bomb' interesting hui and then instantly post it on Facebook. Our team had a great time increasing our engagement on Facebook, particularly with use of the 'likes' and 'shares' techniques.

The celebrity endorsement factor was reinforced through posting short web videos by well-known local personalities. The videos were posted on Facebook and YouTube to excite interest and were shared widely among an online audience. We also initiated 'Profile Pic Tuesday', essentially encouraging our members to change their Facebook profile picture every Tuesday. This was a simple and popular means of enabling others to join in on our kaupapa without too much effort. The Māori Party's Twibbon application – a 'microsite' that allowed people to show their support – was well used in this regard.

The social media approach we took to Election 2014 also showed many of us that we had so much more to learn. We are now far more savvy about the need to ensure our key messages resonate, and aware that there are many different aspects of the strategy that we could devote more time to. While the fortunes of other political parties were being determined by bloggers, we failed to occupy the blogger space. We realise that the strategic use of infographics was a sure-fire prescription for drawing attention to our policy gains. And on reflection we accept that some of our members got distracted by arguments put up by our political opponents, a distraction that added little to our campaign. We wanted to appear energetic and kaupapa-driven, and to act with integrity. Engaging in negative banter with trolls appointed by other parties for the sole purpose of taking us 'off-topic' was counter-productive. We needed to be disciplined in promoting the achievements of our party, explaining that we were a relevant, responsive and responsible force for change.

Concluding comments

Our Waiariki campaign revolved entirely around an agenda to protect Māori rights and advance the dreams and aspirations of Māori in the best interests of this nation. We worked assiduously to put Māori issues front and centre, rather than clip them onto another agenda.

We took part in the 'Te Wero' debates (broadcast to the 21 iwi radio stations via Radio Waatea, Auckland's Māori radio station); the Māori Television electorate specials; and the routine candidate panels that form the foundation of any campaign. As co-leader I also had the privilege of participating in the debates featuring leaders from minor parties; the dinner-table conversation with John Campbell was a format that I particularly enjoyed. We pressed the flesh, delivered pamphlets, crafted our radio and television addresses, and attended the plethora of conferences, hui, AGMs and regional forums that filled up every moment of the pre-election schedule. And through it all, our messages were consistent.

We wanted to remind the electorate that our people have dreams, talent, skills and potential; we have that Māori X-factor that this country as a whole will always benefit from. We stuck closely to that belief in ourselves and our whānau to realise our potential. This is why Whānau Ora is so powerful. It comes from kaupapa, values and traditions that have endured the test of time and are still relevant.

But this election we also had a special call to motivate and mobilise us – Tu Māori Mai. We had adopted that call because that is exactly what the Māori Party does every day. It is a call to stand up and be counted.

When we needed to take a stand internationally we stood up and got the Declaration of the Rights of Indigenous Peoples signed. When our people were in cold houses we got them insulated. When our young parents needed support we stood up and advocated to extend Paid Parental Leave and provide free doctors' visits.

If being effective is getting results, then our message was simply to ask New Zealand to vote for our candidates across the country and to give their party vote to the Māori Party. Despite our best efforts, on election day we were disappointed that there were still many New Zealanders who were unconvinced that the Māori Party is for all citizens of Aotearoa. Our party vote at 1.32 per cent was the lowest yet, with just over 31,000 New Zealanders appreciating our vision for a nation of cultural diversity and richness. We lost out on our founding seats, Te Tai Hauāuru (held by Tariana Turia since 2002, intially for Labour and since 2004 for the Māori

Party) and Tāmaki Makaurau (held by Pita Sharples since 2005). It was a bitter blow to our confidence.

There were, however, two results that restored our hope. In Waiariki voters bucked the trend, increasing our margin from the previous election by more than 2,000 votes, attaining 45.56 per cent of the vote. And for the first time we now have a list member in Parliament, bringing in the irrepressible vitality of Marama Fox.

At the end of the day perhaps that was one of the greatest results from our campaign that we could have hoped for. For the first time, rather than electing a representative of a particular demographic, a geographical cluster, we now have the best of both worlds – one co-leader from an electorate base, and the other able to focus her energies across the land. Sure, the margins weren't what we hoped for: a party of two MPs faces a far more gruelling schedule than a party of four or five. But we survived while others didn't; and we have gone on to negotiate an enduring basis for a respectful relationship with the government, at the table, achieving ministerial gains while at the same time maintaining a strong and independent voice for Māori.

To stand is to live – and for the Māori Party we are determined that we not only do our best to pursue the aspirations of all people who call this country home, but we also make sure that every life is a great life; the people deserve no less.

Tu Māori Mai – that's us.

12

HOUDINI ACT: THE 2014 ESCAPE

David Seymour

Dramatis Personae

ACT began 2014 cornered. Its sole MP and leader, John Banks, had stepped down as a minister the previous October due to controversies that would see him resign as an MP by June, following a conviction in the High Court, only to be at least partially vindicated in November when the Court of Appeal overturned the conviction, ordering a new trial. In May 2015 he was vindicated by the Court of Appeal, far too late for the September election, however, so for the purpose of the 2014 campaign the Banks saga capped a five-year litany of ACT meltdowns so fantastic it verges on surreal.

Nonetheless the party entered 2014 in good spirits. Banks had nobly stepped aside to fight his own battles (which, after all, had their origins in his pre-ACT 2010 Auckland mayoral campaign), announcing that he would not stand again. Jamie Whyte presented as the dream ACT leader-in-waiting. A Cambridge PhD steeped deeply in the party's core philosophy, he had played in the big league. He had a regular column in the *Wall Street Journal* and, living in the UK, he had battled socialists on the BBC. Best of all, this finance sector management consultant was prepared to give his valuable time to visit every hall in the country campaigning for ACT, which he very nearly did.

I believed that New Zealand needed Jamie in Parliament, but I felt that he could not do it on his own. We knew that 'wasted vote syndrome', where discerning voters are unwilling to vote for a party that may not achieve either MMP threshold – neither the 5 per cent party vote nor the victory in at least one electorate seat – would plague any small, battered party. We made a pact to divide the workload: I would seek to represent Epsom, freeing Jamie to increase the overall party vote. This pact had another important purpose. Sharing power made a statement that ACT could be disciplined and collegial, and that it had ambitions of being larger than just one person (i.e., its leader).

Despite a late and unconventional play for the leadership and Epsom candidacy by party president and former MP John Boscawen, the board appointed Jamie and me to the roles we sought. Another former ACT MP, Kenneth Wang, was shortly appointed as deputy leader.

Richard Prebble, the party's longest-serving leader, returned in the role of campaign director. ACT had and has an enduring infrastructure, being one of only four parties to win seats in every MMP election. This organisational structure included members, a board, a network of donors with substantial capacity, and highly committed activists and candidates. Drawing all of these together was the party's largest enduring asset, a unique piece of political real estate representing classical liberals.

Goals

By February the party was set to contest the 2014 election. The overarching goal was to return the party to its former glory, wining multiple seats and breaking the 5 per cent threshold by 2017, if not at this election. This required that several sub-goals be achieved:

- A strong campaign in Epsom, showing that electing an ACT candidate was not only good for the centre-right, but would also give Epsom quality representation;
- Getting Jamie Whyte known and liked by voters across the country in order that several additional MPs would be elected.

A secondary goal was to keep the centre-right in power. We felt that, while ACT supporters could conceivably support a government of nominally left-wing parties (for example, the Lange–Douglas Labour government in 1987), the current opposition threatened to undo the 1980s reforms in a more substantial way than any government since had dared consider.

The party vote campaign

The party vote campaign began with research carried out by the party's traditional pollster, Public Opinion Strategies led by Gene Ulm. The research indicated that ACT's potential vote, consisting of those who considered ACT as their first or second choice, could be as large as 11 per cent of all voters. These voters, the research indicated, would respond to a cluster of messages about crime, government waste, racial equality and tax. As the campaign went on, it slowly deviated from this guidance. If there was one fatal flaw in this otherwise high quality research, it was that second-choice ACT voters at the beginning of 2014 had in mind leaders completely different from our new one.

ACT has always been a heavily policy-orientated party. Its founding document is a 300-page manifesto proposing to complete the *Unfinished Business* (Douglas 1993) of the 1980s, comprehensively extending market reforms to the welfare state. ACT's party vote campaign sought to leverage Jamie's brand as an intellectual and his strength communicating policy ideas by releasing a series of substantial policy papers and speeches. These included an alternative budget, a case for lowering the company tax rate at the expense of corporate welfare, an education policy designed to empower state school boards and independent schools as well as expand the Partnership School policy, a policy on applying the British 'three strikes' approach to burglary, and a speech on racial equality.

These pieces amounted to an earned media strategy and gained varying degrees of success. The alternative budget and burglary policy, for examples, were well covered and even received some grudging respect from political adversaries. The racial equality speech and more radical crime announcements later in the campaign received strong media criticism and probably damaged the campaign. The media's fascination with Kim Dotcom's political machinations and the publicity that followed the Internet Party and its association with the Mana Party intensified the competition for attention in the media, and made it harder to obtain rational media analysis of policy.

At the same time as this 'air war' was being carried out, the party was carrying out direct voter contact through several channels. An automated call centre with professional operators was canvassing targeted areas, volunteers around the country delivered direct mail reinforcing the messages of Jamie's speeches and papers, and Jamie travelled to nearly every region of the country to conduct house and public meetings with potential voters.

Social media was also used, but not as strategically or comprehensively as it might have been. Some paid advertising was done and a series of videos, the 'Sunday Series,' where Jamie would outline an ACT position, were released each week for most of the campaign.

In parallel to the English-language campaign, Kenneth Wang waged a comparatively successful Chinese-language campaign. This included direct mail matched to Chinese-surname households, Chinese-speaking call centre operators, a series of very well attended dinners, and appearances by

Kenneth in the Chinese media. The Chinese-language campaign focused on crime and promoting New Zealand as an open and tolerant society, contrasting with the xenophobic campaigns subliminally directed at the Chinese community and indulged in by every opposition party.

Although our 2014 party vote increased on the 2011 result in electorates with a large Chinese-speaking population, the nationwide result was ACT's worst ever, far short of what was needed to bring in its leader as a second ACT MP. The party was hurt by several media blunders by the leader who, despite enormous talents, struggled to adapt to the reality of retail politics. In Jamie's defence, every other party leader had stood for Parliament before (and been elected). The learning curve is steep and unforgiving. It is regrettable that far lesser and largely unknown candidates have been elected to Parliament via party lists without being tested to nearly the same extent as Jamie was.

The effect of the John Banks indictment, trial, conviction and sentencing should not be understated. The loss of momentum after the conviction was palpable. After Jamie Whyte's election as party leader the membership, donations and mood of the party had all risen appreciably. After John Banks' conviction these trends reversed, with the reversal stronger the further one travelled outside Auckland.

This came at a time when a party with such momentum might traditionally expect to rise in the polls. It is likely that the adverse judicial finding against John Banks at the outset of the election campaign deprived ACT of enough votes to prevent its leader and perhaps several other MPs being elected at the 2014 election. A small consolation of the party vote campaign is that it managed to prevent an 'overhang' in Parliament, strengthening the centre-right.

The Epsom campaign

As I was the candidate, my perspective on this campaign is in some ways the worst. People occasionally asked how I thought my campaign was going, to which I always replied that I was the last Epsom voter whose opinion on the matter counted. With that caveat, here is my account.

The Epsom campaign delivered two messages to Epsom electors. The first was that electing me was the most effective way to ensure the continuation of a centre-right government – the overwhelming preference of the electorate. The second was that the electorate would get a committed, competent and capable electorate MP. A sub-message of the second was that the local National Party candidate (Paul Goldsmith) would be re-elected as a list MP even if he were not elected MP for Epsom.

We will never know the comparative importance that voters placed on the twin messages. The best evidence comes from an early August poll by Colmar Brunton that put me 44–32 behind Paul Goldsmith until respondents were prompted with the fact that John Key had recently endorsed me, switching the result to 45–31 in my favour. Probably the best conclusion to be drawn from these levels of support before and after the prompt is that both messages were necessary and neither were sufficient for me to win. Notwithstanding, I knew, having been involved in two prior ACT Epsom campaigns, that Epsom voters were perfectly capable of making up their own minds. Time to get to work.

Lacking prior name recognition and acknowledging that I was the third ACT candidate to contest Epsom in six years, the previous two (Rodney Hide and John Banks) having made ignominious exits, the only way to win was through enormous amounts of sincere person-to-person contact. In total I knocked on 13,000 doors over eight months. This was short of my goal of every household, but I made a conscious decision to talk as long as almost all voters wanted to. In doing so I picked up a number of constituency issues I would have to address as soon as elected. My reasoning was that the contact needed to be sincere, and often I would be invited into people's homes. In addition I reasoned that anybody interested in talking to me for a prolonged period was likely to talk to their friends about politics too.

This doorknocking campaign was supported by an extensive direct mail campaign. In total five drops of 17,000 personally addressed letters were delivered. We must have had the most highly skilled mail team in the world, with several QCs, the occasional former cabinet minister, a former Reserve Bank Governor, and several surgeons getting out to deliver these letters. The messages were aligned with the campaign themes. They addressed local concerns about the cost of council rates, 'intensification' (i.e., increased urban density), and burglary, alongside strategic considerations arising from MMP. We also used the call centre to canvass Epsom voters, measuring progress at several points during the campaign.

House meetings were useful and widely used. Attendance ranged from a dozen to over a hundred, and close to a thousand people must have attended one of these meetings. At each I spoke briefly before answering questions and speaking to as many guests as possible.

We also used some advertising. Prior to the campaign we purchased several commercial billboards to boost my name recognition. We also bought advertising in local magazines and community papers, simply introducing my name and face. My car was loudly decorated with my name and image. The effectiveness of these approaches is still difficult to ascertain.

Social media got an unexpected boost when a somewhat folksy video I made to introduce myself to visitors to my campaign website became a viral hit. By the end of the campaign it had been viewed over 30,000 times, bringing a combination of admiration, notoriety, sympathy and outright rudeness online. On balance, the video served to raise my profile. It was circulated among the political press, leading to several media engagements that might not have otherwise occurred. It gave me recognition among younger voters and added some levity to an eight-month-long campaign.

The Epsom campaign attracted far more media attention than any other electorate campaign. There were two televised all-candidate debates and seemingly every media outlet sent a reporter out doorknocking with me. This level of attention meant that there was little scope for earned media strategy, other than impressing on the press that I was indeed getting out and working. The effectiveness of media engagement is, like much of the Epsom campaign, best judged by others.

A final campaign tactic was the use of human billboards at busy intersections during the final weeks of the campaign. At their peak, up to 30 people participated, waving signs at traffic, with the intention being to show energy and commitment to the electorate.

In the final analysis, the Epsom campaign was a success. I was elected with a majority of 4,250, larger than the 2005 and 2011 results though much smaller than Rodney Hide's whopping 12,882 vote margin (over National's former Epsom MP Richard Worth) in 2008. Moreover, from the point of view of ACT's overall strategy, the press were not questioning that I would win in the final month, sparing the party from 'wasted vote' syndrome.

Conclusion and the future

ACT has survived again, largely due to the enduring Epsom strategy that the party has used to ensure its survival for four elections so far. As a party, we are now well positioned within government to advance core policy objectives, these being Partnership Schools and regulatory reform. After five *anni horribili* – remarkably difficult years – the party is in a place where it can heal its brand, renew its infrastructure, marketing and policies, and attract new people. Having completed more than 20 years since its founding (in 1993–94), such renewal is needed. I believe there is a constituency for a classical liberal party in a nation based on trade, private property and private enterprise. How large that constituency is, and how well the party can serve it, is a matter to be discussed over the next three years.

13

UNITED FUTURE AND THE FUTURE OF MMP

Peter Dunne

About four elections ago in Britain, the Liberal Democrats used John Cleese to do some advertising for them. In one of his more famous advertisements he says to the camera, '60 per cent of you say you'd vote for us if you thought we could win. Now I'm going to go away and make a cup of tea while you just think about that.' And that is the same scenario that is affecting smaller parties in New Zealand.

In 2013 when United Future had some membership issues with the Electoral Commission we were overwhelmed by the rapidity of people renewing memberships, but more importantly, people joining us. And we assumed – not unreasonably, but as it turned out, falsely – that that was the dawn of a rebirth. We have gone back and canvassed those people as to why they reacted so rapidly and so enthusiastically at that time. And the answer, with shadows back to John Cleese, was 'because it's important that you be there'.

The problem which affects parties like United Future, and as I say, the others as well, is that there is an increasing disconnect between that statement and the fact that people have to do something about ensuring you are there. There is a sense almost that it is really good for our system to have a diversity of parties involved, and we quite like what some of them represent, but do not expect us to actually vote for them. That is someone else's responsibility and if they do not get over the line in sufficient numbers, we are very quick to say 'that was a shame, we thought you would have done better'. And that has certainly been our experience over this most recent election, and to a lesser extent, over the last couple as well. So one of the challenges we are now starting to confront, as we do our post-election review and start to move forward, is how to counter that problem.

We noticed from the various online websites that helped people determine their vote that United Future scored very highly when people did the self-assessment as to where they fitted. And we had a number of messages from people saying, 'I've just done On-The-Fence or Vote Compass or whatever it is and guess what! I'm a United Future supporter!' So are you going to vote for us? 'Well, no because I am just not sure . . . no, I'm not.' So you cannot have it both ways. You cannot say that you support what political parties stand for, and then not meet that requirement by casting a vote. I think that one of the challenges that we are going to face – and I suspect, if they are honest with themselves, ACT and the Māori Party will as well – is how do you continue to make an important enough connection to people so that an intellectual commitment actually follows with a vote?

If, when a party is in a crisis as we were, being deregistered by the Electoral Commission, and people feel so aggrieved by that as to spontaneously seek to join, in large numbers, because 'you've got to be there' but then see that as the limit of their commitment, how do you engage them politically? How do you engage them politically when they enthuse about the thoroughness and detail of your manifesto (and we were the only party that produced such a thorough one) – 'You have got policies on everything! Fantastic! I agree with them' – but then refuse to vote for those policies? And then, after the election, these same individuals come to you and say, 'now about your confidence and supply agreement: these are the things that we hope you will be pushing to include'. This disconnect is very similar to the scenario John Cleese identified under a first-past-the-post (FPP) system all those years ago.

Leaving partisan politics aside, I think the big challenge for the future credibility of our MMP electoral system is in resolving that conundrum. Because what the 2014 election showed abundantly was that when faced with the perception of a crisis – and the crisis came with the sense that there were external forces trying to buy the election – people immediately flock to one or other of the major parties: in this case, one (National) predominantly. And yet, looking back, when we moved to MMP it was because people wanted to curb the power of the major parties. Just four elections ago, in 2002, the smaller parties in Parliament commanded more than a third of the seats (i.e., 41 of 120). We have seen a continual reduction in that proportion since that election. And the question that has to be posed is whether, in fact, under the guise of proportional representation we are actually seeing a return to FPP politics. The challenge which that then gives rise to is about public expectation of a more diverse, open and fluid political environment.

If you see what people are talking about at the moment, it is riven with contradiction. On the one hand, people tell us that they like strong and effective government; on the other hand, they tell us that they like multi-party government because that gives an opportunity for a wider range of views to be represented. They do not want tails to wag dogs, which is fair enough, but they like the fact that there is the capacity for a wider range of opinions to be part of the government process and for other experiences to be brought to bear. But they do not really see that they have anything to do with creating that situation. And frankly, I fear for the future of our current system, long beyond United Future's time in politics, while that disconnect remains.

Now what to do about it? Well, you could look at the spectrum and say it is time for political parties to stake out their particular ground and attract a support that flows with that. And I would say in return that the three parties that I have mentioned have done so. The Māori Party has certainly staked out its ground and has been very effective in government over the last two terms. And yet it suffered from the syndrome of people saying, 'I think we will vote Labour because they are likely to have more numbers and therefore be more effective'. From Opposition? The ACT Party has certainly staked out its ground. And United Future, as a liberal democratic party in the centre, has also done so.

There are New Zealanders who adhere to the particular values of the parties described. The problem is, increasingly, that they do not see those values as sufficiently important to vote for the parties that espouse them. And I think that that is the challenge that the 2014 election makes plain for all of us. Now we can do the work – and we will, in terms of re-examining our organisation, our approach to funding, and all those sorts of things – but I think it will count for very little in the long term if the situation remains as I have described it. Of course, 2014 did have some unusual features attached to it. The Dotcom intervention was the most bizarre, and I note that when he was announcing the launch of the Internet Party in the United States, he said, as a throwaway line, that Hillary Clinton should be worried. I think that says more about him than it does about her. The timing of the release of the *Dirty Politics* book, and the influence that was intended to have, did produce a reaction from people saying, 'that's it, I've had enough, I am drawing the line here'. And the line that was drawn was a blue one, for National, and drawn very heavily on the Monday and Tuesday after the televised 'Moment of Truth'.

So: an unusual election? Certainly. But I think that there are some lessons that have become clear in a very stark way, ones that we will have to start to think about for the future. Now I guess the driving force for all political parties is your commitment to an ideal – your commitment to a view that you hold, one that gives your party a place in the political spectrum. And that certainly remains true for us, and we will progress on that score.

I want finally to draw attention to the current range of confidence and supply agreements, because they are a little different from those that have preceded them. I do not think their full worth has been completely understood. The previous pattern has been basically for a pretty crude system: a confidence and supply agreement in which the major party of government agrees to support certain initiatives proposed by the smaller partner on the understanding that the partner will support the broad sweep of key measures proposed by that government. This is a pretty crude trade-off: open, but basic. The agreements this time, however, were concluded at a time – before the final vote count, including special votes, had been confirmed – when the National Party thought that it had an outright majority. As a result, it decided that it was not going to make any policy concessions to its three partners (ACT, the Māori Party and United Future). On the face of it, this could be said to have been a blow to the smaller parties; but equally, however, the agreements did not demand anything of the smaller parties in return other than the commitment to approve confidence and supply. Unlike previous agreements, therefore, each of the three support parties is in a situation where we can determine our own position, issue by issue. While we do not have that threat of the power of numbers that might have been there previously, what we do now have is the ability to be much more clear and direct in terms of what we want, and of what we will and will not support, without that threat of, 'well, we will pull the confidence trick on you if it all gets too tough'. In many ways we have actually ended up in a more open and free environment, and over the next three years, as everyone gets to grips with this – both the partners and the National Party – I think that a different and more positive dynamic will develop. So that is an observation for the future.

To conclude: on all fronts the results of the 2014 election speak for themselves. However, I think that the bigger issue is about the nature of our MMP system and how we, as voters, think about it in order to get the maximum benefit from it. It used to be said that our essentially two-party political system under FPP was a choice between Tweedledee and

Tweedledum (or Tweedledum and Tweedledumber). Having so actively moved away from that in the 1990s, the question is whether we are now, by stealth, returning to it. Our next election, in 2017, will give us more of an answer.

MEDIA PERSPECTIVES

14

PARACHUTING INTO A POLITICAL NO MAN'S LAND: A JOURNALIST'S PERSPECTIVE ON A CHARACTER-BUILDING CAMPAIGN

Jane Clifton

This campaign had similar qualities to, say, one's first parachute jump, or a night spent stranded in the bush. It was exhilarating, character-building and instructive – but one hopes not to have to go through it again anytime soon. If ever.

The political configuration invited, practically demanded, certain alluring assumptions to be made which, alas for the media, turned out to be wrong. It was also unavoidable to focus on a range of issues and questions which, for similar reasons, turned out not to be important at all in the end. That's not entirely just a fancy way of saying, 'We got quite a lot wrong.' But in the end, the only right answer is the one that came out of the ballot box, and plenty of people disagree with that, too. Suffice it to say, the media never wins an election campaign.

It was nevertheless both a bonanza and a challenge for journalists and certainly the most exciting and tense election I've seen since 1984. It was intensively personality-driven, as was 1984, but the difference was that then, there wasn't much doubt about who was going to win. There was a lot of fun and nervous tension getting there, but it was clear from the beginning that David Lange's Labour was coming in and Sir Robert Muldoon's National was on its way out. This time there was a genuine sense that it could go either way. In this assumption we were almost certainly wrong, but more of that in a minute.

Though Labour's vote was always obviously destined to stay depleted, the arithmetic was tantalising. With the Greens, New Zealand First and the possibility of an Internet Mana (IM) vote, Labour could conceivably get the heft to form the government. Conversely, the possibility of the Conservative vote fattening up could save National's bacon.

So we felt duty-bound to focus heavily on the tiddlers, IM and Colin Craig. Frankly, that wasn't a chore. They were both colourful and maddeningly contradictory – what was not to like? For once, politicians were big entertainment fodder, and even our news editors were happy. Various orthodox polls suggested they could each bring as many as four MPs in, so our fixation on them was justified.

They operated as a sort of seesaw for each other.

The more menacing and potent Internet Mana looked, the more that National supporters flirted with the idea of voting for the Conservatives, to the point where at one stage they looked like getting up to 5 per cent without an electorate MP. Considering last election the Conservatives were a laughing stock and IM not a year old, that was heady stuff.

The problem is, we and the voters were shadow-boxing.

We didn't really know to what extent either of these parties were on the move up or down, or even registering, because the best poll in the world doesn't measure below the margin of error reliably. There could have been twice as many votes or zero votes for either or both parties; we just didn't know and that made it incredibly stressful. Equally, the Conservative vote was heavily conditional on the IM vote. A lot of people who contemplated voting Conservative were only doing so to counter IM. And those saying they were voting IM were – as we now know pretty conclusively – not terribly sincere. It was a rark-up. There's a tendency among voters to tell others, including pollsters, that they're going to vote X or Y for shock value. My hairdresser, for instance, adored annoying her husband by claiming she was voting for Winston when secretly she had no intention of so doing.

So we were flying blind – but with no choice but to keep going in the general direction of IM and the Conservatives being important.

The other thing we didn't know was what Winston Peters was going to do. We always knew we wouldn't know what Winston would do because he has made a virtue and a trademark out of smiting his brow and saying he must wait Till The Voters Have Spoken. It's maddening, but it's an honourable, defensible position. And it gives the whole political firmament much displacement activity in terms of second-guessing what he might do, and trawling his every inflection and tic for clues. But again, it's stressful and confusing for voters, and renders every conclusion you might reasonably reach conditional.

Beyond all this fear and loathing and personality-mongering, what we should have figured out was that there was never really a prospect of Labour forming a government. There are a number of reasons for that, but the overall one is that, despite the obvious proviso – that you need enough seats or potential blocs to support you on all or most issues to run a government – there is a little more to it than arithmetic. Labour faced an irreducible psychological barrier to achieving the lead.

You can form a government under MMP without being the largest party, and you can be a minority government, but there is a question about how far off the majority you can be. In this case, the leading coalition party only had 25 per cent. Labour never looked like crossing the 30 per cent threshold – and that, alas for it, is about the psychological tipping-point at which you start to look like you 'deserve' to form a government. Lower than that, and irrespective of overall MMP maths, voters feel you're taking a liberty; you haven't earned it. Labour never looked like being within cooee of a righteous lead role, and for that reason I think that the Greens would not have done a deal to support it. I don't think Winston would have either. It might seem counter-intuitive that parties that have a majority of seats wouldn't form a government. And boy, had it come to that, would their supporters have been bitter. But in this particular planetary alignment, there was practically every factor militating against taking advantage even of a parliamentary majority.

One is that in this case it would likely have meant working in a government which depended for its majority on Internet Mana. That would have been toxic. Everybody – the media, the public, the parties themselves – would have been mistrustful and beady for signs that the IM MPs were having too much influence. Or any. And I don't think Labour would have been happy to base a government on that level of skepticism.

Depending on IM would have put all these parties' reserves of public goodwill at risk. And there was immense personal enmity in play as well toward IM's members, especially given the defection of Laila Harré from the Greens to be IM co-leader. Russel Norman let rip about his antipathy to IM after the election, and it was heroic he waited so long. IM really did queer the left's pitch.

A second reason is that the Greens and Labour had just failed to make a peace treaty and de facto alliance. The two parties got very close to a deal, but Labour then said no. That failure wouldn't have been so bad were it not, for some bizarre reason, made public. Now, telling the public that you're going to get on like a house on fire in the Beehive when you have just publicly flunked even a soft non-hostility pact, and done so in an atmosphere of no little acrimony, is not an easy sell to the voting public.

Add to that the fact that Winston is allergic to the Greens, and that's an extra non-gelling agent in the mix. New Zealand First and the Greens have a lot in common, supporting radical monetary reform and opposing free trade. But their constituencies are absolutely antithetic to one another.

So it turns out that sometimes in politics you have to do more than just count. There is a psychological element in terms of what the public will accept and even what the parties themselves can bear.

To belabour this point even further, the public were by now painfully aware that most of the Labour caucus didn't support the Labour leader. 'Prime Minister No Mates' was not going to be a triumphant opening image for David Cunliffe's ninth-floor occupancy.

All of that made a ticklish problem for the media. We believed in the maths, that this election could go either way; and even had we sensibly discounted the maths for all of the above reasons, we would not fairly have been able to describe those reasons with too much conviction, because we would then have been open to bias charges.

There was, too, an awful lot of media coverage devoted to issues which, while they were engrossing at the time, turned out to be utterly irrelevant – some of which still remain a complete mystery because they are now so irrelevant it would be a waste of time following them up.

What, for instance, was the deal behind the sudden resignation, at the eleventh hour, of Colin Craig's press secretary? It was a bombshell at the time. People do storm off in the heat of battle, but it's generally hushed up and smoothed over. This was unprecedented. We still don't know what it was about. Craig didn't appear to know even at the time.

We still don't know either what the heck happened to that Labour–Green deal. It was well advanced in the positive discussion stage before someone pulled the plug on the Labour side. We don't know who that was. We don't know why that was. And whatever the cause, the animus seems to be alive and well – at least as the Greens infer it from Labour – even under new leadership.

We still don't know what on earth happened to Hone Harawira. He went mysteriously off-piste during the campaign. Various uncorroborated explanations were advanced, including that he'd had to go overseas. He was treated very shabbily by the party adopting a pro-marijuana policy knowing how deeply he feels about what that drug has done to his constituency, so it is possible he had major temper outage. But we still don't know. He wouldn't say, Laila Harré wouldn't say, and Pam Corkery told us Kim Dotcom didn't have to talk to us about anything at all because we were 'puffed up little shits' and 'glove puppets of Cameron Slater'. But as all of the above ceased to matter after election night, we will probably never know where Hone hid.

We still don't know for absolute sure what Winston had in mind. We do know he was a very cross chap on election night, as he had expected to end up with the balance of power. But quite how he would have styled his – I am guessing here – refusal to support a Labour-led government with the Greens, and/or what torture he would have inflicted on a National-led minority one, is destined to stay a secret till his memoirs.

Something else we still don't know: *what the hell was Laila Harré thinking?* There may not *be* an answer to that.

For the media, it was a harrowing campaign, and a landmark one reputationally – not in a good way. I don't need to elaborate about the pressure media companies are under for sheer viability, but there are fewer and fewer journalists (well, actually working as journalists, and not as government communications staff), very few sub-editors checking our work before publication, sometimes none at all; and with respect to politics, incontrovertible evidence (as in, we can count the clicks) that in the main, politics is a turnoff to readers, listeners and viewers – at least in as much as media businesses are able to gain audiences and sell advertising. Add to that, we are all having to do one another's jobs. The other day, a stranger was in the press gallery of the House taking photos, and was introduced as 'Radio New Zealand's photographer'. Take a second to process the implications of that job description. A few years ago, radio was just an on-air job. Now it has to be a written, spoken, video and pictorial service. As does a newspaper, and a television channel. My old deadlines as a morning paper reporter started to cut in around 5 pm. Now they are constant. All reporters have to feed the internet and social media beast at all hours, from instant tweeting through live-blogging to recording and posting videos, to cutting television news items, to long-run written features.

As a result, journalists on the campaign trail were even more exhausted than usual. As well as the beast-feeding, there is an increasingly strident pressure from news bosses to be more tabloid, more populist. They want more stories on MPs' weight loss secrets, perks abuses and love lives, and as few as is get-away-with-about on carbon emissions, constitutional debates and benefit abatement rates. This creates extra tension with the media and politicians and their handlers, who feel we trivialise or ignore important issues.

But as hard as journalists worked, voters were often minded to ignore us anyway – or at least reject our news judgement and sense of editorial priority. This, for me, was a real facer. The things that we hammered, people just didn't buy. Colin Craig is a good, simple example. Pretty much every time we featured Colin we did so mockingly – and I put my hand up to this as much as anybody – but the more the public saw of him, the more his vote went up, and he nearly got 5 per cent. It's absolutely astonishing for a man with his ambivalent profile, and whose party was a laughing stock at the previous election. He made a fantastic target for humour: the come-hither billboards, the strange changes in his increasingly spooky campaign photos, the press secretary fiasco, and the contradictory and sometimes confrontational policies. Yet the more people saw of him, the more they disregarded our framing of him, and the more seriously they entertained having him in Parliament. Even allowing for the IM-countering factor fuelling the Conservatives' vote, this was remarkable. In fact, if the polls hadn't detected late signs that IM was tanking, he would probably be an MP now.

The other obvious element of this election, that people will be discussing for many years to come, is that the more we have of 'dirty politics' in the news, the less people view it as a factor in their voting decisions. The more we told them – via the tone and magnitude of our reportage of Nicky Hager's book – the more firmly a majority of voters discounted it. In fact, the voters seemed at least as suspicious of the media as they were of the politicians, spin doctors and business people Hager implicated. We had become part of the mix of factors that the public no longer trusts, and that's a very hard thing to bear when you're doing your best to report on news that should be valuable to people, and issues you sincerely judge as worthy of scrutiny and debate.

We were slammed from all possible directions. I got a larruping for expressing a degree of skepticism about the illegal provenance of Hager's information, and the dot-joining he did. Others were castigated for being too credulous and uncritical of his activism. The media came under pressure to ban anyone mentioned in the book and the public to observe a blackout of Whale Oil's advertisers.

There was profound dispute over what was the actual news here.

A lot of what was styled as revelatory about the operation of the *Whale Oil* blog was not new, secret or particularly mysterious. As to the ethics of it, they'll be debated forever. But one of the criticisms we copped was that we'd complacently or deliberately kept Whale Oil's workings a secret. This was nonsense. There's nothing secret about a blog, especially one with as many daily hits as that one. Any attentive reader will have detected campaigns, some on individuals, some on issues, and drawn a reasonable inference of sponsorship and/or systematic promoting or rubbishing.

Yet had we, before *Dirty Politics*, reported on his activities, we would have fetched the criticism of giving Whale Oil too much oxygen. Or of persecuting him, given there are all manner of, shall we say, 'acquired taste' blogs out there; why pick on his?

Then we were criticised because some *Herald* journalists had been secretly swapping news tips with Whale Oil – prising open the massive can of worms about colluding with activists. Why was it bad to collude with Whale Oil over stories, but okay to collude with Nicky Hager? Or vice versa? And by some other lights, how *dared* we compare the one with the other?

Obviously much of this depends on taste, and one's political and ethical compass. Journalists are not supposed to have a political compass, just an ethical one – but boy, are they hard to distinguish sometimes. As to taste . . . that's one thing we're generally happy to leave to fashion-page gushery.

And then there was the blogosphere itself. Somehow, while we were trying not to look and hoping traditional news audiences weren't looking either, some blogs, not least Whale Oil's, had become part of the mainstream media. They were a player – part activist, part media – in the election. Only they were not bound by the same conventions as are supposed to bind journalists.

These are not simple good-versus-evil issues, but it certainly felt like it, being a journalist trying to report fairly and proportionately on *Dirty Politics*. I've seldom felt New Zealand to be so divided since the Springbok Tour. Irrespective of its lack of impact on the election, the issue seemed to demand on either of its sides a complete denial of light and shade.

It has been argued that the ultimate criticism of the media, which was reflected in the National Party's massive vote, came from the many people in our audience who wished to tell us not just that they supported the government, but that they were sick of us banging on about dirty politics, which was a tautology and was not, in their view, news but more likely an attempt to railroad them. It's hard to not see merit in that theory – the more so as it led only to still more criticism from the opposite direction, that we had criminally underplayed dirty politics, because the public wasn't taking it seriously.

Finally, there was the niggling, demoralising reality – that our every bulletin and story was apt to be critiqued by an instant Twitter/comment-thread chorus, often excoriatingly. We learn to be tough, and must always remember that news reporting by its very nature inflicts misery on many of those reported about. We should analyse criticism, not respond defensively. But this new stuff can be corrosive. When disgruntled viewers and readers can, anonymously, in front of the world at large, repeatedly call us ugly and thick, or speculate that we're on the take or in adulterous relationships with sundry MPs, it can have a subconscious chilling effect on the way we report. (It also really upsets our mums.) I would go so far as to say that some high-profile reporters are systematically bullied, and even stalked, via social media and comments threads. There are individuals who spend unwholesome amounts of time obsessing into their computers, unable to bear it that views different to their own can be countenanced, and seemingly determined to intimidate others into silence. Sometimes, the bullies even do this under their own names, so socially acceptable has viciousness come to seem. It's a nasty new by-product of our business, and it can take a lot of self-steeling to persuade oneself that such vileness says way more about the ugliness of the Tweeter/commenter's soul than the professional competence of his or her target.

All up, I come out of this campaign pretty pessimistic about the media. The changes we have made in media style across many of our companies do not seem to be arresting audience decline or building positive new audience engagement. Certainly not so as to make the money to ensure adequate, experienced staffing. I like to think our image and influence cannot sink much further before media company shareholders revolt and force editors to reverse the tabloid/jolly lifestyle/*Ten Celebrities Who Hate Broccoli!* trend. But I fear that can only happen when we get some signal that people value serious news reporting enough to start paying for it again. As we know from other aspects of reporting on election campaigns, a willingness to part with more money is not a signal people give readily.

15

BLOGGERS, BOTTOM FEEDERS AND DISRUPTION:
TECHNOLOGY AND THE 2014 GENERAL ELECTION
CAMPAIGN

Corin Higgs

Introduction

The role of technological change in the conduct of politics has long been a popular topic of study. In the 21st century the effect of technological development based around the internet is seen by many as a catalyst for greater and deeper citizen engagement, possibly reversing the steady decline in voter engagement and participation. Although each of the past five New Zealand general elections has been touted as the 'internet election', the promise of increased voter interest has never quite eventuated. While it is certainly much easier for citizens in 2014 to proactively interact with politics through online communications, many choose not to and voter turnout remains on a stubborn downward trend from the modern-day high (93.7 per cent) reached in 1984 (Electoral Commission 2014c).

There is an understandable, albeit superficial, allure to the notion that technology will 'disrupt' contemporary politics, leading to a 'revolution' in political engagement. Recent technological development has largely improved the organisational aspect of election campaigning for political parties. The internet and its associated tools have made it easier for academics, political parties and other organisations to quantify and measure aspects of political activity. Yet at the same time the selective nature of internet communications allows greater disengagement from politics for the mass public, allowing citizens to tune out from politics much more easily. The advent of click-and-forget 'slacktavism', Twitter trolls and attack bloggers, and the proliferation of online echo chambers, has made it easier for many political activists to eschew mainstream mass engagement in preference for inward-facing validation of their political views by their peers.[1]

The 2014 general election campaign provided a number of cases of the influence of technological change on the conduct of election campaigns, although the technology involved and the impact was not always as expected. This chapter will briefly examine five examples of the role of technology as it affected the 2014 election campaign from a voter's perspective. The rise of the techno-utopian Internet Party dominated political discussion during the campaign, yet amounted to little on election day. Television New Zealand developed the online 'Vote Compass' tool to inform voters and generate media stories, yet it seemed to confuse many. The role of so-called 'social media' affected the election campaign, but not in ways that were predicted. During the campaign the role of right-wing political blogs in the 'dirty politics' scandal contrasted with the irrelevance of the 'hipster politics' of left-wing political blogs. Yet ultimately, it was a centuries-old technology – the printed word in the form of two books, Nicky Hager's *Dirty Politics* and *John Key: Portrait of a Prime Minister* by John Roughan – that was arguably the most influential in the 2014 election campaign.

Techno-utopianism and the failure of the Internet Party

In the late 2000s, a number of political parties based around the use of the internet began to emerge throughout the world. Commonly named 'pirate parties', such movements, emerging primarily in Europe, utilised internet technologies to collaborate and organise, campaigning largely upon issues of copyright and patent reform as well as nternet security and 'freedom'. While initially attaining some limited success in national and European parliaments, such parties largely faded away as the initial wave of enthusiasm from their supporters collided with the reality of campaigning, fundraising and political representation. In 2014, the Internet Party was founded in New Zealand and was claimed by its proponents to be a 'force of innovation' that would harness the power of digital, social and internet media to 'revolutionise' politics. The party was incorporated and funded largely by Kim Dotcom, in part as a response to the internet entrepreneur's legal difficulties.

But much like the pirate parties of Europe, the Internet Party did not match the weighty expectations of its supporters, failing both politically and electorally. The party formed an agreement with the Mana Party to run a joint party list, hoping to use the electoral 'coat-tail' of MP Hone Harawira's Te Tai Tokerau electorate to circumvent the 5 per cent party vote threshold required to gain parliamentary representation. With millions of dollars of funding provided to the party by Mr Dotcom, a few months before the September election the Internet Mana Party was expected to gain as many as five of the 120 seats in Parliament. Yet the party ultimately gained just 1.42 per cent of the party vote and Harawira lost his electorate seat to Labour's Kelvin Davis. Neither the so-called 'revolutionary' Internet Party nor the Mana Party gained representation in the 51st Parliament.

The reasons for the failure of the Internet Party were numerous, but ultimately it was due to political naïveté and a fundamental misunderstanding of how political parties actually work. The party's organisers believed that technology and money could substitute for the long-term graft of grass-roots organisation and activism. The Internet Party had planned to develop aspects of its organisation and policies around crowd-sourcing (i.e., soliciting ideas via social media) and online discussion forums. It was, however, a much-hyped online policy development idea that went largely unused by most members. Despite being founded on the vague principle of internet freedom, the most popular topic of discussion on its online policy platform was not copyright reform or cyber security, but the legalisation of cannabis. Through over-reliance on technology the party perversely enabled its leaders, members and supporters to more enthusiastically pursue and promote their individual political interests rather than aggregate those interests to form a cohesive political movement.

There was also a fundamental disconnect between the party's ideals of collectivism via internet aggregation and its status as the political plaything of Kim Dotcom. The party's belief in the overwhelming power of 'new' media was shown to be short-sighted as Kim Dotcom came under sustained criticism in the 'old' media of television and print for a number of gaffes, including owning a Hitler-autographed copy of *Mein Kampf* and publishing an expletive-laden chant about Prime Minister John Key at a concert. This collision between 'old' and 'new' media reached its apex in the final week of the campaign when Kim Dotcom hosted the 'Moment of Truth' event at the Auckland Town Hall, streamed live on the internet. The event featured appearances by US journalist Glenn Greenwald and whistleblower Edward Snowden, with evidence that they claimed would prove the Prime Minister had misled the public regarding spying allegations. But the event was ultimately derailed by an angry diatribe by Mr Dotcom against prominent journalists at the press conference following the event.

The prominence and supposedly radical nature of the Internet Party and its founder provided the incumbent National Party with many opportunities to demonise it as an almost existential threat to New Zealand democracy. From the left, the Labour and Green parties' attitude to the party deteriorated from grudging acknowledgment to outright resentment at the party's existence, as it was believed to be frightening centrist voters towards National. Following the election, it became conventional wisdom among left-wing politicians that the Internet Party was largely responsible for the Labour Party's worst result in living memory. While this view somewhat papers over the serious and fundamental failings of the Labour campaign, there is some irony in the technological revolution promised by the Internet Party instead leading to an increase in the number of seats for the conservative National and New Zealand First parties. The Internet Party and Kim Dotcom had believed that, through money and technological solutions, the wheel of politics could be re-invented. Instead they were crushed by it.

Vote Compass

In 2014, media organisations also attempted to use technology to encourage voter engagement. 'Vote Compass', promoted by Television New Zealand, had previously been used in Australian and Canadian elections and was claimed to be the most 'sophisticated survey of voter attitudes that has ever been undertaken in New Zealand' (TVNZ 2014b). The tool took the form of an online survey that aimed to stimulate engagement by assisting voters to compare party policies by answering a series of arbitrary and often ambiguous multiple choice questions. The initiative was backed by academics from New Zealand universities and received financial support from the Electoral Commission.

The survey relied heavily on involvement from political parties, which were asked to provide their own responses to policy questions on a scale from 'strongly agree' to 'strongly disagree'. Some parties, including the Conservatives and the Internet Party, were initially excluded from the survey, supposedly because they had not released policies at the time, even though many other parties were yet to release policies in several key areas. Within the 'Vote Compass' analysis that was provided to voters there was no assessment of the intent and ability for parties to carry out promises. Many answers provided by parties were based upon wishful rhetorical perception rather than policy reality. For example, a voter who strongly agreed with the statement that 'free tertiary education should be restored' was matched with United Future, the Green Party and the Mana Party even though only the latter had free tertiary education as a definitive policy for the 2014 election.

The survey was also hampered by occasionally clumsy language open to broad interpretations, such as 'How much control should Māori have over their own affairs?' as well as references to an 'anti-smacking law'. Such loaded questions produced predictable results that were then dutifully reported on television news. For a tool that purported to provide clarity it seemed to confuse voters more than anything, with many users perplexed as to why they should consider voting for United Future, a party never expected to gain more than one electorate MP and which ultimately won just 0.22 per cent of the party vote (McIvor 2014). This was possibly due to the survey's default bias, where a respondent that chose the neutral option to all questions would tend to be matched with the National and United Future parties. Surprisingly, given the involvement of several political scientists in the project, there was little emphasis on 'valence issues' such as competence and leadership, which have been significant factors in National's and John Key's recent electoral success.

'Vote Compass' was another example of the tendency towards reductionist data-driven mechanisation that fails to capture the full essence of contemporary politics. While more sophisticated than similar tools such as Massey University's gimmicky 'On the Fence' website, 'Vote Compass' fell somewhat short of its promise and appeared to exist more as an opinion gathering device that generated stories for the 6 pm news. The choice of the Electoral Commission to provide financial support to what was ultimately a commercial media initiative was somewhat questionable given that the Commission took an actively dissuasive approach to other voter engagement campaigns such as 'RockEnrol' (Rapira 2014).

'Vote Compass' was based upon the belief that many people do not vote because they lack the information to make an informed decision. But lack of information is not the sole reason for many New Zealanders not voting. It is possible that the expectations for 'Vote Compass' to significantly increase voter stimulation and engagement were too high, as it requires much more than just an online survey to politically inspire people. Nevertheless, if reworked and founded upon a more sophisticated and wider scope of political science literature, beyond the largely redundant two-dimensional axis of 'economic' and 'social' policies, it may yet become an increasingly valuable electoral tool for voters.

'Social media': selfies and the 'Rawshark' disruption

So-called 'social media' has become an increasingly popular topic of study within political science, as political parties have devoted greater attention and resources to the medium in recent years. Many studies of contemporary election campaigns (including within this volume) analyse the role of social networks such as Facebook and Twitter in assisting parties and candidates to engage with constituents and gain votes. While there has possibly been an over-emphasis on this aspect of electioneering, particularly by younger political scientists and activists, the evolving world of social media continues to produce interesting challenges to the political status quo.

As noted, this volume includes a detailed chapter regarding social media and the 2014 election campaign, but there were a couple of interesting developments in this area that were not predicted by many. A significant advancement in the political use of social media was John Key's strategic utilisation of the 'selfie' (self-taken photograph) as he met with the public on the campaign trail. Typically, during his visits to shopping malls and other open spaces, the Prime Minister would be mobbed by young and old. As he worked the crowds on such visits, Key used a well-refined and efficient approach to interacting with the public. He would greet, shake hands, exchange banter and move on swiftly to the next person, typically taking less than a minute to do so. Particularly among younger people, the Prime Minister was constantly posing for casual 'selfie' photographs.

The willingness of the Prime Minister to utilise the 'selfie' served a dual effect: he was seen to be popular, blessed with the common touch, on the evening news but also on social media such as Facebook, as the 'selfie' photograph was often shared by the participants on their social networks. The Prime Minister, who has successfully cultivated a persona as an apolitical 'celebrity', was further humanised in the view of the people he shared a 'selfie' with as well as with their Facebook contacts. It is difficult to quantify the viral effect of the 'selfie' with precision, but if the Prime Minister posed for a 'selfie' with an average of 50 people a day over 30 days, that is up to 1,500 people who may share the photograph with 200 friends (the estimated median number of Facebook contacts) – providing a potential reach of up to 300,000 people. One of the benefits of such interactions is that they are not overtly political, which is of great benefit during an election campaign where candidates are attempting to engage with large sectors of the population rarely concerned with the machinations of politics. The simple yet politically savvy appropriation of the 'selfie' by

John Key in the campaign arguably delivered greater voter engagement and conversion than the tens of thousands of dollars spent by political parties on social media campaigns (Leyland 2015).

Although far less popular than Facebook and geared by design towards the selective interests of its users, the short-messaging service Twitter took on greater prominence in the 2014 election. Twitter has become a popular communication tool for political activists and journalists despite its relative political obscurity for many outside those minority groupings. John Key once described Twitter as the realm of 'bottom feeders and trolls' engaging in 'cyber bullying' (Luscombe 2014). His point may well have been proven correct as the election campaign intensified, as far from being an arena for political discourse that enhanced New Zealand's democracy, Twitter often descended into a toxic cesspool of abuse for many users. Several journalists complained about the constant abuse they received from members of the public on the service. The ease of anonymity that is possible on Twitter allowed many political operatives to make expletive-laden and unwarranted attacks on journalists for reporting stories they disliked, without the accountability of attaching their real name to their statements.

Perhaps the most surprising and politically consequential development relating to Twitter during the campaign was the emergence of 'Rawshark'. This anonymous person (or group of people) used Twitter as a means to publish the raw and uncensored leaked material that had formed the basis of Nicky Hager's book, *Dirty Politics*. The information was allegedly obtained via unauthorised access to the computer of National-aligned blogger Cameron Slater. Over a period of weeks, and on a near daily basis through the campaign, using the Twitter account Whaledump, 'Rawshark' published links to a number of transcripts of online conversations between blogger Cameron Slater and other National Party operatives. While *Dirty Politics* was strongly vetted to avoid unnecessary personal injury and slander, and Nicky Hager attempted to put the leaked material in the correct context, there was no such discretion in the 'Rawshark' information releases. 'Rawshark' also provided other politically damaging material to selected journalists to pursue. The information leaks created a sense of panic within National Party circles, as it was unknown what information (and from whom) 'Rawshark' would release next.

Based on information provided by 'Rawshark', Fairfax journalist Matt Nippert had worked up a news story around the attempts of blogger

Cameron Slater and his associates to intimidate the head of the Serious Fraud Office, Adam Feeley (Nippert 2014a). An associate of Slater, Cathy Odgers, who was involved in the plot against Mr Feeley, became aware that Nippert was pursuing leads based on information provided by 'Rawshark'. Unaware of the nature of the information that 'Rawshark' had and when and how it would be published, Odgers panicked and contacted the Office of the Prime Minister. Odgers subsequently provided information that inferred that Judith Collins, then Minister of Justice, was also involved in the campaign against Mr Feeley (TVNZ 2014c).

Acting quickly and decisively, the Prime Minister immediately sacked Collins as a Minister. Yet the information that the Prime Minister acted upon to sack Collins, a supposed 'smoking gun' email from Cameron Slater, was not among the material held by Nippert or 'Rawshark'. The uncertainty created by 'Rawshark', through the immediacy of the new media of Twitter and the meticulous nature of the 'old' media, had caused the downfall of a powerful and popular Minister just three weeks from election day. While Twitter is a not a substitute for vigorous journalism, in this case the actions of 'Rawshark' inflamed the political consequences of an important story.

The political blogosphere: 'dirty politics' vs 'hipster politics'

Political blogs have become an increasingly important element of the New Zealand political environment since emerging in the early 2000s. Although digested by a minority of New Zealanders, political blogs are read by many political journalists, commentators and activists and often provide alternative viewpoints that can affect wider political discourse. The relevance of blogs goes right to the top of New Zealand politics. For example, Prime Minister John Key has stated that he talks to 'lots of blogsters' [sic] to derive political insight and gossip (Fox 2014b).

Broadly, New Zealand's political blogosphere can be divided between left-wing and right-wing blogs. The most popular right-wing blogs, *Whale Oil* and *Kiwiblog*, tend to be written in a gossipy, engaging style that provides a crossover appeal for the mainstream and requires little translation into political stories for mainstream journalists. Both blogs had early success in the election campaign, achieving successful cut-through in the political media through highlighting Kim Dotcom's 'F*** John Key' video and characterising a video of the burning of a supposed effigy of John Key at a party as a political act. These media stories helped to reinforce the National Party's underlying campaign theme for voters: 'don't put it all at risk'.

The publication of Nicky Hager's *Dirty Politics* as the 2014 election campaign got under way put an unprecedented focus on the role of blogs in New Zealand politics. Hager's book alleged that *Whale Oil* and *Kiwiblog* operated as part of a 'two-track' media strategy headquartered in the Office of the Prime Minister. The government would allegedly use blogs to conduct 'dirty' 'attack' politics, separate and distinct from the Prime Minister's 'nice guy' persona. Following the book's publication, the effectiveness of these blogs in publicising National-friendly stories during the campaign diminished due to the preoccupation of the authors in defending themselves against Hager's allegations and the increased scepticism of mainstream political journalists towards *Kiwiblog* and *Whale Oil* (Fisher 2014). Yet by the end of the campaign, the political role of the blogs that were lambasted in *Dirty Politics* seemed largely unchanged. David Farrar, author of *Kiwiblog*, was explicitly thanked in John Key's victory speech on election night (although ostensibly for his role as a pollster, not a blogger) and it was later revealed that the Prime Minister continued to remain in contact with Cameron Slater despite the *Dirty Politics* scandal (Rutherford 2014).

A comparison of the role of the left-wing aligned blogs in the election campaign with those aligned with the political right brings to mind the Oscar Wilde quip that 'There is only one thing in the world worse than being talked about, and that is not being talked about.' While *Whale Oil* and *Kiwiblog* allegedly practised 'dirty politics', the major blogs of the left, *The Standard* and *The Daily Blog,* perpetuated what can be called 'hipster politics'. 'Hipster' is a term used to describe a subculture focused on self-image and individuality to perpetuate a feeling of elitism and superiority to others. Culturally, hipsters focus on music, clothing and activities that are outside a supposed 'mainstream'. For example, a stereotypical hipster believes that a vinyl pressing of an obscure band's first album is better than anything on commercial radio. The political hipster typically uses social media and blogs to insulate themselves from, and attempt to shame, those who do not possess their self-professed superior political and moral fibre.

The tendency of the major left-wing blogs to engage in 'hipster politics' hindered their influence on the mainstream media and, by extension, their relevance to swing voters. Unlike their counterparts on the right, left-wing blogs provided little assistance to political parties in achieving their electoral aims. Instead of seizing the opportunity provided by the *Dirty Politics* scandal, the major left-wing blogs instead amplified their often shrill and condescending tone, opining on ideological and philosophical topics rather than stories that exemplified and reinforced underlying political themes. Although it may in part relate to the timing of the political cycle, blogs and other emerging technologies seemed to have enabled many on the activist left in New Zealand to withdraw further into individual silos and become increasingly detached from mass engagement. Yet those on the right seem to have largely used the technology to better position themselves and their parties within the mainstream political zeitgeist.

Books: the game-changing technology of the 2014 election

Despite the hype about modern technology revolutionising electoral politics, and the extraordinary events of 2014, from 'Rawshark' to the 'Moment of Truth', it was arguably a 600-year-old technology that was the defining feature of the election campaign. That technology was the printed word, in the form of two influential books: John Roughan's *John Key: Portrait of a Prime Minister* and Nicky Hager's *Dirty Politics*. Although approaching the John Key-led government from radically different perspectives, both publications may have assisted the National Party to victory in the 2014 election.

Portrait, written by an experienced *New Zealand Herald* journalist, was claimed to be 'unauthorised', in that the subject did not have the opportunity to read the book prior to publication. Despite this, John Key happily agreed to be interviewed for the book on multiple occasions and headlined the public launch of the book. Signed editions were used as National Party fundraisers and copies were even given as parting gifts to retiring members of National's parliamentary caucus.

The book helped to maintain political focus on the person that is the prime minister, rather than on his policies or principles. In the increasingly presidential style of New Zealand politics, the book fitted perfectly with the idea of 'Team Key', one of National's central campaign themes. The biography portrays Key as likeable, honest, trustworthy and a team-builder. Although interesting in its story of John Key's formative years, the latter half is a largely anodyne, curiously incurious retelling of the Prime Minister's political life. Yet the book was of great assistance in reinforcing and perpetuating the Prime Minister's image as that of a competent and approachable 'man of the people'. It also added to John Key's political stature – as a potential 'great Prime Minister' – that he would have such a tome written about him. Although even without the book's publication

National would almost certainly have won a third term in government, the biography also helped to consolidate the contrast between John Key and Labour leader David Cunliffe, who was viewed with a degree of anxiety by much of the public.

There was no doubt that Nicky Hager's *Dirty Politics* was unauthorised. The book alleged deliberate coordination between ministerial offices and right-wing blogs in order to smear and intimidate political opponents. Following publication, the allegations dominated political news coverage for weeks. Even though the Prime Minister vigorously rebutted the entirety of the book's content throughout the campaign, an investigation conducted by the Inspector-General of Intelligence and Security after the election subsequently verified one of the book's principal allegations, namely, that John Key's office and the New Zealand Security Intelligence Service had acted incorrectly regarding the release to Cameron Slater of information concerning then Labour leader Phil Goff. Yet during the election campaign, John Key's robust defence against Hager's allegations proved sufficient and the scandal appeared to have no material effect on the election outcome.

Conclusion

Due to National's comprehensive election victory, many commentators have written off the political consequences of *Dirty Politics*, but that ignores other possible factors involved in the election result. Although some centrist voters may have been uneasy regarding the *Dirty Politics* allegations, Labour's lacklustre campaign and public scepticism about the party's leadership left many without a viable alternative to the premiership of John Key. It has also been claimed that New Zealanders generally don't care about so-called 'beltway' issues, yet in opposition National ran successful campaigns regarding the finer details of electoral finance law and the legality of donations to New Zealand First. While many people didn't fully comprehend the specifics of those issues, the public gained a general impression that something untoward was occurring under the Clark government and they didn't like it.

It is possible that the political consequences of the allegations raised in *Dirty Politics* are yet to be fully realised. The Watergate scandal was just beginning to be uncovered in the months prior to Richard Nixon's landslide 1972 US presidential victory, yet within two years he had resigned in disgrace. Although the *Dirty Politics* scandal is unlikely to have such extreme consequences, it is possible it will have a corrosive effect on the political fortunes of John Key in his third term as prime minister. By the time of the 2017 election, future electoral success and the historical legacy of John Key may well be determined by which image has greater prominence in the minds of the voting public.

16

#PEAKCRAY: MAKING CURRENT AFFAIRS TELEVISION DURING THE STRANGEST ELECTION IN NEW ZEALAND'S HISTORY

Nicola Kean

On 19 September 2014, the day before the election, Labour leader David Cunliffe made a last-ditch appearance on TV3's late night *Paul Henry Show*. Apparently overtired and on a campaign high, he gave what Henry called, to his face, a 'bizarre' performance. He encouraged viewers to party vote Labour in a pirate voice.[1] When Henry asked him if bad weather meant Labour voters would sit by the fire instead of casting their ballots, he shouted that his supporters couldn't afford fires. He mocked the Conservative Party leader Colin Craig. 'Cunliffe. Paul Henry. Wow,' tweeted *3News* press gallery reporter Brook Sabin. 'We've finally reached #peakcray,' his colleague Tova O'Brien replied.

The #peakcray hashtag, a reference to the colloquial term for crazy, developed on Twitter as the campaign took one weird turn after another. After all, the election year began with the then ACT Party leader Jamie Whyte saying that he had no issues with consensual incest and ended with a world-famous rapper suing the National Party over a campaign ad that used music suspiciously similar to his. In between there was *Dirty Politics*, a ministerial resignation, a spying scandal, and the ill-fated marriage between the Mana Party and a party founded by a German millionaire facing deportation on copyright charges.

And it wasn't just Twitter users who thought the 2014 election had reached new levels of crazy. During the interview with Cunliffe, Henry presented a graphic of the more bizarre episodes of the campaign and asked for his thoughts. 'I think it will go down in history as the craziest, and in some ways the most unfortunate, campaign in recorded memory,' he replied (Henry 2014). It certainly wasn't unfortunate for the National Party, which initially gained an unprecedented parliamentary majority but subsequently found itself reliant on a support partner after the special votes came in.

For Labour it was a different matter: the party gained its lowest vote in decades and the result triggered a leadership contest. In the post-defeat positioning that began with his comments on election night, Cunliffe blamed Labour's inability to break through to voters partially on 'forces outside mainstream politics' sucking oxygen out of the debate between the two large parties (Owen 2014a). While Labour's problems went well beyond not being able to get a word in during the *Dirty Politics* saga, did Cunliffe have a point? Did the media focus too much on the bizarre and not enough on policy? This chapter is an exploration of that question and, from the viewpoint of a producer for the weekly politics television show *The Nation*, an explanation of how decisions about coverage, topics and guests are made.

The hi-vis election

The Nation, TV3's weekend politics show, was relaunched at the beginning of 2014 with new staff and an election to cover. The long-time TVNZ reporter and former foreign correspondent Lisa Owen came on board as the presenter, with *3News* political editor Patrick Gower frequently co-hosting. Under executive producer Tim Watkin, formerly of TVNZ's *Q+A*, the Auckland-based team consisted of senior producer Catherine Walbridge, reporters Torben Akel and Lucy Warhurst, and video editor Stuart Mackay. As the Wellington producer, I work alongside the *3News* political team in the Parliamentary Press Gallery.

In such a competitive industry, the Press Gallery is oddly collegial. Political journalists from all of New Zealand's major media organisations work cheek by jowl in a small annex of the Beehive. In weeks when Parliament is sitting, the day is generally structured around opportunities to question politicians on the fly – the Prime Minister's post-Cabinet press conference, the Tuesday caucus meetings, and on the 'bridge' before Question Time, where Ministers and their media advisors run the gauntlet of the press pack on their way from the Beehive to the House.

But during the campaign period the gallery became something of a ghost town as the action moved away from Parliament and on to the campaign trail. Organisations with larger staff numbers, like Radio New Zealand and the two main print companies, assigned a reporter to a particular party or two for the length of the campaign. Other media, such as TV3, made the decision to send reporters out to party campaign events on merit. Both approaches had their advantages and disadvantages, but it also reflected the differing requirements of the organisations. The election coverage tended to be a mix between the proactive and reactive – events such as major policy announcements were covered, but having journalists follow politicians on the road provides opportunities to dig up other stories. O'Brien's exposé on the falling out between Internet Mana's Hone Harawira and Laila Harré was one example (O'Brien 2014a).

For *The Nation*, covering the election was a matter of balancing long-planned set pieces with breaking news. The process began several months out from the election, with planning sessions among the production staff and the placing of bids with the relevant ministers – what would be the most important issues of the campaign? Who would be the best people to debate them? The economy was a no-brainer. Housing was something that affects everyone, whether you're a struggling first-home buyer in Auckland, a tenant facing massive rent increases in Christchurch, or a baby boomer with all your retirement savings invested in a house. It was also, like education, an area where the two parties likely to be leading the government had vastly different policies that reflected their respective philosophies. The environment was more of a sleeper issue, but one that is intrinsic to New Zealand's future wealth and security.

The Nation is split into four segments, with advertising breaks splitting up the content. The usual format is one interview or track per segment, which results in interviews between 10 and 13 minutes long. With a panel of experts and commentators taking up most of the final segment, the campaign debates in the six weeks before the election were allocated between two and three segments — depending on what else had been in the news that week. That's a significant amount of time in television solely devoted to discussions about party policy and the contest of ideas.

But while two politicians debating policy was the aim, it didn't always go to plan. *The Nation*'s election coverage began officially in August, when the House rose, with the infamous wealth debate between the Economic Development Minister Steven Joyce and Labour spokesperson Grant Robertson. What was intended to be a debate about New Zealand's economic future quickly descended into the pair shouting over each other, largely at Joyce's instigation. Things got even more heated during the ad break, when Joyce reportedly called Robertson an 'angry little man' and Robertson responded by telling Joyce to get out of his face (Owen 2014).

Owen tried to calm the men during the break, while Watkin told them they would each have 30 seconds at the top of the next part to sum up their arguments thus far. Devised as a way for both men to shake off their frustration, get their main points off their chest, and re-engage viewers, Robertson later acknowledged it was the TV equivalent of being 'put on the naughty step'. So by the second break it had quieted down, but it was too late to stop Joyce's performance in particular becoming the 'talk of the Beehive' (Watkins 2014). Having spent several days reading economic reports and brainstorming questions, this was a disheartening result for the producers.

Most of the debates pitted National and Labour candidates against each other. The Green Party co-leader Russel Norman represented the left wing in the environment debate with the then Minister Amy Adams, as a way of recognising the Green's status as the biggest of the minor parties. The reason we gravitated towards the two larger parties wasn't because we misunderstood MMP, which was an accusation leveled at us via social media. Debates are not easy things to organise, and in order for them to be worthwhile the government has to be represented. In order for the government to be represented the minister has to agree to appear. It's a process that can sometimes take weeks or even months of delicate negotiations. We already had to contend with a government-wide rule that ministers would not debate prior to the official campaign period.[2]

But we were very conscious of the role smaller parties had to play during the campaign. During the year *The Nation* ran two debates with the leaders of the minor parliamentary parties – one about the economy, just before the Budget was released in May, and another, which took a dramatic turn, during the campaign. We also held an Epsom candidates' debate in June, and in July, before the House rose, we hosted a debate on Māori issues between Te Ururoa Flavell and Hone Harawira (their first other than on Māori Television) and another between Jamie Whyte and Colin Craig ('the fight for the right').

The Nation vs Colin Craig

The first indication that *The Nation*'s minor parties debate was not going to go smoothly came on Tuesday, 5 August, in the form of an email from the Conservative Party's press secretary Rachel MacGregor. Planning for the debate had started a few weeks previously, and we were in the process of eliciting final confirmations from the leaders, carrying out research, and brainstorming questions. In the early production meetings there was discussion about who should be invited; the consensus was the leaders of the six parliamentary parties. We had six podiums, room for six speakers plus a host, and 34 minutes of airtime. Given the polling and deal-making, all the parties included were virtually guaranteed to make it back into Parliament. And anyway, once you went outside of those parties, where did you stop? What threshold could you set that didn't rely utterly on the vagaries of polling? There had to be a line in the sand, as executive producer Watkin later wrote in his affidavit to the court:

> We felt that this criteria would be readily understandable to *The Nation*'s audience. We also considered that a line needed to be drawn at some point – to invite parties outside of Parliament would have resulted in us being required to make incredibly difficult assessments as to who ought to be included and to develop any cogent, consistent and readily understandable selection criteria (Watkin 2014a, p. 2).

Under those criteria, both the Conservative Party and the Internet Party were excluded from the debate.

Craig objected to his exclusion. He would later argue in court that the decision was arbitrary and unreasonable given that the Conservative Party polled higher, both at the previous election and in media polls, than other parties invited and that it had 'enjoyed significant media profile' in the campaign (Gilbert 2014, p. 2). Indeed, the Conservatives had enjoyed significant coverage – Craig had already been on *The Nation* four times in the lead-up to the debate, as many appearances as the Prime Minister himself. But it was the inclusion of the ACT Party and New Zealand First in the debate that Craig seemed to find problematic. His lawyers noted during the court hearing that with John Banks' resignation ACT no longer had a sitting MP:

> Mr Craig complains that there can be no proper basis for inviting the ACT Party but excluding the Conservative Party from the debate in circumstances where, he says: a) Neither ACT nor the Conservative Party has an MP in Parliament; b) The Conservative Party won more votes in the 2011 election than ACT; and c) The Conservative Party has consistently polled higher than ACT since the last election (Gilbert 2014, pp. 2–3).

Craig and MacGregor met with Watkin and TV3's Head of News, Mark Jennings, on the Wednesday. In that meeting, Craig also complained that we had not chosen to interview him about the sale of the Lochinver Station to Shanghai Pengxin (a story he had broken) the previous week, instead speaking to New Zealand First leader Winston Peters – who had a better chance of being involved in a future government – in the hope of moving the story along. When this was explained he said he could not accept his direct competitor being on the programme two weeks in a row on the issue of foreign ownership (Watkin 2014a, p. 5). The discussions continued over the next few days, with Watkin attempting to make other arrangements in a bid to avoid legal action. But on Thursday evening, just one working day before the debate was scheduled, Craig told us he'd see us in court.

On Friday afternoon Watkin and Jennings donned ties and headed down to the court. The rest of the team continued with the debate preparation. Hours passed without word. Then suddenly, before anyone from our team had a chance to call, it was all over Twitter. Auckland High Court judge Justice Gilbert had found that Craig had a case – it was arguable that the decision to exclude the Conservatives was unreasonable – and he restrained *The Nation* from holding the debate without him. He said:

> If Mr Craig is excluded from the debate, his prospects and those of his party at the forthcoming election are likely to be diminished. He is therefore likely to suffer irreparable damage which cannot be adequately met by an award of damages. The public will gain the impression that MediaWorks has determined that Mr Craig does not 'make the cut' and is not eligible to participate in the minor leaders' debate.

And:

> It seems to be the additional cost and inconvenience to MediaWorks of rescheduling the debate at another venue, if necessary, is clearly outweighed by the harm that Mr Craig is likely to suffer if the injunction is not granted (Gilbert 2014, p. 5).

Even though it was an interim injunction, the timing of the court action meant the full case would never be argued. We had no choice but to go ahead with Craig, a worrying intrusion into editorial independence.

The first reports out of court said differently, however. As the judgment was handed down, social media had exploded with rumours that the debate would be cancelled. That was never really an option – we couldn't just cancel the debate and have an hour of static or, a running joke within the production team, Lisa Owen filling in by tap dancing. Outside broadcasts ('OBs' in TV speak) require weeks of work, a venue, extra crew, various trucks carrying the necessary technology, tens of thousands of dollars to pay for it all, and production experience that our team didn't have.[3] So that option was out. Should we squeeze him in with a podium different to the others, so he stood out? We had to accept a ruling against us with good grace, and that meant somehow finding seven podiums with 24 hours' notice. This was much easier said than done, and how I found myself desperately cold calling furniture rental companies. The end result, as one viewer wrote in to my despair, was a set of podiums that looked akin to Fisher and Paykel washing machines. But, frankly, we were lucky to get those.

Dirty Politics

Late in the afternoon of 13 August 2014, what seemed like half of Wellington attempted to cram into Unity Books for the launch of investigative journalist Nicky Hager's new book. The subject was a well-kept secret and a topic of discussion among gallery journalists. The best guess was that Hager had got his hands on some of the Edward Snowden documents relating to the activities of intelligence agencies in New Zealand. The reality was more like *The Hollow Men* 2.0[4] and would propel the election campaign into a whole new level of cray.

As the clock ticked closer to the 6 pm bulletin and journalists jostled for position, Hager arrived and gave a short speech. He had obtained a series of emails and instant messages between the *Whale Oil* blogger Cameron Slater and other political figures, including the former Prime Minister's Office staffer Jason Ede, public relations consultant Carrick Graham, and former Justice Minister Judith Collins. It revealed, among other things, that Ede had accessed a supposedly secure database on the Labour Party's website; that Collins had supplied the name of a public servant whom Slater had gone on to attack on his blog; and that the Official Information Act had been misused in Slater's favour (Hager 2014).

It was a fast-moving story. The two major news channels went live from Unity Books with the basics. Further details, along with responses from various parties involved, emerged over the next few days. Hager's *Dirty Politics* was a short book, but there was a lot in it. The first step to figuring out how to cover it on a weekly show was to read it. The book had only been released in Wellington so, like many in the Press Gallery, I stayed up half the night working my way through it.

Then it was a question of who would be on the show. With breaking news of this level, the plans we had for that weekend were thrown out and we started from the beginning. We wanted to give our viewers something new and interesting about the *Dirty Politics* revelations, beyond commentators providing analysis of the political implications. But while most of the politicians mentioned in the book would front for so-called 'stand up' press conferences from the campaign trail, they would not come into the studio for an extended interview. We requested interviews with John Key, Judith Collins and Steven Joyce, who all declined to appear. Slater was travelling in Israel, but we managed to get in touch with him and he agreed to be interviewed remotely. Hager also agreed to fly to Auckland to be interviewed in the studio, along with former Labour leader Phil Goff, who was the subject of a number of the messages between Slater and others, and Green Party co-leader Metiria Turei, who had laid a number of complaints over the content of the book. Our reporter Torben Akel also summed up the main events of the week in a short taped piece, following that up with an in-depth piece on *Dirty Politics* the following week.

After the rush of the first week, we continued to cover *Dirty Politics* as more emerged from the 'Rawshark' leaks and as the initial allegations continued to develop. When Judith Collins resigned on 30 August – a Saturday afternoon, after we had broadcast the live show but before the repeat the next morning – we remade the show rather than screening an out-of-date version on Sunday.[5]

During the *Dirty Politics* coverage there was a recurring theme of feedback from some viewers: why aren't you covering the issues that really matter? And it wasn't just ordinary viewers – it was an almost constant refrain from the National side and what David Cunliffe was referencing when he made his 'forces outside of mainstream politics' comment. Victoria University political scientist Kate McMillan has completed qualitative research on the *Dirty Politics* coverage elsewhere in this volume, but at *The Nation* we made a great deal of effort to cover policy through our debates and interviews. A total of 123 minutes of the show was devoted solely to policy debate during the campaign period, with 42 minutes about *Dirty Politics*.[6] On TVNZ, *Q+A* had a similar debate format. Other current affairs shows like *Campbell Live* tackled policy. On Radio Live's evening show, Andrew Fagan and Karen Hay ran lengthy discussions with MPs. Radio New Zealand's *Nine To Noon* aired probing interviews with party leaders. Across the media, there were journalists and producers working hard to ensure New Zealanders were informed about policy when they walked into the polling booth.

Secondly, *Dirty Politics* is an issue that matters. While I don't endorse the hacking of anyone's personal information, what was revealed highlighted some ethically dubious and inappropriate behaviour by politicians and others involved in the political sphere. It was about leadership and trust, two factors voters often rank as high priorities in election campaigns. Further, it led to the resignation of a high-ranking government minister and spurred a number of investigations. One, by the Inspector-General of Intelligence and Security, found that a spy agency had released inaccurate information in an Official Information Act request that led to 'misplaced criticism' of an opposition leader (Gwyn 2014). Policy is important, but so is the way political power is wielded.

The morning after

After an exhausting campaign period, 20 September felt oddly quiet. The rules around broadcasting political content on election day meant that it was impossible for *The Nation* to stay in its usual Saturday slot. It would also have been much less interesting had we done so. Instead, we planned a one-and-a-half-hour special show beginning at 8 am the morning after.

Most of the main players had been lined up in advance, barring John Key, who had declined all interviews for that morning. Between the politicians we had two panels organised: a media panel with Radio Live host Duncan Garner and political scientist Bryce Edwards, and a pollster panel with Labour's Rob Salmond and National's David Farrar. The final shape of the rundown, however, was largely dependent on the result. If National was the most likely to be able to form a government, we wanted to speak with Steven Joyce first. If Labour looked like it could claw together a coalition, David Cunliffe was a natural top interview. Around midnight we hit the phones to confirm the final line up – or as final as it could be.

Back at the studio later that morning, getting the show to air was like a game of Tetris. Everyone was operating on little or no sleep and the order had to constantly be revised, with some politicians only available at certain times, some arriving late, and others wanting to leave. The late arrivals of New Zealand First leader Winston Peters and Internet Party leader Laila Harré required a reshuffle of the whole rundown, and changes had to be made when we decided at 1 am to add in an interview with former Labour leader David Shearer. The restrictions of the set we were using added another level of complication. The presenters, Lisa Owen and Patrick Gower, were doing interviews at opposite ends of a single studio desk, which meant we only had short windows of time to get the guests in and out, and microphones on and off. But while the adrenaline was pumping in the control room, the end product came out relatively smooth.

In the midst of this, Mana leader Hone Harawira had gone AWOL. The plan initially was for him to fly down from Te Tai Tokerau, the electorate he no longer held, late on Saturday to speak in the morning. Calls to him and his press secretary went unanswered. By the morning we received a group text message saying he would not be doing interviews. We had planned to squeeze Harawira's rival, Labour's Kelvin Davis, into the show, but now we needed him. Davis had already scheduled back-to-back interviews, including one at Māori Television, during the time slot we had open. I jumped in a cab and went to the Māori Television headquarters in Parnell, where I spoke to Davis and a very kind producer. We could do the interview while he was waiting to go on air, but the catch was that the truck that would beam the interview back to TV3 couldn't get reception outside the Māori Television studio building. We ended up having to run up the street and do the interview outside a random Parnell apartment block. Then, of course, it started to rain.

Conclusions

My own personal peak cray came on the morning of the 21st, standing in a late September sun-shower on a street in Parnell, holding an umbrella over the head of a newly elected Member of Parliament while he did a sound check for a live interview with a presenter who'd had emergency retinal surgery ten days prior and was reading the autocue one-eyed.[7] But the examples I've discussed here are just the tip of the cray iceberg. There was the 'Moment of Truth', the 'Rawshark' Twitter dumps, the resignation of Colin Craig's press secretary Rachel MacGregor two days before polling day and, not to be forgotten, the Eminem lawsuit.

Some of those things mattered more than others, but they all helped shape the course of the election. *Dirty Politics* and the 'Rawshark' revelations had the largest impact on the campaign itself, even if the scandal didn't appear to affect the final outcome. It dominated the headlines, and rightly so, given the seriousness of the book's contents. Did all the attention on the more bizarre aspects of the campaign mean the coverage of policy was neglected? For once David Cunliffe and John Key have something in common: their answer to that question is yes. Cunliffe argued that 'forces outside of mainstream politics' hamstrung the policy debate. Key's constant refrain during the *Dirty Politics* scandal was that the issue wasn't one that mattered to New Zealanders (Wong 2014a).

From my perspective the answer is no. *The Nation* ran six debates about policy from the first week we were able to get representatives of the government into a studio, plus five other debates prior to that. We continued those debates throughout the campaign, providing substantial screen time to a contest of ideas – although it didn't always work out as intended. We ran two minor party debates, one almost solely devoted to economic policy. And we weren't the only ones to do so; as pointed out above, the debate format was a popular one across a variety of media organisations. At the end of the day – to use a popular election campaign phrase – the unprecedented amount of cray undoubtedly took some media time from other issues. Nevertheless there was a generous smorgasbord of policy debate on the menu for anyone wanting to consume it.

17

BLACK OPS, GLOVE PUPPETS AND TEXTUAL RELATIONS:
THE MEDIA'S CAMPAIGN 2014

Kate McMillan

Introduction

'Chaos and Mayhem', the roguish name bloggers Cameron Slater and Cathy Odgers and public relations consultant Carrick Graham give their corporate spin doctoring activities (Slater 2014; Hager 2014, p. 89), might equally be used to describe the 2014 election campaign. With the release of Nicky Hager's book *Dirty Politics* less than six weeks before the election, the chaos and mayhem Slater and co. had covertly sought to inflict on their adversaries was suddenly thrown into the spotlight. By election day it had brought into its orbit the government, the media, and, for some, the entire political system.

Hager's book made Slater the poster boy of 'dirty politics' in New Zealand. The question that divided public opinion thereafter was who should be counted as his supporting cast. Was dirty politics a new minority sport played primarily by the pugilistic network of right-wing bloggers and lobbyists exposed in Hager's book? Or, as Hager alleged, were Prime Minister John Key, members of his Cabinet and senior National Party advisors complicit in the bloggers' dirty work, and thus themselves very grimy? What about Nicky Hager? His book was based on thousands of stolen emails and Facebook messages; did that make him equally – maybe even more – guilty of dirty politics than Slater? In fact, given their profession's demand for the scurrilous and sensational, were some or all journalists responsible for creating the conditions necessary for dirty politics to survive? Or, more broadly still, were Slater and co. simply doing on the right what bloggers, politicians and lobbyists on all sides of politics do and have always done? Was politics itself, and all those involved with it, just fundamentally filthy?

Equally divisive was the other major story of the 2014 election campaign: the claims and counter-claims arising from the Internet Mana

Party's 'Moment of Truth', at which it was alleged that New Zealanders were subject to mass surveillance, despite the Prime Minister's repeated denials. New Zealanders were asked to decide whether they believed the international triumvirate of Edward Snowden, Julian Assange and their American journalist advocate Glenn Greenwald, or the local trio of the New Zealand Prime Minister, the head of the New Zealand Government Communications Security Bureau (GCSB) and the CEO of Southern Cross Cable Network (the company in charge of the cable linking New Zealand telecommunications with the rest of the world). Evidence for both sides was inconclusive, making a fully informed decision difficult.

These were rich pickings indeed for the news media. Not only did *Dirty Politics* and the mass surveillance claims raise multiple questions about the honesty and integrity of Key's government at precisely the time it was seeking a third term in office, they also pointed to deeper, more systemic questions about the political challenges and changes wrought to New Zealand politics by digital technologies. Some of these concerned the media themselves, particularly their ability to survive the dual onslaught of commercialisation and digitisation. Who or what, if anything, now set journalists and journalism apart from public relations and 'churnalism',[1] or from partisan bloggers, tweeters and Facebook posters? Equally, many of the stories threw into focus evolving and unsettling debates about the appropriate balance between protecting private digital communications and protecting the public interest.

With the exception of the Internet Party, for whom the mass surveillance claims were centrally important, these were not issues on which the political parties themselves were campaigning. Many were frustrated that front-page coverage of the historical activities of right-wing bloggers and lobbyists was displacing coverage of their campaign launches, policies, leaders' debates, coalition deals and performance on the campaign trail (Wong 2014). Moreover, although much of the content of *Dirty Politics* had the potential to reflect badly on the National Party, intense media scrutiny of Key and his ministers at least kept the National Party in the forefront of voters' minds. In defending himself and his government against the barrage of allegations, Key was given plenty of opportunity to exercise his political skills in front of a camera. Opposition parties, on the other hand, found it even harder than usual to get into the media spotlight. Further, politicians of all stripes found themselves competing for media attention with the 'media' themselves. Journalists, bloggers, spin doctors, hackers, leakers and 'dumpers' emerged as major news makers during the campaign period.

It was also not clear how important the *Dirty Politics* and mass surveillance issues were for many voters. Public opinion polls throughout the campaign did not register major changes in support for the National government as a result of the *Dirty Politics* or 'Moment of Truth' stories, although there was a wobble midway through (Young 2014). On polling day the government was returned with a slightly increased vote and, despite predictions that the negative tone of the campaign would put people off voting, turnout was higher than at the 2011 election.

That the stories which dominated much of the campaign period neither directly concerned the parties' formal campaigns, nor appeared to greatly affect the election result, gave rise to further questions about the relationship between the media and politics in contemporary New Zealand.

This chapter examines what the election campaign told us about the state of the media in 2014 and the years leading up to it, focusing on two related issues. First, what was revealed during the campaign about the relationship between journalists, politicians and spin doctors in New Zealand politics, and how did journalists themselves respond to the suggestion that they were implicated in the 'dirty politics' Hager identified? Second, how did accusations of media bias manifest and play out during the election, and with what implications for the media's credibility? Before turning to these questions, however, the chapter outlines the most significant stories arising out of the *Dirty Politics* and 'Moment of Truth' allegations in order to set the scene for the following discussion. This is by no means a comprehensive survey of the many and often extraordinary stories that gained coverage, nor of the coverage given to campaign-related matters such as party policy, coalition deals, campaign speeches and so on.[2] Rather, the goal is to highlight the stories that had the most political and legal significance for the media.

Dirty Politics and the 'Moment of Truth'

Dirty Politics dominated media coverage for the first three weeks of the campaign. The book was based on a selection of the thousands of Facebook and email conversations between Cameron Slater and his 'political associates' provided to Hager by an individual who claimed to have hacked into Slater's personal computer. If these were indeed an accurate transcript of Slater's exchanges, they appeared to reveal the orchestrated role Slater's often controversial *Whale Oil Beef Hooked* blog played in the National

Party's core communications strategy.

Hager's argument in *Dirty Politics* was that *Whale Oil,* and National's use of it, represented a 'new kind of attack politics that was rapidly changing the political environment in New Zealand' (Hager 2014, p. 10). He saw National as operating a two-level strategy, with Key maintaining the popular, friendly, and laid-back public face of the National Party while behind the scenes a network of National Party-aligned bloggers, spin doctors, lobbyists and PR consultants operated a nasty 'covert attack machine' (Hager 2014, p. 13) working constantly to undermine the reputations of opposition candidates and policies with gossip and innuendo, transmitted through a network of right-oriented bloggers and lobbyists. The mainstream media was seen as having had an important role in this strategy by publishing and thus legitimising stories picked up from influential right-wing blogs such as *Whale Oil* and David Farrar's *Kiwiblog.*

Slater's often aggressive email and Facebook exchanges painted a picture of a group of National Party activists with a no-holds-barred approach to political strategy and a frank enthusiasm for political revenge. Hager supported his claim that this was a dirtier, nastier form of politics than that of the past with reference to the virulently aggressive tone of some of the exchanges. Hager questioned whether it was ethical, or at the very least, becoming, for senior politicians, including the Prime Minister (Hager 2014, p. 123), to be in regular contact with such people, and to leak information to them knowing that the information would be published on blogs that were not required to conform to journalistic ethics or standards.

In his narration of a selection of Slater's emails and Facebook messages Hager also raised some constitutionally significant allegations against John Key's 'office' and against National Party minister Judith Collins. The most damaging was his suggestion that prime ministerial advisor Jason Ede had primed Slater to lodge an Official Information Act (OIA) request that would reveal information embarrassing to the then Leader of the Opposition, Phil Goff. This information was contained in briefing notes from the New Zealand Security Intelligence Service (SIS), purportedly showing that Goff had received a security briefing that he subsequently denied having had. Further, Key's office was said to have then expedited the OIA request so as to allow Slater to make political mileage out of the information on his blog. The implication was that the government was improperly manipulating both SIS resources and the OIA process for partisan purposes. Hager also suggested that Ede, while paid by the taxpayer as a Ministerial Services employee in the Office of the Prime Minister, worked alongside Slater to access a Labour Party website containing the names of Labour Party donors, with a view to publishing donor details on *Whale Oil*. Ede was apparently known within the Beehive as the 'black ops' man (Hager 2014, p. 21; Garner 2014).

Other significant allegations concerned the then Minister of Police Judith Collins' seeming approval of Slater's revelation that a police source was going to leak police evidence to him about the 2007 Urewera police raids, and her provision to Slater of the name of a public servant whom Slater then identified as having leaked embarrassing information about Deputy Prime Minister Bill English's expenses to the Labour Party. Death threats against that individual appeared subsequently in the comments section of *Whale Oil*.

The book also appeared to reveal that many posts on *Whale Oil* were written and paid for by corporate lobbyists on behalf of their clients from the tobacco, alcohol and grocery industries, despite appearing under Slater's name. These included posts that explicitly attacked the credibility and reputation of health researchers.

A week after the release of *Dirty Politics*, and using the pseudonym 'Rawshark', the hacker who provided Hager with the material for his book began to release additional email conversations between Slater and others via a Twitter account called 'Whaledump'. Media companies APN, Fairfax and MediaWorks were also provided with copies of emails dating between 2009 and 2014. Among other things, the leaked emails appeared to show more conversations between Slater, Graham and Odgers about how *Whale Oil* and Odgers' blog *Cactus Kate* could be used to promote the interests of Graham's corporate clients.

Gaining the most prominence was a story concerning 2011 correspondence between the three in which they discussed strategies to discredit the Serious Fraud Office (SFO) and the Financial Markets Authority (FMA) on behalf of Graham's client Mark Hotchin. Hotchin, a former director of finance company Hanover Finance, which lost hundreds of millions of dollars of investors' money, was under investigation by both the SFO and the FMA at that time. The story escalated into a political scandal after the release of an email in which Slater implied that Collins, then Minister of Police and thus responsible for the SFO, was complicit in the smear campaign against the SFO and its then Chief Executive Adam Feeley. Slater is quoted as saying 'I spoke at length with the Minister responsible today. She is gunning for Feeley. Any information that we can provide her on his background is appreciated' (Nippert 2014c).

Collins was already under pressure from an earlier simmering controversy about her taxpayer-funded visit to the Chinese branch of a milk exporting company, Oravida, in which her husband was a director (Bennett and Young 2014). Key was said to have told her before the campaign that she was on her 'last chance' (*New Zealand Herald* 2014). Now, three weeks out from the election, the SFO claims seemed likely to take up several more days' worth of media coverage during a campaign already dominated by allegations of National's 'dirty politics'. Although Collins strongly denied Slater's claims and protested that she herself was the victim of a smear campaign, the Prime Minister accepted her resignation on 30 August. Departing, she asked the Prime Minister to establish an enquiry into the allegations so that she could clear her name.[3]

Collins' resignation was not, however, sufficient to stem the flood of *Dirty Politics* and 'Whaledump' stories. Rawshark continued to release emails, including some that backed up Hager's allegations relating to Slater's publication of blogs deriding health spokespeople on behalf of another of Graham's clients, Katherine Rich (Hager 2014, pp. 80–89). A former National MP, Rich had left politics to become CEO of the New Zealand Food and Grocery Association and was concurrently a government appointee to the Health Promotion Agency. The email correspondence appeared to show Slater publishing posts that attempted to discredit people whose public statements were seen as bad for the grocery industry, such as alcohol addiction expert Professor Doug Sellman of Otago University. In characteristically macho language Graham described these posts as 'hits' (Fisher 2014a).

Rawshark's Twitter 'dumps' of Slater's correspondence continued until 5 September, when Slater's case for an injunction to be placed on Rawshark, APN, Mediaworks and Fairfax was heard at the Auckland High Court. The judge imposed a temporary injunction on Rawshark (the 'unknown defendants'), but declined to impose a similar injunction on the media companies, deferring that decision to a fuller inquiry scheduled for the following week. Rawshark announced there would be no more 'dumps', saying, Bond-ishly, that 'By the time you read this, every device used in this operation will have been destroyed and disposed of along with all the decryption keys' (Wong 2014b). On 10 September Slater reached an agreement with the three media companies that they would not publish any of the personal details about him or his family contained in the leaked emails in return for him dropping his case for an interim injunction against their publishing of the leaked materials.[4]

Two days later Slater was back in court, this time on the other side of an argument about stolen emails. He had been sued in 2013 for defamation by Auckland businessman Matthew Blomfield, about whom he had written a series of derogatory blog posts in 2012. The posts were based in part on extracts from emails allegedly stolen from Blomfield's computer hard drive. As part of his defamation action Blomfield had requested that Slater reveal the identity of the person who had supplied him with the emails (Fisher 2014b). Slater had declined on the grounds that he was a journalist and was therefore protected by the Evidence Act 2006, section 68 of which allows journalists to protect their sources. In late 2013 a District Court judge had rejected this defence, ruling that the relevant sections of the Evidence Act did not apply to blogs. Slater appealed this decision to the High Court. On 12 September 2014, High Court judge Justice Asher reversed the earlier decision, arguing that a blogger could, indeed, be a journalist and could, therefore, invoke the protections of the Evidence Act (Fletcher 2014). In this case, however, Judge Asher also ruled that Slater's blogs did not meet the second requirement of the Evidence Act for those wishing to protect their sources: namely, that as Price (2013) put it, the 'public interest in disclosure outweigh the negative impact on the source and the general impact on the flow of information to journalists'. Slater was thus winner and loser; he had been recognised as a journalist but had nonetheless been ordered to comply with the disclosure requests.

Meanwhile, the second major political storm of the election was about to break – one that was to dominate news coverage for the final four days of the campaign. Organised by the Internet Mana Party, the 'Moment of Truth' was scheduled for 15 September, five days before the election. It promised revelations about New Zealand's participation in the 'Five Eyes' Alliance, and evidence that the Prime Minister had been lying about the extent to which New Zealanders were subject to mass surveillance (Kilgallon 2014a). American investigative journalist Glenn Greenwald, who had published extensive reports based on leaked classified US government documents, flew in to New Zealand ahead of the event, while the source of those documents, fugitive security analyst Edward Snowden, would be beamed in by satellite. Further, Internet Party founder Kim Dotcom was reportedly poised to present 'incontrovertible documentary evidence Prime Minister

John Key lied about his knowledge of Dotcom before the infamous FBI-inspired raids on Dotcom's Coatesville mansion – something Key has consistently denied' (Kilgallon 2014a). In the days leading up to the event, Greenwald was interviewed at length on TV3's *The Nation* (*3News* 2014b) and TV One's *Q+A* (TVNZ 2014), stimulating much media speculation about what was about to be revealed and reviving the story of how the Government Communications Security Bureau (GCSB) had been found to have illegally intercepted Kim Dotcom's digital communications in 2012 (*3News* 2012, Kitteridge 2013, Vance 2013).

The 'Moment of Truth' took place in a packed Auckland Town Hall, with a live stream going out to an international online audience (Brown 2014), and live-blogged by *The Guardian* (Manhire 2014). Kim Dotcom was joined on stage by Internet Party Leader Laila Harré, Glenn Greenwald, and Greenwald's lawyer Robert Armstrong. Beamed in by video link was not only the fugitive leaker of US security communications, Edward Snowden, but also Julian Assange, founder of Wikileaks, who was holed up in the Ecuadorian Embassy in London to avoid extradition to Sweden on sexual assault charges.

Much like those in *Dirty Politics,* the allegations raised by Asssange, Snowden and Greenwald were both sensational and bewilderingly complicated. Snowden's central claim, however, was not difficult to understand: New Zealanders were subject to mass surveillance and the Prime Minister was lying when he said they were not (Vance 2014). Further, he claimed, there were two National Security Agency (NSA) spying bases in New Zealand, which the Prime Minister knew about. The evidence on which these claims were based came from his experiences working as an NSA infrastructure analyst in Hawaii, where he said he was routinely able to access the private communications and metadata of New Zealanders via a programme known as 'X-Keyscore' (Vance 2014a). These communications included New Zealanders' email correspondence, text messages, internet searches, and Facebook postings and friends. The data was obtained, he claimed, using 'taps' on the Southern Cross Cable, along which New Zealand's internet traffic flows.

In response to Snowden and Greenwald's allegations about mass surveillance John Key released several declassified documents detailing two other surveillance programmes: Operation Speargun and Project Cortex. The former, he said, was never developed even as as far as a 'business case' because it was seen as being too intrusive. Instead, the government adopted Project Cortex, designed, Key argued, primarily to defend New Zealand government agencies, businesses and significant infrastructure providers against cyberattack (Pullar-Strecker 2014). This seemed to contradict PowerPoint slides presented by Greenwald which quoted leaked security intelligence communications: 'GCSB's cable access programme SPEARGUN phase 1; awaiting new GCSB Act expected July 2013; first metadata probe mid-2013' (Pullar-Strecker 2014). Greenwald's inference from this was that the GCSB Act 2013 was passed in order to legalise the mass collection of metadata via Operation Speargun (Greenwald and Gallagher 2014; Keall 2014).

The GSCB rejected this understanding, claiming that the 'metadata probe' referred to in Greenwald's slides referred to cyber-protection rather than collection of personal data. Key refused to discuss whether or not New Zealand employed the X-Keyscore programme Snowden was referring to, citing national security, but both he and the chief executive of the Southern Cross Cable Network, Anthony Briscoe, denied there was any capacity for 'tapping' into the Southern Cross Cable (Southern Cross Cable Network 2014). Snowden's response to Briscoe's statement was, apparently, to laugh, saying, 'I would have to ask that gentleman what makes your company unique, out of every telecommunications provider in the world, that you would know when the GCSB, when the NSA are tapping your lines when no one else can?' (Vance 2014). Neither side of the argument seemed to be able to provide conclusive evidence that their version of events was the correct one, although Key did later suggest that X-Keyscore might be able provide information to the GCSB, but only when they had approved the appropriate legal permission to access such information (Vance 2014c).

Equally unforthcoming was conclusive evidence that John Key was lying when he said that he had not known of Dotcom's presence in the country until the day before the police raid on Dotcom's house in 2012 (TVNZ 2014a). Prior to the town hall meeting, an email purportedly from Warner Brothers chairman and chief executive Kevin Tsujihara to the Motion Picture Association of America (MPAA) was released to the media. The email had Tsujihara telling his MPAA associate 'John Key told me in private that they are granting Dotcom residency despite push back from officials about his criminal past. His AG will do everything in his power to assist us with our case. VIP treatment and then a one-way ticket to Virginia' (Trevett and Fisher 2014).

If genuine, the email would confirm Dotcom's theory that Key had not only heard of Dotcom prior to the raid in 2012, but that he had been actively working with the Americans to get Kim Dotcom deported to America to face copyright charges. Key denied any memory of such an agreement taking place with Tsujihara, and Tsujihara dismissed the email as a fake. The email was not, however, discussed at the 'Moment of Truth' because by then it had been referred by Mana MP Hone Harawira to Parliament's Privileges Committee, and Dotcom said he was not, therefore, free to talk about it. The Privileges Committee, moreover, said it was unable to consider the matter before the election, postponing any definitive answers about the email's veracity until after the election.

The 'Moment of Truth' spying allegations and email claims consumed considerable media attention in the last three days of the campaign. On the Tuesday before the election, data analytics firm Qrious reported that the 'Moment of Truth' had taken over from *Dirty Politics* as the most tweeted about subject under the hashtag #NZpol (Election Data Consortium 2014).

Collectively, the *Dirty Politics*, 'Whaledump' and 'Moment of Truth' stories formed the context in which the rest of the campaign played out. Extraordinary in terms of their potential political significance and shock value, and their complexity, the sheer number and variety of stories raised by the Slater files was a challenge for journalists. Hager's allegations led to the establishment of two government inquiries,[5] the results of which were not going to be known until after the election. Moreover, many of the stories concerned the journalistic profession itself. Journalists were required to report therefore not only on parties and candidates, policies and politics, but also to reflect on their own profession's role in New Zealand politics. The next section turns to these reports and reflections.

Dirty Journalism? The relationship between journalism, public relations and politicians

A central contention of Hager's book was that 'news organisations, in exchange for easy stories, co-operate in a government's PR plans' (Hager 2014, p. 135). The problem as he saw it was not partisan or even lazy newsrooms and journalists, but under-resourced ones: pressured to break stories in a highly competitive media market, and often required to produce stories in multiple formats in downsized newsrooms, journalists had been too easily tempted to take the pre-packaged stories provided by government or corporate spin doctors. Many spin doctors, moreover, were themselves former journalists, well experienced in newsroom practices and able to craft stories that neatly fitted what they knew to be the needs and news values of media organisations. An understaffed media was crucial to the success of National's PR strategy, which worked only because of the amplification and legitimacy that 'tips' fed out from Ede or Collins, via Slater or Farrar, subsequently acquired through publication or broadcast in the mainstream media. Hager identified two factors as further facilitating this strategy: the frequent use of partisan commentators by mainstream media organisations, and a weakening of some journalists' and editors' resolve to speak truth to power, due to fear of the kind of retribution Slater meted out. The result, according to the blog *The Political Scientist*, was a 'thoroughly embedded network that threads like a mat of convolvulus rhizomes through the body politic, the media and parts of the corporate world' (*The Political Scientist* 2014).

Correspondence included in Hager's book afforded the public a behind-the-scenes glimpse into Slater's corporate and political campaign strategies, including the relationships he and his colleagues cultivated with journalists. *New Zealand Herald* reporters David Fisher and Jonathan Marshall, and gossip columnist Rachel Glucina, were all mentioned as beneficiaries of his 'tipline' (Hager 2014, pp. 53, 69, 75, 77, 114, 117, 124). In correspondence with Graham and Odgers, seemingly about the campaign to discredit SFO boss Adam Feeley on behalf of Mark Hotchin, Slater says, 'Agree. Let's go to war on FMA. Hotchin keeps quiet. We do the hitting. We now own herald and nbr so best we keep them cool with that' (Nippert 2014a). Later, he wrote to them again about progress with the campaign:

> Today is the 4th day straight of stories of headlines and additional revelations about Feeley. I am maintaining daily communications with Jared Savage at the Herald and he is passing information directly to me that the Herald can't run and so are feeding me to run on the blog. I also have additional information flowing in via my tipline. The information will be drip fed into the media or via my blog. (Savage 2014)

Slater lists four *New Zealand Herald* articles critical of Feeley, then goes on to say:

> Cathy [Odgers] can outline her contact with O'Sullivan separately. Basically though the media are now picking up our lines . . . So far the Herald has been running this . . . [line], expect the NBR to

publish on Friday. Cathy will be chatting with Jock Anderson and I will cover [then *National Business Review* journalist] Matt Nippert. (Savage 2014)

Slater's perception that journalists were obediently adopting the framing and terminology he and Odgers suggested to them invoked a variety of responses from journalists. These ranged from outraged denial to rueful reflectiveness, with some cynical 'tell us something we don't know' in between.

Among those who dismissed the claims as nonsense were two of the *New Zealand Herald* journalists discussed in the Hotchin strategy email. Savage, O'Sullivan and their *New Zealand Herald* editors denied Slater's inference that in publishing stories containing criticism of Feeley they had been either willing or unwitting accomplices to Slater's PR strategy. Savage acknowledged that he had been naïve not to realise that information he provided to Slater might have been forwarded to others, but denied that Slater had been the source for any of the six stories he had written about Feeley, and stated that although he kept in touch with Slater he always did so with an awareness that Slater had a right-wing agenda and that it was his job as a journalist to 'sort the wheat from the chaff and only publish what was accurate, fair and true' (Savage 2014). O'Sullivan simply dismissed as 'risible' the inference that Odgers had any influence over her columns. *New Zealand Herald* editor-in-chief Tim Murphy and editor Shayne Currie defended their journalists' Feeley stories as 'independent of *Whale Oil*', 'good journalism', and 'in the public interest' (Savage 2014). From their perspective, Slater was wildly overestimating his own influence, mistaking or misrepresenting the 'horsetrading' (Savage 2014) common between journalists and their sources as real influence over them, perhaps for the benefit of their client Hotchin.

Another journalist named in that email, Matt Nippert, however, admitted that he had used the lines developed by Slater and co. in his reporting of the Feeley story and subsequently apologised to Feeley for doing so (Māori Television 2014a). He agreed with Hager's view that, on occasions, pushed-for-time journalists could be tempted to take a story that was 'handed to them on a plate' by a source (Māori Television 2014b).

Then there were the 'it's not pretty, but it's not new, and everyone is doing it'-type responses. Long-time Press Gallery journalist and *Listener* columnist Jane Clifton did not dismiss the possibility that journalists were unwittingly acting as megaphones for National Party PR, but in her view what Hager had done in receiving, selecting, narrating and publishing Slater's hacked correspondence, without giving Slater a right of reply, was on a 'continuum' with what he accused Slater of doing: spinning and framing illicitly obtained materials to 'fit [his] desired world view' and 'advance a political cause' (Clifton 2014). While this did not make grubby politics OK, she argued, it was nonetheless true that the left and right sides of politics were as bad as each other.

Stuff's political editor Tracy Watkins thought it unlikely that many journalists would be surprised by Hager's outing of Ede as the source of many of Slater's tips, given how regularly inside government information made its way into his blog. She did, however, question John Key's dismissal of this practice as just 'the modern world', writing, 'Hager's book raises legitimate questions about whether people like Ede and Slater are a response to the modern world, or a tool to reshape the modern world to better suit a government's political ends' (Watkins 2014a). According to Watkins, no Fairfax journalist had received a call from Ede in years, despite Key describing 'briefing journalists' as Ede's main job. Ede preferred to feed information to partisan blogs, in her view, because it assured him anonymity, and because there were 'much better odds of it reflecting the spin that has been put on it'. This desire to duck media scrutiny was also evident, she argued, in Key's strategy of 'avoiding at all costs' a situation where he might be 'blindsided' by journalists' questioning. However, like Clifton, she saw no reason to believe that such tactics, whether illegal or just a bit underhand, were confined to the right side of politics.

Others, like *New Zealand Herald* journalist David Fisher, gave more credence to the view that Slater wielded a new and unholy influence over journalists, through both fear and favour. Like Savage, Fisher acknowledged Slater had been a contact, but admitted to becoming less confident over time of his own ability to extract the non-partisan, factual 'wheat' from the PR 'chaff' Slater fed him. He said he had come to wonder 'who was manipulating Slater and whether I, in turn, was being made to do another's bidding'. Uneasy, he 'stepped back' from the relationship and found himself 'outside the tent' (Fisher 2014). His description of his subsequent experiences with Slater undermined his fellow *Herald* writers' and editors' more benign view of Slater's influence: 'If you're in Slater's tent,' he said,

> it's warm and cosy. There is information which only those well connected would know. Almost exclusively, the tips are for stories [that] are good for National and bad for anyone in its way. If you're

outside the tent, which is where I fetched up, it is cold and hard. This is what journalism should be. You should work for your readers, and work hard. But when I started writing stories on issues which went against Slater's interests, I became someone he wanted to 'smash'. At that point, I was away from the tent and out in the wilderness. He launched a personal assault with what I believed were threats of violence and created an atmosphere in which I was personally and professionally denigrated. Those who post comments on his website made awful slurs. It is as horrible an online environment as you will find anywhere. (Fisher 2014)

Fisher's experience was echoed by *New Zealand Herald* columnist Wendyl Nissen, who described how her weekly columns on health issues had been the subject of several complaints from Food and Grocery Council CEO Katherine Rich to both the Press Council and her editors at the *Herald*. Contemporaneously, she had become the target of what she described as a smear campaign by Slater and Odgers. She wrote that 'the regularity of the posts against me made me think that someone was paying for them' (Nissen 2014).

Radio Live host and former TV3 political editor Duncan Garner, and *Metro* editor Simon Wilson, similarly highlighted the new danger to journalism presented by the 'stick' aspect of Slater's tactics, although they downplayed the 'carrot' side. Garner said he had been fed stories directly by Ede; indeed, he said, 'black ops' Ede was well known around Parliament as the source of many leaks. This was par for the course – politics was a dirty, grubby business, and leaks were simply a routine and integral part of that business. In Slater's 'blackmailing and stand-over tactics', however, Garner saw a 'mafioso' quality that was a 'new and horrible development' (Garner 2014). This followed revelations in *Dirty Politics* that Slater had requested a prostitute friend dig for sexual dirt on Garner after he had done a negative story on Slater; as Slater's email is quoted as saying, 'It is never wise to piss off the whale' (Peacock 2014). Wilson interpreted as insidious and threatening Slater's blog post about having correspondence with journalists from other media companies that he was willing to leak to prove that he was more than just a minor cog in the media landscape (Simon Wilson 2014).

Radio Live host Sean Plunket saw things differently. For him, 'dirty politics' was evident in Kim Dotcom's role in establishing and funding the Internet Mana Party. By his reading, the extensive media coverage of the 'Moment of Truth' showed the New Zealand news media to be weak and easily manipulated. They had been, he said, 'conned and seduced by the glitz and the headlines, and the money and the intrigue that Kim Dotcom has created ... and they have lapped up his putrid offerings with remarkable keenness' (Radio New Zealand 2014).

Slater himself both accepted and rejected Hager's claims. On the one hand, he agreed with Hager that overworked or, in his view, lazy journalists were easy targets for spin doctors; indeed, he had long referred to journalists on his blog as 'idiot repeaters' and 'churnalists' (Slater 2010). On the other, he contested Hager's claim that Slater was exploiting that vulnerability in order to practise dirty politics. Instead, he argued, given that Hager's book was based on a selection of illegally obtained materials, it was Hager who was the real purveyor of dirty politics. Further, rather than the media being complicit in a giant right-wing conspiracy, their excessive focus on *Dirty Politics* during the campaign illustrated the influence of a conspiracy led by Hager, a left-wing journalist – one set on destroying Key's National government. This argument chimed with the Prime Minister's own dismissal of Hager as a 'screaming left-wing conspiracy theorist' (Armstrong 2014). In words that could have been written by Hager, Slater bemoaned that 'Our democracy and our elections are being hijacked by a criminal political conspiracy and the guardians of that democracy (the media) are part of it, enabling instead of holding to account' (Slater 2014a).

Further analyses of the mainstream media's reaction to Hager's allegations were to be found on Māori TV's *Media Take* and Radio New Zealand's *Mediawatch*. A number of high profile New Zealand journalists also blogged about the media's role in political communications, with sustained criticism of the media coming primarily from left-leaning blogs (*3News* 2014a, Bracewell-Worrall 2014, Geddis 2014, McCulloch 2015, *The Political Scientist* 2014, Thompson 2015, Tiso 2014 and 2014a, Watkin 2014). However, Tim Watkin (executive producer of TV3's *The Nation*) remained optimistic about journalism's effects during the campaign, praising the media for having pursued the Collins story to the point that Cathy Odgers, thinking the *New Zealand Herald*'s Nippert already had it (he didn't), pre-emptively released the incriminating email that led to Collins' resignation (Māori Television 2014b). Moreover, in the heat of a campaign in which accusations of media bias, failure and manipulation were being hurled from every side, many journalists had continued pursuing the stories that were important, and 'at the core of the business is that determination to check and ask and check again. And that's why ... journalism is different from most blogging and something to be appreciated'(Watkin 2014).

Much less optimistic was Keith Ng's *Public Address* post 'Sunlight Resistance' (Ng 2014), in which he diagnosed the New Zealand news media as impotent in the face of National's PR strategy. Despite being neither lazy nor biased in their pursuit of the *Dirty Politics* stories, he said, the media had nonetheless failed to 'disinfect' politics by exposing wrongdoing to the 'sunlight' of journalistic scrutiny. 'What happens,' he asked, 'when you crank up the sunlight, and the brightly-lit a**holes just stand there staring back at you, giving you the fingers?' In his view, the Parliamentary Press Gallery's typically strategic framing of politics was partly to blame, as it 'contributed to a culture where "political engagement" means to cynically understand "the game"'. 'Can we be surprised then,' he asked, 'that this has finally permeated into public consciousness, and anything and everything is all just part of the game?' Like Tracy Watkins, Ng perceived National to be operating a deliberate strategy of trying to sideline the media altogether:

> The scariest possibility is that National have finally achieved full-spectrum dominance over the media. That the combination of sophisticated polling and focus-grouping . . . Key's personal brand, and media management system (including the use of back channels like Slater and . . . others) now allows them to subvert the media's every move. They know that the cost of completely ignoring your questions is negligible. They know that they can negate a bookful of allegations just by calling Hager partisan. They know you'll give up on Ede if they just hide him for long enough. They know they can throw a bunch of CORTEX-CYBERHACKING-ANTIVIRUS-BUTTS-MALWARE-METADATA obfuscations into the air, and simply choke a story with irrelevant facts (Ng 2014).

Lastly, there were those, such as journalist Alison McCulloch, blogger Martyn Bradbury, and Hager's sister, author Mandy Hager, who saw the media as not only under-resourced but also biased: in McCulloch's case, in favour of their corporate owners, and in Bradbury and Mandy Hager's case, also towards the right side of politics (McCulloch 2015, Bradbury 2014, Mandy Hager 2014).

How edifying was all this? Did we learn enough during the campaign to establish whether the media were a part of the problem or part of the solution to 'dirty politics'?

Among the allegations, denials, mea culpas and 'so whats', light was shone on several aspects of the media's performance that had previously been more obscure. First, clearly Slater was an active source of leaks to several prominent journalists, using information sourced from the Beehive, despite the highly aggressive and sometimes vitriolic nature of his blog. Further, as Nippert's admission testifies, Slater could claim at least some success in getting journalists to run with the PR line developed on behalf of his corporate and political clients. This was, at best, embarrassing to the journalists concerned who, as many pointed out in their analysis, needed to be able to tell when they were being 'played' by their sources. At worst, it left them open to allegations of partisan bias. Most significant in this respect was the revelation that the *New Zealand Herald*'s Jared Savage was providing tips to Slater as well as receiving them. Presumably, these were for stories that did not pass the *Herald*'s journalistic standards.

Second, many agreed that a combination of underfunded newsrooms and sophisticated media strategies on the part of politicians and corporates was making it increasingly difficult for journalists to hold politicians and other powerful interests to account.

Third, although a number of Press Gallery and other 'beltway' analysts professed to finding little that was surprising in Hager's book, for others less inured to Wellington politics, the PR anatomy lesson of Slater's correspondence provided more information than had hitherto been publicly available about how informational power was traded between the mainstream media, bloggers, politicians and the corporate world. The consequences of this greater awareness will play out in New Zealand's politics in the years to come. It seems highly probable that it will affect levels of trust in both the media and politicians, levels of partisanship, and political participation.

Fourth, even accepting the commonly held view that leaking is a commonplace activity within Parliament, and that leaking to partisan bloggers is merely a new manifestation of an age-old practice, questions remained about the probity of a government communications strategy that relied in part on a blogger who attracted such controversy, whose site appeared to offer comment for cash as well as hosting vitriolic and sometimes violent commentary, and who was seen by many journalists as attempting to silence public debate through bullying and intimidation (Nippert 2014b). The Prime Minister was questioned repeatedly about the extent of his communications with Slater, and about whether it was acceptable for his Justice Minister to have leaked to Slater the name of a public servant who received serious death threats as a result (Radio New Zealand 2014a). His initial denials, then concession that he had made contact with Slater in November 2014 regarding the release of the SIS report (Rutherford 2014) – spoofed by Radio Live political reporter Lloyd Burr with the line 'I did not have textual relations with that blogger' (Burr 2014) – did not lead to an explicit effort by the government to distance itself from the communication strategy identified in the book.

Fifth, *Dirty Politics* raised questions about how many of the partisan commentators upon whom the mainstream media rely for political discussions have commercial as well as partisan interests. Although Odgers, who had been scheduled to be a 2014 campaign commentator by the *New Zealand Herald*, withdrew from that role after the Hotchin/SFO scandal, many others with links to both National and Labour continued to appear as regular guests on radio and television, and as columnists for daily newspapers. Nothing has yet been done to ensure that these commentators are required to declare any other interests they may have. Moreover, the *Sunday Star Times'* decision to publish weekly columns by Judith Collins and Phil Goff after the 2014 election will have done little to ease public anxiety about the publicity opportunities afforded by the mainstream media to clearly partisan interests.

Finally – although there are many other issues that could be canvassed here – perhaps the most striking development revealed, and probably exacerbated, by the campaign was the degree to which the New Zealand news media's credibility was under threat. As illustrated above, most journalists continued to defend the concept of journalistic independence and to see as a profound threat to the profession the suggestion that they were becoming a mouthpiece for either politicians or corporate lobbyists. Yet accusations of journalistic bias within the mainstream media proliferated, and were made more difficult to refute by changing definitions of and expectations placed on journalists. A perception that the news media are seriously biased has corrosive effects on both the media and the political system, and it is to these perceptions and effects that the next section turns.

Media bias and credibility

Prior to the beginning of the campaign, the then Labour leader David Cunliffe's staff were reported to have complained about Television New Zealand's (TVNZ's) selection of *Seven Sharp* host Mike Hosking as the host for their major party leaders' debates, on the grounds that he had previously referred to Cunliffe as a 'moron' and endorsed John Key's leadership (Vance 2014b). The Prime Minister responded that TV3's choice of host for their leaders' debate, John Campbell, was biased towards the left, referencing Campbell's 2003 statement that he had voted for the Alliance. Both Hosking and the Prime Minister appeared satisfied, however, that it was possible for a journalist to leave his or her political views outside the studio (Trevett 2014a). This debate mirrored one that had taken place earlier in the year after revelations that Shane Taurima, General Manager of Māori and Pacific Programmes at TVNZ, had used TVNZ's resources to campaign for the Labour Party. National's Minister for Social Development, Paula Bennett, and National MP Tau Henare both then claimed that Taurima had been biased in his interviews with them (Vance, Kirk and Fox 2014). TVNZ undertook a review of Taurima's work to see whether his political biases had influenced the editorial content of the work he undertook, finding they had not.[6]

These stories formed the prequel to a campaign in which questions of media neutrality and credibility came to the fore (Edwards 2014). One of the more memorable moments of the campaign was Internet Mana's press secretary, former Alliance MP (1996–99) Pam Corkery, yelling at TV3 reporter Brook Sabin 'You work in news, you puffed up little sh*t!' (Fox 2014a). This scene occurred outside the party's launch, at which Kim Dotcom had boasted that he had hacked both the German credit rating system and a former German Chancellor, the latter, he said, 'because I didn't like the guy'. Television footage, however, focused on Corkery's response to journalists' questions about what Kim Dotcom had meant when he had said 'and we have all figured out by now there is another prime minister I don't like' (Fox 2014a). Corkery was reportedly frustrated at the media's focus on Dotcom rather than on the questions raised by Snowdon's revelations, and after telling the reporters repeatedly that Dotcom wasn't going to talk with them, let fly with 'When will you glove puppets of Cameron Slater just p*ss off?' (Fox 2014a). Corkery's accusation of media bias echoed similar cries from other parties and pundits, but there was no matching agreement over whose hands were manipulating these journalistic 'glove puppets'.

Anxiety about media bias is nothing new. In 1993 only a third of New Zealanders surveyed agreed that 'the New Zealand news media's coverage of politics could be characterised as "fair and unbiased"' (Roberts and Levine 1996, p. 207). Moreover, partisans frequently considered that the media favoured their opponents: National voters, for example, were more likely than Labour voters to think the media favoured Labour, while Labour voters were more likely than National voters to see the media as having a consistently pro-National bias (Roberts and Levine 1996, p. 205). Minor-party voters were even more likely than major-party voters to perceive media bias operating against the party they supported. These findings conformed to the frequently-cited 'hostile media phenomenon' (Vallone et al. 1985) in which partisans from both sides of the Arab-Israeli conflict judged the same media reports of the conflict as biased against their side.

Perceptions of bias nonetheless remain highly problematic for the news media. Journalists' power, such as it may be, lies largely in their ability to inflict reputational damage, which in turn relies on their own credibility. Any reduction in the latter affects the former. According to the traditional model of 'objective' journalism, journalistic credibility relies on journalists respecting basic professional principles such as the collection and presentation of verified facts, the clear separation of fact from opinion and advertisements, and the maintenance of independence from those they cover. According to the Pew Research Center:

> journalists in . . . [news] organizations must maintain allegiance to citizens and the larger public interest above any other if they are to provide the news without fear or favor. This commitment to citizens first is the basis of a news organization's credibility, the implied covenant that tells the audience the coverage is not slanted for friends or advertisers. (Pew Research Center, n.d.)

As the previous section illustrated, a number of New Zealand journalists and media organisations defended this model of journalism and their own adherence to it in the face of allegations of partisan or corporate media bias. But by 2014 the mainstream news media no longer had the media landscape to themselves. Instead, they found themselves reporting in an environment in which other models of journalism competed with and undermined the objective, neutral model on which they staked their credibility. The competition presented by these other models of journalism was particularly challenging during a period of reduced advertising revenues, and in the face of declining public trust in the media internationally (Dugan 2014).

One response to the growing perception that the media harbour partisan or corporate biases has been to dismiss the very possibility of 'neutral' reporting. Glenn Greenwald, discussed above, is a leading advocate of the 'subjective, activist, adversarial' (Greenslade 2013) genre of journalism, which contends journalists would have more credibility if they openly declared their biases. According to this view, practising 'advocacy journalism' would spare journalists the contortions required for them to repress their opinions and take on a false but god-like neutrality. Audiences would then be saved the trouble of trying to detect and resist hidden or suspected biases and be free to make up their own minds as to which among many partisan arguments on offer they found most convincing (Greenslade 2013, Keller 2013, Burns 2014, Miller 2014). Greenwald's prominent role in the latter part of the campaign, as a guest of the Internet Mana Party, provided this alternative model of what 'journalism' looked like in 2014, one in which journalists were not afraid to associate themselves with a political party.

Further undermining of the traditional model of 'journalism' was the enormous range of political websites operating independently of the mainstream news media's online presence. Few of these adhered to traditional journalistic principles, and most of the focus during the campaign was on those blogs, such as *Whale Oil*, that did not. Yet Slater's claim that he was a 'journalist' won support from two powerful sources in election year. In May *Whale Oil Beef Hooked* was awarded the Canon Media Best Blog Award 2014 for its work exposing Auckland Mayor Len Brown's extra-marital affair (Canon Media Awards 2014). Newspaper Publishers' Association chairman Rick Neville described the Canon Media Awards as 'New Zealand's premier journalism awards' and 'a brilliant showcase for journalism' (Canon Media Awards 2014a). This ringing endorsement from the journalistic establishment was echoed, less ringingly, by the legal establishment in September 2014, with Justice Asher's ruling in the Auckland High Court that Slater was a journalist (Field and Downes 2014).

Hager himself presented additional challenges to the mainstream news media's credibility, although he also advocated in favour of strong, independent journalism. Aside from the allegations discussed in the previous sections about journalists' vulnerability to PR messages, there was the incontrovertible fact that a journalist who operated entirely independently of the major news media organisations was able to dominate the news agenda for most of the election campaign. Moreover, although Hager was careful to dissociate himself from any political party, and his previous books had been critical of both National- and Labour-led governments (Hager 2002), there was a widespread perception that his politics fell very much to the left of centre, a perception compounded by his own and the Prime Minister's counter-positioning of him in relation to a 'right-wing' blogger, Slater.

Combined, these factors contributed to a campaign media environment profoundly undermining of the idea that journalism was characterised by dispassionate, objective presentation of verifiable facts. While an understanding of the long-term effects of these changes to journalism on levels of public trust in the New Zealand media will require local empirical research, international research suggests that the perception that media outlets are highly partisan can, among other effects, polarise political debate and increase a tendency for partisans to view as reliable only those media sources that align with their own partisan preferences (Levendusky 2014). Indeed, this latter effect forms one explanation for why the media's focus on *Dirty Politics* and the 'Moment of Truth' appeared to have so little impact on the election results. It is possible that the highly partisan flavour of the campaign contributed to a situation where *what* people believed about dirty politics and government surveillance depended on *who* they believed.

Conclusion

The 2014 election campaign told us perhaps as much about the media in New Zealand as the media told us about the campaign. The issues raised were many and complex, and pointed to the realities of a media landscape that is in a state of extreme flux. While the two inquiries established during the campaign had both reported back by the end of November 2014, questions remained about the implications of the Gwyn Inquiry's finding that the information released by the SIS to Slater about Goff was redacted in such a way as to make the information misleading (Gwyn 2014). Moreover, a great number of other questions about the media's role in New Zealand politics remained unanswered.

Foremost among these unresolved questions was: what kind of journalism will characterise the news coverage of future elections? All commercial mainstream news organisations in New Zealand are struggling to develop a model of funding that will sustain their operations, while the primary public broadcaster, Radio New Zealand, has been operating on a frozen budget for several years. Different types of funding models are likely to result in different types of journalism; it remains an open question as to whether a model can be found that will sustain a variety of high quality, comprehensive news services which retain an emphasis on public good reporting. How the funding question is resolved is also likely to have a series of complex and inter-related effects on various matters, including government transparency, levels of trust in the media and the political system, and levels of partisanship and political participation.

Also highlighted by the 2014 campaign were a range of new and difficult questions arising from the widespread use of digital information technologies. Hager defended his publication of hacked private communications on the grounds that releasing such information was in the 'public good'. The New Zealand government similarly used a 'public good' argument to defend the collection of New Zealanders' private communications for security purposes. Snowden, Assange, Greenwald and Hager are among those who have used leaked security communications to argue that state surveillance is a breach of the right to privacy, and have themselves deployed a 'public good' argument to justify their publication of classified security documents. In a variety of ways, then, the 2014 campaign underlined the political significance of an emerging debate over the balancing act between the right to privacy and the 'public good'. This is a debate that is likely to impact significantly on journalism in terms of both what kind of material journalists will be permitted to publish in the future, and the extent to which they can preserve the privacy of their own information and sources. It also has important implications for broader issues of free speech, both during and outside of election times.

Lastly, the question of which cast of players belonged on a *Dirty Politics* poster appeared unresolved at the campaign's conclusion. The re-election of John Key's government suggests that those who voted to re-elect National either did not believe Hager's allegations, did not fully understand them, considered that all parties practised dirty politics but preferred National's brand, or did not think the book and its allegations were relevant to their voting decision. Similarly, whether any of the New Zealand media, including bloggers, were practising 'dirty politics' was an issue over which there was little agreement, even among the media themselves.

Such disagreement is the stuff of politics. The outcome of efforts by those wishing to create a viable business model, or sustain sufficient public funding for the collection and dissemination of political news, will determine how such disagreements, on this and other political issues, will be reported and debated in future New Zealand elections.

THE 2014 PARLIAMENTARY ELECTIONS –
THE CAMPAIGN AND THE RESULTS

18

VOTER TARGETING: DEVELOPMENTS IN 2014

Rob Salmond

Two statisticians went hunting. Spotting a prize stag, they prepared to shoot.

BANG! The first statistician fired, missed the stag five yards to the left, startling it into a mad dash for survival over a nearby ridge.

The second statistician followed the stag's upwards gallop in her scope. CRACK! She fired, missing the stag five yards to the right.

As the stag ran safely over the ridge, both statisticians leapt up, whooping and giddy with delight.

'We got him on average!'

This chapter is about how election campaigns are changing. Parties no longer try to persuade voters on average. Instead, modern parties are returning to their pre-broadcast roots, trying to persuade voters one unique individual at a time. But the tools they use are anything but pre-broadcast.

In past election cycles, campaigns in New Zealand have focused more heavily on broadcasting a single core message to everyone. That message was usually subject to deep scrutiny before it was released, making sure it had the widest appeal across New Zealand. Once selected, it was plastered across TV advertisements, radio spots, billboards, leaflets, bumper stickers, and other bumpf. 'For a decent society' trumpeted National to all corners of New Zealand in 1990. 'Jobs, growth, health' said the Labour Party to everyone in 1993.

On the occasions where parties did engage in one-on-one communication with voters, at street corner meetings, over the phone, or through the letterbox, they often ended up talking with their strongest supporters. That was the parties' priority. Making absolutely sure that the 'red dots' in a Labour campaign, or the 'blue dots' in a National campaign, came out to vote was a top priority for activist teams. Meetings were held, reminders were sent, rides were offered.

In recent years, political parties around the world have shifted this focus substantially. Parties came to understand that cajoling their strongest supporters to the polls was probably a waste of everyone's time. A party's strongest supporters, being actually interested in politics, are overwhelmingly likely to vote under their own steam. They don't need any help.

Instead of looking for red dots and blue dots, modern parties go looking for 'purple people'. These marginal voters *might* be supporters, but need to be convinced. Parties target them in order to convince them.

Parties also started to realise that some messages with broad appeal across everyone had no deep appeal to anyone. They would persuade the population on average, but only by missing millions to the left and millions to the right.

Parties have figured out that voters are more open to being persuaded by their friends and neighbours than by a stranger in their ear. And they figured out that voters are more persuadable in person than through the TV.

None of this was rocket science; people are social creatures when they are being voters, just as they are the rest of the time.

Before, parties broadcast a single message to everyone they could find, but with some extra attention given to their best supporters. Now, parties send a series of linked but distinct messages to different segments of the community, with their extra attention saved for their most marginal supporters: i.e., those at greatest risk of failing to vote the right way if left alone.

These campaigning developments were mainly pioneered in the USA, home of billion-dollar election budgets and campaigns teeming with quantitative activists. One particular innovation, which sits above a lot of the newfangled campaigning techniques, is called 'microtargeting'. It aims to paint as rich a picture as possible about the circumstances, preferences, hopes and fears of every individual who could vote in an election. With that picture, parties can campaign more effectively than ever before.

This chapter is about microtargeting in New Zealand in 2014, with a particular focus on the Labour Party campaign. I begin by establishing what parties with functionally unlimited budgets can do with a microtargeting database overseas, and then discuss what New Zealand parties, whose budgets are anything but unlimited, have so far aimed to do as they make and deploy similar databases here.[1]

Microtargeting

Targeting has a long history in politics. Under New Zealand's old first-past-the-post electoral system, parties would target many aspects of their campaigns on the few marginal seats dotted around the country.[2] Within those marginal seats, parties would target their strongest sectors – whether those sectors were geographic suburbs or workplaces or demographic cohorts. In those sectors, parties would send in carload after carload of activists – often from out of the area – to knock on doors, wave signs at malls, and drive people to the polls.

That is 'targeting', but it is not 'microtargeting'. Targeting is venerable; microtargeting is new. The distinction between the two is that while targeting looks to identify broad *groups* of people to solicit for votes, microtargeting seeks to identify targets on the basis of their unique *individual* circumstances. It's the difference between choosing to contact 'retired women' and choosing to contact 'Clare Salmond'.

The promise in narrowing a list of targets via microtargeting lies in minimising the mistakes. If, for example, the National Party decided to contact 'retired women' they might contact Clare Salmond. But if they were making decisions one at a time about whether to contact each individual retired woman and noticed that Clare's son had worked for Labour in Parliament, they might come to a different decision. With that knowledge, National would estimate that contacting Clare is at best a probable waste of their resources, and at worst may be deepening Clare's determination to vote for their opponents.[3]

Microtargeting was born in the USA. It underwent significant development in Republican campaigns run by Karl Rove, and was later advanced further again by Howard Dean's and Barack Obama's Democratic campaigns. These are now vast and enormously sophisticated campaigning datasets.

Microtargeting datasets usually start with the electoral roll, to which political parties have access in most of the democratic world. Exactly what information the parties get varies from place to place. In the US state of Ohio, for example, parties can access the name, address, age, party registration (Democrat or Republican or neither), and voter turnout history for every person enrolled to vote in that state. In New Zealand, there is no party registration or turnout information included in the electronic files, but there is information about each person's occupation. In Australia, by contrast, the rolls provide no occupational information.

The process of developing a microtargeting database is painstaking, usually relying on multiple other datasets and a considerable quantity of statistical code. New information is added to the system one piece at a time, sometimes in the form of known facts, other times as estimates. For example:

- If a party knows a person's first and middle names, and has access to a list of typical boy names and another list of typical girl names, it can make a good guess at most people's gender.[4]
- If a party knows a person's gender and age, and has access to a separate database about the age-gender structure of mobile phone usage, the party can make a good initial guess about whether the person has a mobile phone. That may help them decide what method to use to contact the voter.
- If a party knows a voter's occupation, and also has access to census information about the qualifications typically held by people in that occupation, the party can make a good initial guess as to the person's likely educational qualifications.
- And if a party has good information about a person's age, gender, occupation, and other demographics, and has access to some polling indicating the political leanings of people based on their demography, it can build a better-than-a-pie-in-the-face estimate of each individual's most likely vote choice.

The dramatic qualifier on that final estimate, better-than-a-pie-in-the-face, is deliberate. The partisan estimates, usually built on multiple other imperfect demographic estimates, are by no means foolproof, and continue to make errors. Political parties the world over therefore have to calculate the level of errors likely to be made using a microtargeting model to select its targets, and then consider how that compares to the level of error made using its next best targeting method. If microtargeting performs better than the next-best option (which typically it does), then microtargeting is worthwhile, even if it involves making lots of mistakes.

High-water

Of course, microtargeting models are no use to a campaign on their own. They are simply a tool that campaigns use to decide which voters to get in touch with, and what to say when they make contact. Microtargeting will never be a replacement for person-to-person or party-to-person contact; its only role is to make that contact more efficient.

One good way to understand the promise of microtargeting approaches is to observe what the most high-budget, sophisticated political campaigns do with the datasets they have developed. At present, the high-water mark for campaign sophistication is, without doubt, the USA, from where the following two examples are drawn. These two accounts draw heavily on the work of the American journalist Sasha Issenberg, both in his book *The Victory Lab* (2012) and in his columns on *slate.com*.

TV

By 2012, both the Barack Obama (Democrat) and Mitt Romney (Republican) campaigns had put together new tools that aimed to better understand the TV viewing habits of their persuasion and mobilisation targets. And Obama's campaign had negotiated access to the minute-to-minute viewing habits of TV viewers, as recorded by a cable TV provider.

Obama's campaign would send the cable company two lists: one of persuadable voters, one of mobilisation targets. When the cable company found a match to their billing records, it sent Team Obama an anonymised record of the person's viewing habits. Across tens of thousands of matches, and paired with overall ratings data, the campaign was able to find the shows that most efficiently reached its target voters. This deal alone cost Obama's campaign US$350,000, but the investment was repaid in substantially more efficient TV advertising, getting Obama's messages in front of more of the right people per ad dollar spent. (Romney's operation was engaging in similar work, but without quite the sophistication of Obama.)

The most noteworthy aspect of this deal was that it combined all Obama's microtargeting intelligence, itself a complex combination of many other data sources, with an entirely new form of data: TV habits. It is this creativity of analysis – which in this case involved taking non-anonymous voter targeting records and treating them as anonymous once more in order to procure the new data – that sets the best modern campaigns apart from the rest.

Direct mail

These outside-the-box innovations were not limited to the official party or candidate campaigns. In fact, there were some innovations that appeared so toxic that the candidates themselves could not put their names to them. Doing so would have made them ineffective because it would have made the voters angry at whichever candidate had deployed them. But there were legions of third party campaigns that did not have to worry much about a backlash from angry voters. They were free to use these aggressive techniques, more or less with impunity. There is nowhere to vote against an interest group on the ballot.

One such technique is the 'vaguely threatening turnout letter'. It has been long established in psychology that humans are susceptible to peer pressure or social proof – i.e., the idea that we are more likely to do something if we're told that other people do it too (or that not doing it is 'weird'). It is also well established that people do not like to be publicly shamed for engaging in frowned-upon behaviour, such as failing to vote. Several US interest groups and academics combined these two psychological insights into new and very aggressive direct mail.

The most aggressive version of this approach, which experiments in the US suggest increased turnout by up to nine percentage points in some races, is a letter that looks like this:

> Mr Rob Salmond
> 123 Fourth Street
> Five Town
>
> Dear Rob,
>
> Your turnout records are public, and in them I have noticed that you have only voted in two of the last four elections. This is below average in your neighbourhood.
>
> Did you know that your neighbor Jo Smith has voted in all four of the most recent elections? Her husband Jim voted in three of the last four, and your other neighbour Bill Jones voted in all four as well.
>
> I plan to write to everyone in your neighbourhood after the election to give an updated report on everyone's participation in the election.
>
> Please vote on 27 September, so I can write to your neighbours with good news.
>
> Best regards,
>
> Ann Taylor
> Coalition for Voting

This letter is, of course, both highly invasive and quite threatening. That is why it works. For this reason, political parties have generally shied away from this most aggressive of approaches, because to the extent that it leads people to the polls, it also makes them very angry with the party that drove them there, often leading them to vote the other way.

Instead, political parties have been more likely to create direct mail appeals that use softer, more friendly-sounding variants on the same insight.

For example, instead of telling a person they are in the minority if they don't vote (which sounds menacing), parties will more likely use an upbeat variant such as 'More than 2 million people will vote on Saturday. Be among them.'[5] And instead of explicitly threatening to write to your neighbours to tell them whether you voted, parties will more likely just note that they may run a follow-up survey after the election. This cues the fear of being observed voting or not voting, without triggering quite the backlash of the more explicitly aggressive approach.

Microtargeting New Zealand

At first, it may seem that any New Zealand attempt to adopt these new campaigning tools is doomed to failure, because of the massive disparity in available resources. The 2012 Obama campaign spent around $985 million on his re-election (*New York Times* estimate), and won around 66 million votes. That works out to $15 per vote. In New Zealand, by contrast, a party that spent every last cent of its allowable campaign spending, including its broadcast allowance, and received one million votes (a little over 40 per cent) would be spending around $4 per vote.

So how do parties in New Zealand look to save at least 75 per cent on the American costs per vote?

First, New Zealand campaigns do not have to do a lot of the path-breaking research that lies behind the US campaigning advances. Instead, they simply have to buy the books written about those campaigns, and try to reverse engineer the techniques from there. The most influential of these has been *The Victory Lab*.

Second, there are some parts of the US enterprise that New Zealand parties simply cannot replicate. Sometimes this makes the New Zealand task more complex. For example, US parties have access to a database listing approximately 120 million people who self-identify as Democrat or Republican via their party registration; New Zealand parties do not.

At other times, however, New Zealand's microtargeting algorithms may be simpler and cheaper. For example, some of the US microtargeting is built on exabytes of consumer data, recording who subscribed to *Field and Stream* magazine or who was watching *Ice Road Truckers* on Sunday night. That kind of data is likely beyond the means of even an extremely well-funded New Zealand campaign, leading their microtargeting to be marginally less effective but substantially less expensive as well.

Labour's broad approach

In previous terms, the Labour Party had only been able to individually target people who had been personally contacted by volunteers asking for their vote preference. Most other targeting had been based around geographic areas.

For 2014, Labour overhauled its data-driven campaigning, creating room for a series of predictive models that covered everyone on the electoral roll. This allowed Labour to individually target across the entire electoral population.

Labour's approach followed the published accounts of the American microtargeting databases fairly closely, excluding those elements that were based on data that is either unavailable or prohibitively expensive in New Zealand. Starting with the electoral rolls, Labour progressively incorporated data from multiple other sources, both free and paid, including census information, previous election results, social science research findings, the party's own canvassing, some polling information, and so on.

The method Labour used for this add-on process was sometimes simply based on matching. A person's address is linked to a census meshblock, for example, and Statistics New Zealand allows anyone to freely download a meshblock-level set of demographic breakdowns. This allows Labour to have a picture of the neighbourhood characteristics for everyone in New Zealand.

At other times, Labour's procedure was based around Bayes' Rule, a widely used formula in statistics which requires a series of estimates of a particular probability of interest, based on several known characteristics of a person.

If a party, for example, wants to know the ethnicity of a person called Rob Salmond who lives in one corner of Kelburn, a Wellington suburb, then the first estimate of his ethnicity might be the known distribution of ethnicities in his census meshblock.[6] In this case, this initial estimate would produce an 85.6 per cent probability that Rob is Caucasian, armed only with the knowledge of where he lives.

But parties know more about Rob than his address. Crucially, they also know his full name, which very often provides ethnic clues (for a review of this literature see Mateos 2007). Labour developed methods that allowed it to estimate ethnicities based on names as well. In order to use Bayes' rule, these probabilities had to be written in a slightly unusual way. The formula needed to know, as it tried to update its estimate of how likely Rob Salmond was to be a Caucasian, the proportion of Caucasians in New Zealand who have the last name Salmond (~0.00476 per cent), as well as the proportion of the overall population who have the last name Salmond (~0.00419 per cent).

Armed with those three pieces of information, along with the overall proportion of the New Zealand population who are Caucasian, Labour's database could update the estimated probability that Rob is Caucasian, using Bayes' rule:

$$\Pr\left(A|B\right) = \frac{\Pr\left(A\right) * \Pr\left(B|A\right)}{\Pr\left(B\right)}$$

Using the specific example of updating the probability that Rob is a Caucasian given that his last name is Salmond, we can make Bayes' rule more specific:

$$\Pr\left(Caucasian|"Salmond"\right) = \frac{\Pr\left(Caucasian\right) * \Pr\left("Salmond"|Caucasian\right)}{\Pr\left("Salmond"\right)}$$

The Pr(Caucasian) term here represents Labour's best guess at Rob Salmond's ethnicity before learning his last name, in this case the probability he is Caucasian based on where he lives, 85.6 per cent. We can then put the numbers into the formula:

$$\Pr\left(Caucasian|"Salmond"\right) = \frac{0.856 * 0.0000476}{0.0000439}$$

$$= 0.928$$

In this case, learning Rob's last name increases the estimated probability he is Caucasian from 85.6 per cent to 92.8 per cent, which is helpful, though not overwhelmingly so. Some last names are more informative than this (for example Anderssen, Fatialofa, Xu); others are almost entirely uninformative.

Repeating this process across all major ethnicities, across a person's first and middle names as well, and across all 3.1 million people on the electoral roll, gives a set of estimates for the ethnicity of every voter in New Zealand.

There were, of course, some people this process would get wrong. Jami-Lee Ross, a National MP partly of Māori descent, has a registered residential address in a heavily Asian area $(Pr(Asian) > 0.6)$ and has the word 'Lee' in his name. Labour's database thought, incorrectly, that he was Asian. Some of those errors could be fixed via other means; others remained uncorrected.

Labour repeated variants on this Bayesian process for several other demographic characteristics, and also for their likely political, issue and voting turnout preferences.

Once this database had been created, and then updated regularly as new information came in from Labour's army of volunteer canvassers, it would be used to decide which households should receive communications from Labour. It also allowed Labour to match the content of those communications to the likely circumstances of the family receiving them. Households listing typically low-waged occupations on the electoral roll, for example, might receive information highlighting Labour's measures and policies aiming to help lower paid workers. Those who Labour felt were likely to have young children in the home, on the other hand, were given information highlighting Labour's proposed education reforms. Likely first-home buyers were given information highlighting Labour's housing package.

Other parties

National, too, spent a considerable part of the 2011–2014 election cycle developing various models to predict voter behaviour across the entire electoral roll, and to make campaigning decisions based on those predictions. As with Labour, National started with the electoral roll, looking to supplement that information with whatever else it had or could buy. National used those models to decide which neighbourhoods to contact for 'Get Out The Vote' campaigning, who to write to or call, and what to say to them.

National's 'Get Out The Vote' operation was accidentally made public via an over-excited activist tweeting a photo of a confidential slide. The slide showed National using a combination of historic polling-booth-level results and survey-powered demographic modeling of turnout to pick which census houses and meshblocks its activists should target with 'Get Out The Vote' messages.

Evidence about National's direct mail programme was easier to find – it gets delivered to letterboxes nationwide. A Labour staffer, who lives with his partner and young child, received a mailout from National that was focused on its claimed achievements in education and housing quality. A couple in the same electorate but with different demographics, by contrast, received an item promoting New Zealand's economic record under National instead. These were not accidents.

This microtargeting strategy represents a change from National's electioneering in 2011, just as it does for Labour. Campaign finance records show, for example, that in 2011 National spent around $150,000 sending the same piece of generic, unaddressed mail to all 1.6 million households in New Zealand. Other mail, this time addressed, contained only two variations (one for Ōhāriu, one for the rest of the country) across almost 280,000 households in target areas. That, in 2011, is the kind of campaigning a party undertakes when it does not have an effective microtargeting database. Now, in 2014, National does.

There were, as is usual, competitive tensions between National and Labour about whose system was more powerful or accurate. A nerdy spat broke out online between National's campaign director Steven Joyce and myself over the partisan history of the so-called 'missing million' – the almost 1,000,000 people in New Zealand who were enrolled to vote in 2011 but did not cast a ballot. Steven Joyce felt that most were latent National supporters. I disagreed. We waved sanitised pieces of data analysis at each other, sometimes via surrogates. Nobody will ever know for sure who was right.

Almost certainly there were differences in the information going into National's system, compared to Labour's. Labour received multiple reports of National cold-calling people's cell phones and greeting them by name, indicating that National had purchased a commercial list of many thousands of cell phone users. Labour, by contrast, held no information about mobile phones, and only called landlines as part of its microtargeted voter contact. There were other data advantages that likely ran in the other direction (see endnote 1).

The Greens did not engage in the same kind of electoral roll-based predictive modelling as Labour and National, preferring instead to derive their lists of potential supporters via online activity. When people interacted with the Greens' posts on websites and via social media such as Facebook, they became targets for the Greens.

This online version of microtargeting is more accurate than many electoral roll-based methods, because those people who actively engage with a party online are very likely to be at least somewhat warm towards the party. But it has dramatically lower reach than the electoral roll methods, because it relies on the voter making the initial active engagement with the party's campaign. While a party can make this connection easier for people, for example by hosting populist petitions which voters 'sign' using their email address, it is the voter, not the party, that has to take the initiative to become a microtarget.

The Greens did not, of course, rely exclusively on the web for their targeted communications. They sent customised letters, for example, to nurses, teachers and public servants. That activity, however, is targeting in the traditional group-based sense, not individual-level microtargeting.

Internet Mana also avoided roll-based microtargeting strategies and opted instead for online engagement, which is unsurprising given its roots. Internet Mana's web presence was polished, although one major and unusual piece of web technology never saw the light of day.

Internet Mana staff developed a system called Mobilise that allowed people to commit to voting on election day, without having to address which party they were intending to vote for. People who used Mobilise could also recommend it to their friends. There were even monetary incentives for signing up friends, which is where things became controversial. If person A recommended Mobilise to person B, and if person B then used the system to commit to vote, then Internet Mana would pay person A $1.00.

This, naturally, led to some concerns, both from people within Internet Mana and from the relevant authorities, that Mobilise may represent a form of 'treating' – directly buying influence over a person's vote – even though the person receiving the payment was not the person committing to vote, but rather their friend. 'Treating' is illegal in New Zealand and in most democracies. Rather than risk losing in court and enduring weeks of negative newspaper headlines about the case (regardless of the eventual result), Internet Mana decided not to deploy Mobilise.

What next?

Voter microtargeting is, in basic terms, the political application of a decades-long evolution of advertising practice, where businesses attempt to gather more and better information about their potential customers before making contact so that their pitch can be as relevant and persuasive to the individual person as possible. Businesses, advocacy groups and political parties the world over invest heavily in these techniques because they pay dividends. For political parties, this may mean more voters coming to the polls or more donations going into party bank accounts.

American developments of this kind of political marketing have been dramatic over the most recent generation, thanks to the efforts first of Karl Rove on the Republican side, and latterly Howard Dean and Barack Obama on the Democratic side. But, like rust, competitive pressure will never sleep. New Zealand parties can be expected to constantly attempt to make their microtargeting databases ever broader and more accurate.

In the 2014–17 period, New Zealand parties will likely look to their competitors as sources of competitive inspiration. Labour and National will have both seen the Greens outperform them in making meaningful online voter contact, and both can be expected to improve their offerings in this area. The Greens know that their two bigger cousins are using new microtargeting tools to find potential supporters offline, and I expect they will have their own database ready to deploy by the time of the next election campaign.

Advertising is an arms race in any competitive market, and probably even more so in politics, where the dynamics are so different from most commercial markets. Instead of having many dollars, each person has only one vote. In most markets, people can split their investment between multiple parties – that is not really possible in politics. In politics, there is no option to 'save' your vote this time and have two to spend next time. The differences are many, all of them leading to a sharper competitive environment for political parties than for business firms. Anything that increases the efficiency with which parties' efforts are translated into votes will be keenly exploited. Microtargeting is one such tool, and it is assuredly here to stay.

19

THE SEARCH FOR STABILITY

Morgan Godfery

While the rest of the country abandoned the Labour Party in 2014, Māori electorate voters returned. After securing 41 per cent of the valid votes cast, the Māori electorates became a kind of consolation prize for Labour in an otherwise disastrous election. Or at least that is how the post-election narrative goes. The truth is more complex: there could be no return to the Labour Party because there was never a departure. The difference between the Labour Party's result in the Māori electorates at the 2011 and 2014 general elections was an additional one per cent of the party vote and one extra electorate seat. Thus, rather than emerging out of a new empirical reality, the narrative emerged simply out of a stark contrast: while the Labour Party enjoyed a slight increase in its support in the Māori electorates, its national vote collapsed to a measly 25 per cent.

Former Māori Party leader Tariana Turia found the contrast 'curious' and wondered why 'Māori voters decided to place their vote with a party that would suffer its wors[t] defeat in 92 years' (Turia 2014). Commenting on the contrast, Rotorua District Councillor Merepeka Raukawa-Tait was moved to ask 'are we thick or what?' (*Marae Investigates* 2014). Yet there is nothing particularly curious or 'thick' about the result. After ten years of conflict in Māori politics, Māori voters sought the security of the status quo. In the Māori electorates the status quo is a strong Labour Party. Thus the Māori electorates delivered a conservative result within the context of a conservative election. The difference is that the conservatism of the Māori electorates manifests itself differently from conservatism in the general electorates.

The results in the Māori electorates, then, were not entirely out of step with the rest of the country. But the results in the Māori electorates do represent a dramatic departure from the more radical results of some recent MMP elections. The Māori Party, which only a decade ago seemed rich in emancipatory promise, has been reduced to one electorate (and, in 2014, a list seat). Mana, which argued that it would take emancipation from promise to reality, has no seats whatsoever. This chapter will use three electorates – Te Tai Tokerau, Te Tai Hauāuru and Waiariki – to demonstrate why conservative sentiment prevailed in the Māori electorates and how the Labour Party candidates succeeded in exploiting it.

Te Tai Tokerau

Would Kelvin Davis prove four times unlucky? The Labour Party MP ran against Mana leader Hone Harawira in the 2008 general election, the 25 June 2011 by-election and the 2011 general election. Each time Davis was defeated. In 2008 he polled almost seven thousand votes behind Harawira. Although Davis reduced that gap to a little over one thousand at the 2011 general election, few political commentators expected him to secure a win in 2014. Yet after the provisional results were delivered and an official recount was undertaken, Davis won with a 743-vote majority. What was it that made Davis fourth time lucky?

The answer is obvious, if implausible only three years earlier: Kim Dotcom. On election night the contrite Internet Party founder was moved to take 'full responsibility for this loss tonight because the brand – the brand Kim Dotcom – was poison for what we were trying to achieve' (Hutchison 2014). This was a far cry from the optimism which followed confirmation that the newly formed Internet Party would contest the election with Mana. In a low-key announcement in May 2014, both Harawira and Internet Party chief executive Vikram Kumar announced that their respective parties would contest the election as a combined entity. The memorandum of understanding between the two parties granted Mana first, third and fourth places on the combined party list while the Internet Party took second, fifth and sixth places.

The alliance seemed a strategic triumph. The combined party generated intense media coverage, public interest and political momentum, yet it is – in hindsight – better described as a short-term tactical win and a long-term strategic disaster. After the initial optimism wore away it became clear that the two parties did not have enough in common to sustain the short-term momentum their alliance had generated. September 16 may have been the first sign that this was the case. Released the day after the much publicised 'Moment of Truth', the Māori Television Reid Research poll in Te Tai Tokerau revealed a 1 per cent gap between Harawira (38 per cent) and Davis (37 per cent). Internet Mana needed Harawira to win if it was to exploit the coattail rule allowing a party with less than 5 per cent support to elect list MPs if successful in winning an electorate seat. Without that electorate seat Internet Mana had no hope of parliamentary representation.

Davis did not need that poll to know that Dotcom and the alliance with the Internet Party were Harawira's weak spots. In August, leaked emails revealed that the Davis campaign team had discussed creating a campaign website asking for donations to prevent the Internet Party from entering Parliament (O'Brien 2014). That same month, Davis took to Facebook and wrote, 'I'm just an ordinary Māori living up north trying to stop the biggest con in New Zealand's political history from being pulled against my whānau, my hapū, my iwi' (Davis 2014).

Hyperbole aside, this was not a typical political situation and Davis knew it. Thus his campaign strategy revolved around reminding the voters of the north to *vote against Dotcom*. The framing was very deliberate; the last three elections had proven that in a straight contest between Harawira and Davis the voters would opt for Harawira. Davis and his team had to shift the framing, from an election against Harawira to a moral judgement on Dotcom and Internet Mana. Thus Davis framed himself as the 'ordinary Māori' fighting to 'stop [Kim Dotcom] from buying the seat of Te Tai Tokerau with his three million dollars' (Davis 2014). Harawira was largely incidental to this framing, only relevant when being portrayed as a proxy for Dotcom.

After his election win Davis acknowledged the Internet Mana deal and Dotcom as Harawira's 'Achilles heel' (Nippert 2014) while condemning the alliance as 'all steam and no hangi' (Fox 2014). Davis was not the only politician to use the Dotcom framing in Te Tai Tokerau. For the first time, New Zealand First leader Winston Peters endorsed a candidate from another party. Peters told reporters that the MP for Te Tai Tokerau should not be 'contaminated with an arrangement by a crooked German [who has] been here for five minutes' (Cheng 2014). Peters then suggested that New Zealand First voters should support Davis. Several other MPs also reinforced Davis's framing, including the Prime Minister, who told reporters that, were he a voter in Te Tai Tokerau, he would vote for Davis. These cross-party endorsements may be unprecedented in New Zealand politics.

Almost the entire political establishment fell in behind Davis, not because he was an irresistible candidate, but because reframing the election in Te Tai Tokerau as a referendum on Dotcom worked well in the context of the general election as a whole. For example, the Prime Minister could redirect the cynicism *Dirty Politics* had released against Dotcom rather than the National Party. Davis knew he could channel this cynicism too: thus the language about 'con jobs' and Dotcom 'buying the election'. Faced with this unrelenting cynicism and conflict the choice in Te Tai Tokerau was a straightforward one – remove the apparent cause: Harawira.

Even Mana Party members and candidates were suspicious. Former Green MP Sue Bradford left Mana shortly after the Internet Party alliance was endorsed at Mana's national hui, while former Labour MP Georgina Beyer, Internet Mana's candidate in Te Tai Tonga, likened Dotcom to a puppet master and suggested Hone Harawira was sacrificing his principles for political expediency (Fallow and Fox 2014). Harawira was opposed both internally and externally, but rather than trying to shift the debate to where he is strongest – for example, child poverty – Harawira strayed off message and fought the election in Davis's territory.

Harawira started defending Dotcom and the Internet Mana alliance. That suited Davis because it was a constant reminder of the principle that he was asking Te Tai Tokerau voters to vote on: the integrity and mana of the seat. When Harawira accepted the grounds on which Davis had defined the Te Tai Tokerau election he was as good as done. Thus it was not Peters' or Key's unprecedented endorsements which secured the Te Tai Tokerau seat for Davis and the Labour Party. Instead, it was the framing and creation of a hostile political environment. In doing so Davis and the Labour Party managed to transform the Internet-Mana alliance from a short-term tactical triumph to an electorally strategic disaster.

The result in Te Tai Tokerau demonstrates the relationship between mainstream politics and Māori politics. To a certain extent the Māori electorates constitute their own separate polity with their own unique logic and character, yet what Davis revealed is the overlap between Māori politics and mainstream politics. What was happening with Dotcom – a situation that would usually be considered a mainstream issue rather than a Māori issue – became central to the result in Te Tai Tokerau, whether it was politicians from across the political spectrum intervening to add their endorsements for Davis, or Internet Party funds finding their way into Harawira's campaign budget.

And that final fact was heavily emphasised, even though it was not known at the time precisely how much Harawira had – or might not have – received. Unfortunately, issues such as education – the most important issue in Te Tai Tokerau according to the Native Affairs Reid Research

Poll (Māori Television 2014) – became secondary to questions of political relationships and political integrity. Faced with such conflict, voters sought the security of the status quo. Fairly or unfairly, Davis represented the stability that Harawira and Internet Mana did not provide. And the Labour Party – as the dominant party in the Māori electorates from the postwar era onwards – also represented a kind of political continuity that Internet Mana was unable to provide.

The result seems counterintuitive: although Davis did his best to increase and exploit the conflict he was also the primary beneficiary. Yet the preference for Davis and the Labour Party makes sense in the context of the last decade in Māori politics. From 2004 to 2014, Māori politics has been characterised by significant conflict: between Māori and the National Party under Don Brash after his antagonistic Orewa speech which condemned 'Māori privilege'; between the Labour Party and the Māori protest movement (which would later form the Māori Party) over the Foreshore and Seabed Act; and, in the last three years, between Mana and the Māori Party over the very nature and purpose of Māori politics. Davis represented a clean break from that era of conflict. He was not associated with the Labour government which passed the Foreshore and Seabed Act, nor was he associated with the internecine battles between Mana and the Māori Party.

When the result is placed in that larger context a return to the Labour Party is neither 'curious' nor 'thick'. Internet Mana had become a lightning rod for further conflict in Māori politics, the sort of conflict that sits uncomfortably in Māori society. Māori politics is currently adversarial and majoritarian, yet it traditionally operated on a consensus model (even into the 20th century). Certainly in pre-colonial and colonial times political decisions – from war to the allocation of resources – were not majoritarian decisions but rather were made on consensus. The focus was on preserving relationships, and only contesting them in tightly controlled situations, and the residue of that emphasis on relationships is preserved in places like the Māori Party constitution – such as clause 5.1, which holds that 'all decisions of the Māori Party shall be made by consensus' (Māori Party 2013).

Internet Mana, a source of conflict and adversarialism, was on the wrong end of the short-term history of Māori politics – i.e., the ten-year phase of conflict beginning with Brash's Orewa speech and the fifth Labour government's passage of the Foreshore and Seabed Act. It was also on the wrong end of the long-term history of Māori politics – i.e., the focus on consensus. Although Labour Party candidate Adrian Rurawhe relied on different political tactics in Te Tai Hauāuru, he too would benefit from that history.

Te Tai Hauāuru

Labour Party candidate Adrian Rurawhe did not have to rely on framing to win the election in Te Tai Hauāuru. Arguably the framing in Te Tai Hauāuru favoured Māori Party candidate Chris McKenzie. The incumbent, Māori Party founder and co-leader Tariana Turia, was retiring and the party was confident it could retain the seat. McKenzie, as a former advisor to Turia, was largely seen as her successor. In an election where the overarching goal was a return to stability, McKenzie could frame himself as the candidate who best represented political continuity and stability. Moreover, as a former Treaty settlement negotiator, able to speak fluently in te reo Māori and with whakapapa connections across the electorate, McKenzie seemed like the candidate out of central casting.

But it was not enough on election day. Rurawhe won the electorate with a 1,554-vote margin over McKenzie. That may seem surprising in the context of a Māori polity seeking the security of the status quo. Surely McKenzie, as the obvious successor to Turia's legacy, had the political advantage with a sort of de facto incumbency and inherited mana. However, that misreads the role that the Māori Party has played over the last decade. The Māori Party emerged in 2004 when Māori politics was at a low ebb; it then presided over a quick recovery. Yet after securing its key demands, including repealing the Foreshore and Seabed Act and replacing it with the Marine and Coastal Areas Act, the conflict in Māori politics intensified as the struggle went from an external one – the Māori political movement against the state – to an internal one, with the Māori political movement pitted against itself.

The Māori Party proved unable to manage the tension of its insider-outsider status, leading to a split and the formation of Mana. The party enjoyed insider status in the sense that it entered government in 2008; yet it remained an outsider in that its ministerial roles were held outside of Cabinet. It was also an insider in the sense that it was a parliamentary party, but an outsider for having emerged out of the Māori protest movement (specifically the 'hikoi' against the Foreshore and Seabed Act in 2004). This insider-outsider tension quickly turned to conflict. Actions such as the party's vote for the Emissions Trading Scheme started to form a creeping narrative which held that the party stood for alleged iwi elites rather than the majority of Māori (thus confirming a quasi-insider rather than outsider status).

The narrative gathered strength during the party's first term when Harawira labelled the 2010 Budget and the proposed rise in the rate of GST – which the Māori Party was obliged to vote for under its confidence and supply agreement – an 'attack on the poor' (Watkins 2010). An increasingly dissatisfied Harawira sought to exploit the Māori Party's insider-outsider status – where the party leadership were framed as insiders and Harawira the outsider – in an opinion column for the *Sunday Star Times* (Harawira 2011). The column was written before the Marine and Coastal Areas Bill – the replacement for the Foreshore and Seabed Act – had its final reading. Harawira called on the Māori Party to:

> Oppose National's Marine and Coastal Areas bill. Just because we were consulted on it doesn't mean we have to support it. The bill is National's. It does not reflect the hopes and dreams of either the Māori people or the Māori Party, and was opposed by most Māori during the select committee hearings. If we support this bill, we're effectively saying that our coalition with National is more important than our commitment to Māori – surely not?

Facing expulsion from the party for the column, Harawira went on to form Mana. However, Harawira's party was fighting for the same political ground as the Māori Party – two sides of the same movement fighting for the middle ground. The adversarial nature of the contest did not fit well within the context of Māori politics, intensifying the conflict which had begun in 2004. The Labour Party had its opening as the party not tainted by the new form the conflict had taken. Rurawhe's win in Te Tai Hauāuru occurred in this political context. Rurawhe had two other additional advantages. He was the stability candidate because he was actually the political continuity candidate, but not in the sense that McKenzie was.

It can be said that there was a return to whakapapa-based politics in 2014. Whakapapa considerations have always played a role in Māori politics. The preference for candidates with political lineage is often attributed to mere cultural preference, but there is also a more prosaic element: political continuity. The most conspicuous example is in Te Tai Tonga (formerly Southern Maori) where the first Rātana MP, Eruera Tirikatene, was succeeded by his daughter, Whetu Tirikatene-Sullivan, in 1967. After 15 years out of the hands of the Tirikatene whānau the seat returned to

Whetu's nephew and Eruera's grandson, Rino Tirikatene, who defeated the Māori Party incumbent, Rāhui Kātene, in 2011 by 1,475 votes, easily retaining the seat in 2014 with a 3,554-vote margin over the Māori Party candidate.

In 2014 there were other Labour Party winners with distinguished whakapapa. Labour's candidate for Tāmaki Makaurau, Peeni Henare, elected in 2014, is the great-grandson of Northern Maori MP Taurekareka Henare and the nephew of former National Party MP Tau Henare. The seat had been held by Māori Party founder and co-leader Pita Sharples who, like Turia, retired at the 2014 election. In Hauraki-Waikato, Labour's Nanaia Mahuta – the daughter of Sir Robert Mahuta, the lead Treaty settlement negotiator for Waikato-Tainui and brother to the late Māori Queen Te Atairangikaahu – retained her seat with an increased majority.

Rurawhe also represents this search for stability through whakapapa. He is the grandson of former Western Maori (now Te Tai Hauāuru) MPs Matiu Rātana and Iriaka Rātana as well the great-grandson of the Rātana Church founder himself, Tahupōtiki Wiremu Rātana. This is the contradiction in the Labour Party. If any party is directing a return to whakapapa-based politics rather than class politics then it is Labour, not the Māori Party. Rather than adhering to some grand cultural imperative, the return to whakapapa-based politics signals that voters in the Māori seats, in 2014, were merely looking for the stability political continuity provides.

Whakapapa and stability are not, in and of themselves, enough to always secure an election win. For instance, neither Turi Carroll (National candidate, 1949), the nephew of former deputy prime minister Sir James Carroll (in 1893 the first Māori to win a general electorate seat), nor Henare Ngata (National candidate, 1969), the son of Sir Āpirana Ngata (MP for Eastern Maori, 1905–43, for, in turn, the Liberal, United and National parties), could win back Eastern Maori from the Labour Party. James Henare (National candidate on five occasions, beginning in 1946 and ending in 1963), the son of Taurekareka Henare (MP for Northern Maori, 1914–38, first for Reform and then for the National Party), could not win back Northern Maori either. Although it is a truism that whakapapa is important in Māori electorates, it can be subordinate to party affiliation and campaign tactics.

In Te Tai Hauāuru, Rurawhe and his campaign team relied on their organisational advantage rather than political framing. This was crucial if he was to turn his political advantage – as the whakapapa candidate and the Labour Party candidate – into a reality. In an electorate bigger than Belgium, with an internet access rate similar to Serbia and a voter turnout rate consistently lower than that of the general population, a sound campaign organisation becomes essential. This is the advantage of standing for the Labour Party: candidates have access to the party's institutional knowledge, software and volunteers.

This is particularly important in an electorate where voters are scattered. Targeting voters through Labour Party software and teaming up with Labour Party volunteers in places like New Plymouth and Whanganui allowed Rurawhe to expand his reach in a way the other candidates contesting the electorate could only struggle to match. When the *Wanganui Chronicle* asked Rurawhe what was the best thing he had done in the past year, he told them that it was his team's voter canvassing programme (Wills 2014).

Taking advantage of the search for stability in the Māori electorates turned on the mundane in Te Tai Hauāuru: voter turnout. At 54 per cent, the turnout rate in Te Tai Hauāuru was the second highest in the Māori electorates, behind only Te Tai Tokerau (unsurprisingly). In a lower profile campaign like Te Tai Hauāuru, of little interest to the national media, candidates have to rely on smart allocation of scare resources, and use what is affectionately known as the 'Parekura Method' – named for long-time Labour MP Parekura Horomia – which is shorthand for a kind of ad hoc visibility in the community. Such an approach is at a disadvantage when up against a more systematic effort, however, particularly in an unfavourable political context.

Waiariki

Yet there is one politician who refused to submit to the logic of Labour Party dominance: Te Ururoa Flavell, the Māori Party's co-leader – successor to Sharples – and MP for Waiariki. Perhaps his win exposes the problems with the stability theory – and the misguided attempt at ascribing motives to voters – unless he too was, in his electorate, the stability candidate. Flavell was the overwhelming winner, endorsed with 9,726 votes. His closest rival, Labour's Rawiri Waititi, secured 5,837 votes. Internet Mana's candidate – Mana's president Annette Sykes – finished third with 5,482 votes. Flavell increased his share of the candidate vote from 43 per cent in 2011 to 45.6 per cent in 2014.

How, then, was Flavell the stability candidate? It might be argued that the search for stability involved voters making judgements based on their view of the overall competence of the candidates. Flavell is considered reliable and technocratic, 'a gentle man who cries at happy news' (Trevett 2014). Trevett named Flavell her politician of 2014 – no small achievement in an active and intense political year.

Yet Flavell made a decision more crucial than his perceived competence – or, framed another way, a decision which proves his competence – when he:

> refused to let the Māori Party be dragged into the dirty politics furore, even at the cost of invisibility during the campaign. The Māori Party got a pounding. But it was less of a pounding than Hone Harawira got for all his efforts at maximising his vote. (Trevett 2014)

Thus, although the Māori Party is associated with the last ten years' conflict in Māori politics, Flavell astutely removed himself and the party from the primary conflict of the 2014 campaign period. If there was one party of the Māori political movement which was associated with 'dirty politics' it would be Mana, not the Māori Party, and the results in Te Tai Tokerau (Harawira, defeated) and Waiariki (Flavell, re-elected) demonstrate as much.

Of course Flavell could not entirely insulate himself and his party from association with the conflicts of the previous ten years, but his opponents lacked the advantages the other successful challengers possessed. Davis had framing; Rurawhe had whakapapa and organisation; Waititi did not enjoy these advantages in the same degree. As for Sykes, while she could rely on her political experience and name recognition, the association with Dotcom and the Internet Party proved too much. Nor could Waititi and Sykes rely on intense media coverage, as Davis had in Te Tai Tokerau, further strengthening Flavell's position. As the incumbent he could rely on his existing networks across the electorate to carry his messages.

Māori politics: end of an era

Even though the Māori Party survived the election, it appears that 2014 represents the close of a distinct period in Māori politics. As noted, the decade opened with the Orewa speech and the passage of the Foreshore and Seabed Act; it closes with the National Party having abandoned the politics of Orewa and the Labour Party having earned apparent forgiveness for the Foreshore and Seabed Act. But within that ten-year period Māori politics has been characterised by remarkable (and atypical) conflict. Two new political parties emerged out of that conflict – the Māori Party and Mana – yet only one remains in Parliament, as Māori voters, in a search for stability, have largely opted for Labour.

Why would Māori voters overwhelmingly endorse a party at least partly responsible for creating the conflict? Indeed, how does the Labour Party, from the postwar era onwards, manage to repeatedly succeed in excluding and defeating independent Māori political movements? It was believed with the rise of the Māori Party, and Mana, that Māori politics would revert to its old form: iwi and hapū-led. That assumption appears to have been mistaken. Even though exceptions to Labour Party dominance have arisen in the last century – from the Young Maori Party (prominent from 1909 through to around 1930) to New Zealand First – the social forces which led to Labour Party dominance have not disappeared. As Sorrenson notes, Māori support for the Labour Party has 'since 1935 exactly paralleled the shift in their socio-economic position from a rurally based people [to] a largely urban based proletariat after the Second World War' (Sorrenson 2014, chapter 9). A largely 'urban based proletariat' remains the primary Māori occupational condition, even in the Treaty settlement era.

Thus the wider social and economic context still favours the Labour Party in the Māori electorates. However, in the past the party's success did not rely solely on notions of class. For much of the 20th century the Labour Party's support in the Māori electorates rested on its relationship with the Rātana Movement (i.e., the Rātana Church). However, by 1984, Rātana support had become 'incidental'; trade union membership was about to plummet; and while 'Labour's Māori support was based on class . . . most of its Māori representatives . . . were now from the professional middle class' (Sorrenson 2014, chapter 9). The old notions of class and religious affiliation were about to weaken and the Labour Party had to find the right response if it were to remain relevant in the Māori electorates.

Labour turned to factors usually associated with iwi and hapū-led politics, including whakapapa. The importance placed on traditional ties is reflected in the selection of candidates like Rino Tirikatene, Adrian Rurawhe, Peeni Henare and Nanaia Mahuta. This return to whakapapa-based politics reflects shifting social forces, among them a reversal of some of the effects of urbanisation (such as disconnection from iwi and hapū family ties). Māori urbanisation is no longer – and in many respects never was – a one-way process where the migrant leaves his or her cultural base and replaces it with a class base in New Zealand's cities and suburbs (Williams 2015, chapter 9).

Links with a migrant's iwi and hapū base were often kept alive and, for those who lost connection, new generations have begun to reactivate old links and reclaim their place in the iwi and hapū. The same economic forces which drove urbanisation may now be driving a kind of retribalisation, with a return to whakapapa-based politics and a search for stability in Māori politics to compensate, at least in part, for the instability in the economy. The Labour Party, far from being the natural party of Māori, has merely been the most capable party at adapting and exploiting the social forces which shape Māori politics.

Conclusion

Some might view the Māori electorates as a hotbed of left-wing radicalism, continually supporting the left-wing Labour Party. The Māori electorates are better described as left-wing in political outlook, but deeply conservative in nature and sentiment. To continually support a single party is a sign more of conservatism than radicalism. It is a conservatism, however, that, far from being 'curious' or 'thick', is perfectly explainable. In an election where Māori voters were searching for stability, a reaffirmation of bonds with the Labour Party made impeccable sense.

20

SURVEY FINDINGS AND THE 2014 ELECTION

Stephen Mills

The 2014 election

All elections are interesting but the 2014 election was more interesting than most.

Despite all the sound and fury of *Dirty Politics* and the 'Moment of Truth' there was actually very little change from the 2011 results (Table 20.1).

The largest vote movements were a 2.4 per cent drop in the Labour Party vote, a 2.1 per cent increase for New Zealand First and a 1.3 per cent increase in the Conservative vote. The next highest movement was a 0.4 per cent drop for ACT (although this did represent a loss of more than a third of its 2011 party vote).

It was still, in the end, as in 2011, a close result – between National or New Zealand First being in charge of coalition formation.

Table 20.1: The vote – 2011 vs 2014

Party	2011 Election	2014 Election	Change
National	47.3	47.0	−0.3
Labour	27.5	25.1	−2.4
Green	11.1	10.7	−0.4
New Zealand First	6.6	8.7	+2.1
Māori	1.4	1.3	−0.1
Internet Mana	1.1	1.4	+0.3
ACT	1.1	0.7	−0.4
United Future	0.6	0.2	−0.4
Conservative	2.7	4.0	+1.3

In the first two years of the 2011–14 term it had promised to be a close contest between National, with its client parties ACT and United Future, and the core centre-left parties Labour and the Greens.

As outlined in Table 20.2, in UMR Research's monthly telephone omnibus surveys throughout 2012, the Māori Party (making the assumption that it held its three electorate seats) would have held the balance of power five times; there would have been a Labour-Greens government three times; a National, ACT and United Future government three times; and New Zealand First holding the balance of power once.

Table 20.2: The balance of power, 2012–2014

Month	Year		
	2012	2013	2014
January	NZ First	Māori Party	NZ First
February	Māori Party	Right Majority	Māori Party
March	Māori Party	Left Majority	Right Majority
April	Māori Party	Left Majority	NZ First
May	Māori Party	Left Majority	Right Majority
June	Right Majority	Māori Party	Right Majority
July	Left Majority	Right Majority	Right Majority
August	Left Majority	Left Majority	Right Majority
September	Right Majority	Left Majority	Right Majority
October	Māori Party	Left Majority	Right Majority
November	Left Majority	Left Majority	
December	Right Majority	Māori Party	

Question: Under MMP you have two votes. One for the candidate in the electorate you live in, and the second for a party. Thinking about this party vote only, if the general election were held today which party would you vote for? (Based on UMR's telephone omnibus surveys[1])

Those results arguably pointed to a greater likelihood of a centre-left government. The Māori Party would for the first time have been in the position of having to choose between a National-led government and a Labour-Greens government, rather than a National-led government and being in opposition. The Māori Party leadership may have preferred

National in such circumstances but they would have been acting against the wishes of a majority of their own voters in doing so.[2]

A critical current metric in New Zealand politics is whether the combined Labour-Greens vote is greater than the vote for National. In 2013 the centre-left had a clear edge. There would have been a Labour-Greens government after seven of the twelve monthly surveys, a National-led government in two of the surveys and the Māori Party in the position to decide the outcome in the other three. There were clear breakouts for the centre-left from March to April and from August to October (Figure 20.1).

Figure 20.1: The Vote – Left vs Right, 2012–2014

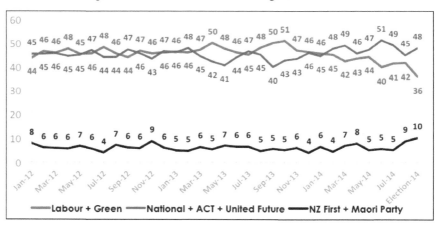

Question: Under MMP you have two votes. One for the candidate in the electorate you live in, and the second for a party. Thinking about this party vote only, if the general election were held today which party would you vote for? (UMR telephone omnibus surveys[3])

National timed its run well in 2014. New Zealand First held the balance of power in January and April and the Māori Party in February; otherwise it was all clear centre-right majorities. National had worked itself into a strong enough position leading into the election to forego the insurance option of throwing the Conservative Party an electorate seat.

National in 2014 wriggled clear of fundamental trends pointing to a possible change in government in 2014. Perceptions of whether the country is heading in the right direction or the wrong direction, averaged year-on-year from monthly UMR readings, tend to coincide with the rise and decline of New Zealand governments (Figure 20.2). That indicator slid for National in 2012 and 2013 but reversed direction in 2014. National's vote followed the same path (Figure 20.3).

Figure 20.2: The Mood – annual averages, 1991–2014

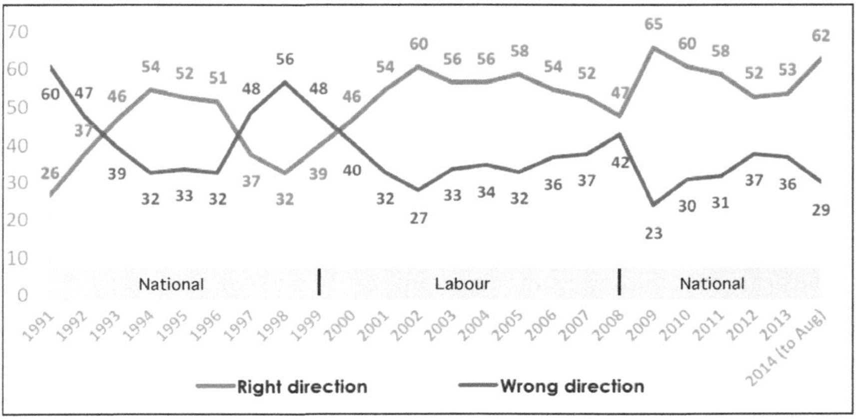

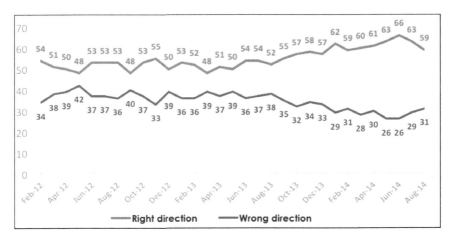

Question: Generally speaking are things in New Zealand heading in the right direction or are they off on the wrong track? (UMR telephone omnibus surveys)

Figure 20.3: The Mood – National's second term, 2012–2014

Question: Generally speaking are things in New Zealand heading in the right direction or are they off on the wrong track? (UMR telephone omnibus surveys)

The final election result was an especially disappointing one for the two centre-left parties. After being competitive through 2012 and 2013 they were not in the frame after the first quarter of 2014. Labour supporters may have been braced for a fall in the party vote in the 2011 election but certainly would not have expected a further 2 per cent drop in 2014. The final party vote was the lowest recorded by Labour in the seven MMP elections to date.

The Labour vote began to decline in UMR surveys in the last quarter of 2013 and dropped away sharply from May 2014 (Figure 20.4). The highest profile political events in that month were the Budget and the formation of the Internet Mana Party. The Budget showcased National's credibility on the economy with the forecast surplus, and provided some delivery on social policies with the extension of paid parental leave, extending free healthcare for children from 6 years up to 13 years old, and a slightly later announcement of free breakfasts to low decile schools.

Figure 20.4: The Labour vote, 2013–2014

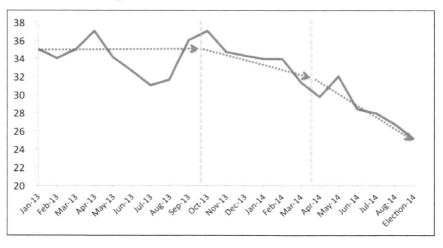

Question: Generally speaking are things in New Zealand heading in the right direction or are they off on the wrong track? (UMR telephone omnibus surveys)

The Budget was very well received, with 38 per cent of those surveyed believing overall that the Budget was good for New Zealand and only 5 per cent believing that it was bad for the country. This was the best net rating (percentage responding 'good' minus percentage responding 'bad') ever recorded in polling on this question going back to 1996 (Figure 20.5). It was also the equal-highest 'good' rating ever recorded in this series.[4]

Arguably the election was almost as bad a result for the Greens. While their vote remained stable, the combination of a struggling Labour Party and *Dirty Politics* potentially highlighted their more idealistic positioning, seeming to represent a breakthrough opportunity. The Greens often claimed that they had been the 'real opposition' to National in the previous three years. None of this paid any obvious electoral dividend.

National's success and the centre-left's failure was founded on the powerful bases of economic credibility, stability and leadership. These were the core messages from National in the 2014 campaign.

Economic confidence began rising rapidly in the last quarter of 2013 and remained strong through to the election (Figure 20.6).[5]

That rising economic confidence gave National a strong narrative. National could argue that it had seen New Zealand through very tough times while keeping it in much better shape than most other countries in the Western world, and that things were now improving. There were vulnerabilities on housing, inequality, and the squeeze of stagnant wages and rising prices, but the fundamentals of confidence in the direction of the country and of the economy were strong for National in 2014.

National, by the end of the campaign, had an overwhelming lead as the better party for economic management. The 69 per cent to 18 per cent lead enjoyed by National over Labour on the eve of the campaign was the highest ever recorded in an intermittent series of UMR polls on this question going back to 2001 (Figure 20.7). In a September post-election telephone survey, among those who declared the economy to have been the single most important election issue, 80 per cent voted National and only 9 per cent Labour.

If in any sense the election was close from around May, it was close between National and its tiny client parties and a combination of Labour, the Greens and New Zealand First, and potentially also Internet Mana, a scenario in which Winston Peters would once again have been the key player in any post-election coalition formation. This gave National the considerable advantage of being able to position itself as a stable government up against an unconvincing alternative.

Figure 20.5: Opinions of Budgets, 1996–2014 – was it good overall for the economy?

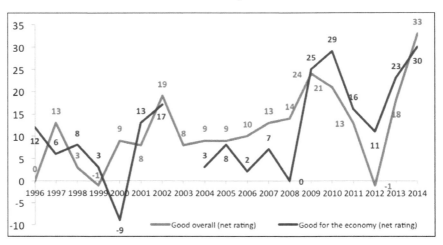

Question: As you may be aware the Government Budget was released today, Do you think the Budget will be good for New Zealand overall (the New Zealand Economy), bad for New Zealand overall (the New Zealand Economy) or not make much difference (UMR telephone omnibus surveys)

Figure 20.6: Economic Confidence – National's second term, 2012–2014

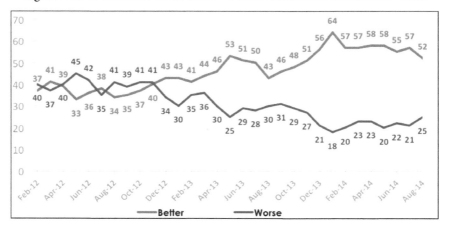

Question: Do you expect the following [the economy] to get better or worse in the year ahead (UMR telephone omnibus surveys)

Figure 20.7: Better party for economic management, 2001–2014

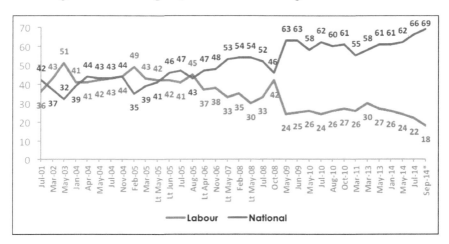

Question: Irrespective of who you are supporting, do you think a Labour-led Government or a National-led Government would be better at handling the following issues? (UMR telephone omnibus surveys, UMR online election tracker survey[6])

In UMR's September 2014 omnibus survey, 59 per cent of those surveyed thought a National-led government would be more stable, but only 25 per cent thought a Labour-led government would be more stable.

The third critical advantage for National was leadership. John Key's favourability rating wobbled a little in 2013, touching a low of 52 per cent favourable and 43 per cent unfavourable in October (Figure 20.8). His numbers throughout his second term were similar to those of Helen Clark in her third term (2005 to 2008), which did not save her from defeat.

But critically, neither David Shearer nor David Cunliffe were able to challenge the incumbent prime minister as John Key had done as opposition leader before the 2008 election. In the final media polls prior to the 2008 election Key was ahead of Helen Clark in preferred prime minister match-ups by eight points in the Fairfax Media Nielsen poll and by four points in the *One News* Colmar Brunton poll. The two leaders were even in the TV3 TNS poll and Key trailed by 0.6 per cent in the *Herald* Digipoll.

In the final public polls leading into the 2014 election John Key was ahead of David Cunliffe by 48 points (64 per cent to 16 per cent) in the *Herald* Digipoll, 32 points in the *3News* Reid Research poll (44 per cent to 12 per cent) and 31 points in the *One News* Colmar Brunton poll (43 per cent to 12 per cent).

Figure 20.8: John Key's Favourability – National's second term, 2012–2014

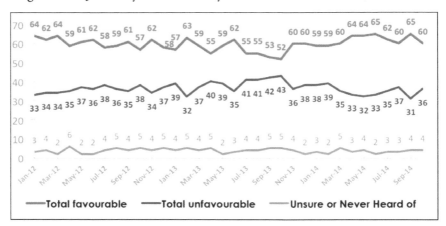

Question: Thinking about the following politicians tell me if you generally have a very favourable, somewhat favourable, somewhat unfavourable or very unfavourable opinion of them. If you do not know enough about them just say so. (UMR telephone omnibus surveys)

Among those who declared in a post-election September UMR survey that leadership had been the single most important election issue, 89 per cent voted National and 5 per cent voted for New Zealand First: only 3 per cent voted Labour.

Post-election polling confirmed these drivers of the National Party vote. In an open-ended question in a post-election September telephone survey, the main reasons given by National Party voters for their vote were the economy, stability and leadership.

In prompted testing in a UMR post-election online survey on the importance of different factors, the themes of economy, leadership and stability, as well as contrasts with the opposition parties, emerged as the main reasons for National Party votes (Figure 20.9).

There were much thinner pickings for the centre-left parties. National had established an advantage on employment and had essentially neutralised education and health: all areas where the centre-left was traditionally strong (Figure 20.10). There were still opportunities for the centre-left on inequality, child poverty, cost-of-living pressures and, to a lesser extent, housing.

Figure 20.9 Reasons for voting National (prompted), 2014 election

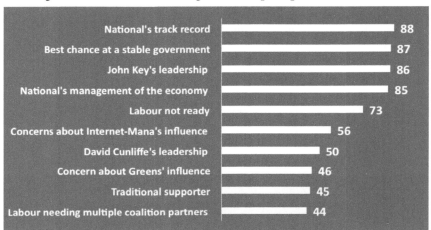

Question: For the final time, in terms of finally deciding which party you were going to vote for in the 2014 election, would you say the following factors were . . . critically important to you/ one of the main things you considered?[7] (UMR online omnibus survey[8] – September 2014, post-election)

Figure 20.10: Better party for issues, 2014 election

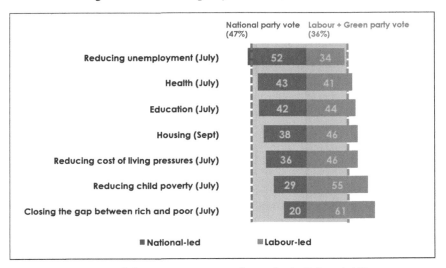

Question: Irrespective of who you are supporting, do you think a Labour-led Government or a National-led Government would be better at handling the following issues? (UMR telephone omnibus survey, 2014)

The major factors driving Labour Party votes that emerged in open-ended questioning in a post-election telephone survey included looking after people, poverty and unemployment.

In prompted testing in a UMR post-election online survey on the importance of different factors, Labour voters were most concerned about child poverty and inequality, National becoming more arrogant and not listening, the minimum wage, the Kiwi Build policy and the environment (Figure 20.11). This did not add up to anywhere near as coherent or powerful a message as the economy, stability and leadership.

Figure 20.11: Reasons for voting Labour (prompted), 2014 election

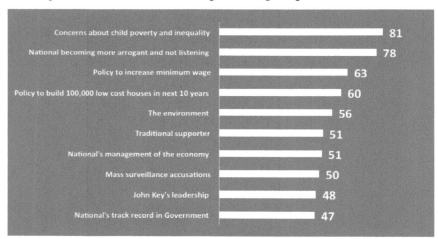

Question: For the final time, in terms of finally deciding which party you were going to vote for in the 2014 election, would you say the following factors were . . . critically important to you/one of the main things you considered (UMR online omnibus survey – September 2014, post-election)

Nicky Hager's book *Dirty Politics* smashed into the election campaign on 13 August, just over five weeks before the 20 September election. From that point it dominated the campaign. The lasting memory of the 2014 election may well be the press pack hounding John Key over the multiple charges in Hager's book and subsequent further Twitter releases of emails and Facebook messages by Hager's original source (the anonymous Rawshark).

The 'Moment of Truth' was a much hyped Internet Mana rally held at the Auckland Town Hall the Monday before voting. It featured American journalist Glenn Greenwald, with whistleblower Edward Snowden and

WikiLeaks founder Julian Assange on video feeds. It purportedly revealed evidence of New Zealand's role in mass global surveillance and challenged John Key's credibility on the issue.

A previous Hager book, *Seeds of Distrust* (2002), accusing the then Labour-led government of covering up the contamination of imported corn with genetically modified seeds, had a huge impact on the election result. In UMR's June 2002 survey prior to the July election, Labour was on 53 per cent, National 29 per cent, New Zealand First 4 per cent and United Future 0.7 per cent. The final results for these four parties were quite different: 41 per cent, 21 per cent, 11 per cent and 7 per cent (the Greens remained unchanged on 7 per cent). While these dramatic vote movements can certainly not be entirely attributed to *Seeds of Distrust*, the fallout from the book was the most important factor in changing that election result from an almost certain Labour-Greens government into a Labour/Progressive-United Future coalition.

There were more charges – arguably more serious charges than in *Seeds of Distrust* – in *Dirty Politics*, centring on a political 'dirty tricks' operation run out of the Prime Minister's Office, including the misuse of New Zealand's security services.

What is clear, however, is that neither *Dirty Politics* nor the follow-up 'Moment of Truth' persuaded even a small percentage of voters to cross the right–left political divide.

There was only a small, temporary impact on the polls. The National vote in UMR polling briefly dipped to the 45 per cent danger level, an outcome that would have made dealing with Winston Peters necessary for a government to be formed (Figure 20.12).

Dirty Politics did create some disquiet about John Key. In the immediate aftermath of the book's release, 29 per cent of those who had shown at least a little interest in the story thought Key was handling the issue well, and 44 per cent badly. Two weeks later, in the middle of the campaign, this rating had improved for the Prime Minister, with 36 per cent of those with at least a little interest in the story considering that he was handling the issue well and the same proportion (36 per cent) badly (Figure 20.13).

Campaign polling also showed that although John Key did not necessarily win the argument on 'dirty politics', what really mattered for National was that it did not lose votes.

Given a choice, 37 per cent went for the argument that 'dirty politics' was essentially a left-wing smear, while 58 per cent considered that there were serious issues at stake (Figure 20.14).

Figure 20.12: Party Vote – the impact of *Dirty Politics*

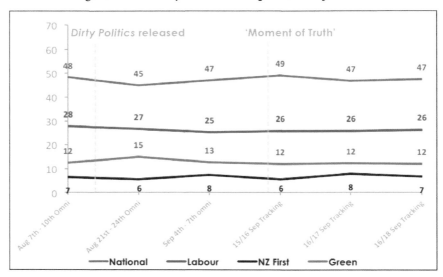

Question: Under MMP you have two votes. One for the candidate in the electorate you live in, and the second for a party. Thinking about this party vote only, if the general election were held today which party would you vote for? (UMR telephone omnibus survey, UMR online election tracker survey)

Figure 20.13: John Key's handling of *Dirty Politics*

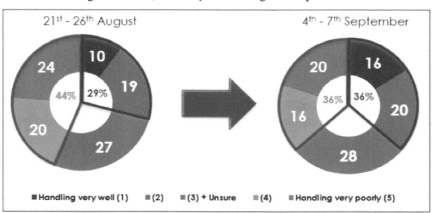

Question: Using a scale of 1 to 5 where 1 means Very well and 5 is Very poorly, please tell me how well John Key is handling the issues around the book *Dirty Politics* and Judith Collins (UMR telephone omnibus survey, base: respondents who claim to be following the issue)

Figure 20.14: *Dirty Politics* statement testing

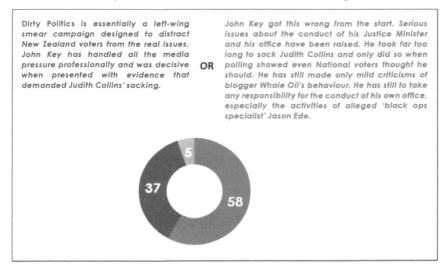

Dirty Politics is essentially a left-wing smear campaign designed to distract New Zealand voters from the real issues. John Key has handled all the media pressure professionally and was decisive when presented with evidence that demanded Judith Collins' sacking.

OR

John Key got this wrong from the start. Serious issues about the conduct of his Justice Minister and his office have been raised. He took far too long to sack Judith Collins and only did so when polling showed even National voters thought he should. He has still made only mild criticisms of blogger Whale Oil's behaviour. He has still to take any responsibility for the conduct of his own office, especially the activities of alleged 'black ops specialist' Jason Ede.

Question: Regardless of your vote which of the following is closer to your own view even if not quite right … (UMR telephone omnibus survey, September 2014, base: respondents that claim to be following news stories on *Dirty Politics* and Judith Collins' resignation)

Figure 20.15: Is John Key telling the truth on Goff story?

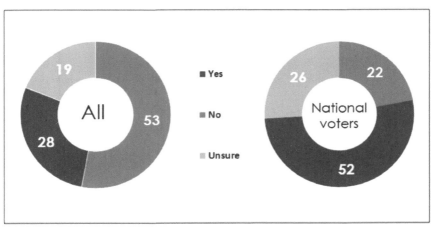

Question: Regardless of your vote do you believe that John Key is telling the truth when he says he had no knowledge at all of the organised leaking of a report by the Security Intelligence Services to blogger Whale Oil? This was designed to embarrass then Labour leader Phil Goff in the lead up to the 2011 election. (UMR telephone omnibus survey, September 2014, base: respondents that claim to be following news stories on *Dirty Politics* and Judith Collins' resignation)

UMR polling also showed that only 28 per cent of New Zealanders thought John Key was telling the truth about not knowing anything about the release of the Phil Goff/SIS briefing documents; 53 per cent thought that he was not being truthful (Figure 20.15). Among National voters, 22 per cent did not believe John Key on this issue. If about a third of those doubting National voters had switched to centre-left parties, Winston Peters would have been 'kingmaker'.

But of course they did not, and despite the ferocious barrage John Key's favourability rating barely budged (Figure 20.16).

Figure 20.16: John Key's Favourability – the impact of *Dirty Politics*

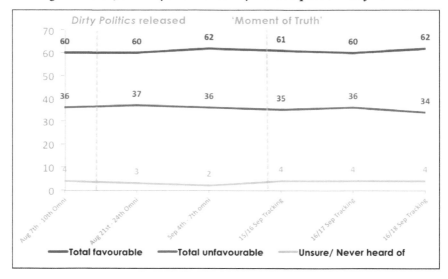

Question: Thinking about the following politicians, tell me if you generally have a very favourable, somewhat favourable, somewhat unfavourable or very unfavourable opinion of them. If you do not know enough about them just say so. (UMR telephone omnibus surveys, UMR online election tracker survey)

The 'Moment of Truth' certainly failed to shake National voters. National Party claims that it actually added 1–2 per cent to the National vote in the last week of the campaign are plausible.

A UMR survey showed 23 per cent of New Zealanders thought the 'Moment of Truth' raised serious doubts about whether John Key had been truthful; 65 per cent thought that the event had been unpersuasive. Even core Labour voters were unimpressed. The percentage of Labour voters who thought that the 'Moment of Truth' raised serious concerns about John Key (41 per cent) was actually slightly less than the number who thought it was a flop (42 per cent).

There are a number of reasons for this double failure.

Neither Nicky Hager nor Kim Dotcom were ever going to reach most National voters. Considerable political research in the last decade has shown that partisan voters of all colours are adept at rationalising negative information and twisting and turning facts to defend their original voting intentions (Westen et al. 2006).

Hager's favourability rating among all New Zealanders soon after the release of *Dirty Politics* was 20 per cent positive and 43 per cent negative; among National voters Hager was assessed as follows: 7 per cent positive; 64 per cent negative.

In qualitative research among 'soft' National voters – i.e., those at least prepared to consider voting Labour – they batted away the charges in Hager's book: the pre-election timing was seen as deeply suspicious; they repeated John Key's initial defence that it was all a left-wing smear; Nicky Hager was just selling books; no notice should be taken of a book based on stolen emails; 'they all do it'; and, tellingly if perhaps not rationally, 'there is no alternative'.

The multiple issues raised by *Dirty Politics* may have been too complex to communicate effectively in the heat of a political campaign. There was a lot for voters with low levels of interest in politics to take in, and when *Dirty Politics* did narrow down to a simple story, critically it was Judith Collins and not John Key in the crosshairs. Already seriously weakened by the Oravida scandal, Collins became the perfect campaign sacrifice.

It can certainly be speculated whether *Dirty Politics* could have had a greater impact on the election result if it had been handled differently. Winston Peters was withering in his charge that anyone with such a huge fund of damaging material should have known to drip-feed it rather than release it all in one rush (see chapter 10). Another, more neutral, author without a history of disrupting election campaigns would probably have made life more difficult for John Key.

It is possible too that *Dirty Politics* could have been decisive if the left had offered a more credible opposition in the 2014 campaign. The book did create doubts among some National voters, but John Key and National had more than enough going for them to retain their support.

As for the 'Moment of Truth', this was never going to turn the election. The credibility of the accusers was weak. In 2012, after the American movie-style raid on his home, New Zealanders were evenly divided about Kim Dotcom: 38 per cent had a positive view and 36 per cent a negative view. Before the 'Moment of Truth' his rating had already collapsed to 16 per cent positive, 74 per cent negative. After the Auckland Town Hall performance the Monday before the election, Dotcom's rating dropped even further – to 11 per cent positive, 82 per cent negative.

The other main players involved in the 'Moment of Truth' were not much better: Laila Harré (20 per cent positive, 50 per cent negative); Julian Assange (15 per cent positive, 42 per cent negative); and Edward Snowden (21 per cent positive, 45 per cent negative). These numbers are all even worse among the National voters that the centre-left had to win: Laila Harré (14 per cent positive, 63 per cent negative); Julian Assange (5 per cent positive, 55 per cent negative); and Edward Snowden (9 per cent positive, 63 per cent negative).[9]

The issues involved in the 'Moment of Truth' were even more complex than for *Dirty Politics*. With codenames such as Project Cortex, Operation Speargun and X-Keyscore flying around, there was far too much for voters to process in just five days before voting.

Politicians on the left throughout the campaign complained that *Dirty Politics* took away the media time they needed to make a successful case for a change in government. That is, at best, arguable. The fundamentals of a growing economy and, more importantly for voting, rising economic confidence, offering a more stable coalition and a strong leadership advantage were always going to work for National. While polling certainly suggests that New Zealanders were prepared to consider a change of government in 2012 and 2013, from around May 2014 New Zealand voters appeared to have decided that there was no viable alternative on offer. From that point a clear change to a centre-left government was never on the cards. However, the workings of MMP meant that even with the National vote in the high 40s it was a close call between National remaining in charge on its own and having to deal with Winston Peters.

The political landscape in 2015 looking towards the 2017 election is very similar to that in 2012 looking ahead to the 2014 election. It will only take a tiny swing, far less than the expected fraying of support for a government in its third term, to propel Winston Peters into the 'kingmaker' role. By contrast, there is a lot more work required for Labour and the Greens to get into a position where their combined vote is above that for National and its client parties.

The problem for the centre-left is that now National is totally dominating the centre, and winning more left votes than Labour and the Greens are winning right votes.

Asked to define themselves on a 0-to-10 left-to-right scale – based on their degree of support for government provision of services, the need for governments to intervene in the economy and a progressive tax system – 30 per cent of New Zealanders were clearly left (0–3 on the scale); 42 per cent were in the centre (4–6); and 25 per cent were clearly right (7–10).[10] As is often observed, the centre is the battleground in New Zealand politics.

If the 42 per cent on the centre bloc are split up further, 12 per cent go left, 10 per cent go right, and 20 per cent remain in the middle of the scale. That leaves 42 per cent on the left, 35 per cent on the right, and 20 per cent dead centre. At first sight this appears promising for centre-left parties. But among the 'clearly left' Labour has 42 per cent, the Greens 25 per cent, National 19 per cent, and New Zealand First 10 per cent. In the centre National has 56 per cent, Labour 18 per cent, the Greens 12 per cent, and New Zealand First 9 per cent. Among the 'clearly right' National has 76 per cent, Labour 13 per cent, New Zealand First 4 per cent, and the Greens just 1 per cent.

To sum up: National is winning much more support away from its base than Labour. Only 39 per cent of National's current party vote is from 'clearly right' voters; 46 per cent is from the centre, and 12 per cent is from the 'clearly left', whereas 54 per cent of Labour's vote is from the left, 31 per cent from the centre, and 14 per cent from the right. The Greens have a stronger left profile, with 59 per cent of its vote from the left, 38 per cent from the centre, and only 1 per cent from the right.

John Key's flexible political positioning and popularity is an obvious obstacle to Labour and the Greens driving out National's inroads into the left base and improving the left's appeal to the centre. John Key has some appeal to the left and he has strong appeal to the centre. His favourability rating with the 'clearly left' is 31 per cent positive, 64 per cent negative. Among the critical centre bloc he rates 67 per cent positive, 30 per cent negative.

Analysis of vote by self-declared social class shows a similar pattern. In an October 2014 UMR telephone survey, 28 per cent of New Zealanders said that they were 'working class', 32 per cent 'lower middle class', 31 per cent 'upper middle class' and only 2 per cent 'upper class'. As shown in Figure 20.17, National led by 9 per cent among 'working class' voters; by 20 per cent among 'lower middle class' voters; and by 50 per cent among 'upper middle class' voters.

Figure 20.17: The Vote by social class, 2014 election

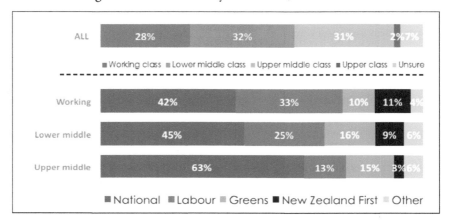

Question 1: If you were asked to choose one of these four names for your social class, which would you say you belong to – the working class, the lower middle class, the upper middle class or the upper class? Question 2: Under MMP you have two votes. One for the candidate in the electorate you live in, and the second for a party. Thinking about this party vote only, if the general election were held today which party would you vote for? (UMR telephone omnibus survey – October 2014)

It may be some solace to Labour that most voters see the party's problems as just part of the normal political cycle. Given a choice, only 13 per cent think that Labour 'has no place in modern politics and is going to fade away'; 78 per cent think 'its current problems are just the usual political cycle and [Labour] remains the alternative major political party that people will turn to when they get tired of John Key and National'.[11]

But that political cycle at the time of writing – six months after the general election – had yet to turn.

APPENDIX: REASONS FOR 2014 VOTE, BY PARTY

Table 20.3: Reasons for voting National, 2014 election

National	per cent Critical + Main reason
National's track record in government	88.4
National having the best chance to establish a stable government	86.6
John Key's leadership	86.4
National's management of the economy	85.4
Concerns that Labour was not ready to lead a government	72.6
Concerns about the influence of Internet Mana on a Labour-led government	56.2
David Cunliffe's leadership	50.2
Concern about the influence of the Greens on a Labour-led government	46.3
Traditional supporter of party I vote for	45.3
Labour having a much smaller party vote than National and needing at least two and possibly three more parties to form a government	43.6
Concerns about child poverty and inequality in New Zealand	34.5
David Cunliffe's problems explaining details of Labour's capital gains tax	30.4
John Key's charges that Labour will introduce 5 new taxes	28.6
The environment	28.3
John Key's debate performances	24.4
National's grants to new home buyers	22.2
Labour and Green policy to increase the minimum wage	21.2
National proposing possible small tax cuts in the next term	20.6
John Key effectively sacking Judith Collins for allegedly undermining the head of the SFO	17.4
David Cunliffe's debate performances	17.2
Labour's policy to build 100,000 low cost houses in next 10 years	12.9
Wanting to vote for a coalition partner that will act as a check on National	11.0
Judith Collins leaking a public servant's name and contact details to blogger Whale Oil	7.5
National becoming more arrogant and not listening	7.3
Accusations of mass surveillance of New Zealanders by our security agencies	5.8
The information in the book *Dirty Politics* generally about the way the National government operates	4.1
The alleged use by John Key's office of information from the SIS to embarrass Phil Goff in the 2011 election	2.8

Table 20.4: Reasons for voting Labour, 2014 election

Labour	per cent Critical + Main reason
Concerns about child poverty and inequality in New Zealand	80.7
National becoming more arrogant and not listening	77.7
Labour and Green policy to increase the minimum wage	63.5
Labour's policy to build 100,000 low cost houses in next 10 years	60.4
The environment	56.0
Traditional supporter of party I vote for	51.4
National's management of the economy	50.8
Accusations of mass surveillance of New Zealanders by our security agencies	49.6
John Key's leadership	47.8
National's track record in government	47.2
The alleged use by John Key's office of information from the SIS to embarrass Phil Goff in the 2011 election	43.0
Judith Collins leaking a public servant's name and contact details to blogger Whale Oil	42.9
David Cunliffe's leadership	42.0
The information in the book *Dirty Politics* generally about the way the National government operates	39.8
Labour having a much smaller party vote than National and needing at least two and possibly three more parties to form a government	35.6
Wanting to vote for a coalition partner that will act as a check on National	34.6
John Key effectively sacking Judith Collins for allegedly undermining the head of the SFO	30.5
David Cunliffe's debate performances	29.9
National proposing possible small tax cuts in the next term	22.7
Concern about the influence of the Greens on a Labour-led government	22.5
Concerns that Labour was not ready to lead a government	21.8
Concerns about the influence of Internet Mana on a Labour-led government	19.1
John Key's debate performances	17.1
National's grants to new home buyers	17.0
National having the best chance to establish a stable government	16.2
John Key's charges that Labour will introduce 5 new taxes	15.5
David Cunliffe's problems explaining details of Labour's capital gains tax	15.2

Table 20.5: Reasons for voting Greens, 2014 election

Greens	per cent Critical + Main reason
The environment	90.3
Concerns about child poverty and inequality in New Zealand	78.2
National becoming more arrogant and not listening	68.1
Labour and Green policy to increase the minimum wage	62.2
National's management of the economy	57.3
National's track record in government	46.4
Accusations of mass surveillance of New Zealanders by our security agencies	43.2
Judith Collins leaking a public servant's name and contact details to blogger Whale Oil	40.7
John Key's leadership	39.5
The alleged use by John Key's office of information from the SIS to embarrass Phil Goff in the 2011 election	35.1
David Cunliffe's leadership	33.7
The information in the book *Dirty Politics* generally about the way the National government operates	33.5
Wanting to vote for a coalition partner that will act as a check on National	32.9
Traditional supporter of party I vote for	31.2
Labour's policy to build 100,000 low cost houses in next 10 years	30.5
Labour having a much smaller party vote than National and needing at least two and possibly three more parties to form a government	27.9
Concerns that Labour was not ready to lead a government	27.4
Concern about the influence of the Greens on a Labour-led government	26.2
John Key effectively sacking Judith Collins for allegedly undermining the head of the SFO	20.8
National having the best chance to establish a stable government	19.4
Concerns about the influence of Internet Mana on a Labour-led government	18.6
David Cunliffe's problems explaining details of Labour's capital gains tax	17.0
National proposing possible small tax cuts in the next term	13.5
David Cunliffe's debate performances	10.7
National's grants to new home buyers	9.6
John Key's charges that Labour will introduce 5 new taxes	9.4
John Key's debate performances	8.0

Table 20.6: Reasons for voting New Zealand First, 2014 election

New Zealand First	per cent Critical + Main reason
Wanting to vote for a coalition partner that will act as a check on National	63.3
National becoming more arrogant and not listening	62.1
National's management of the economy	54.9
Concerns that Labour was not ready to lead a government	52.5
National's track record in government	52.0
John Key's leadership	50.4
Concerns about child poverty and inequality in New Zealand	46.4
Concerns about the influence of Internet Mana on a Labour-led government	41.2
David Cunliffe's leadership	37.4
Concern about the influence of the Greens on a Labour-led government	35.9
John Key effectively sacking Judith Collins for allegedly undermining the head of the SFO	35.3
Labour having a much smaller party vote than National and needing at least two and possibly three more parties to form a government	33.0
Judith Collins leaking a public servant's name and contact details to blogger Whale Oil	29.4
The environment	28.5
Labour's policy to build 100,000 low cost houses in next 10 years	26.9
The alleged use by John Key's office of information from the SIS to embarrass Phil Goff in the 2011 election	24.0
National having the best chance to establish a stable government	23.2
Accusations of mass surveillance of New Zealanders by our security agencies	22.8
Labour and Green policy to increase the minimum wage	22.7
David Cunliffe's problems explaining details of Labour's capital gains tax	18.8
The information in the book *Dirty Politics* generally about the way the National government operates	18.4
Traditional supporter of party I vote for	15.3
National proposing possible small tax cuts in the next term	13.8
National's grants to new home buyers	13.5
David Cunliffe's debate performances	12.0
John Key's charges that Labour will introduce 5 new taxes	11.6
John Key's debate performances	9.7

21

SOCIAL MEDIA IN THE 2014 GENERAL ELECTION

Matthew Beveridge

'The internet is a well-established part of daily business, political and social life in New Zealand . . .' This is how Anthony Deos and Ashley Murchison opened the social media chapter of *Kicking the Tyres: The New Zealand General Election and Electoral Referendum of 2011* (2012, p. 234). What they observed in 2011 is even more the case in 2014. There are businesses that exist today that are only possible because of the growth of the internet. However, the internet not only affects the way that people and businesses operate, but also how political parties operate.

This chapter looks at the presence of political parties on Facebook and Twitter, focusing on the last month of the 2014 campaign, from Writ Day on 20 August up to and including 19 September (i.e., the day before the election). This period is used for two reasons: it represents the peak period of campaigning during the election period; and it also corresponds to the period used by Deos and Murchison (2012) in their comparable chapter in the previous book in this series looking at Facebook, as well as Murchison (2013) assessing Twitter. This allows for a more accurate comparison of the changes in political use of social media in New Zealand.

The 2014 election was one of 'dirty politics', 'moment(s) of truth' and 'selfies'. All three of these elements were present, and highly discussed on social media. Added to this, a new well-funded political party aimed at the internet generation, and the larger parties dedicating more resources to social media, helped to generate an overall higher level of use and engagement. This resulted in a highly contested social media space.

The 2014 election offers the first opportunity to track changes in how New Zealand political parties have used certain social media platforms. This chapter focuses on how political parties used the two main social media sites in New Zealand – Twitter and Facebook. There have been a number of other social media options launched since the 2011 election, including Tinder, Snapchat, Pinterest and so on. However, these are, in a political sense, marginal, rarely used[1] and difficult to track. The use of some of these smaller platforms will be touched upon towards the end of the chapter.

During the period concerned, all of New Zealand's largest political parties – National, Labour, the Greens, New Zealand First, the Māori Party, ACT, United Future, the Conservative Party, Mana and the Internet Party – had a presence on Facebook. Nearly all were present on Twitter as well, other than the Conservative Party (which had no account in its name) and Mana (whose account went unused). As in 2011, the National Party ran two Twitter accounts, @NZNationalParty and @NatFeed, the content of the latter consisting of links to the party's website. This account stopped tweeting on 28 August and is discounted from the statistics used in this chapter. Nevertheless the approach on that account reinforces the conclusions reached about the main @NZNationalParty Twitter account.

Moe and Larrson (2012) highlight a key issue in social media research: there is no agreed method to collect data. This issue is compounded by the lack of standard methods to assess the use and impact of social media. However, for this chapter there is a counterpart that offers a useable baseline from which to work. As the basis for comparison, this chapter looks to the work done by Deos and Murchison (2012) in the previous book in this series.

Methodology

The findings in this chapter are based on an analysis of Facebook pages and Twitter accounts of nine parties contesting the 2014 general election. These parties were selected on the basis that they were either already in Parliament or were seen by commentators as likely to be there after the election. As noted, the data covers the period between 20 August and 19 September. The Twitter data was collected via a third party analytics website[2] that allows for the download of the last 3,200 tweets sent by an account. Facebook posts were captured manually, via screen grabs and the counting of individual comments. Unlike the 2011 analysis, the number and content of posts by other users to the timeline of the party pages were not counted. Instead, only content posted by the parties themselves – and comments by users on that content – was counted for the 2014 election.

The posts by the parties' Facebook pages, and the tweets by their accounts, were coded based on whether they were an original post, were posts sharing content from another place on Facebook, or involved retweeting other accounts. Posts were coded if they contained a link; if so, they were then additionally coded based on what that link was to – the party website, a mainstream media website, YouTube, Facebook, Twitter, another social media site, a blog, or a website that did not fit in one of the above categories. Posts were also coded based on whether they contained a photo or graphic. In relation to Twitter, a photo or graphic was counted as a link as well. Posts were coded for content regardless of whether they were original or shared posts.

Since 2011, there have been a number of changes to the way that Facebook operates. In 2011 it was common to include just a link, photo or graphic in a post. In 2014, however, it was common to have both a graphic and a link within the associated text. While in 2011 it was possible to code a post into a single category, in 2014 it was common for a post to be included in two categories. As a result, the total of each of the categories for some parties adds up to more than the number of posts by the party.

Other changes that have been made during the three years since the 2011 election will be noted where appropriate.

Labour

In the 2014 election, Labour showed the greatest increase from 2011 in the number of posts made by the party during the last month of the campaign. During this period in 2014 Labour posted 107 posts on Facebook. This was a 48 per cent increase on the same period in 2011. The style and content also changed from 2011. Of the 107 posts in 2014, only nine were shared from other Facebook sources. There was only one post (0.93 per cent) that was a simple status message with no other content. This is a significant change from 2011 when 10 posts (13.9 per cent) were simple 'status posts' (i.e., an information update of one kind or another). In a similar vein, images and graphics became much more prevalent in 2014. In 2011, 21 posts (29.2 per cent) contained an image; during the 2014 campaign this had increased to 75: 16 (15.0 per cent) containing photos and 59 (55.1 per cent) with a graphic of some sort. Twenty-one of the posts with graphics included a link to a website that fitted within one of the above categories. The inclusion of these links within posts with graphics is a sign that Labour learned to use the changes that Facebook released in the three years since 2011.

During the last month of the election, Labour's posts received 90,061 likes, a 2,115 per cent increase from 2011. When the increase in number of posts is taken into account, the average number of likes per post represented an increase of 1,391 per cent. In 2011, 47 per cent of Labour's posts received fewer than four likes, with the most liked post gaining 238 likes. In 2014, only four of Labour's posts received fewer likes than the 2011 peak; the party's most liked post received 2,775 likes, with eight posts receiving more than 2,000 likes. Labour posts were shared a total of 14,223 times in the final month, compared to 503 total shares in 2011 – a 2,728 per cent increase. Only eight posts went unshared in 2014, compared with 56 in 2011. The most shared post in 2014, a supplied graphic to be used as a profile photo, had 991 shares (Labour Party 2014b). The total number of comments on Labour's posts in 2014 was 11,959, up from 2,081 in 2011. The most commented-on post, a graphic about Labour's minimum wage policy, gained 668 comments; this was also the party's most liked post (Labour Party 2014a).

National

National represented the mirror image of Labour on Facebook. In the final month of the 2011 campaign, National had 179 posts. In 2014 this dropped to 97, a decrease of 46 per cent. In 2014, National placed less emphasis on linking directly to its party website, with only 30 links to party websites across 97 posts (30.93 per cent), compared with 47.5 per cent in 2011. In 2011, only 15.6 per cent of National posts contained an image (either photo or graphic), while in 2014, 55.67 per cent of posts contained a graphic (as opposed to a photo). Taken together, these two changes may be related to an attempt to increase the reach of its posts so as to convey a policy message to more people. Unlike Labour, which only had one text-only 'status post', National had nine (9.28 per cent) among its 97 posts. This is still a decrease from 2011, when 15.6 per cent of their posts were text-only. The conclusion reached in 2011, that most of the text-only 'status posts' were shared posts (rather than original), has not changed significantly, with four out of nine being shared posts in 2014.

It is in the area of interaction that National's statistics have changed significantly. In 2011 National received 1,062 likes across all of its posts. In 2014, this number was 78,567, which, while still less than Labour and the Greens in 2014, represents an increase of 7,298 per cent. Of the 97 posts made by National, 25 gained more than 1,000 likes, with two gaining more than 2,000. This compares with a peak of 28 likes on a single post in 2011. The most-liked post, a graphic on a prison work policy, gained 5,806 likes, and also gained the most shares, 504 (National Party 2014a). This post gained 604 per cent as many shares as all of National's posts in the last month of the 2011 election campaign. Only nine (9.28 per cent) of National's posts failed to gain at least one share in the last month of the 2014 election campaign (compared with 83.2 per cent going unshared in 2011). This resulted in a total of 6,816 shares during the final month of the campaign – a 9,778.26 per cent increase in shares. This high level of growth extended to the number of comments received on posts as well, which increased from 339 in 2011 to 18,032 in 2014 – a rise of 5,219.17 per cent. National's most commented-on post, which focused on the different answers given by Labour to questions around the party's capital gains tax, gained 945 comments (National Party 2014), compared to a peak of 23 comments on a post in 2011.

One element that set National apart was its use of its leader's Facebook and Twitter accounts. Both of these had significantly more followers than the National Party's own accounts. As at 22 August, the National Party's Twitter account had 6,717 followers; John Key's Twitter account had 115,930 followers – a massive difference. As for Facebook, as at 17 June the National Party's page had 12,900 likes; John Key's Facebook page, by contrast, had 147,500 likes (following a merger of his page and profile). For most other parties the reverse was true: the parties' accounts had more followers than the leaders' accounts. The data for National, and for John Key, is consistent overall with the focus on Prime Minister Key's popularity. A principal manifestation of this in the area of social media can be seen in the hashtag that National chose for 2014 – #TeamKey. As a single point of comparison, @JohnKeyPM sent 146 tweets. These messages gained 2,148 retweets and 3,610 favourites. The National Party's own account – @NZNationalParty – sent 271 tweets, which elicited only 1,239 retweets and 1,181 favourites.

Greens

Despite being a medium-sized party, the Greens fell roughly in the middle between National and Labour in regard to the number of Facebook posts made, with 100 posts, up 49.25 per cent from 2011. However, the Greens gained more likes and shares than Labour or National. The only category of engagement where the Greens did not lead the field was in the total number of comments (in which it was third). The Greens experienced strong growth in their level of engagement compared with 2011. In 2011, posts by the Greens gained a total of 3,153 likes, whereas in 2014 the Greens' posts received 97,718 likes, a 2999.21 per cent increase. A similarly strong rise was seen in the increase in shares, from 526 in 2011 to

16,587 in 2014, a 3,053.42 per cent increase. The growth in the number of comments – while still the second highest among all the parties for which data are available – was not as strong as the growth in the number of likes and shares. In 2011 the Greens received 866 comments; in 2014 the party received 9,508 comments, an increase of 997.92 per cent. As in 2011, no post by the Greens went unliked; however, their least liked post gained 36 likes, up from 7 in 2011. Their most liked post, a photo of comedian Guy Williams casting an advance vote with text encouraging others to do the same, gained 2,904 likes, up from a maximum of 223 in 2011. Their most commented-on post, a link to Metiria Turei's appearance on TV3's *Firstline* on 12 September, gained 224 comments (Green Party 2014), up from 54 in 2011.

Māori Party

In 2011 the Māori Party was the second most active of the measured parties. In 2014 they have gone one better, becoming the most active of the five parties that were also measured in 2011. This is despite being less active in 2014 than in 2011 (131 posts versus 140, a decrease of 6.43 per cent). As with National, this drop in activity did not prevent the party experiencing a significant increase in engagement. Just as in 2011, links to the mainstream media were the most common type of post made by the Māori Party; however, the proportion they represented was less (from 33.6 per cent to 23.66 per cent). As with other parties, the number of posts containing photos or graphics rose: from 16.4 per cent in 2011 to 38.17 per cent in 2014. There was a significant drop in the percentage of posts that contained links to the Māori Party website: from 28.4 per cent to 14.5 per cent. These two elements – more images and graphics, fewer party website links – may be related, with the party focusing on using graphics to get its message across, as opposed to directing people to the party's website.

In 2014, posts by the Māori Party gained 12,549 likes, up from 760 in 2011 – an increase of 1,551.18 per cent. The rise is explained not only by an increase in the highest number of likes, up from 16 to 492, but also a decrease in the number of posts with no likes, down from 55.4 per cent to 0 per cent. In 2014, the least liked post, a link to a tweet, gained six likes. As with other parties, there was growth in the number of comments: in 2011 the party's posts received 249 comments; in 2014 there were 1,336 comments, an increase of 436.55 per cent. This growth was once again supported by two elements: the percentage of posts with four or fewer comments declined from 92.8 per cent to 32.58 per cent, while the most commented-on post, a link to the party website in which co-leader Te Ururoa Flavell criticised the Labour Party for how it had dealt with the Māori Party, both recently and in the past, gained 70 comments (compared to 16 for the most commented-on post in 2011; Māori Party 2014b). The total number of shares for Māori Party posts in 2011 was 38. In contrast, the total number of shares in 2014 was 2,030, and the most shared post, encouraging people to enrol, gained 167 shares (Māori Party 2014a).

ACT

As with most of the smaller parties, there was little change in the number of posts made by ACT during the last month of the campaign: 66 versus 68, a 3.03 per cent increase. There was a much larger increase in engagement, however, although not to the same extent as other parties. In 2011, ACT received 563 likes across all of its 66 posts. In 2014 this increased to 3,423 likes across the party's 68 posts, an increase of 507.99 per cent. The most likes gained by a single post showed an increase slightly higher than the overall increase in likes – from 21 in 2011 to 134 in 2014. The most liked post in 2014 was a graphic encouraging supporters to 'Vote your values' (ACT 2014a). Only one post failed to gain any likes. Like many parties in 2011, ACT struggled to get shares on its posts, 85 per cent of them going unshared during the last month of the campaign. In 2014, the percentage of posts unshared dropped to only 33.82 per cent. This helped lift its overall number of shares from just over 20 in 2011 to 299 in 2014. Alongside this overall increase, the most shared post went from two shares to 47. This most shared post was one explaining how 50,000 party votes for ACT could deliver three MPs, as opposed to 65,000 party votes for National delivering just one extra MP (ACT 2014b). In the area of comments, growth was drastically lower at 120.54 per cent – 370 comments in 2011 rising to 816 in 2014. The comments in 2014 were a lot more evenly distributed, with only 45.59 per cent of posts having four or fewer comments, as compared to 81.7 per cent in 2011.

Parties not measured in 2011

Due to a lack of data it is not possible to analyse changes in activity or engagement on Facebook by other New Zealand political parties since 2011. However, it is still possible to assess how they used the platforms in 2014 and how they performed in relation to each other.

New Zealand First

New Zealand First, along with all of the parties in this section, made over 100 posts (142) during the final month of the campaign. Of these posts, 23 (16.20 per cent) were shared posts, with the rest being original content from New Zealand First. These posts gained 6,202 likes, 890 comments and 602 shares. These figures give New Zealand First between 2.5 and 4.4 per cent of the level of engagement per post that the larger parties achieved. Most of the posts (96, or 67.61 per cent) contained links to mainstream media. Unlike the larger parties, New Zealand First did not post links with graphics or photos. This may partially explain the lower level of engagement, as the New Zealand First posts may not have been seen by as many people due to the algorithm-driven nature of Facebook (which shows posts to users based on a combination of content and engagement).

United Future

Despite being the second most active party on Facebook (behind Mana) with 150 posts, United Future was the only party to receive fewer than 1,000 likes across all of its posts. The average number of likes per post that United Future attracted – 3.91 – was around 0.40 per cent of the Green Party's. Compared to ACT, a party of comparable size in relation to MPs and votes gained, United Future only gained 7.77 per cent the number of average likes per post. United Future also had the lowest number of likes, still not having broken 1,000 likes after the election (United Future 2015). This low level of engagement is most likely due to the party's inability to generate engaging content, both before and during the campaign. These outcomes, in turn, reflected highly limited resources, consistent with the party's issues around membership numbers in 2013 (Chapman 2013) and consequent difficulties with fundraising.

Mana

Mana performed better in many categories than most of the other minor parties, even outperforming some of the major parties in some measures. Mana was the most active of the parties on Facebook, with 176 posts, 29 of them being shared. Mana gained more likes – both as an absolute number, 58,973, and on a per post basis, 335.07 – than the Internet Party. The Internet Party gained more comments than Mana's 4,081, however. Mana did well with shares, gaining 10,865, or 61.73 per post, compared with National's 6,816 shares. Mana's success in numbers of shares can be attributed to two posts in particular, both of them focusing on the issues that the National Party had with the music used in National's TV ads (Mana Movement 2014a; 2014b).

Mana also made use of 'paper.li', a self-generated online 'newspaper', to aggregate content focused on its campaign from news media and other social media sources. This was published on Mana's Facebook page, as well as the personal Twitter account of one of its members. The amount of traffic this publication received is impossible to measure from the outside; however, it is a sign that some of the smaller parties were trying different methods to bring together content to present to followers and supporters.

Internet Party

The Internet Party was the newest of the parties to join social media. It did not contest the 2011 election, having only been established in March 2014. With 132 posts on Facebook during the final month of the campaign, the Internet Party sits towards the high end of range when it comes to activity. Despite this high level of activity, its large number of likes, and its focus on the use of digital and social media to campaign (StopPress Team 2014), it did not reach the same level of engagement as the major parties. The Internet Party received a total of 42,768 likes (324 per post), 7,389 comments (55.98 per post) and 9,308 shares (70.52 per post). Its most engaged-with post was about its policy on marijuana decriminalisation, which gained 1,498 likes, 359 comments and 443 shares (Internet Party 2014).

In the lead-up to the election the Internet Party was able to build a solid base of page likes, with 17,400 likes as at 17 June. As can be seen by the engagement figures, likes on a page are not indicative of engagement and are not necessarily indicative of support at the ballot box.

Conservatives

The Conservatives were not highly active on social media like many of the other small parties. Their activity falls in line with the larger parties of National, Labour and the Greens, with 102 posts. The Conservatives also stand out as the only party that did not share content from anywhere else on Facebook. All of its posts were original ones. Despite the Conservatives' small size on Facebook – around 3,000 page likes, similar to ACT – the Conservatives were able to generate overall higher levels of engagement, with 10,217 likes, 642 comments and 1,062 shares. Their most liked and shared post – a graphic about a vote for the Conservatives not being a wasted vote – produced 215 likes and 88 shares (Conservative Party 2014b). The party's most commented-on post, with 26 comments, was related to a poll result showing them nearly in Parliament (Conservative Party 2014a).

Twitter

Facebook is the largest social media network used by New Zealand political parties. The number of likes on party Facebook pages is much higher (30,000–70,000 for the three major parties) than the number of followers on Twitter (8,500–16,000). While Twitter may provide fewer followers for political parties, those who do follow parties on Twitter are seen as potential conduits for helping to spread party political messages. This effect may be more relevant to individual candidates than to parties, as Green MP Gareth Hughes has observed: 'as an MP and candidate a post on Twitter, due to its strong beltway element, is more likely to generate a news story than a post on Facebook' (Ross and Bürger 2014). This fits with research from the United States that has found that both the Obama and Romney campaigns in 2012 used Twitter as a way to potentially influence how the media viewed events (Uberti 2014). The study found that in the US context, Twitter was being used by reporters as a gauge of public opinion and as a means of judging how to present political stories. If political parties are able to flood Twitter with messages that reflect their position, this can influence how reporters cover a story. Further primary research is required, however, to establish whether this kind of process is occurring in New Zealand.

Given its fairly recent development, when it comes to the use of Twitter in a New Zealand election there is only a single data reference point – the 2011 election (Murchison 2013). As with Facebook, the available data covers National, Labour, the Greens, the Māori Party and United Future, with the added element of National having had two active accounts in 2011. The party's second account, @natcampaign, focused on campaign-related posts (Murchison 2013); in 2014 the main account (@NZNationalParty) carried those campaign-related messages, and the secondary account, @natfeed, stopped during the campaign, carrying solely likes to items posted on the National Party website.

Due to the 'scrolling' nature of Twitter, and the fact that a user's feed is for the most part unmediated by the service itself, it is possible for parties to post more content without overwhelming the user. This is evident for five of the eight parties on Twitter, with only the Māori Party, United Future and New Zealand First 'tweeting' less than they posted on Facebook.[3] For the Internet Party and the Greens, the difference between the two platforms was significant, with tweets exceeding Facebook posts by 555.03 per cent and 1,202 per cent, respectively. For National and Labour (whose tweets exceeded their Facebook posts by 179.38 per cent and 194.39 per cent, respectively) the difference, though not as large, was still significant.

The increased level of Twitter activity did not translate into a greater level of content sharing overall or per post. The only party which had more retweets than shares – 527 vs 299 – was ACT. National, on Facebook the least shared, on average, of the major parties, still had nearly five times as many shares per post (70.27 per cent) as the most retweeted party, Labour, gained in retweets on Twitter (14.98 per cent).

This difference in engagement across the two social media sites is highlighted by looking at the Greens, which had 55,000 page likes on their Facebook page (Beveridge 2014a) and 13,000 followers on Twitter.[4] Per post the Greens had an average of 165.87 shares on Facebook; on Twitter the Greens had an average of 9.16 retweets. This failure to engage on Twitter was not only in the area of content sharing. 'Favouriting' a tweet is the Twitter equivalent of liking a post on Facebook. The Greens gained a total of 97,718 likes, or 977.18 per post on Facebook, while on Twitter the Greens only gained 6,640 favourites, or 10.26 per new tweet.[5] The difference in Greens followers between the two platforms is around 400 per cent; the difference in engagement, on a per post basis, is between 1,700 per cent and 9,500 per cent. Even though Twitter is aimed at encouraging users to share content, New Zealand political parties were, on the whole, unable to leverage this in 2014 to gain a similar, or larger, level of engagement as on Facebook.

Engagement by Parties

Unlike other forms of mass political communication, such as billboards or advertisements (whether in print or on television or radio), social media has the potential for two-way communication. In this way it is more akin to a community hall or street corner meeting. However, to achieve this two-way communication requires a commitment by the parties concerned to actively engage with their followers. It is not clear that this commitment is being made in New Zealand.

One measure of the level of a party's engagement with its followers and commenters is the average number of times they commented on their own posts on Facebook. Another is in the proportion of tweets which were replies.

As shown in Table 21.1, none of the parties had an average of even one comment per Facebook post. Outside of the Greens and the Internet Party, none of the parties averaged above 0.35 comments per post. They did better on Twitter: although National was the worst performer, with replies making up only 1.11 per cent of their tweets, all of the other parties had replies making up between 8.5 and 25.38 per cent of their tweets. Despite the lower level of active engagement from followers, those who opted to send tweets were more likely to experience interaction from the parties. Due to the 'scrolling' nature of Twitter, however, these interactions were less likely to be seen by other users, unless the user actively took steps to scroll through the responses.

Table 21.1 – Facebook comments and tweets per party (2014 campaign)

Political party	No. of comments by party on their own Facebook posts	Average no. of comments by party per Facebook post	No. of tweets by party in response to other Twitter users	Percentage of all tweets by party that were replies to other Twitter users
National	22	0.22	3	1.11
Labour	32	0.30	39	12.38
Greens	73	0.73	150	11.52
Māori Party	21	0.16	13	12.15
NZ First	7	0.05	4	14.29
Mana	62	0.35	n/a	n/a
Internet Party	91	0.69	73	8.44
ACT	21	0.31	134	25.38
Conservatives	9	0.09	n/a	n/a
United Future	21	0.14	20	16.67

Conclusion

What was apparent during the last month of the 2014 election campaign was that New Zealand's political parties had improved their understanding (since 2011) of how Facebook and Twitter work and what sort of material was likely to generate engagement from users. The number of New Zealanders who use Facebook has increased, though the extent of engagement has not entirely kept pace. Some of the engagement from users is likely to have been driven by advertising, now possible on both Facebook and Twitter, but even so, engaging content is still needed if the advertising is to be effective. Parties did not achieve the same level of engagement on Twitter as on Facebook, although for some people, Twitter allowed a greater level of interaction with the parties.

The electoral consequences of social media engagement, for candidates and parties, is more difficult to determine, and remains a topic for further and more extensive research. The same can be said for the effects of Facebook, Twitter and other sites on voter turnout. The significance of social media for campaigns, and for politics more generally, is evident, however. Social media is here to stay as part of the online landscape, and as part of New Zealand's political landscape as well.

22

STANDING BACK AND LOOKING FORWARD:
THE 2014 ELECTION IN PERSPECTIVE

Therese Arseneau and Nigel S. Roberts

Election cycles tend to have a certain rhythm, with an ebb and flow of support for the sitting government. International research suggests that governing is costly, with governments losing support over the course of their incumbency (Rose and Mackie 1983; Nannestad and Paldam 2002). A survey of New Zealand elections since 1945 reveals that while winning a third term is not uncommon, especially for National, it does tend to be difficult, with elections for a third term typically hard-fought affairs. This is particularly true of two recent elections under MMP, in 1996 and 2005, when the governing party sought and obtained a third term. Both had cliffhanger results on election night followed by longer, relatively complicated government formation periods – it took about eight weeks in 1996 and four weeks in 2005 to form a government. In both cases the government formed had an element of surprise: in 1996 New Zealand First – somewhat unexpectedly – supported National, and in 2005 Labour favoured confidence and supply arrangements with New Zealand First and United Future, and not with the Greens, despite the two parties expressing a willingness to work together during the campaign (see Boston 2007).

In some ways the 2014 election fits this pattern: National did win a third term and the campaign was tumultuous and bruising. But unlike 1996 and 2005, the election result itself was not a nail-biter and this became clear quite quickly in the evening when the very large advance vote – roughly one-third of all ordinary votes – was reported.

The post-election government formation also lacked suspense. There was no doubt that National would continue to govern, the only uncertainty being whether it might be in a position to govern on its own. Indeed, until the special votes were counted and the writs returned, National appeared to have an absolute majority of 61 seats in a 121-seat Parliament and thus the possibility of the first ever MMP single-party majority government. Ultimately National's allocation receded to 60 out of 121 seats in Parliament:

still an MMP record high, but not enough to govern on its own.

In the interim, National had already made the decision to renew confidence and supply arrangements with its governing partners from the previous Parliament: ACT, the Māori Party and United Future. The governing arrangement (see Church, chapter 4) provided National access to four extra votes on confidence and supply and a possible working majority of 64 seats in a 121-seat Parliament.

The 2014 election will likely be remembered primarily for its campaign rather than its result. Prime Minister John Key described the campaign as 'most unusual', with *Dirty Politics* and Kim Dotcom hijacking much of the discussion away from policy (as noted by the Prime Minister in chapter 5). Yet the result itself was seemingly unaffected, the election producing a Parliament that was little changed. In this sense the campaign appeared strangely detached from the election itself. What explains this fundamental disconnect between the campaign and the result? What factors best explain this status quo result? And looking forward, what are the realities of MMP that shape both the party system and the shifting blocs of governing and opposition parties?

Key factors in the election

The election result is best explained by examining the broader context of political science literature, starting with the classic question: why do people vote the way they do? The contemporary emphasis is on four factors: the economy, party leaders, party competence and political issues (Hague and Harrop 2004, p. 158).

The first factor – the economy and economic conditions, including disposable income, unemployment and inflation – has an important impact on voters' evaluation of governments (Dorussen and Taylor 2002). Voters are described as 'fair weather friends' (Nadeau, Nieme and Yoshinaka 2002), punishing governments in times of economic downturn and, perhaps, rewarding them in times of prosperity. There is strong evidence that New Zealanders have long made the connection between economic conditions and voting choices (Aimer 2014, p. 21; Vowles 2001, p. 180). It is interesting that more important than objective measures of the state of the economy is a voter's perception of economic health, often based on personal experience in relation to economic conditions (Vowles 2003, p. 197).

The impact of the second factor, political leadership, on election outcomes is much debated. The leader is the chief spokesperson for the party and has certainly become the media focus, particularly in television coverage. Even more than this, leaders have become the personification of their parties: 'for most people . . . the parties spring to life through their leaders' (Vowles and Aimer 2004, p. 173). Televised leader-focused events, such as leaders' debates, can significantly influence elections (Johnston 1998, pp. 70–72). Nevertheless, it is still difficult to measure definitively the importance of leadership among the other factors affecting a voter's choice. Two points are important. First, even if the effect of leadership is small, it may still be significant in a close election (Bean 1992). Second, leadership is most important in terms of its mobilising and reinforcing effects: a leader should make it easier for voters who are uncommitted, or merely leaning towards a party, to make the decision to vote for that party (Vowles and Aimer 2004, p. 181).

A party's competence, and in particular its perceived ability to cope with the varied and unpredictable demands of governing, is the third factor identified as significant to voting choices (Hague and Harrop 2004, p. 158). Competence has certainly become an important marketing asset for parties and is especially important to a sitting government; according to Fiorina's theory (1981) of 'retrospective voting', voters increasingly evaluate a government's performance and then cast their votes based on this assessment. The question they ask of governments is 'what have you done for me and the country lately?' A change of government requires widespread dissatisfaction with the government's performance as well as an opposition giving voters confidence that it is a capable government-in-waiting.

The last major factor in voting choices is that, increasingly, people vote based on specific issues. Election campaigns are expected to provide voters with the policy information they need to make their voting choices. This leads parties to emphasise their more popular policies while downplaying less popular ones. In this sense, success in elections is very much based on a party's ability to set the policy agenda, thus influencing what issues are discussed during the election campaign (Johnston et al. 1992, p. 3).

While policy took a back seat in 2014, the other three factors were decisive to the election outcome. First, New Zealand's economy was strong, especially in comparison to other western democracies, including our closest neighbour Australia. New Zealand was labelled a 'rock star economy' (Bloxham 2014). Although Labour tried to counter the claim by pointing to growing inequality and an excessive reliance on dairying and Christchurch rebuilding expenditure, the label stuck – it resonated well with voters and was a mantra often repeated through the campaign. UMR polling confirmed that economic confidence remained strong throughout the election campaign and that National was greatly preferred to Labour as the party better able to manage the economy (see Mills, chapter 20). The Prime Minister acknowledged Finance Minister Bill English's important role in the election victory, symbolised by English joining Key onstage at National's election-night victory party.

Second, Prime Minister John Key was the preferred prime minister in every poll and by a very wide margin. Colin James describes Key as a 'macro-personality'; in the 2014 election he personified the National government and attracted voters who might not otherwise vote National (James, chapter 2). This is backed-up in UMR polling – 86 per cent of National voters cited Key's leadership as a main reason for giving National their vote (Mills, chapter 20). In contrast to this, David Cunliffe, Labour's third leader in six years, failed to win the confidence of voters or his own parliamentary colleagues; leaks about caucus dissatisfaction dogged Cunliffe and Labour, even during the campaign. Although the finger was repeatedly pointed at Cunliffe as the cause of Labour's poor showing, so too was it with David Shearer and Phil Goff before him. This does raise the question of whether leadership woes were more a symptom of much wider problems rather than a cause of Labour's poor 2014 election results.

The third factor, party competence, is crucial to understanding the 2014 result. As is discussed elsewhere in this book, National was seen to have performed well during its time in government and had a 'good track record' (Mills, chapter 20). It had the 'stronger team' (Key, chapter 5), run at its apex by a 'tight trio' of Key, English and Joyce (James, chapter 2). But perhaps the best indicators of voters' assessment of a government's performance, and therefore the likelihood of its re-election, are the various surveys that ask voters for their perception on whether the country is heading in the right direction. Polling conducted throughout 2014 leading up to the September election consistently found that over 60 per cent of New Zealanders believed the country was on the right track (Roy Morgan 2015). There was, in short, neither the anger nor the angst required for a change of government; on the contrary, the mood indicated widespread satisfaction with the direction the country was headed under National.

In sharp contrast, and as has been acknowledged by new Labour leader Andrew Little, the public saw Labour as divided, inward looking and ill-disciplined; its policies were too 'cluttered and complicated' and managed to turn the voter off (see Little, chapter 7). At the start of the campaign, Labour seemed to rebuff the Greens' attempt to work cooperatively, and Labour also ruled out governing with Internet Mana and the Māori Party. The sense that Labour was not ready to govern, combined with confusing messages about preferred coalition partners, fuelled voters' perception of a lack of viable alternative government.

This, more than anything, might explain the lack of effect of the charges of 'dirty politics'. It is the Prime Minister's contention that voters 'didn't care about' the issues raised (Key, chapter 5). This is likely an accurate assessment – for some voters. Equally though, it could be argued that some voters did care about the issues, but cared even more about electing a viable, stable government. For this latter group, the accusations made during the campaign could have longer-term consequences. The question of whether National abused its power – both in terms of 'dirty' political techniques and surveillance – may indeed be the cause of growing unease. In particular, disquiet about John Key's handling of these issues could, ultimately, do the most damage by hitting National where it is strongest – leadership and performance.

The election results: the major parties[1]

Three main factors that typically structure the vote – party performance, leadership and the economy – were all very strongly in National's favour; and the 2014 election results clearly reflect this. For National there was much to celebrate. Its seat count increased by one, from 59 in 2011 to 60 in 2014, and National was the party vote winner in 60 of 64 general electorates – up from 56 in 2011. This included an absolute majority (i.e., more than 50 per cent) in 33 electorates. National's percentage of the party vote increased in 31 of 71 electorates, with the largest increase being in New Lynn, the seat held by then Labour leader David Cunliffe (see Farrar 2014).[2] To balance this, National's percentage of the total party vote decreased – slightly – from 47.3 per cent in 2011 to 47 per cent in 2014, including a decreased share in 39 electorates. The one-seat gain in 2014 was due to National receiving a higher share of the effective vote on a higher wasted vote; parties that failed to cross the threshold accounted for 6.2 per cent of the 2014 vote, compared with 3.4 per cent in 2011 (see Electoral Commission 2014b).

In sharp contrast, Labour had little to celebrate. Its 2014 party vote dropped 2.3 per cent. The number of Labour electorate MPs increased by five, but the party was entitled to seven fewer list MPs, resulting in two fewer MPs overall. Labour's party vote share decreased in 65 of 71 electorates (Farrar 2014) and dropped to a 90-year low of 25.1 per cent (but still not as low as National's 20.5 per cent in 2002). Labour was the party vote winner in just 11 electorates (four general electorates and all seven Māori electorates), with an absolute majority in only three: the south Auckland electorates of Mängere, Manukau East and Manurewa.

Figure 22.1 shows the full extent of National's dominance over Labour in 2014. Using the number of party votes won by the two major parties in each of the 71 electorates, it ranks each electorate from best to worst for National and worst to best for Labour. The solid lines are the results of the 2014 election; the dashes are 2011. The longer lines are the general electorates; the shorter ones on the right are the Māori electorates.

In terms of the sheer number of party votes, National is up and Labour down across the general electorates. The Māori electorates defied this trend, Labour increasing its party vote on 2011's. Labour's best electorate in 2014 (Mängere, with 18,470 party votes) was not close to National's best (Tāmaki, with 24,091 party votes) and was lower than National's 30 best electorates. The 2014 crossover point in the general electorates, where Labour first outperforms National in terms of number of party votes, is well through the diagram in the general electorate ranked 60th (out of 64 for each party), making it Labour's fifth best versus National's fifth worst general electorate.

Labour's party vote decline was despite an overall increase in voter turnout; official turnout was 77.9 per cent, up from 74.2 per cent in 2011. Turnout based on estimated voting-age population (rather than on those enrolled) was also up on 2011 – from 69.6 per cent to 72 per cent in 2014 (Electoral Commission 2014c; Electoral Commission 2015, p. 46). This is another troubling outcome for Labour, as the party focused attention and resources on its voter mobilisation strategy. It hoped mobilising the 'missing million' voters who were absent in 2011 would be the key to a Labour victory in 2014 (see Salmond, chapter 18). The strategy made sense. Under MMP, because of the party vote (in which 'every vote counts'), elections can now be won and lost based on a party's ability to get out its vote. In recent elections between 20 and 30 per cent of New Zealand's voting-age population have not voted. Some are serial non-voters; the rest are better described as intermittent non-voters. Surveys have found these non-voters often favour Labour over National by a large margin (New Zealand Election Study; see Arseneau 2010).

Figure 22.1 The number of party votes for National (from best to worst) and for Labour (from worst to best) cast in electorates in the 2011 and 2014 New Zealand general elections

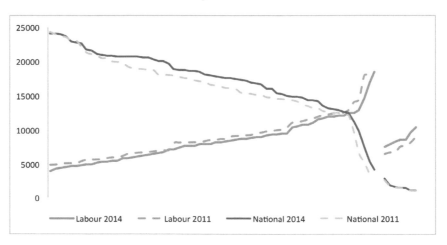

Source: Data from New Zealand Electoral Commission, www.electionresults.govt.nz

The importance of turnout is best viewed in Labour's 'heartland'. Table 22.1 first lists Labour's top ten electorates based on percentage of the party vote received and, second, the party's top ten electorates in order of number of party votes received. The highlighted electorates in both columns indicate electorates that are among New Zealand's ten lowest in terms of official voter turnout.

While the top three electorates in both columns remain unchanged, the rest are significantly different. This highlights the impact and importance of voter turnout. The seven Māori electorates and the three South Auckland seats are typically among Labour's best in terms of the percentage of the party vote, but they are also typically among the electorates with the lowest voter turnout as well. Given Labour's focus on voter mobilisation and the importance of these electorates to Labour, both the results and the voter turnout in these electorates tell an important story.

At first glance the story is a positive one for Labour in Māngere, Manukau East and Manurewa – the only electorates where Labour received an absolute majority of the party votes (something these electorates have done since 2002). In 2014, though, the percentage share of the party vote for Labour dropped, on average, around 4 per cent across these three electorates compared to a drop of 2.35 per cent nationally (see Farrar 2014); and while official voter turnout was up in Māngere, Manukau East, and Manurewa by around 2.5 per cent, this was less than the national average of 3.7 per cent (Electoral Commission 2014b).

Table 22.1: The Labour Party's top ten electorates in the 2014 New Zealand general election – by percentage of the party vote, and by the number of votes cast

Electorate	Labour's party vote as a percentage of all the votes cast	Electorate	The number of party votes cast for Labour
Māngere	67.56	Māngere	18,470
Manukau East	63.70	Manukau East	16,925
Manurewa	53.03	Manurewa	14,579
Ikaroa-Rāwhiti	48.09	Kelston	12,934
Hauraki-Waikato	46.50	Mana	12,601
Te Tai Hauāuru	42.23	Dunedin South	12,518
Kelston	42.13	Maungakiekie	12,199
Tāmaki Makaurau	40.84	Rimutaka	12,176
Waiariki	38.77	Mt Roskill	12,086
Te Tai Tonga	36.92	New Lynn	12,085

Highlighted electorates are among the country's ten lowest in terms of official voter turnout.
Source: Data from New Zealand Electoral Commission, www.electionresults.govt.nz

It was in the Māori electorates where Labour had cause for some celebration. Labour's percentage share of the party vote increased from 2011 in only five electorates; four of these were Māori electorates (Farrar 2014). On average across all seven Māori electorates Labour's share of the party vote increased by 3 per cent compared to a 2.8 per cent decline nationwide. The 6.9 per cent increase in the average turnout of enrolled voters in the Māori electorates also exceeded the nationwide increase of 3.7 per cent. Coupled with renewed success in the electorate vote – with six of the seven

Māori seats now held by Labour – these electorates provided Labour with some good news that could have long-term significance for the party. The Māori seats had long been a Labour stronghold, breached only by New Zealand First in 1993 and 1996 and the Māori Party and, briefly, Mana in the wake of the foreshore and seabed legislation. The 2014 result might signal Māori voters returning home to Labour – although most never left it in terms of the party vote – and provide Labour with a base from which to rebuild.

Labour's stronger showing in the electorate vote more generally was, perhaps, another bright spot in an otherwise rather dismal result. Although MMP elections are largely determined by the party vote, winning an electorate is still highly prized. The two major parties continue to see it as a point of honour, even though electorate contests for them have no effect on their total number of seats. Also important from an individual MP's perspective is the issue of incumbency. Under MMP the rate of turnover for list MPs is over twice that of electorate MPs (Vowles 2012). In 2014, for example, only one incumbent electorate MP was defeated – Hone Harawira, under circumstances particular to Te Tai Tokerau.[3] Electorates therefore provide a more secure bolt-hole for an incumbent MP and thus a better route to a sustainable parliamentary career.

It has been suggested (in reference to the 2011 election result) that Labour's percentage of the electorate vote is a truer indicator of the party's underlying support than its party vote. There were also claims that the rather lopsided 2014 result in terms of the number of Labour electorate versus list MPs elected (27 and 5 respectively) was symptomatic of the party's and leader's unpopularity. The analysis of split voting suggests caution on both counts. Supporters of smaller parties are far less likely to vote for their party's electorate candidate, if there is one (Aimer and Vowles 2004, p. 25). Instead, a majority of these split voters vote for the electorate candidate from the major party that is closest to them in terms of party ideology.

Table 22.2 uses Electoral Commission data to analyse Labour's electorate votes more closely. The data show that Labour party voters were the largest source of Labour's electorate votes – indeed, over 82 per cent gave Labour 'two-ticks'. This accounts for just under two-thirds of Labour's electorate vote. The rest came predominantly from Green and New Zealand First party voters. It is striking that more Green and New Zealand First party voters voted for a Labour electorate candidate than voted for a candidate from their own party. Thus Labour's greater success in the electorate vote is owed, in part, to votes from electors who gave their party votes not to Labour, but to probable or possible electoral allies for the Labour Party.

Table 22.2: Straight- and split-ticket voting statistics for the 2014 New Zealand general election

Straight-ticket voting: nationwide statistics	
National	83.28%
Labour	82.26%
Māori	49.75%
Internet Mana	42.42%
Conservative	40.28%
Green	34.61%
ACT	25.64%
New Zealand First	22.16%
United Future	9.06%

Party vote . . .	% electorate vote for Labour	Number of votes*
Labour	82.26	497,290
Green	47.39	121,962
New Zealand First	37.48	78,070
Internet Mana	27.50	9,375
United Future	22.06	1,166
Māori	19.54	6,223
ACT	13.42	2,240
Conservative	10.09	9,560
National	5.95	67,324

Source: Electoral Commission 2014. http://www.electionresults.govt.nz/electionresults_2014/ elect-splitvote-Overall.html
* Calculated by the authors, based on the percentage of votes (the exact numbers are not provided in the official results).

Interestingly, just over 67,000 party-voted National while voting for a Labour electorate candidate. The motivations behind this split voting are likely varied, making it impossible to say with certainty which vote is the 'sincere' vote – i.e., whether these voters are better described as National voters who supported a Labour candidate, or lapsed or latent Labour supporters who gave their party vote to National in 2014. In any case, it is the party vote that matters most in MMP elections and is therefore the truer indicator of support. A mark of Labour's demise in 2014 is revealed by viewing the commission's split-vote analysis through a different lens. While over 80 per cent of Labour party voters voted for a Labour electorate candidate, the reverse – Labour electorate voters supporting Labour in the party vote – was only true for 62 per cent. The main recipients of the remainder included the Greens (15 per cent), New Zealand First (9.7 per cent) and National (8.4 per cent). By contrast, roughly 87 per cent of people who voted for a National electorate candidate also party-voted National, and therein lies the important indicator of support in 2014.

The election results: the intermediate and smaller parties

In 2014, for the third election in a row, the combined party vote share of the intermediate and smaller parties increased (21 per cent, 25 per cent and 28 per cent in 2008, 2011 and 2014), as did their number of seats (21 seats in 2008, 28 seats in 2011 and 29 seats in 2014). However, this is still well below the support the smaller parties attracted in the first three elections under MMP, and must be set against the electoral dominance of National in 2014 (see Vowles 2014, pp. 32–33).

Despite a declared target of 15 per cent of the party vote, the Greens maintained a status quo 14 seats on a reduced party vote, despite a much weakened Labour Party. Mana – combined with the Internet Party in 2014 – had a slight rise in its percentage of party vote but at the expense of Hone Harawira's Te Tai Tokerau seat, leaving it below the threshold and out of Parliament. Meanwhile ACT, the Māori Party and United Future experienced the ongoing curse of smaller parties in government under MMP – without exception, smaller parties that are formally part of the government (whether in full coalition or through confidence and supply agreements) have lost party support in the following election. In 2014 all three government support parties lost party vote share, and in the case of the Māori Party it also lost two electorate seats, but with the compensation of its first ever party list MP.

The Conservative Party received 3.97 per cent of the party vote. Although this was an increase of 1.3 per cent on its 2011 vote share, with neither 5 per cent of the party vote nor an electorate MP it failed to win election to Parliament. The 2014 election was a positive one for New Zealand First, however, and a story of continued resurgence. New Zealand First increased its seat count by three and is the *only* current parliamentary party that was returned with an increased share of the party vote. This may be cold comfort for a party that hoped to be a 'kingmaker' but is instead sitting yet again on the crossbenches.

Table 22.3: Party vote change in the 2014 New Zealand general election by blocs

National-led governing bloc parties	
Party	Party vote percent change
National	−0.27
ACT	−0.38
Conservative	+1.32
Māori	−0.11
United Future	−0.38
TOTAL:	+0.18
Opposition and cross-bench parties	
Party	Party vote percent change
Green	-0.36
Labour	-2.35
Internet Mana	+0.34
New Zealand First	+2.07
TOTAL:	-0.30

Source: Data from New Zealand Electoral Commission, www.electionresults.govt.nz

The 2014 result is best viewed through a wide-angle lens – by stepping back and looking at the changes Parliament-wide. Table 22.3 shows the change in party votes from 2011 to 2014 with parties grouped together according to where they sit, sat (Mana) or were likely to sit (Conservatives)

in Parliament. It shows that while the 2014 election resulted in some shifting of seats between parties within the governing versus non-governing party groupings, the big picture is that of a status quo election, with the 51st Parliament looking remarkably similar to the 50th. The combined party vote for National and its three support parties decreased by 1.1 per cent from 2011; however, when the Conservative Party is added, the overall vote change for the National-led bloc is a negligible increase of 0.2 per cent. The non-governing bloc's party vote, including New Zealand First sitting on the crossbenches, dropped a miniscule 0.3 per cent.

The lack of change is most evident when looking at seats. Table 22.4 compares the two blocs' change in seats from 2011 to 2014. On the government side, National gained a seat while its support partner, the Māori Party, lost one – overall, no change. Similarly there was a reshuffling of seats on the other side of the House: Labour lost two seats and Mana one, while New Zealand First's tally increased by three.

Table 22.4: Seat change in the post-2014 New Zealand Parliament by blocs

National-led governing bloc parties	
Party	Change in number of seats in Parliament
National	+ 1
ACT	No change
Māori	– 1
United Future	No change
TOTAL:	No change
Opposition and cross-bench parties	
Party	Change in number of seats in Parliament
Labour	– 2
Green	No change
Mana	– 1
New Zealand First	+ 3
TOTAL:	No change

Source: Data from New Zealand Electoral Commission, www.electionresults.govt.nz

There are four other ways of examining the 2014 general election that emphasise the static nature of the results. The first is to look at the number of political parties in Parliament. Instead of simply counting the number of parties (and thus regarding large ones and tiny ones as if they were similar-sized entities), we have used a widely accepted formula to calculate the *effective* number of parliamentary parties (ENPP).[4] After special votes had been counted and the final allocation of seats had been made to the seven parties that cleared either MMP's 5 per cent party vote threshold or the one-seat waiver, the effective number of political parties in New Zealand's 51st Parliament was 2.96. This figure can be placed in perspective by examining Table 22.5, which shows the average ENPP data for three periods in New Zealand's post-war political history.

Table 22.5: The effective number of parliamentary parties in New Zealand, 1946–2014

Electoral period	Electoral system	ENPP*
1946–1993	First-past-the-post	1.96
1993–2002	MMP	3.66
2005–2014	MMP	2.93

*Effective number of parliamentary parties

It is immediately obvious that the effective number of parliamentary parties was wholly in line with what has been occurring in New Zealand since 2005. The introduction of MMP witnessed a significant rise in the effective number of parties in the House of Representatives. New Zealand's Parliament jumped from being effectively a two-party legislature under FPP during the period from 1946 to 1993 to being a three-and-a-half party system during the 1996 to 2002 period (i.e., the period following the first three MMP elections). However, there was then a distinctive shift in the pattern of parliamentary representation: each of the four MMP elections from 2005 through to and including 2014 has produced what is, in effect, a three-party Parliament.[5]

The second way in which the results of the 2014 election were wholly static is that only the two major parties – Labour and National – cleared both the 5 per cent and the one-electorate-seat electoral system thresholds. This was the fourth consecutive general election in which only the Labour and National parties were able to do so.

The fate of New Zealand's two intermediate-sized parties – that is, the Greens and New Zealand First – was the third way in which the 2014 election results were unchanged. Since 2005, whenever these two parties have qualified in a general election for a share of all the seats in Parliament, it has only been by crossing the 5 per cent party vote threshold. The Greens have not won an electorate seat in Parliament since the party's former co-leader, Jeanette Fitzsimons, lost the Coromandel electorate in 2002 – and that was also when New Zealand First last won a seat in a general election (namely, Tauranga).

The fourth indication of the static nature of the overall results is the fate of the country's minor parties. Whereas only one or (at most) two parties were represented in Parliament in the first three MMP elections solely because they scaled the one-seat threshold, ever since 2005 a minimum of three, and more often four, parties have fallen into that category. In the 2011 general election, four of the eight political parties in the House of Representatives – the ACT, Mana, Māori and United Future parties (accounting for a combined total of six MPs, 5 per cent of the total membership of the House) – were represented in Parliament despite their inability to cross MMP's 5 per cent party vote threshold. With the sole exception of Mana, these parties were returned to Parliament in 2014 because, once again, each managed to win an electorate seat, and as was the case three years earlier, neither ACT nor United Future qualified for any further seats in the House of Representatives.

Looking forward: the realities of MMP

The defining feature of the 2014 election result was thus an overall lack of change. While there were some swings and roundabouts within each bloc, the net change between the government and opposition was zero. Reconfiguring seats within the Labour-led opposition bloc did not threaten the government. By the same token, National gaining a seat did not expand the governing bloc because the Māori Party lost one. In this most fundamental sense then, neither the governing bloc nor the opposition bloc made any headway at all.

In MMP elections it can be misleading to look at results in terms of individual parties alone. The key to winning an election under MMP is to maximise the size of a potential governing bloc by attracting either more votes or more support partners – or both. This is made more complicated by certain MMP realities. First, the source of a vote gained is at least as, if not more, important than the vote itself. Second, votes taken from a rival party are more important than votes taken from a potential coalition partner. Third, the most useful vote of all for either Labour or National is one taken from its major party rival.

The importance of thinking in terms of blocs rather than individual parties is made clear by looking at the National Party. It is by far the largest party in Parliament, but is relatively short of viable support parties. This dates back to the 2005 election when, under the leadership of Don Brash, National nearly doubled its party vote – from 20.9 per cent in 2002 to 39.1 per cent in 2005. But this increase was largely at the expense of its then potential coalition partners: ACT, New Zealand First and United Future. Rather than significantly increasing the size of its potential governing bloc, National essentially consolidated votes from within the centre-right.

For the National Party to win in 2017 it needs to maintain or even grow the size of its bloc. This could be achieved by maximising its bloc's votes and/or by increasing the number of parties in its bloc. One way National could consolidate the strength of its parliamentary bloc would be to ensure that as many of its allies' votes as possible are not wasted. It is worth noting that if the votes cast for the political parties in 2014 had been exactly as they were with one small exception – namely, that the Conservative Party had won 4.0 per cent of the party votes rather than the 3.97 per cent it actually obtained – and if the seats in Parliament had been distributed in accordance with the Electoral Commission's 2012 recommendations, the Conservatives would have won five seats, National would have had three fewer seats, and Labour and the Greens would each have had one fewer seat. (These results would have been in a Parliament of 120 MPs, as the Electoral Commission had also proposed abolition of the provision for overhang MPs.) While such a result would have seen a reduced number of National MPs, at the same time National would have had a somewhat stronger bloc in Parliament, with 65 National, ACT, Conservative, Māori Party and United Future MPs. In these circumstances National could even have formed a 'minimum winning coalition' majority government with the Conservative Party alone (together the two parties would have had 62 seats in Parliament) – something National could not have done in these circumstances with any of the other parties in its bloc of electoral allies.

Looking ahead to 2017, though, a more likely scenario is that National will need to gather up a significant proportion of the votes that were cast for the Conservative Party at the last election but were wasted because the Conservatives neither crossed the 5 per cent threshold nor won one electorate. In this case, increasing National's vote at the expense of what was once a potential ally would make sense as those votes would actually count.

However, New Zealand First might also be well-positioned to plunder Conservative votes in 2017, and this draws attention to another – and potentially more significant – way that National could increase the size of its bloc in Parliament: that is, by bringing New Zealand First within the ambit of its governing coalition. Not only would any Conservative votes poached by New Zealand First be preserved for a National-led bloc, but, more importantly, this strategy would also substantially expand National's bloc at the expense of Labour and its allies. Unlike ACT, the Conservatives and the Greens – all of which can be viewed as 'captive' parties nearer the further ends of the left–right ideological spectrum than are the National and Labour parties, and thus highly unlikely to support a government of the opposite 'hue' – New Zealand First prides itself on being a potential 'kingmaker', positioning itself as a pivot which, depending on the outcome of any particular election, could determine the formation of a National-led or Labour-led government. This is precisely what New Zealand First did in 1996 when it chose to govern with National, and in 2005 when it cast its lot with Helen Clark's Labour-led government. There is strong evidence that New Zealand First is viewed by voters as a centre party, positioned between the two major parties on the left–right ideological spectrum (see Vowles 2014, p. 50) and regularly attracting voters from both left and right, including from both Labour and National in roughly equal measure (see, for example, Colmar Brunton 2014; Aimer and Vowles 2004, p. 23).

When considering National's options for the future, it should also be stressed that its post-2014 allies – all of which have been National's confidence and supply partners ever since the John Key-led government assumed office in November 2008 – are, without exception, the parliamentary minnows. None crossed the 5 per cent party vote threshold and each is present in Parliament only as the result of winning an electorate. An interesting question is whether these very small parties have a future or whether they are nearing the end of their life cycle. As we have already noted, Labour made significant gains in 2014 in the Māori electorates at the Māori Party's and Mana's expense.

Both ACT and United Future experienced a fall in party votes in 2014. At 0.7 per cent and 0.2 per cent respectively, they received a smaller share of the party vote than the Conservatives (3.97 per cent) and Internet Mana

(1.4 per cent). United Future (with 5,286 party votes) received roughly half the votes of the Aotearoa Legalise Cannabis Party (10,561) and was a mere 173 votes ahead of the Ban 1080 Party. Despite their poor performance in the race for party votes, ACT and United Future each won one electorate – David Seymour in Epsom and Peter Dunne in Ōhāriu – mainly due to accommodations with the National Party, because National expected these deals to be advantageous. However, this was, in fact, *not* the case. The data are quite clear: had neither Seymour nor Dunne won their seats (and had either National or Labour won those two electorates instead), National would have won 61 seats – an absolute majority in a Parliament with 120 members (120 because Dunne wouldn't have been present as an overhang MP). This therefore begs the question: is National likely to continue with accommodations in Epsom and Ōhāriu? And without these arrangements, are ACT and United Future likely to survive?

One other way for the National Party to increase its (and its bloc's) vote would be to continue to ensnare votes directly from Labour. However, this option is possibly the least likely to be fruitful in 2017 because the 2014 election may well prove to have been the high-water mark for National and, correspondingly, the low-water mark for Labour.

Turning the spotlight onto the political parties in the non-government bloc in the House of Representatives, it is clear that the Labour Party needs to increase its share of the vote. The most effective way to do so is for Labour to win the support of some of the people who voted National in 2014. Labour needs to hone the image and impact of its leaders and policies to entice voters directly from National. At the same time, the party needs to regain the support of people who have dropped out of the electoral process. Labour has long been aware of the importance of increasing turnout, especially in its electoral strongholds, but the party should bear in mind the fact that converting a National voter to the Labour cause is twice as effective as regaining the support of a former non-voter.

Both the Labour and the Green parties need to increase the number of party votes they win, but to do so at each other's expense is pointless. It would be cannibalising the bloc's support (in a manner akin to National's rise in 2005) instead of reinforcing the centre-left's overall support. This raises a major question for the Greens. Can the party grow without hurting its natural allies? To do so, the Greens will need to consider a repositioning that would allow it to be more of a pivotal party and less of a captive party. The Green Party's new leadership team has a unique opportunity to transform the party into a vital component in New Zealand's complex proportional representation party system. If it fails to do this, the Green Party faces the prospect of continuing irrelevance, destined to languish on the margins of power and influence.

New Zealand First was the sole party in Parliament to win an increased share of the party votes cast in the 2014 election. Nevertheless, the party is inextricably associated with its founder and leader, Winston Peters, and no matter how well the party is currently faring, it is also a fact that Winston Peters turned 70 in 2015. No politician is immortal, and it is therefore dangerous for any party to rely on a politician it regards as indispensible. In the very hour of its success New Zealand First needs to start considering a succession plan if the party is to have a long-term future. If the party survives – and this is looking ahead not just to 2017, but also to the 2020 and 2023 general elections – then there is little doubt that it could play a crucial role in choosing and working within the framework of future governments.

Conclusion

A viable government in waiting is one of the fundamental roles of the opposition, and under MMP this means not just the official opposition, but the wider grouping of parties who could govern together. The very different configuration of the National-led versus the Labour-led bloc is important. The centre-right has consolidated in National which, with 60 seats, is the dominant party in its governing bloc. The opposition/cross-benches is a more evenly spread three-party grouping; Labour is still clearly the major party, but with two robust potential support parties. What are the implications for elections to come?

Constitutionally there is no issue with the second largest party in Parliament forming and leading a government, even if it comes second by a reasonable margin. The fundamental principle of New Zealand's Westminster parliamentary system is that the government must maintain 'the confidence' of the House of Representatives. This means that the government is formed by the party or grouping of parties that can muster a working majority in Parliament. And while, so far, under MMP this has been led by the largest party in Parliament, it doesn't have to be.

There is, however, a difference between what is constitutional in terms of government formation and how the configuration is perceived by the voter. The perception of a strong, united bloc versus a more fractured one can have a significant impact on voting choice. This perception was something National effectively capitalised on in its rowing advertisements during the 2014 election campaign. National was depicted as a well-coordinated and unified rowing eight, while their opposition was portrayed as an ill-disciplined lot paddling a dinghy in circles. It effectively illustrated the potential 'risk' of a Labour–Green–Internet Mana–New Zealand First government.

In future elections, in order to look like a viable alternate government, it may not be enough simply for Labour to focus on getting its own house in order. Unless it can significantly consolidate the centre-left vote, Labour will need to work on clear messaging, cooperation and coordination with its support parties. The great unknown is whether New Zealand First and the Greens could work together in a Labour-led government, and if not, which is Labour's preferred partner?

This chapter began with the observation that election cycles have a certain rhythm, an ebb and flow of support for incumbent governments. While third term governments are not uncommon in New Zealand, it should be noted that fourth term governments are exceedingly rare. MMP election results, including seemingly one-sided affairs such as in 2014, are typically more finely balanced when viewed in overall perspective. Stepping back, the pattern is clear: the tide of an incumbent government does, inevitably, recede; and when it does, even a small shift in support can be decisive. Looking forward, that is the promise as well as the prospective peril for political parties contesting New Zealand's next general election.

EPILOGUE

23

LOOKING TOWARDS 2017

Jon Johansson

Leadership as adaptive response

New Zealand's continued economic and social development and its future well-being relies, in part, upon the quality of the country's leadership in fashioning a local response to the global opportunities and challenges that confront our small trading nation of 4.5 million people. This is adaptive work and it requires leadership, a collaboration, including leaders inside and outside of government. Projecting forward over the next three years, one can see that the accelerated technological revolution we are experiencing will continue to interact with a global economy that is still experiencing traumatic and uneven post-Global Financial Crisis responses from sovereign governments. Complicating concerns about economic prospects are the new threats to international stability that are themselves a maladaptive drain on scarce resources.

While comparatively speaking New Zealand seems well placed to respond to these challenges – with an abundance of water, strong global demand for our dairy, meat and seafood products, and a reputation for corruption-free, transparent government processes – continual adaptive work is required to overcome our still narrowly based national economy and an entrenched tail of under-achievement that serves as an anchor-weight on our progress. The bizarre nature of the 2014 election – where a wholly unequal contest and ephemeral diversions about peripheral distractions shielded New Zealanders from any substantive debate about how best to respond to these global forces – means that the quality of Prime Minister John Key's plans for the next three years passed largely untested through the campaign. A lack of electoral competition may be variously celebrated or bemoaned by party partisans but it cannot be good for New Zealanders, as any complacency or hubris risks impeding the country's ability to make the necessary adaptive responses. What, then, are the prospects for a more competitive election in 2017?

A fourth term?

After the 2011 election there was an 8.77 per cent gap between the centre-right National Party and the two major centre-left parties, Labour and the Greens. Three years on National is in an even more ascendant position. The gap between them has grown to 11.21 per cent and a party vote chasm has opened up between National and its historical rival, Labour – now a staggering 21.91 per cent. John Key commands New Zealand politics from a position of complete dominance. Analysis also shows that the rate of vote decay after their second terms, for four previous National governments, averaged 3.22 per cent. Yet at the 2014 election National's vote only declined by 0.27 per cent of the party vote, nearly three points less than its historical average. This underscores the current electoral strength of National, overwhelmingly based around the personal popularity of Prime Minister John Key and positive perceptions built upon his deputy and Minister of Finance Bill English's prudent management of the economy.

If this imbalance wasn't foreboding enough for opposition parties to contemplate as they consider post-election strategy, then another piece of electoral history further strengthens John Key's electoral outlook for 2017. What follows, then, is an analysis of the vote decay for the four previous three-term National governments in our political history, only one of which – Keith Holyoake's second National government, in 1969 – actually won a prized fourth term:

- Syd Holland/Keith Holyoake (1949–57): Vote loss between third win (1954) and fourth election (1957) (–0.01 per cent)
- Keith Holyoake (1960–72): Vote gain between third win (1966) and fourth election (1969) (+1.60 per cent)
- Robert Muldoon (1975–84): Vote loss between third win (1981) and fourth election (1984) (–2.90 per cent)
- Jim Bolger/Jenny Shipley (1990–99): Vote loss between third win (1996) and fourth election (1999) (–3.34 per cent)
- Average loss (1954–99): –1.16 per cent vote decay between third and fourth election

The outlier government in the sample was Jenny Shipley's unsuccessful bid for electoral success in 1999, to give her a mandate to build upon the three Bolger possessed before she replaced him in December 1997. Having effectively usurped the voters' choice, Shipley's inherited third term government was beset by a difficult economy and multiple scandals until it limped to the 1999 general election. Shipley's larger than average vote decline coincided with Labour leader Helen Clark's 10.55 per cent surge, which allowed her to comfortably win that election. Key's government is so far tracking more like Keith Holyoake's similarly cast, steady-as-she-goes, incrementalist government than Shipley's performance-challenged one, so the centre-left parties should as a matter of prudent strategy anticipate that John Key is likely to replicate his last two election performances and maintain National's level of voter support in the mid-40 per cent range.

The severity of the challenge facing Labour leader Andrew Little – now John Key's fifth Labour opponent (following Clark, Phil Goff, David Shearer and David Cunliffe)[1] – is highlighted by analysing how much the Labour Party's vote increased during elections when it won office from National. From this history an equally daunting picture emerges for a Labour Party facing its centenary in 2016:

- 1932–35: Michael Joseph Savage gained 12.1 per cent of the vote to lead Labour to its first term in office;
- 1954–57: Walter Nash gained 4.2 per cent of the vote to end the Holland-Holyoake tenure;
- 1969–72: Norman Kirk gained 4.2 per cent to defeat Holyoake's successor, Jack Marshall;
- 1981–84: David Lange gained 4.0 per cent to end the Muldoon years;
- 1996–99: Helen Clark gained 10.55 per cent of the vote to lead Labour to its first victory under MMP;
- 1932–99: Average electoral gain of 7.01 per cent to win office.

Even if Andrew Little matches the most historic rise in electoral fortunes ever achieved by a Labour Party leader – the 12.1 per cent surge of support that carried Savage and his party to victory in 1935 – Labour will still only have managed to lift its share of the vote to 37 per cent of the party vote. An average seven-point increase – a still not inconsiderable challenge against a popular opponent – would get Labour to only 32 per cent of the party vote. Crucially, in even its best case scenario, Labour would still need either the Greens or New Zealand First (or both) to credibly offer an alternative government to the voting public at the 2017 election. The challenge for parties on the centre-left is, therefore, to establish a path dependency in the minds of the New Zealand public, by starting to fix in the public mind the idea that parties on the centre-left will cooperate to form a government, while giving people some sense of the policies that such a collaboration would produce. Only by doing so can voters be given a genuine and viable opportunity for considering a credible alternative to John Key's National-led government.

The reason why creating a credible path to power is crucial to offering a choice at the next election is that the situational dynamic since 2008 is one that it is new to post-MMP politics. As things stand, one side of New Zealand's politics is hugely centralised around one dominant party, National, while the other is fragmented into three distinct parties (Labour, the Greens and New Zealand First) with areas in common as well as fundamental differences, identities and histories. Helen Clark's Labour Party faced no legitimacy issues in 1999 when it won office. It led National in all polls leading up to the final poll on election day. However, as discussed, even in the unlikely event that an Andrew Little-led Labour Party outperforms its own party's history, it will still likely finish behind National in 2017. Making a change in government, in such circumstances, is a challenge for a political culture still adapting from its deeply conditioned winner-takes-all mentality. Additionally, the literature on pre-coalition deals suggests that it is in more disproportional electoral systems than ours that such deals are made; or they occur when potential coalition partners are sufficiently similar ideologically, or when constituent parties to a pre-coalition deal are similarly sized (Golder 2006). So it seems there are barriers to, as well as opportunities for, Labour developing with the Greens an overarching cooperative framework that also provides for maximum competition. Perhaps, after seven MMP elections, we have indigenised it to the point where theories based on the European experience hold less relevance. Regardless, the onus is firmly on Labour and other opposition parties to adapt to their novel and difficult circumstances. Certainly, if they do not act differently from the past they can only expect to replicate their last term's failure.

Flagging new and unfinished business

In the first confidence and supply agreement signed between National and the Māori Party, agreement was reached to conduct a constitutional review. Subsequently a panel was constituted which heard over 5,000 submissions about aspects of New Zealand's constitutional architecture. The report, delivered in December 2013 without fanfare, and meeting with a predictably muted reaction, examined several constitutional and political dimensions, including, among other things, the size of Parliament; the length of the parliamentary term; the role of the Treaty of Waitangi in New Zealand's constitution; the Māori electoral option and the existence of Māori seats in both national and local politics; and the the idea of establishing a written constitution (Constitutional Advisory Panel 2013).

Interestingly, there was no explicit question about whether New Zealand should become a republic, although the panel did acknowledge that the role and functions of the Head of State and symbols of state were raised by some submitters. Pita Sharples, on behalf of the Māori Party, and Deputy Prime Minister Bill English, for the National Party, were the two Cabinet Ministers who led the constitutional review process. Prime Minister Key kept his distance, showing little interest in it. Afterwards, however, he suddenly announced – out of nowhere – that he wished to hold a referendum on whether New Zealand should have a new flag. His reasons included the current flag's close similarity to the Australian flag – long a source of potential embarrassment for every New Zealand and Australian Prime Minister forced to select one from an array of international flags – and he thought a new flag would provide better 'branding' (clarity) for New Zealand and its businesses. Key was quick to rule out any wider referendum on whether New Zealand should have its own Head of State – labelling himself the 'biggest constitutional monarchist you'll meet' (Fuatai 2015) – and he intends to hold a two-stage referendum process during the 2014–17 parliamentary term. The first stage will ask, by way of a postal ballot, which of four flag designs – to be designed by an expert panel, themselves chosen by an all-party group (excluding New Zealand First, which has declined to participate) – New Zealanders prefer. The second referendum will then put the flag that wins a preferential vote in the first referendum up against the nation's existing flag.

The flag referendum will be the second one that the Key government has initiated, and the fourth to have occurred during its terms in office. Its first, the referendum on electoral systems, saw the public support the retention of MMP at the 2011 election, on the understanding that an improved version of the system would emerge from a post-referendum review. The post-referendum review exercise was followed by Minister of Justice Judith Collins stating that party unanimity could not be achieved around widely supported changes recommended by the Electoral Commission in its review. These included a lowering of the electoral threshold from 5 to 4 per cent and removal of the one-seat coattailing provision that has caused most of the public disquiet about electoral politics under MMP. Opposition parties claimed that there was no good faith attempt to lead or consult by Collins, in contrast with what her predecessor Simon Power had achieved in winning Parliament's support when designing the MMP referendum process in the first place. The unfinished business from this first National-initiated referendum will remain until either public opinion or the government changes.

The second referendum, on the government's 'mixed ownership model' for the previously fully state-owned energy companies, was nominally a citizens-initiated one. In reality it was organised by the opposition parties and groups like the Council of Trade Unions and Grey Power on behalf of New Zealanders opposed to the government's privatisation policy. The result of the referendum – where voters rejected the government's policy by 67.3 per cent to 32.4 per cent, but on a low voter turnout of 45.1 per cent via postal ballot (Electoral Commission 2013) – was completely ignored by the government. All sides claimed victory but nothing changed, and the Prime Minister made much of the expense ($9 million) that the opposition had put on the taxpayer on a matter he felt his election win in 2011 had already mandated.

The idea for the flag referendum is a curious and somewhat surprising one. Any New Zealander with republican sensibilities would likely welcome it just to see the back of the Union Jack: 'free at last', if only on cloth. Many other New Zealanders, especially older and more conservative ones, and perhaps more recent migrants from the United Kingdom, will resist what they will see as an attempt to foist a flag change upon the country. The first phase of the flag referendum will also be a postal ballot, and the projected cost of both referendums is $26 million. If turnout does not significantly increase from the partial-asset-sales postal ballot in 2013, it will be difficult to argue that a flag design which wins on a preferential basis, in a low turnout postal ballot, is going to have any legitimacy for changing the national cloth New Zealanders proudly wave around the globe. There has also been no clamour from below for change. Indeed, the republican spirit has momentarily atrophied in New Zealand, and from a very low base. Every argument employed to promote a new flag does possess the double gift of also explaining how natural it would be to contemplate, as a country, whether New Zealand should have its own Head of State rather than a British monarch, residing in the UK, in that role. Many might think that a flag change flows logically from resolving this latter and more substantive question first. If it changed in this organic fashion there would be reason to celebrate a new flag because it would mean that the citizenry, drawn from every background, had unified around a new and widely shared idea of ourselves as New Zealanders. Successful or otherwise, the flag referendum will undoubtedly attach itself to John Key as part of his distinctive legacy.

Let's not forget

Christchurch has been one of the strongest contributors to New Zealand's economic 'rock star' status ever since the reconstruction phase of the earthquake recovery effort began to accelerate. Driven by insurance payouts in the billions and similarly massive infrastructure spending by central government, the Canterbury region is experiencing its own post-earthquake boom phase of strong economic activity. During election year, for instance, labour force participation and employment rates in Christchurch were comfortably ahead of the New Zealand average, and the unemployment rate was significantly lower (Ministry of Business, Innovation & Employment 2014). Without quite replicating Auckland, the Canterbury property market has been exceptionally buoyant, and sometimes in suburbs not accustomed to such appreciation. Given this context, it was hardly surprising that voters in the six Canterbury electorates solidified their support for the National Party from three years earlier. The margin between the electorate votes received by National Party candidates and their Labour opponents, across the seats – with four held by National (Christchurch Central, Ilam, Selwyn and Waimakariri) and two by Labour (Christchurch East and Port Hills) – went from 25,021 in National's favour in 2011 to 31,084 in 2014. The party vote margin – with National polling the most party votes in each of the six seats in 2014 – also increased, from 56,335 to 64,182 across the region. Even in Christchurch East, the electorate alongside Christchurch Central worst affected by earthquake damage, National easily won more party votes than Labour (Electoral Commission 2014b).

The Labour Party's failure to offer itself as a credible alternative to National is reflected in these voting statistics. Whatever the levels of ongoing frustration being experienced – with insurers; the Earthquake Commission (EQC); the Christchurch Earthquake Recovery Authority (CERA); the Christchurch City Council; the Minister for the Canterbury Earthquake Recovery, Gerry Brownlee; and the Key government more generally – Canterbury voters stuck firmly with the leadership they were used to, for both good and ill. They, more than voters elsewhere, needed stability and predictability. As an alternative, Labour offered them neither. Only National did.

Another positive development in Christchurch has been the infusion of foreign workers to help in the city's reconstruction. The greater ethnic diversity that workers from Southeast Asia, South America and the Pacific – as well from Australia, the United Kingdom and Western Europe – have brought with them has added a new vibrancy to a population that has been, historically, less diverse than its counterparts in the North Island.

While a new Christchurch slowly begins to emerge from the rubble of the old, recovery from a natural disaster like the Canterbury earthquakes in 2010 and 2011 is thought to take between five and ten years. In that sense the current economic growth somewhat obscures the longer term picture for the city. There remain real issues to be resolved: not least how to attract the private capital investment needed if the central city is going to be economically viable over the long haul, beyond the boom cycle it is currently experiencing. The true test of the Christchurch recovery will be how well it survives the next inevitable downturn. As the locus of economic activity has necessarily shifted away from the central city to Christchurch suburban satellites, the inertia of business owners, currently enjoying a bright 'new normal' in the suburbs, will be hard to shift.

Continual flooding in the low lying suburbs of St Albans and Mairehau, known as the Flockton Basin flood area, points to the earthquakes' ongoing, uncertain effects. Many people who were living in Christchurch and its surrounds – particularly those living in the eastern suburbs, badly affected hill suburbs, and northern beach communities – suffered life-changing disruption to their lives after the earthquakes. For them life has been a gruelling psychological exercise in coping with frustration and, sometimes, despair. These Cantabrians have, through their perseverance, already proven themselves a resilient and adaptable people. They've needed to be so because the rest of the country has slowly moved on from their initial wave(s) of sympathy and support, impatient for their own cities and regions and their needs, urgent or routine, to be addressed. Some New Zealanders, affected through kinship, have maintained links with their families in the Garden City, and some Cantabrians have themselves taken the opportunity caused by the earthquakes' disruption to live and work far from the scene of the disaster. For many New Zealanders, however, new demands replace old concerns for the emotional and physical welfare of Cantabrians.

For some who did stay in their wounded city, committed long term to seeing it through, their 'new normal' can also camouflage the psychosocial effects lingering from the original earthquakes and their aftermath. Post-traumatic stress reactions, anxiety, loneliness and other effects from the earthquakes can manifest in all sorts of anti-social behaviours and they can impact on an individual's work, relationships and finances. Not everyone can diagnose themselves either, and so these people can make bad choices for the wrong reasons, causing hurt and confusion to those around them. Many of these Cantabrians will need understanding from within their communities as they struggle to regain a sense of control over their lives.

The loss of a sense of self-efficacy can be debilitating, and so it has been for Cantabrians, facing a highly centralised power configuration that continues to drive the Christchurch reconstruction. From 1 February 2015, CERA has been run out of the Prime Minister's Office, although former prime minister Jenny Shipley is working as Advisory Board Chair with representatives of local and regional government, as well as community and business interests, to transition CERA's power back to these other agencies. Regional democracy, however, remains suspended, still in the hands of a small group of commissioners who report directly to Cabinet, although in October next year seven elected councillors with sit with six government appointed commissioners, before full democracy is restored in 2019. Mayor Bob Parker has given way to Mayor Lianne Dalziel, and CERA head, Roger Sutton, is gone, while Gerry Brownlee provides continuity as the Canterbury Earthquake Recovery Minister, supported by Associate Minister Nicky Wagner. The infusion of new leaders, picking up from those who bore the brunt of the initial crisis response, is a good thing, as different skills are required at different stages of the recovery process and new perspectives cannot but help to re-energise the decades-long reconstruction effort.

Leadership capital and duty of care

Prime Minister John Key has unprecedented reserves of leadership capital (see Bennister, t'Hart and Worthy 2014).[2] How he chooses to spend his capital during the next phase of his leadership will go a long way to shaping his immediate legacy once he does eventually choose to leave politics. The ongoing adaptive work required in Christchurch competes with Auckland's infrastructure demands as well as those of provincial regions. Deeper issues and challenges face the country, including New Zealand's economic competitiveness; the crippling society-wide effects of inequality; how New Zealanders relate to each other during a looming post-treaty settlement phase of politics; dramatic technological and demographic changes; and a generational transition that is happening, if only haphazardly. Confronting these issues (and others) will require significant leadership investment if Prime Minister Key is to leave the country in better shape than he found it.

The Prime Minister's duty of care is, as he appreciates, to all of New Zealand, not just to those citizens who voted for National at the 2014 election. Leadership scholar Ronald Heifitz (1994) underscored this truism when he described the leadership strategies that were guaranteed to impede necessary adaptive work: scapegoating; externalising perceived opponents; using distracting issues or events; and jumping to premature conclusions. Unity of purpose, however, alongside a leader fostering consensus through their public leadership so as to help facilitate necessary change – rather than relying solely on the exercise of power or personal prerogative – characterises an adaptive leadership response. New Zealand is too small, and the global challenges too large, for the country to drift. The challenge for Prime Minister John Key and his government is to offer leadership that is inclusive of all, tolerant of difference and dissent, and effective in advancing the nation's prosperity and prospects.

Preface

1   *The Twilight Zone* was a television programme (1959–64), its first season's opening words (narrated by the programme's creator, Rod Serling) describing 'the twilight zone' as a place situated 'between the pit of man's fears and the summit of his knowledge'. The outcome of a journey to 'the twilight zone' was seldom positive.

1. Stephen Levine, 'Moments of Truth: the 2014 New Zealand general election'

1   The opening passage for this chapter draws upon two Hollywood western movies: *The Man Who Shot Liberty Valance* (1962), depicting a legend in the making; and *High Noon* (1952), starring Gary Cooper and Grace Kelly – inspiration for the woman on New Zealand's coat of arms (Levine 2012). In each there is a resolute and determined individual – Jimmy Stewart (in *The Man Who Shot Liberty Valance*) and Gary Cooper (in *High Noon*) – facing a 'moment of truth' while a less heroic citizenry looks on.

2   The speech calling for a new New Zealand flag, given on 11 March 2014 at Victoria University of Wellington, declared the venue appropriate as one 'where ideas are encouraged and discussed'. Remarking that 'I have given careful thought to this', the Prime Minister gave his support to change – 'being respectful of our history does not lock us permanently in the past' – while promising that 'ultimately the decision on whether or not to change the flag will rest with New Zealanders themselves' (see Davison 2014 for the text and video of the speech). Following the 2014 election the government initiated procedures for referendums to be held about the flag and possible alternatives, introducing the New Zealand Flag Referendums Bill on 9 March 2015.

3   Prime Minister Robert Muldoon had promised New Zealanders 'New Zealand the way *you* want it', famously giving, as his prime ministerial goal, the objective of leaving New Zealand 'no worse off' than he found it.

4   *One News* 2014a. Responding to the hip-hop song, *New Zealand Herald* political correspondent John Armstrong wrote that the 2014 campaign had moved 'from dirty politics to the politics of the downright vulgar and vile' (Armstrong 2014c).

5   Maurice Williamson's May 2014 resignation as a minister (but not as an MP) came after it was revealed in April that he had phoned a senior police officer about criminal charges being faced by a businessman. It was also revealed that

Williamson had previously emailed the Minister of Internal Affairs (in November 2010) urging that the individual's immigration application 'be processed as fast as possible', with ministerial discretion subsequently being exercised to grant citizenship on 16 December 2010. The Prime Minister's response to Williamson's telephone call to the police was firm: 'Irrelevant of the purpose of the phone call, it's a very long establishment that MPs don't interfere with police. There's no grey in this; in the end there's a line. The moment he made the phone call he crossed the line. We are a government of high standards' (Manning, Savage and Davison 2014; Young 2014c; Kirk et al. 2014). Despite his resignation Williamson remained an electorate candidate (he was demoted to 35th place on National's party list). As for Judith Collins, the Prime Minister indicated in March that he was 'disappointed' (Radio New Zealand 2014h) with her behaviour in relation to the Oravida issue (see *3News* 2014e for an overview), which led to persistent parliamentary questioning and pressure from March through May, leading to his suggestion in May that she take a brief break from Parliament (Bennett and Young 2014). The subsequent adverse publicity, mid-campaign, in relation to the 'dirty politics' controversy (*One News* 2014d), made her departure inevitable.

6　These two matters – 'dirty politics' and the 'Moment of Truth' – are not elaborated upon in this chapter as they are extensively discussed by contributors elsewhere in this book. The latter – the 'Moment of Truth' broadcast – may be viewed at https://www.youtube.com/watch?v=Pbps1EwAW-0. The post-event media commentary was highly critical: see, for instance, Armstrong 2014d; Fisher 2014c.

7　Amanda Knox is an American woman who spent almost four years in prison in Italy accused of murder until being freed in 2011, when she returned to the United States.

8　See, for example, *Dominion Post*, 17 September, p. A10.

9　Gibson's selection as Labour's Rangitata candidate was summarised thus: 'Labour's first call for candidates in Rangitata attracted no suitable candidates and Gibson was nominated on a second attempt. Removing Gibson would create a vacancy six weeks from the election – not a good look' (O'Neill 2014). The Labour Party also saw fit to place Gibson on its party list, ranked (pointlessly) 56th. Following the election Gibson quit the party, suggesting that Cunliffe should 'jump in the lake', and observing that the campaign had taught him to 'be careful what you say' (Montgomerie 2014).

10　The moa is believed to have become extinct in the 15th century. At one time this large flightless bird was considered symbolic of New Zealand in a way that the much smaller kiwi (also flightless) is today, with 28 of 103 entries for New Zealand's coat of arms (1908) including images of the moa (Worthy 2015; Levine 2012).

11　The Prime Minister, when asked about Cunliffe's apology, said, 'It's a pretty silly comment from David Cunliffe. The problem isn't being a man, the problem is if you're an abusive man . . .' (Rutherford and Dennett 2014). The apology for being a man was followed, in due course, by some expression of regret (in effect, an apology) for having made it. Like many people, Labour's leader was more comfortable apologising for actions for which he was not responsible – as in his membership of the male segment of the species – than for those for which he was. These included his behaviour as a Labour MP during the period of David Shearer's leadership, when Cunliffe was described (by then Labour whip Chris Hipkins) of having 'openly undermined' Shearer's position (Trevett 2012).

12 Lole-Taylor was given a ranking of 16 (compared with eight in 2011) and was thus unable to return to Parliament on the New Zealand First list. She stood as a candidate in Manukau East, winning 1,847 votes (finishing third in the electorate race). Another of New Zealand First's 2011 'class', Brendan Horan, ranked sixth on the 2011 New Zealand First list, also experienced well-publicised difficulties. Expelled from the party in December 2012, he remained in Parliament as an independent, launching the NZ Independent Coalition Party in 2014 and participating (as a party leader) in a televised minor party leaders' debate. The party received 872 votes (0.04 per cent) at the 2014 election. Horan's candidacy in the Bay of Plenty electorate won him 1,281 votes, sufficient for a fifth-place finish (of seven candidates).

13 The idea was reminiscent of Labour prime minister Bill Rowling's offer of a 'baby bonus' at the 1975 general election, an initiative derided by opponents and the media, further undermining Labour's campaign. The election outcome saw a 'landslide' victory for National and its leader, Robert Muldoon.

14 On 19 September the Advertising Standards Authority, considering a Conservative Party pamphlet dealing with the topic of alcohol law reform, ruled that there had been a misleading claim which breached the Authority's code of ethics. While Winston Peters pointed out that the pamphlet had been misleading voters, Craig also claimed vindication, noting that the Authority had dismissed most of New Zealand First's claims (Radio New Zealand 2014e).

15 In 2012 Craig stated that New Zealand has the 'most promiscuous young women in the world' (3News 2012a).

16 Reagan's quip was made at a news conference on 12 August 1986 (http://www. reaganfoundation.org/reagan-quotes-detail.aspx?tx=2079). This was, as it happens, during the peak period of New Zealand's 'Rogernomics' experiment, initiated by Minister of Finance Roger Douglas, subsequently (in 1993) ACT's co-founder and party leader (1994–96).

17 Too late to save his political career, Banks was exonerated on 19 May 2015 of charges that had seen him lose ministerial office, resign ACT's leadership and exit from Parliament (see Stuff 2015).

18 Response to an Internet Mana video clip of a crowd cheering on Kim Dotcom, chanting 'f— John Key', was uniformly negative, becoming one of the reasons why, in Dotcom's words, his 'brand' became 'poison'. Labour MP Chris Hipkins,

responding to the clip, called Dotcom a 'thug': 'It's not political leadership. It's thuggery and megalomania intertwined' (Cheng 2014c; O'Brien 2014c).

19 The denouement for the Internet Mana election launch featured Kim Dotcom running from the building in which it occurred as journalists were sworn at by the party's press secretary, former Alliance MP (1996–99) Pam Corkery (see, for example, Sabin 2014).

20 Jimmy Breslin's popular novel *The Gang That Couldn't Shoot Straight* – published in 1969 and released as a film two years later – is a comical portrayal of an inept and bumbling group of gangsters, a mob not to be taken too seriously despite its tough talk and pretensions. As a result, the phrase – 'the gang that couldn't shoot straight' – is available to sum up any group of less-than-competent characters.

21 The Civilian Party won 1,096 votes (0.05 per cent of the vote). A referendum on Hamilton's separation would almost certainly do better. The Civilian Party won 18 votes in Hamilton West and 23 votes in Hamilton East. See *3News* (2014c) for an interview with its party leader, Ben Uffindell.

22 The Prime Minister watched the results come in at his home in Parnell, Auckland, before going to the Auckland Events Centre, arriving around 11.30 pm. David Cunliffe was in Herne Bay, in Auckland, before proceeding to the New Lynn Community Centre. Winston Peters, also in Auckland, attended a party function at the 'Spencer on Byron' hotel in Takapuna. The Greens took in election night at Hopetoun Alpha, an historic building in central Auckland. Te Ururoa Flavell spent the evening at his marae in Ngongotaha near Rotorua in his Waiariki electorate. Peter Dunne voted in Wellington and attended an election-night function at the Khandallah Bowling Club. The Internet Mana Party's election evening event was held at The Cloud on Auckland's waterfront. The Conservatives held their election night event at the North Shore Golf Club in Albany. The ACT Party's election function was held in Auckland. Hone Harawira followed the results at election night headquarters at Awanui, near Kaitaia.

23 For more detailed discussion of election results (and MPs' backgrounds), see Parliamentary Library (2015). For a further overview of the 2014 election, see Levine and Roberts (2015).

24 Labour's 27 electorate MPs included eight MPs absent from the 2014 party list for one reason or another: incumbent MPs Clare Curran, Ruth Dyson, Kris Faafoi, Trevor Mallard and Rino Tirikatene; new MPs Peeni Henare and Adrian Rurawhe; and returning MP Stuart Nash.

25 See Appendix 4 in the 2011 election book (Johansson and Levine 2012) and in this book for the membership of Parliament before and after the 2014 election. The difference between the 2014 and 2011 Parliaments is to be found not only in the new MPs but also, of course, in the MPs no longer present. Cabinet minister Tony Ryall's February announcement of his retirement from Parliament at the 2014 election added to the significant number of National MPs stating their decision to leave, several having already departed during the

2011–14 term: Lockwood Smith (Speaker; list), replaced in February 2013 by Aaron Gilmore; Gilmore, replaced in May 2013 by Claudette Hauiti; Jackie Blue (list), replaced in May 2013 by Paul Foster-Bell; and Katrina Shanks (list), replaced in January 2014 by Joanne Hayes. National MPs not returning for the 2014–17 term included Shane Ardern, Chris Auchinvole, Cam Calder, Claudette Hauiti, John Hayes, Phil Heatley, Tau Henare, Paul Hutchison, Colin King (challenged at selection), Eric Roy, Tony Ryall, Chris Tremain and Kate Wilkinson. A significant departure on the Labour side was front-bench Labour MP Shane Jones, who resigned from Parliament in April 2014 to take a position as the government's Pacific Economic Ambassador. His exit was an embarrassment for Labour, reflecting a lack of confidence in Labour's election prospects as well as recognition that the former leadership contender's outlook was not entirely welcome in the party's caucus. Other retirements at the end of the 2011–14 Parliament term were Darien Fenton, Rajen Prasad and Ross Robertson (Labour); Holly Walker (Greens); and Pita Sharples and Tariana Turia (Māori Party).

26 At the beginning of its third term (following the 2005 election) Labour's caucus of 50 MPs included only four new MPs (Darien Fenton, Shane Jones, Sue Moroney and Maryan Street); a fifth, Moana Mackey, replaced Graham Kelly (list) in July 2003 when he was appointed High Commissioner to Canada. The appointment of Jonathan Hunt (Speaker; list) as High Commissioner to the United Kingdom led to his replacement in April 2005 by Lesley Soper, who served out the 2005 term (and was not returned to Parliament at the 2005 election).

27 While 12 women were elected as Labour MPs at the 2011 election – the same number as in 2014 – prior to the 2014 election there were 14 women in Labour's caucus, Carol Beaumont having replaced Charles Chauvel (list) in March 2013 and Meka Whaitiri succeeding Parekura Horomia (winning the 29 June 2013 by-election). Other 2011–14 replacements in Labour's caucus – Poto Williams for Lianne Dalziel (30 November 2013 by-election) and Kelvin Davis for Shane Jones (list) in May 2014 – had no effect on gender numbers. Overall, 38 women were elected to Parliament in 2014, representing 31 per cent of the membership, a slight decline from 2011 (39, 32 per cent) and from 2008 (41, 34 per cent, the highest number thus far). The number of women in National's parliamentary caucus, under John Key, remained the largest of any party, having first surpassed Labour in 2008. In 1996 National's caucus included eight women (of 44 MPs); in 1999, nine (of 39 MPs); in 2002, six (of 27 MPs); in 2005, 12 (of 48 MPs); in 2008 – when Key first led National to victory – 17 (of 58 MPs); in 2011, 15 (of 59 MPs); and in 2014, 16 (of 60 MPs). Following the 2014 election, in addition to National (16) and Labour (12), the 38 women MPs came from the Greens (seven), New Zealand First (two) and the Māori Party (one). The number of women MPs rose by one, to 39, with the entrance of Ria Bond as a list MP when Winston Peters became MP for Northland.

28 Of course, Labour could have achieved success in moving towards its goal of 45 per cent women in its parliamentary caucus had fewer male MPs been elected. A caucus of 30 MPs – without Trevor Mallard (whose 709-vote margin over Chris Bishop was the smallest majority of any Labour MP) and Andrew Little (based on a slight reduction in Labour's party vote) – would have moved the total up to 40 per cent.

29 All voting figures given in this chapter are from data posted on the website of the New Zealand Electoral Commission (available at http://www.electionresults. govt.nz/).

30 Beyer gained publicity during the campaign with critical comments about the party and Kim Dotcom, expressing displeasure that the campaign's focus was solely on the party vote rather than on her quixotic quest at winning the Labour-held seat of Te Tai Tonga. She had agreed to be a candidate, she said, having been impressed by Kim Dotcom at Mana's annual meeting in 2014. 'I've travelled with him since. . . . The most telling thing was spending three hours on the ferry crossing with him. Really, I found him to be a distant person who was always utterly consumed in his iPad.' Beyer noted: 'I sort of have an intuition sometimes about people . . . there's something about him I just don't trust' (Goodwin 2014).

31 The observation, traditionally attributed to King Solomon, is found in *Ecclesiastes* (*Kohelet* in Hebrew), verse 10:8.

32 A National candidate, Brett Hudson, remained on the ballot (receiving 16.6 per cent of the vote) notwithstanding the 'signal' from John Key for National voters to give their electorate vote to Dunne. The Labour candidate, Virginia Andersen, received 34.9 per cent of the vote, the Greens' Tane Woodley 7.5 per cent. Dunne's first election to Parliament, in 1984, likewise benefited from a divided opposition as, standing for Labour, he unseated incumbent National MP (and Cabinet minister) Hugh Templeton, with the National vote (in the Ohariu electorate) split between Templeton and New Zealand Party leader/candidate Bob Jones. Dunne's share of the vote was 37.9 per cent, the lowest proportion of any successful candidate at that election (Levine and Roberts 1987, p. 4).

33 Of course, what the Spanish actually call it is '*el momento de la verdad*'.

34 Leaving little to chance, it should be noted that Neil Armstrong was the first human being to walk on the moon – the first person ever to walk anywhere other than on the earth – having done so on 20 July 1969 as part of the historic Apollo 11 mission. If there was ever an event about which it could be said 'the whole world is watching' it was this one.

35 Peters' observation about 'ingratitude' was made in his talk to the 3 December 2014 post-election conference.

36 It might, of course, be noted that National's substantial lead in the party vote still amounted to only 47 per cent of the vote: 53 per cent of the participating electorate voted against the National Party. In another system – the United States – that level of support (47 per cent) was sufficient to leave Republican presidential

candidate Mitt Romney soundly defeated by Barack Obama in 2012.

37 For a New Zealand prime minister to appeal for votes by urging New Zealanders to opt for steak rather than New Zealand lamb – an 'iconic' feature of the country's lifestyle and economy – must represent some sort of cultural 'turning point'.

38 See chapter 4, by Stephen Church, on the post-election confidence and supply discussions and arrangements. The agreements themselves are provided in Appendices 1–3, with the post-election ministry listed in Appendix 5.

39 The other Labour leadership contenders were MPs David Parker and Nanaia Mahuta. The detailed vote results – by voting group (caucus, party and affiliates) and by round (1, 2 and 3, in order to produce a majority result for a candidate) – are given in Trevett (2014i). Labour's president Moira Coatsworth also resigned post-election, standing down in mid-December.

40 The three maiden speeches cited may be read (and viewed) at the official parliamentary website, http://www.parliament.nz. The first speeches made by the 21 other new MPs – the 'class of 2014' – likewise provide insight into their backgrounds, values and goals as they begin their parliamentary careers, and can be accessed at the parliamentary website.

41 The statement, though generally attributed to Lincoln, may actually have been made about him, as his approach to power and leadership in exceptionally testing circumstances displayed an uncommon mix of determination, decisiveness and humility.

2. Colin James, 'Election in a bubble'

1   In practice, it proved difficult to determine which measure of money supply to use; central bankers used inflation as a proxy. This led United States Federal Reserve Chairman Alan Greenspan to run a policy which greatly expanded the money supply by targeting above-zero inflation at a time when strong global forces and technological innovation were reducing manufacturing and some services' costs and prices. This was to become an underlying factor in the global financial crisis of 2007–08.

2   The post-1984 government also ended sports contact with apartheid South Africa, banned nuclear warships from New Zealand waters, thereby adopting an independent foreign policy, and made constitutional changes, including some legislative recognition for the Treaty of Waitangi.

3   Martin Wolf was a 'cheerleader' on behalf of Friedmanite market-liberalism; his April 2014 *Financial Times* column is one of a number in the author's files.

4   An illustration of how trust works in politics is that Australian prime minister John Howard was re-elected in 2004 despite being exposed as having larded the facts in the 2001 campaign over an incident involving would-be illegal immigrants.

5   Labour initially tried to stay out of the controversy so as to leave all the focus on
    Key and National.

3. Jon Johansson, 'Leadership in a vacuum: Campaign '14 and the limits of "followership"'

1   'Dirty Politics' refers to the book by the same name, authored by investigative
    journalist Nicky Hager. Its claims about the National Party's attack politics
    dominated the pre-campaign period. *Dirty Politics* was published some ten days
    before the official campaign period, but spilled into the campaign proper after
    the Prime Minister refused to answer any of its significant claims. The 'Moment
    of Truth' was supposed to reveal John Key's collusion with Warner Brothers in
    offering a preferential deal to resolve an industrial dispute involving moviemaker
    Peter Jackson and his *Hobbit* movies. The email that Kim Dotcom revealed,
    actually before the moment of truth, was soon dismissed as a fake and the actual
    'Moment of Truth' was the claims made by Julian Assange, Edward Snowden and
    Glenn Greenwald that John Key had lied to New Zealanders about the degree of
    mass surveillance of them that was allegedly taking place.

2   National had a 55 per cent probability of winning the 2017 general election in
    late January 2015 (see iPredict 2015).

3   The selectorate for the Labour leadership contests is split 40/40/20 per cent
    between the caucus membership, the party membership, and Labour's affiliates
    (basically unions). In the 2013 contest between David Cunliffe, Grant Robertson
    and Shane Jones, Cunliffe won the leadership with fulsome backing from
    members and affiliates despite receiving only 32.35 per cent support from his
    caucus, revealing their skepticism about their colleague's abilities. In the 2014
    contest, Andrew Little sneaked in by 1 per cent over rival Grant Robertson.
    Little received less support than Robertson from both the caucus and the
    party membership, securing the top job on the back of overwhelming support
    from the affiliates. This was not least because the value of each selectorate was
    disproportionate, with the value of an ordinary member's vote less than that of a
    caucus member which, in turn, was valued less than that of a union delegate (see
    Satherly 2014).

4   The problem with the 40 per cent party vote goal, however appropriate or
    necessary it was thought to be as a long term objective for Labour, was that
    history made Jones' call strategically risible in the situation in which it was
    made, although it was also adopted quickly by Labour's other leadership
    contenders – they could not afford to be seen to be less ambitious, which had
    the effect of compounding Jones' error – and by National-sympathetic writers
    such as John Roughan (2014, p. 225). However, a Michael Joseph Savage-led
    Labour gained 12.1 per cent of the vote to win in 1935, and Labour added 10.55
    per cent under Helen Clark to win in 1999. Even if under David Shearer or

David Cunliffe's leadership – judged as abject failures by, variously, their own members or by the voting public, and therefore judged not to be in the rarified leadership class occupied by Savage and Clark – Labour had been able to match its two best historical performances, against a far more popular leader, John Key, than either a reluctant George Forbes (in 1935) or a discredited Jenny Shipley-led National government in 1999, it still would not have achieved its 40 per cent objective.

5   The writer was shown private polling which revealed that 41 per cent of voters who considered voting for the Greens, but who ultimately gave their party vote to Labour, chose 'strategic voting' as their primary reason for their final vote, with the inference being that these voters were voting to prevent an even greater electoral loss by Labour.

6   The Prime Minister explained his new trust in Winston Peters by referencing his son Max's markedly different visual appearance from 2008 – when Max was 12 years old and Key regarded Peters as poison. Max's ageing seems to have had only this very specific effect on the Prime Minister; other policies, such as lifting the retirement age or giving New Zealand a republic, have not been affected by Max's maturing into adulthood.

7   During the first term National lost MPs Richard Worth, Pansy Wong, Phil Heatley and David Garrett (ACT). During its second term, sackings or resignations of one type or another gathered pace, encompassing MPs Aaron Gilmore, Maurice Williamson, Kate Wilkinson (from the Labour portfolio), Nick Smith, Judith Collins, Gerry Brownlee (from the Transport portfolio), Peter Dunne (United Future) and John Banks (ACT). Backbench MP Mike Sabin resigned from Parliament on 30 January 2015, bringing the total to 13.

8   The first Citizens Initiated Referendum, in 1995, concerned staffing levels for firemen, while the fourth, held in 2009, concerned parents smacking their children.

4. Stephen Church, 'In other news: forming a government in 2014'

1   One reason for single party majority governments having been the norm is that votes were only cast at an electorate level under first-past-the-post. If the candidate for that party did not win the seat, votes cast for that candidate had no impact on the overall allocation of seats in Parliament or the composition of the government. This tended to limit the number of parties represented in Parliament.

2   Votes are more likely to be of instrumental (i.e., as a means to achieve office/policy ends) than intrinsic value. In addition to satisfying short-term office/policy goals, decisions about which party to work with after an election may also be influenced by the anticipated impact on longer term electoral support.

3   Radio New Zealand 2014i. This represented a hardening of Cunliffe's stance of the previous month, when he had said it was highly unlikely that Internet Mana MPs would be ministers in a government he led (Trevett 2014k).

4   This echoed an attempt by the Alliance in 1996 to make the negotiation of a pre-
     election agreement a condition of its post-election participation in government,
     which was also rejected by Labour.

5   The year before the 2014 election Winston Peters rated the chances of being part
     of a coalition that would include the Greens as 'extremely remote' (Moore 2013).

6   Rutherford and Small 2014a. New Zealand First had also ruled out working with
     the Māori Party as it was 'race-based'. Initially, Peters did not consider that the
     Mana Party fit this category (Young 2014e), but he later ruled them out on the
     same basis (Ryan 2014).

7   In 2011, little more than two weeks before the election, John Key and ACT's
     Epsom candidate John Banks met for a highly public 'cup of tea', intended to
     send a message to Epsom voters that Key wanted them to vote for Banks with
     their electorate vote while giving National their party vote. The event, viewed
     by members of the media, unravelled when the conversation between Key and
     Banks was recorded by a cameraman, with the recorded comments leading to
     accusations and controversy, the entire affair making the 'cup of tea' approach a
     less attractive way of communicating to voters.

8   Even if the minor party in such circumstances does not win additional seats in
     this way, their electorate seat will be a net addition to the total number the major
     party can rely upon. These types of accommodations may also be motivated
     by a desire to prevent major party supporters from giving their party vote to
     a potential partner in the hope of getting them over the 5 per cent threshold.
     Despite some understandable squeamishness about such accommodations, they
     arise whenever there are electoral barriers to entry, and so were also a feature of
     the first-past-the-post system. For example, in the 1931 and 1935 elections the
     Reform and United parties attempted, with varying success, to only put up a
     single 'Coalition' candidate from either party in each electorate to avoid splitting
     the vote. This proved to be an important step towards the formation of a single
     National Party in 1936. A similar rationale lay behind the coagulation of left-
     wing independents and parties into the New Zealand Labour Party in 1916.
     More recently, the formation of the Alliance, comprising the New Labour, Green,
     Mana Motuhake, Democrat and Liberal parties, was also an attempt to overcome
     the high threshold for representation under first-past-the-post through a similar
     'restraint of trade' on contesting the same electorates. The Alliance was formed
     in 1991 to improve the chances that one of its constituent parties would win an
     electorate seat by agreeing that the other member parties would stand aside. In
     2014 the temporary merging of the Mana and Internet parties, in an attempt to
     bring in list MPs from both parties by winning the seat of Te Tai Tokerau, was yet
     another example of an electoral accommodation.

9   This was National's approach towards Richard Prebble's bid to win Wellington
     Central for ACT in 1996, and was replicated by Labour in 1999 in favour of the
     Green co-leader Jeanette Fitzsimons in the seat of Coromandel.

10 For example, the resignation of the MP for Northland, Mike Sabin, on 30 January 2015, temporarily reduced National's caucus to 59, confirmed by the results of the 28 March 2015 by-election (in which National lost the seat to New Zealand First).

11 Bennett 2014g. Key later singled out the Māori Party for bringing 'an important dimension to this Government over the past six years' (Bennett 2014h), and that he had 'no doubt that we New Zealanders are better off because of it' (*Stuff* 2014b).

12 This was, at least in part, an attempt to reconcile New Zealand First's acceptance of a ministerial post with its leader's pledge in the prelude to the election that it would support the largest party but not seek 'the baubles of office'.

13 This echoes the terms of the 'enhanced cooperation' agreement between Labour and the Greens in 2005, which saw two Green MPs become non-executive government spokespeople (alongside the relevant minister) on selected issues (e.g., energy conservation and efficiency). Under both arrangements the spokeperson/undersecretary has access to official papers and advice but is not directly accountable to Parliament (e.g., through Question Time).

14 Even so, when I ran ACT's 2011 and 2014 agreements, minus specific policy statements, through an online tool for checking plagiarism, 84 per cent of the words still matched.

15 Rutherford 2014e. At the time of writing, the possibility that National might lose the Northland by-election (see note 10 above), keeping its caucus at 59 rather than restoring it to 60, led United Future leader Peter Dunne to raise the prospect of seeking further concessions from National (Davison 2015).

16 *Stuff* 2014b. See this book's Appendices 1–3 for the text of the three 'confidence and supply' agreements.

8. Tim Barnett and David Talbot, 'The 2014 Labour campaign: a party perspective'

1 In June 2014 David Cunliffe faced calls to resign after an 11-year-old letter that he signed, when supporting Donghua Liu's residency application, was published by the *New Zealand Herald* following Cunliffe's denial of any connection with Donghua Liu (Savage 2014a) [eds.].

2 National's 'Cabinet Club' formed part of its fundraising network, with donors gaining access to National MPs and ministers (O'Brien 2014b) [eds.].

10. Winston Peters, 'Losing an "unloseable" election'

1 During the Northland by-election campaign Prime Minister John Key, seeking to assist National's candidate, repeatedly missed a nail with his hammer while trying to erect a placard. His serial 'nail fail' efforts, captured on camera, were reportedly viewed more than a million times on an image-sharing internet site over a period of only a few days. The Prime Minister subsequently admitted to having less than perfect 'home handyman' skills (*New Zealand Herald* 2015) [eds.].

2   New Zealand First leader Winston Peters, already a list MP, stood as a candidate
     in the Northland by-election, brought about by the resignation from Parliament
     of National MP Mike Sabin (who won the seat in 2011 and was re-elected in 2014,
     with majorities of 11,362 and 9,300 over Labour's candidate; New Zealand First
     did not stand a candidate in the electorate in 2011 or 2014). In the by-election,
     Peters won 16,089 votes; National candidate Mark Osborne received 11,648
     votes; Labour's candidate Willow-Jean Prime won 1,380 votes (see Electoral
     Commission website for further details). As a result, Peters became the MP for
     Northland and New Zealand First increased its parliamentary representation by
     one as Ria Bond, ranked 12th on the 2014 party list, entered Parliament as a new
     list MP [eds.].

11. Te Ururoa Flavell, 'Tu Māori Mai: the Māori Party campaign'

1   Some of the Māori language used in this chapter may be understood as follows:
     hikoi – march; rohe – a Māori tribal territory (or its boundaries); kaupapa –
     policies or plans; whānau – family (extended family); tamariki – children; hui – a
     gathering or meeting; marae – encompasses the complex surrounding a meeting
     house; runanga – governing council/administrative group; whakatauakī – Māori
     proverb; hapū – sub-tribe; iwi – tribe; rangatira – high-ranking and respected
     traditional leaders; kanohi kitea – to be seen in the community; mokopuna
     – grandchildren/descendants; waiata – a song; te reo – the Māori language;
     Whānau Ora – family health, referring to a government programme agreed to
     between the National Party and the Māori Party (following the 2008 election,
     and continued subsequently) for a family-oriented health programme shaped by
     Māori values; Te Wero – the challenge [eds].

15. Corin Higgs, 'Bloggers, bottom feeders and disruption: technology and the 2014 general election campaign'

1   'Slacktavism' – not a complimentary term – describes people who take politically
     motivated 'actions' – such as changing their Facebook picture in support of a
     cause – which require little effort (and often have little practical effect). Twitter
     'trolls' is a term referring to people who use Twitter to engage in abuse and
     harassment [eds.].

16. Nicola Kean, '#Peakcray: Making current affairs television during the strangest election in New Zealand's history'

1   Mercifully, it was also International Talk Like a Pirate Day so there was some
     justification.
2   The ministerial debate rule was the subject of substantial discussion between *The
     Nation* and the Prime Minister's Office. The Prime Minister's Office argued the

rule was first instituted during the previous Labour government, but *The Nation* believes the rule has become much stricter under the Key government.

3   *The Nation* did do two OBs later in the year, one during the Labour leadership contest and the other for the final show of the year. Both required hiring an extra producer and weeks of planning – not something we could arrange with 12 hours' notice.

4   *The Hollow Men* (Hager 2006), based on emails and National Party documents, was an exposé of National Party behaviour during the 2005 general election, with a particular focus on party leader Don Brash. The popularity of the book was such that it was subsequently adapted by Dean Parker to become a popular and critically well-received play [eds].

5   That was one of two times we did an extra edition in 2014. The other was when Labour leader David Cunliffe resigned on a Saturday afternoon following the election, triggering a leadership primary.

6   That excludes one-on-one interviews that included policy discussion along with questioning about other issues, such as possible coalition arrangements.

7   Patrick Gower had suffered a detached retina ten days out from the election. He had surgery and was presenting *The Nation* three days later, reading the autocue with his good eye.

17. Kate McMillan, 'Black ops, glove puppets and textual relations: the media's campaign 2014'

1   'Churnalism' is a term used to refer to the practice of 'churning' out news stories based largely on public relations press releases (Davies 2009).

2   For detailed content analysis of the campaign coverage see Bahador and Boyd 2015.

3   Cheng 2014a. The subsequent inquiry found no evidence that Collins 'inappropriately sought or received information about Feeley or any other party' (Chisholm 2014, p. 4).

4   A subsequent attempt by Slater to have all the leaked materials returned to him was unsuccessful (Daly 2014).

5   One inquiry investigated whether the New Zealand Security Intelligence Service (NZSIS) had acted properly in the disclosure of information about a meeting between the Director of the NZSIS, Dr Warren Tucker, and then Leader of the Opposition, Phil Goff. The inquiry found that the documents released to Slater under the OIA were incomplete, inaccurate and misleading, and led to 'misplaced criticism of the then-Leader of the Opposition, Phil Goff.' For the final report of that inquiry, see Gwyn 2014. The second inquiry (Chisholm 2014) was into the allegations that Judith Collins had acted improperly in relation to the Head of the Serious Fraud Office.

6   Quilliam 2014. The TVNZ report found no evidence of bias in the content for which Mr Taurima was responsible (McAnulty, Francis and Price 2014).

18. Rob Salmond, 'Voter targeting: developments in 2014'

1   Some microtargeting information Labour developed for the 2014 cycle is excluded from the discussion as Labour wants to protect its most sensitive intellectual property for future campaigns.

2   The main exception to this rule was the fundraising campaign, which was targeted at strong supporters.

3   Of course, mistakes happen in the other direction, too. A decision to campaign to 'retired women' might miss other women who are not yet 65 but who otherwise behave just as a retired woman does.

4   In this regard, parents who choose 100 per cent androgynous names like 'Taylor Kelly Smith' for their children do little to endear themselves to their local political parties.

5   Some may notice that this message would actually turn people off voting if rational choice explanations of voter turnout are to be believed. But rational choice models of turnout are, in general, spectacularly inaccurate (Green and Shapiro 1994), making the effectiveness of the 'all your friends are doing it too' mobilisation approach rather less surprising.

6   Specific details in this example are deliberately incorrect; the general structure given for the method is accurate, however.

20. Stephen Mills, 'Survey findings and the 2014 election'

1   The limits of the assumptions behind this table should be noted. New Zealand First, for instance, regularly recorded above 4 per cent but below 5 per cent in UMR polls. It was always a reasonable assumption that the New Zealand First party vote would improve sufficiently in the campaign for the party to remain represented in Parliament. National also had the insurance policy of providing the Conservatives with an electorate seat. It was also doubtful that the Māori Party would hold all three electorate seats.

2   Polling across all of 2012 (total of 202 respondents) shows that 50 per cent of Māori Party voters would prefer a Labour-led government, with 30 per cent preferring a National-led government. Māori Party electorate voters have always shown a strong tendency to split their vote, supporting a Māori Party electorate candidate while giving their party vote to Labour.

3   Questions asked in the UMR Research nationwide telephone omnibus survey. This is a nationally representative sample of 750 New Zealanders 18 years or older. The margin of error for a sample size of 750 for a 50 per cent figure at the 95 per cent confidence level is ±3.6 per cent.

4   38 per cent of respondents also said the 2010 Budget was good for New Zealand overall (17 per cent said it was bad).

5   There were also generally positive trends for other indicators of economic confidence tracked by UMR research, including expected movements in

unemployment and families' standard of living.

6   Online surveys in the final week before the election; sample sizes varied between
      500 and 1,000.

7   The full set of reasons given for voting for National, Labour, the Greens and New
      Zealand First is included in the tables in the Appendix to this chapter.

8   Questions asked in the UMR Research online omnibus survey, a nationally
      representative sample of 1,000 New Zealanders 18 years or older. The margin
      of error for a sample size of 1,000 for a 50 per cent figure at the 95 per cent
      confidence level is ±3.1 per cent.

9   UMR telephone omnibus surveys (September 2012, August 2014); UMR
      election tracker surveys (September 2014).

10   UMR telephone omnibus survey (October 2014).

11   UMR telephone omnibus survey (October 2014).

21. Matthew Beveridge, 'Social media in the 2014 general election'

1   Only one candidate, Labour MP Jacinda Ardern, is confirmed as having used
      Tinder as a campaign tool (Beveridge 2014).

2   Twitonomy.com provides analytics of Twitter accounts. Using premium accounts
      it allows the download of the last 3,200 tweets sent by an account.

3   Mana and the Conservatives are excluded from coverage, either not having a
      Twitter account or having an account from which tweets were absent during the
      election campaign.

4   The data is from a dataset compiled weekly during the campaign, held by the
      author and available on request.

5   A new tweet is original content by the account, not a retweeted comment.

22. Therese Arseneau and Nigel S. Roberts, 'Standing back and looking forward: the 2014 election in perspective'

1   This chapter was written based on the 2014 general election results and does not
      include subsequent changes due to by-elections.

2   The 2011 results come from David Farrar (2014) and have been manually
      adjusted to reflect the 2013 boundary changes. Note: his comparative analysis
      found one electorate – Waimakariri – had no change in party vote share (per
      cent).

3   In 14 electorates the incumbent MP did not contest the seat in 2014: 11 of
      these electorates were won by candidates from the same party as the departing
      MP and the other three were won by candidates from a different party. There
      were also two new electorates in 2014: the newly created electorate of Upper
      Harbour elected National's Paula Bennett (previously the electorate MP for
      Waitakere) and the newly redrawn electorate of Kelston elected Labour's
      Carmel Sepuloni.

4   The formula is N=1 divided by the sum of Seats(i)-squared (see Lijphart 1994, p. 68).

5   The effective number of parliamentary parties for each of the seven MMP elections was 3.76 (1996), 3.45 (1999), 3.76 (2002), 2.98 (2005), 2.78 (2008), 2.98 (2011) and 2.96 (2014).

23. Jon Johansson, 'Looking towards 2017'

1   Helen Clark likewise faced five National Party counterparts (Bolger, Shipley, English, Don Brash and Key) during her period as leader.

2   The concept of 'leadership capital' includes variables other than solely a leader's personal popularity, including: their policy vision; their public leadership performance; their popularity relative to opponents; their length of tenure; the size of their electoral victory; polling popularity; trust ratings; their short-term leadership challenges; their freedom to shape policy; and their parliamentary effectiveness. Key's overall leadership capital rating is stratospheric, comparing favourably with Tony Blair (who was assessed at the peak of his powers, in 2001, before his disastrous Iraq folly). See Bennister, t'Hart and Worthy 2014, p. 14.

3News 2012, 'Govt Admits Illegally Spying on Dotcom', 24 September, http://www.3news.co.nz/politics/govt-admits-illegally-spying-on-dotcom-2012092413#axzz3S4Lp7BPf.

3News 2012a, 'Kiwi women "most promiscuous" – Colin Craig', 9 May, http://www.3news.co.nz/politics/kiwi-women-most-promiscuous--colin-craig-2012050911#axzz3blA6uwXZ.

3News 2014a, 'Journos "Soul-Searching" after Latest Dirty Politics Leaks', 2 September, http://www.3news.co.nz/politics/journos-soul-searching-after-latest-dirty-politics-leaks-2014090210#axzz3TMMaq1lx.

3News 2014b, 'Interview: Glenn Greenwald', http://www.3news.co.nz/tvshows/thenation/interview-glenn-greenwald-2014091311#axzz3S4Lp7BPf.

3News 2014c, 'Interview: The Civilian Party's Ben Uffindell', *The Nation*, 24 May, http://www.3news.co.nz/tvshows/thenation/interview-the-civilian-partys-ben-uffindell-2014052414#axzz3aN7vi8Lt.

3News 2014d, 'ACT: Scrap helmet law to boost cycling', 19 August, http://www.3news.co.nz/politics/act-scrap-helmet-law-to-boost-cycling-2014081911#axzz3aN7vi8Lt.

3News 2014e, 'Timeline: Judith Collins and Oravida', 5 May, http://www.3news.co.nz/politics/timeline-judith-collins-and-oravida-2014050512#axzz3byoaaoLW.

28th Māori Battalion (NZ) Association 2012, 'Ake! Ake! Kia Kaha E!', Final Official Luncheon: http://www.tpk.govt.nz/_documents/28th-maori-battalion-luncheon-booklet.pdf.

ACT 2014, 'Richard Prebble returns to politics in key ACT role', press release by acting ACT president, Barbara Astill, 23 February.

ACT 2014a, 'Every Party Vote for ACT Will Count. It'll Take Just 1.3 per cent of the Party Vote to Get Jamie Whyte into Parliament. These Are His (and Our) Values: If You Share Them, It's Okay to Vote for Them' [Facebook post], 11 September, https://www.facebook.com/actparty/photos/a.453007989118.249029.92043134118/10153280347334119/.

ACT 2014b, 'The Election May Be Decided by Just One or Two MPs. Thanks to Epsom, It Takes Just 28,000 Party Votes (about 1.2 per cent) to Put 2 ACT MPs in Parliament. And the More ACT MPs There Are, the Less Power Winston Has. Learn More at www.act.org.nz/mmp' [Facebook post], 18 September, https://www.facebook.com/actparty/photos/a.453007989118.249029.92043134118/10153293592394119/.

Aimer, Peter 2014, 'New Zealand's Electoral Tides in the 21st Century', in Jack Vowles (ed.), *The New Electoral Politics in New Zealand: The Significance of the 2011 Election*, Institute for Governance and Policy Studies, Wellington.

Aimer, Peter and Jack Vowles 2004, 'What Happened at the 2002 Election?', in Jack Vowles, Peter Aimer, Susan Banducci, Jeffrey Karp and Raymond Miller (eds.), *Voters' Veto: The 2002 Election in New Zealand and the Consolidation of Minority Government*, Auckland University Press, Auckland.

Anderson, Perry 2014, 'The Italian Disaster', *London Review of Books*, 22 May.

Armstrong, John 2014, 'Hager's Claims Light a Fuse under the State of Key', *New Zealand Herald*, 14 August, http://www.nzherald.co.nz/nz/news/article.cfm?c_id=1&objectid=11308460.

Armstrong, John 2014a, 'Labour must cling to the wreckage', *New Zealand Herald*, 21 June, http://www.nzherald.co.nz/opinion/news/article.cfm?c_id=466&objectid=11278362.

Armstrong, John 2014b, 'Spend-big politicians play into National's hands', *New Zealand Herald*, 11 August, http://www.nzherald.co.nz/nz/news/article.cfm?c_id=1&objectid=11306932.

Armstrong, John 2014c, 'Hip-hop song scrapes bottom of rotten barrel', *New Zealand Herald*, 27 August, http://www.nzherald.co.nz/nz/news/article.cfm?c_id=1&objectid=11314681.

Armstrong, John 2014d, 'Moment of "struth" sees Dotcom bubble burst', *New Zealand Herald*, 17 September, http://www.nzherald.co.nz/nz/news/article.cfm?c_id=1&objectid=11325925.

Arseneau, Therese 2010, '2008: National's Winning Strategy', in Stephen Levine and Nigel S. Roberts (eds.), *Key to Victory: The New Zealand General Election of 2008*, Victoria University Press, Wellington, pp. 272–294.

Bahador, Babak and Mark Boyd 2015, 'Media Coverage of New Zealand's 2014 "Dirty Politics" Election: A "weird" Campaign or Business as Usual?', *Political Science*, vol. 67, no. 2.

Bale, Tim, Jonathan Boston and Stephen Church 2005, '"Natural Because It Had Become Just That." Path Dependence in Pre-electoral Pacts and Government Formation: A New Zealand Case Study', *Australian Journal of Political Science*, vol. 40, no. 4, pp. 481–498.

Bean, Clive 1992, 'Party Leaders and Local Candidates', in Martin Holland (ed.), *Electoral Behaviour in New Zealand*, Oxford University Press, Auckland.

Bennett, Adam 2014, 'ACT leader Jamie Whyte stands by incest comments', *New Zealand Herald*, 26 February, http://www.nzherald.co.nz/nz/news/article.cfm?c_id=1&objectid=11210373.

Bennett, Adam 2014a, 'ACT leader "regrets" incest comments', *New Zealand Herald*, 27 February, http://www.nzherald.co.nz/nz/news/article.cfm?c_id=1&objectid=11210507.

Bennett, Adam 2014b, 'PM: ACT leader's incest comments "stupid"', *New Zealand Herald*, 27 February, http://www.nzherald.co.nz/nz/news/article.cfm?c_id=1&objectid=11210988.

Bennett, Adam 2014c, 'Leaders' conflict surfaces in debate', *New Zealand Herald*, 6 September, http://www.nzherald.co.nz/nz/news/article.cfm?c_id=1&objectid=11319891.

Bennett, Adam 2014d, '13 bizarre things David Cunliffe has said in the past 24 hours', *New Zealand Herald*, 30 September, http://www.nzherald.co.nz/nz/news/article.cfm?c_id=1&objectid=11334067.

Bennett, Adam 2014e, 'Key dismisses Dotcom's planned Internet Party', *New Zealand Herald*, 21 January, http://www.nzherald.co.nz/nz/news/article.cfm?c_id=1&objectid=11189704.

Bennett, Adam 2014f, 'Act's Whyte calls for end to race based laws', *New Zealand Herald*, 29 July, http://www.nzherald.co.nz/nz/news/article.cfm?c_id=1&objectid=11301011.

Bennett, Adam 2014g, 'Dunne deal: United Future signs deal with National-led govt', *New Zealand Herald*, 29 September, http://www.nzherald.co.nz/nz/news/article.cfm?c_id=1&objectid=11333482.

Bennett, Adam 2014h, 'Flavell given portfolio re-named to reflect "new focus" on Maori future', *New Zealand Herald*, 6 October, http://www.nzherald.co.nz/nz/news/article.cfm?c_id=1&objectid=11337482.

Bennett, Adam and Jeremy Rees 2014, 'Act candidate quits over leader's speech "stunt"', *New Zealand Herald*, 6 August, http://www.nzherald.co.nz/nz/news/article.cfm?c_id=1&objectid=11304781.

Bennett, Adam and Audrey Young 2014, 'Collins Told to Take a Break from Parliament', *New Zealand Herald*, 5 May, http://www.nzherald.co.nz/nz/news/article.cfm?c_id=1&objectid=11249833.

Bennett, Adam, Audrey Young and Claire Trevett 2014, '"Too late" to change Labour leadership – Williams', *New Zealand Herald*, 19 June.

Bennister, Mark, Paul t'Hart and Ben Worthy 2014, 'Assessing the Authority of Political Office-Holders: The Leadership Capital Index', in *Western European Politics*, European Consortium for Political Research Working Paper.

Beveridge, Matthew 2014, 'Swipe Right with a Difference: A Candidate on Tinder', *Social

Media & the 2014 General Election, 17 August, http://www.matthewbeveridge. co.nz/politics/swipe-right-with-a-difference-a-candidate-on-tinder/

Beveridge, Matthew 2014a, 'Party Facebook Pages: Update 25 August', *Social Media & the 2014 General Election*, http://www.matthewbeveridge.co.nz/politics/ party-facebook-pages-update-25-august/.

Bloxham, Paul 2014, 'New Zealand 2014's "rock star" economy', *Stuff*, 7 January, http://www.stuff.co.nz/business/industries/9583473/New-Zealand-2014s-rock-star-economy.

Boston, Jonathan 2007, 'An Unusual Government: Coalition politics and inter-party arrangements following the 2005 election', in Stephen Levine and Nigel S. Roberts (eds.), *The Baubles of Office: The New Zealand General Election of 2005*, Victoria University Press, Wellington, pp. 389–418.

Bracewell-Worrall, Anna 2014, 'Dirty Politics', *Pantograph Punch*, 19 November, http://www.pantograph-punch.com/post/dirty-politics.

Bradbury, Martyn 2014, 'How Biased Is the NZ Media?', *The Daily Blog*, 8 September, http://thedailyblog.co.nz/2014/09/08/how-biased-is-the-nz-media/.

Brown, Russell 2014, 'Vision and Dumbassery', *Hard News. Public Address*, 16 September, http://publicaddress.net/hardnews/vision-and-dumbassery/.

Burns, James MacGregor 1978, *Leadership*, Harper Collins, New York.

Burns, Shawn 2014, '"Advocacy" Is Not a Dirty Word in Journalism', *Media Shift, Education Shift, PBS*, 16 October, http://www.pbs.org/mediashift/2014/10/ advocacy-is-not-a-dirty-word-in-journalism/.

Burr, Lloyd 2014, 'I did not have textual relations with that blogger: http://www. radiolive.co.nz/Another-Brain-Fade-from-John-Key-PMs-Claims-vs-Cameron-Slater-texts/tabid/615/articleID/62914/Default.aspx' [tweet], retrieved from https://twitter.com/lloydburr/status/537765394056900608.

Canon Media Awards 2014, 'Canon Media Awards 2014 Winners', 9 May, http:// www.canonmediaawards.co.nz/winners-2014.

Canon Media Awards 2014a, 'Newspaper Publishers Regret Attacks on Canon', 15 August, http://www.canonmediaawards.co.nz/announcements/newspaper-publishers-rebuff-attacks-on-canon.

Carlyle, Thomas 1841, *On Heroes, Hero-Worship and the Heroic in History*, John C. Winston, Chicago.

Chapman, Kate 2013, 'United Future Deregistered', *Stuff*, 31 May, http://www.stuff. co.nz/national/politics/8742802/United-Future-deregistered.

Cheng, Derek 2014, 'Te Tai Tokerau: Peters backs Labour's Kelvin Davis', *New Zealand Herald*, 18 September, http://www.nzherald.co.nz/nz/news/article. cfm?c_id=1&objectid=11327170.

Cheng, Derek 2014a, 'I'm the Victim of a Smear Campaign: Judith Collins Resigns', *New Zealand Herald*, 30 August, http://www.nzherald.co.nz/nz/news/article. cfm?c_id=1&objectid=11316644.

Cheng, Derek 2014b, 'Te Tai Tokerau: Peters backs Labour's Kelvin Davis', *New Zealand Herald*, 18 September, http://www.nzherald.co.nz/nz/news/article. cfm?c_id=1&objectid=11327170.

Cheng, Derek 2014c, 'Internet Mana "sinking to such a low"', *New Zealand Herald*, 7 August, http://www.nzherald.co.nz/nz/news/article.cfm?c_id=1&objectid= 11305399.

Cheng, Derek 2014d, 'Winston Peters: Conservatives have no chance', *New Zealand Herald*, 9 September, http://www.nzherald.co.nz/nz/news/article.cfm?c_id=1& objectid=11321237.

Cheng, Derek 2014e, 'Party planning "like Maori ninjas in stealth mode"', *New Zealand Herald*, 14 July, http://www.nzherald.co.nz/nz/news/article.cfm?c_ id=1&objectid=11292882

Chisholm, Lester 2014, *A Government Inquiry Into: Allegations Regarding the Honourable Judith Collins and a Former Director of the Serious Fraud Office*, 24 November, New Zealand Parliament, Wellington.

Church, Stephen 2012, 'The post-election government: formation, "FOMOs" and "frenemies"', in Jon Johansson and Stephen Levine (eds.), *Kicking the Tyres: The New Zealand General Election and Electoral Referendum of 2011*, Victoria University Press, Wellington, pp. 97–115.

Clifton, Jane 2014, 'Dirty Rotten Politics', *The Listener*, 21 August, http://www. listener.co.nz/current-affairs/politics/dirty-rotten-politics/.

Clifton, Jane 2014a, 'Key lands free hit as focus on trusts at question time', *Dominion Post*, 5 March.

Collins, Simon 2014, 'NZ should abandon Security Council bid – ACT', *New Zealand Herald*, 2 September, http://www.nzherald.co.nz/nz/news/article. cfm?c_id=1&objectid=11317981.

Colmar Brunton 2014, http://www.colmarbrunton.co.nz/index.php/polls-and-surveys/political-polls/vote-switching-analysis-2014.

Conservative Party 2014a. 'Conservatives on Brink of Entering Parliament . . . – Vote Conservative NZ' [Facebook post], 11 September, https://www.facebook.com/ ConservativepartyNZ/posts/705806432829030.

Conservative Party 2014b. 'A Vote for Conservative Is NOT a Wasted Vote . . . #standforsomething' [Facebook post], 17 September, https://www.facebook.com/ ConservativepartyNZ/photos/a.177639248979087.44276.155117061 231306/708743519201988/.

Conservative Party 2014c, 'People and Policies You Can Trust' [brochure], http://www.conservativeparty.org.nz/Material/Brochures/004%20Broch%20Key%20People%20Drugs.pdf.

Constitutional Advisory Panel 2013, *New Zealand's Constitution: A Report on a Conversation*, Ministry of Justice, Wellington.

Daly, Michael 2014, 'Slater to Pay Media Costs,' *Stuff*, 14 November, http://www.stuff.co.nz/national/politics/63222219/slater-to-pay-media-costs.

Daly, Michael 2014a, 'David Cunliffe's catastrophes', *Stuff*, 18 June, http://www.stuff.co.nz/national/politics/10173411/David-Cunliffes-catastrophes.

Dastgheib, Shabnam 2014, 'ACT novice wins in Epsom but still gets a rap over the knuckles', *Sunday Star Times*, 21 September, p. 4, http://www.stuff.co.nz/national/politics/10525450/ACT-novice-Seymour-victorious-in-Epsom.

Davies, Nick 2009, *Flat Earth News*, Vintage Press, London.

Davis, Kelvin 2014, 'I was on *3News* last night . . .' [Facebook status update], 4 August, https://www.facebook.com/KelvinDavisLabour/posts/832926910072491,

Davison, Isaac 2014, 'NZ flag vote to be held after election', *New Zealand Herald*, 11 March, http://www.nzherald.co.nz/nz/news/article.cfm?c_id=1&objectid=11217658.

Davison, Isaac 2014a, 'PM challenged over "Cabinet Club" meetings', *New Zealand Herald*, 8 May 2014, http://www.nzherald.co.nz/nz/news/article.cfm?c_id=1&objectid=11251849.

Davison, Isaac 2015, 'Peter Dunne wants rethink if Winston Peters wins Northland', *New Zealand Herald*, 28 February, http://www.nzherald.co.nz/nz/news/article.cfm?c_id=1&objectid=11409251.

de Winter, Lieven, and Patrick Dumont 2008, 'Uncertainty and Complexity in Cabinet Formation', in Kaare Strøm, Wolfgang Müller, and Torbjörn Bergman (eds.), *Cabinets and Coalition Bargaining: The Democratic Life Cycle in Western Europe*, Oxford University Press, Oxford, pp. 123–157.

Deos, Anthony, and Ashley Murchison 2012, 'What's on Their Mind? Political Parties and Facebook in the 2011 New Zealand General Election', in Jon Johansson and Stephen Levine (eds.), *Kicking the Tyres: The New Zealand General Election and Electoral Referendum of 2011*, Victoria University Press, Wellington.

Dominion Post 2014, 'Keep New Zealand Working' [advertisement], 17 September, p. A10.

Dominion Post 2014a, 'A pact with ACT not a great look', 4 February, p. A8, http://www.stuff.co.nz/dominion-post/comment/9681210/Editorial-A-pact-with-ACT-not-a-great-look.

Dominion Post 2014b, 'Editorial: The crowd goes mild at Budget', 16 May, p. A8, http://www.stuff.co.nz/dominion-post/comment/editorials/10049744/Editorial-The-crowd-goes-mild-at-Budget.

Dominion Post 2014c, 'One Law To Rule Us All and other crazy thinking' [advertisement], 14 July, p. A7.

Dominion Post 2014d, 'Party Vote Conservative: People and Policies you can Trust' [advertisement], 19 September, p. A6.

Dominion Post 2014e, 'Voters deliver Key sweeping mandate', 22 September, p. A6, http://www.stuff.co.nz/dominion-post/comment/10527392/Voters-deliver-Key-sweeping-mandate.

Dominion Post 2014f, 22 September, p. A2.

Dorussen, Hans and Michael Taylor (eds.) 2002, *Economic Voting*, Routledge, London.

Douglas, Roger 1993, *Unfinished Business*, Random House, Auckland.

Duff, Michelle 2014, 'Nothing stuck to Teflon John', *Sunday Star Times*, 21 September, p. A3.

Dugan, Andrew 2014, 'Americans' Confidence in News Media Remains Low', *Gallup*, 19 July, http://www.gallup.com/poll/171740/americans-confidence-news-media-remains-low.aspx.

Dunne, Peter 2014, 'Dunne Tells United Future to "Go Back to Basics"', press statement, *Scoop*, 15 November, http://www.scoop.co.nz/stories/PA1411/S00202/dunne-tells-unitedfuture-to-go-back-to-basics.htm.

Easton, Paul 2014, 'Greens leaders stand firm but still left out in the cold', *Sunday Star Times*, 21 September, p. A5, http://www.stuff.co.nz/national/politics/10525464/Greens-leaders-stand-firm-still-left-out-in-cold.

Edwards, Brian 2001, *Helen: Portrait of A Prime Minister*, Exisle, Auckland.

Edwards, Bryce 2014, 'Bryce Edwards: Media Bias and Election Coverage', *New Zealand Herald*, 4 April, http://www.nzherald.co.nz/nz/news/article.cfm?c_id=1&objectid=11232322.

Election Data Consortium 2014, 'Wordcloud: Dirty Politics Replaced by The Moment of Truth', press release, 16 September, http://www.scoop.co.nz/stories/HL1409/S00128/wordcloud-dirty-politics-replaced-by-the-moment-of-truth.htm.

Electoral Commission 2013, *Citizens Initiated Referendum 2013: Final Result*, http://www.electionresults.govt.nz/2013_citizens_referendum/.

Electoral Commission 2014, '2014 General Election Split Voting Statistics – All Electorates', http://www.electionresults.govt.nz/electionresults_2014/elect-split-vote-Overall.html.

Electoral Commission 2014a, *General Elections 1853–2014 – Dates and Turnout*, http://www.elections.org.nz/events/past-events/general-elections-1853-2014-dates-and-turnout.

Electoral Commission 2014b, *Elections: New Zealand Election Results*, http://www.electionresults.govt.nz/.

Electoral Commission 2015, *Report of the Electoral Commission on the 2014 General Election*, Wellington.

Fallow, Michael and Michael Fox 2014, 'Beyer takes Harawira to task over Dotcom', *Stuff*, 2 September, http://www.stuff.co.nz/national/politics/10448666/Beyer-takes-Harawira-to-task-over-Dotcom.

Farrar, David 2014, '2014 New Zealand General Election: Analysis of results by electorate, area and region', http://www.nbr.co.nz/sites/default/files/249022205-2014-Final-Election-Results.pdf.

Field, Michael and Siobhan Downes 2014, 'Court: Cameron Slater a Journalist, but Must Disclose Sources', *Stuff*, 12 September, http://www.stuff.co.nz/national/10492707/Court-Cameron-Slater-a-journalist-but-must-disclose-sources.

Fiorina, Morris 1981, *Retrospective Voting in American National Elections*, Yale University Press, New Haven.

Fisher, David 2014, 'David Fisher: My history with Cameron Slater', *New Zealand Herald*, 25 August, http://www.nzherald.co.nz/nz/news/article.cfm?c_id=1&objectid=11313962.

Fisher, David 2014a, 'Rawshark Emails Reveal Details of "Hit" Jobs', *New Zealand Herald*, 3 September, http://www.nzherald.co.nz/nz/news/article.cfm?c_id=1&objectid=11318445.

Fisher, David 2014b, 'Ex-Pizza Boss Matt Blomfield: Whaleoil and Me', *New Zealand Herald*, 9 October, http://www.nzherald.co.nz/nz/news/article.cfm?c_id=1&objectid=11339962.

Fisher, David 2014c, 'Dotcom turns up empty-handed', *Otago Daily Times*, 16 September, http://www.odt.co.nz/news/election-2014/316079/dotcom-turns-empty-handed.

Fletcher, Hamish 2014, 'Slater Must Reveal His Sources, Judge Rules', *New Zealand Herald*, 12 September, http://www.nzherald.co.nz/nz/news/article.cfm?c_id=1&objectid=11323615.

Fox, Michael 2014, 'Kelvin Davis blasts Mana Party', *Stuff*, 21 September, http://www.stuff.co.nz/national/politics/10527144/Kelvin-Davis-blasts-Mana-Party.

Fox, Michael 2014a, 'Corkery Hacked off with the Hackers', *Dominion Post*, 25 August, http://www.stuff.co.nz/national/politics/10419322/Corkery-hacked-off-with-the-hackers.

Fox, Michael 2014b, 'Looks like Slater is Key's Peters source', *Stuff*, 14 February, http://www.stuff.co.nz/national/politics/9723130/Looks-like-Slater-is-Keys-Peters-source.

Fox, Michael 2014c, 'Greens open to talks with Mana', *Stuff*, 15 April, http://www.stuff.co.nz/national/politics/9943442/Greens-open-to-talks-with-Mana.

Fox, Michael 2014d, 'Kelvin Davis blasts Mana Party', *Stuff*, 21 September, http://www.stuff.co.nz/national/politics/10527144/Kelvin-Davis-blasts-Mana-Party.

Fox, Michael and Laura Walters 2014, 'National to stick with ACT, United Future and Maori', *Stuff*, 28 July, http://www.stuff.co.nz/national/politics/10320342/National-to-stick-with-ACT-UnitedFuture-and-Maori.

Fuatai, Teuila 2015, 'Waitangi Day: Anti-StatOil Protest group rounds out hikoi', *New Zealand Herald*, 6 February, http://www.nzherald.co.nz/nz/news/article.cfm?c_id=1&objectid=11397526.

Garner, Duncan 2014, 'My Story about the Real "Dirty Politics"', http://www.radiolive.co.nz/My-story-about-the-real-Dirty-Politics/tabid/506/articleID/52158/Default.aspx.

Geddis, Andrew 2014, 'Cri Du Coeur', *Pundit*, 17 August, http://pundit.co.nz/content/cri-du-c%C5%93ur.

Gilbert, J., 2014, 'Oral Judgement of Gilbert J.', Colin Graeme Craig v Mediaworks TV Limited, Auckland High Court CIV-2014-404-001972 [2014] NZHC 1875, 8 August.

Godfery, Morgan 2012, 'The fragmentation of Māori politics', in in Jon Johansson and Stephen Levine (eds.), *Kicking the Tyres: The New Zealand General Election and Electoral Referendum of 2011*, Victoria University Press, Wellington.

Golder, Sonar Nadenichek 2006, 'Pre-Electoral Coalition Formation in Parliamentary Democracies', *British Journal of Political Science*, vol. 36, no. 2, pp. 193–212.

Goodwin, Eileen 2014, 'Georgina Beyer lashes out at Dotcom, Internet party', *Otago Daily Times*, 2 September, http://www.nzherald.co.nz/nz/news/article.cfm?c_id=1&objectid=11317634.

Graham, Kennedy 2014, 'Why green isn't just a shade of red', *New Zealand Herald*, 9 October, http://www.nzherald.co.nz/nz/news/article.cfm?c_id=1&objectid=11339340.

Green, Donald P. and Ian Shapiro 1994, *Pathologies of Rational Choice,* Yale University Press, New Haven.

Green Party 2014, 'Who Knew Such a Great Poll Result Would Cause Such a Fuss!', 12 September [Post removed from Facebook page between data capture and time of writing].

Green Party 2015, 'Candidates for male co-leader of the Green Party', https://www.greens.org.nz/page/candidates-male-co-leader-green-party.

Greenslade, Roy 2013, 'Greenwald vs Keller – Adversarial Journalism vs Mainstream Journalism', *The Guardian*, 29 October, http://www.theguardian.com/media/greenslade/2013/oct/29/new-york-times-newspapers.

Greenstein, Fred 2000, *The Presidential Difference: Leadership Style from FDR to Clinton*, The Free Press, New York.

Greenwald, Glenn and Ryan Gallagher 2014, 'New Zealand Launched Mass Surveillance Project While Publicly Denying It', *The Intercept*, 15 September, https://firstlook.org/theintercept/2014/09/15/new-zealand-gcsb-speargun-mass-surveillance/.

Gwyn, Cheryl 2014, *Report into the Release of Information by the New Zealand Security Intelligence Service in July and August 2011*, Public Report, Wellington, Office of the Inspector-General of Intelligence and Security, 25 November, http://www.igis.govt.nz/assets/Inquiries/FINAL-REPORT-INTO-THE-RELEASE-OF-INFORMATION-BY-NZSIS-IN-JULY-AND-AUGUST-2.pdf.

Haass, Richard N. 2014, 'The Unravelling: How to respond to a disordered world', *Foreign Affairs*, November–December.

Hager, Mandy 2014, 'Mandy Hager Sends Patrick Gower To The Spin Bin', *Spin Bin*, https://www.spinbin.co.nz/mandy-hager-sends-patrick-gower-to-the-spin-bin/.

Hager, Nicky 2002, *Seeds of Distrust: The story of a GE cover-up*, Craig Potton, Nelson.

Hager, Nicky 2006, *The Hollow Men: A study in the politics of deception*, Craig Potton, Nelson.

Hager, Nicky 2014, *Dirty Politics: How attack politics is poisioning New Zealand's political environment*, Craig Potton, Nelson.

Hague, Rod, and Martin Harrop 2004, *Comparative Government and Politics*, sixth edition, Palgrave Macmillan, Bristol.

Harawira, Hone 2011, 'Crunch Time for Māori Grumbles', *Sunday Star Times*, 16 January, http://www.stuff.co.nz/sunday-star-times/columnists/4545920/Crunch-time-for-Maori-grumbles.

Hargrove, Erwin 1998, *The President as Leader: Appealing to the Better Angels of Our Nature*, University Press of Kansas, Kansas.

Heifetz, Ronald 1994, *Leadership Without Easy Answers*, Harvard University Press, Cambridge.

Hemingway, Ernest 1932, *Death in the Afternoon*, Charles Scribner's Sons, New York.

Henry, Paul 2014, 'Cunliffe on craziest moments of the election', *The Paul Henry Show*, 19 September, http://www.3news.co.nz/tvshows/paulhenryshow/cunliffe-on-craziest-moments-of-the-election-2014091923.

Herald on Sunday 2014, 'Editorial: Key has a right to savour this moment', 21 September, http://www.nzherald.co.nz/nz/news/article.cfm?c_id=1&objectid= 11328618.

Hutchison, Jonathan 2014, 'New Zealand's Ruling National Party Is Re-elected', *New York Times*, 20 September, http://www.nytimes.com/2014/09/21/world/ asia/new-zealands-ruling-national-party-is-re-elected.html?_r=0.

Internet Party 2014, 'Internet Mana Wants a Complete Review of New Zealand Drug Law, with an Immediate Focus on Cannabis Law Reform' [Facebook post], 4 September, https://www.facebook.com/InternetPartyNZ/photos/a.49722980 7050128.1073741828.466067543499688/569565659816542/.

iPredict 2015, 'Collins picked to return to Cabinet before next election', press release, *Scoop*, 27 January, http://www.scoop.co.nz/stories/PO1501/S00090/collins-picked-to-return-to-cabinet-before-next-election.htm.

Issenberg, Sasha 2012, *The Victory Lab: The Secret Science of Winning Campaigns*, Broadway Books, New York.

Issenberg, Sasha 2012a, 'How Obama's team used big data to rally voters', *MIT Technology Review*, 19 December, http://www.technologyreview.com/ featuredstory/509026/how-obamas-team-used-big-data-to-rally-voters/

James, Colin 2014a, 'The foundation and a pillar of good government', *Otago Daily Times*, 25 August, http://www.colinjames.co.nz/the-foundation-and-a-pillar-of-good-government/.

James, Colin 2014b, 'Investing, not spending. A tougher way of thinking', *Otago Daily Times*, 14 October, http://www.colinjames.co.nz/investing-not-spending-a-tougher-way-of-thinking/.

Johansson, Jon 2005, *Two Titans: Muldoon, Lange and Leadership*, Dunmore, Wellington.

Johansson, Jon 2009, *The Politics of Possibility: Leadership During Changing Times*, Dunmore, Wellington.

Johansson, Jon and Stephen Levine (eds.) 2012, *Kicking the Tyres: The New Zealand General Election and Electoral Referendum of 2011*, Victoria University Press, Wellington.

Johnston, Richard 1998, 'Issues, Leaders, and the Campaign', in Jack Vowles, Peter Aimer, Susan Banducci and Jeffrey Karp (eds.), *Voters' Victory? New Zealand's First Election Under Proportional Representation*, Auckland University Press, Auckland.

Johnston, Richard, André Blais, Henry Brady and Jean Crete 1992, *Letting the People Decide: Dynamics of a Canadian Election*, Stanford University Press, Stanford.

Keall, Chris 2014, 'PM Releases Declassified Docs, Says They "Set the Record Straight"', *National Business Review*, 15 September, http://www.nbr.co.nz/article/pm-releases-declassified-docs-says-they-set-record-straight-ck-162439.

Keller, Bill 2013, 'Is Glenn Greenwald the Future of News?', *The New York Times*, 27 October, http://www.nytimes.com/2013/10/28/opinion/a-conversation-in-lieu-of-a-column.html.

Key, John 2006, 'Address to Inaugural Jenny Shipley Memorial Lecture', Canterbury Manufacturers Association Conference Room, Christchurch, 14 December, http://www.johnkey.co.nz/archives/39-Address-to-Inaugural-Jenny-Shipley-Lecture-part-one.html

Kilgallon, Steve 2014, 'Labour rout the lowlight on painful night for Left', *Sunday Star Times*, 21 September, p. A2.

Kilgallon, Steve 2014a, 'Kim Dotcom to Reveal Spying Details', *Sunday Star Times*, 14 September, http://www.stuff.co.nz/national/politics/10496502/Kim-Dotcom-to-reveal-spying-details.

Kilgallon, Steve and Simon Day 2014, 'Skiing holiday puts Cunliffe on slippery slope', *Sunday Star Times*, 20 July, http://www.stuff.co.nz/national/politics/10287781/Cunliffe-I-work-as-hard-as-anyone.

Kirk, Stacey and Amanda Parkinson 2014, 'Greens push river protection plan', *Dominion Post*, 14 July, p. A2, http://www.stuff.co.nz/national/politics/10262956/Greens-push-river-protection-plan.

Kirk, Stacey, Vernon Small, Laura Walters and Shabnam Dastgheib 2014, 'Maurice Williamson resigns over police call', *Stuff*, 1 May, http://www.stuff.co.nz/national/politics/9996560/Maurice-Williamson-resigns-over-police-call.

Kitteridge, Rebecca 2013, *Review of Compliance at the Government Communications Security Bureau*, March 2013, http://www.gcsb.govt.nz/assets/GCSB-Compliance-Review/Review-of-Compliance.pdf.

Labour Party 2014a, 'Labour Will Put People First . . .' [Facebook post], 10 September, https://www.facebook.com/NZLabourParty/photos/a.352820246451.152168.337477311451/10152369761066452/.

Labour Party 2014b, 'Are You Voting Labour This Saturday?' [Facebook post], 17 September, https://www.facebook.com/NZLabourParty/photos/a.352820246451.152168.337477311451/10152382540041452/.

Levendusky, Matt 2014, 'Are Fox and MSNBC Polarizing America?', *The Washington Post*, 3 February, http://www.washingtonpost.com/blogs/monkey-cage/wp/2014/02/03/are-fox-and-msnbc-polarizing-america/.

Levine, Stephen 2012, 'Coat of Arms', in *Te Ara*, the New Zealand Ministry for Culture and Heritage, online *Encyclopedia of New Zealand*, http://www.teara.govt.nz/en/coat-of-arms.

Levine, Stephen and Nigel S. Roberts 1987, 'Parties, Policies, and Personalities: A Study of Two Electorates [Miramar and Ohariu] in the 1984 General Election', *Political Science*, vol. 39, no. 1, pp. 1–16, http://pnz.sagepub.com/content/39/1/1. full.pdf+html.

Levine, Stephen and Nigel S. Roberts 2015, 'The General Election of 2014', in Janine Hayward (ed.), *New Zealand Government and Politics*, sixth edition, Melbourne: Oxford University Press, pp. 334–344.

Leyland, Patrick 2015, 'Digital Campaigning in New Zealand', *The Progress Report*, 28 February, http://theprogressreport.co.nz/2015/02/28/digital-campaigning-in-new-zealand/.

Lijphart, Arend 1994, *Electoral Systems and Party Systems: A Study of Twenty-Seven Democracies, 1945–1990*, Oxford University Press, Oxford.

Lipsmeyer, Christine and Heather Pierce 2011, 'The Eyes that Bind: Junior Ministers as Oversight Mechanisms in Coalition Governments', *The Journal of Politics*, vol. 73, no. 4, pp. 1152–1164.

Lowe, Josh 2014, 'Simon Danczuk: Hayward and Middleton by-election was a wake-up call for Labour', *Prospect*, 10 October.

Luscombe, Jane 2014, 'PM: Twitter full of "trolls, bottom feeders"', *3News*, 6 May, http://www.3news.co.nz/politics/pm-twitter-full-of-trolls-bottom-feeders-2014050618.

Makhlouf, Gabriel 2014, 'Economics: Teaching, Applying, Learning', speech to the GEN annual conference, The Treasury, 5 November.

Mana Movement 2014a, 'Muahahahahahahahahahhahahaha' [Facebook post], 16 September, https://www.facebook.com/ManaMovement/photos/pb.103911136362306.-2207520000.1420333708./699435193476561/.

Mana Movement 2014b, 'A Message to John Key from Eminem Wink Emoticon #keyidiot #keydiot #photoshopped' [Facebook post], 18 September, https://www.facebook.com/ManaMovement/photos/pb.103911136362306.-2207520000.1420333708./700189716734442/.

Manhire, Toby 2014, 'Greenwald, Dotcom, Snowden and Assange Take on "Adolescent" John Key', *The Guardian*, 15 September, http://www.theguardian.com/world/2014/sep/15/moment-truth-greenwald-dotcom-snowden-assange-new-zealand-john-key.

Manning, Brendan 2014, 'Jamie Whyte: ACT brand is "tarnished"', *New Zealand Herald*, 21 September, http://www.nzherald.co.nz/nz/news/article.cfm?c_id=1&objectid=11328860.

Manning, Brendan, Jared Savage and Isaac Davison 2014, 'Maurice Williamson "crossed the line" – PM', *New Zealand Herald*, 1 May, http://www.nzherald.co.nz/nz/news/article.cfm?c_id=1&objectid=11247628.

Māori Party 2013, 'Māori Party Constitution', http://maoriparty.org/wp-content/uploads/2014/01/Constitution-2013-Ratified-Version-08.12.13.pdf.

Māori Party 2014, 'Tame Iti stands for the Māori Party', 25 August, http://maoriparty.org/panui/tame-iti-stands-for-the-maori-party/.

Māori Party 2014a, 'We're Sending out the Kereru! Share with Your Whānau and Friends Overseas. They Can Enrol, Check, Update Their Details, and Vote in the Election This Year. http://bit.ly/voteoverseas2014 for More Info' [Facebook post], 20 August, https://www.facebook.com/MaoriParty/photos/a.225433844134443.67647.194480190563142/833152173362604/.

Māori Party 2014b, 'Māori Party – 'When Labour Get into a Tight Spot They Dump Māori . . .' [Facebook post], 8 September, https://www.facebook.com/MaoriParty/posts/842845822393239.

Māori Television 2014, 'Te Tai Tokerau poll results highlight voter concerns', *Native Affairs*, 16 September, http://www.maoritelevision.com/news/galleries/te-tai-tokerau-poll-results-highlight-voter-concerns.

Māori Television 2014a, 'Extended interview with Matt Nippert and Raymond Miller', *Media Take*, 2 September, http://www.maoritelevision.com/tv/shows/media-take/S01E001/media-take-episode-10-extended-interview.

Māori Television 2014b, 'Series 1, Episode 10', *Media Take*, 2 September, http://www.maoritelevision.com/tv/shows/media-take/S01E010/media-take-series-1-episode-10.

Marae Investigates 2014, 'Māori voting pattern defies non-Māori voting pattern', https://www.youtube.com/watch?v=8ob226dr9ck&index=3&list=PLQ4mqbMg3-7mDgY9xXgBHOJyMqBYygN80.

Mateos, Pablo 2007, 'A review of name-based ethnicity classification methods and their potential in population studies', *Population Space and Place*, vol. 13, no. 4, pp. 243–263.

Mateparae, Lt Gen Rt Hon Sir Jerry 2013, 'Speech to a dinner in honour of the Parliamentary Press Gallery, Government House', Wellington, 9 November, http://gg.govt.nz/content/press-gallery-dinner.

McAnulty, Brent, Bill Francis and Steven Price 2014, *TVNZ Report into Alleged Misconduct within Māori and Pacific Programmes Department*, Television New Zealand, 12 May, http://images.tvnz.co.nz/tvnz_images/about_tvnz/independent-report.pdf.

McCulloch, Alison 2015, 'Stop The Press: The State of NZ News Media – A Public Conversation', *Scoop*, 16 January, http://www.scoop.co.nz/stories/HL1501/S00060/stop-the-press-alison-mcculloch.htm.

McIvor, Kerre 2014, 'Vote Compass party picker offers weird choices', *New Zealand Herald*, 24 August, http://www.nzherald.co.nz/opinion/news/article.cfm?c_id=466&objectid=11313363.

Miller, Geoffrey 2014, 'Moderator "bias" in TV Leaders' Debates – Mike Hosking vs. John Campbell' [blog post], 25 July, http://www.geoffreymiller.info/2014/07/moderator-bias-in-tv-leaders-debates-mike-hosking-vs-john-campbell-2/.

Ministry of Business, Innovation & Employment [MBIE] 2014, 'Canterbury Monthly Job Matching Report: April 2014', MBIE, Wellington.

Mitchell, Paul, and Benjamin Nyblade 2008, 'Government Formation and Cabinet Type', in Kaare Strøm, Wolfgang Müller and Torbjörn Bergman (eds.), *Cabinets and Coalition Bargaining: The Democratic Life Cycle in Western Europe*, Oxford University Press, Oxford, pp. 201–235.

Moe, Hallvard and Anders Olof Larsson 2012, 'Methodological and Ethical Challenges Associated with Large-Scale Analyses of Online Political Communication', *NORDICOM Review*, vol. 33, no. 1, pp. 117–24.

Montgomerie, Jack 2014, 'Steve Gibson quits Labour Party', *Timaru Herald*, 30 September, http://www.stuff.co.nz/national/politics/10559052/Steve-Gibson-quits-Labour-Party.

Montgomerie, Jack and Hamish Rutherford 2014, 'Cunliffe on Labour candidates' outbursts', *Timaru Herald*, 6 September, http://www.stuff.co.nz/national/politics/10468244/Cunliffe-on-Labour-candidates-outbursts.

Montgomerie, Tim 2015, 'The world's most successful conservative? Ten observations about New Zealand's John Key', *Conservative Home*, 22 January, http://www.conservativehome.com/international/2015/01/the-worlds-most-successful-conservative-ten-observations-about-new-zealands-john-key.html.

Moore, Bill 2013, 'Old warhorse leading the charge', *Nelson Mail*, 11 November, http://www.stuff.co.nz/nelson-mail/lifestyle-entertainment/weekend/9385507/Old-warhorse-leading-the-charge.

Müller, Wolfgang and Kaare Strøm 2000, *Policy, Office, or Votes? How Political Parties in Western Europe Make Hard Decisions*, Cambridge University Press, Cambridge.

Müller, Wolfgang and Kaare Strøm 2000a, 'Conclusion: Coalition Governance in Western Europe', in Wolfgang Müller and Kaare Strøm (eds.), *Coalition Governments in Western Europe*, Oxford University Press, Oxford, pp. 559–92.

Murchison, Ashley 2013, 'Changing Communications? Political Parties and Facebook in the 2011 New Zealand General Election', in *Social Transformations and the Digital Age*, World Social Science Forum, Montreal, Canada, 13–15 October.

Nadeau, Richard, Richard Nieme and Antoine Yoshinaka 2002, 'A Cross-National Analysis of Economic Voting: Taking Account of the Political Context Across Time and Nations', *Electoral Studies*, vol. 21, no. 3, pp. 403–23.

Nagel, Jack H. 2014, Review of Jon Johansson and Stephen Levine (eds.), *Kicking the Tyres: The New Zealand General Election and Electoral Referendum of 2011*, in *Party Politics*, vol. 20, no. 2, pp. 304–5.

Nannestad, Peter and Martin Paldam 2002, 'The Cost of Ruling: a foundation stone for two theories', in Hans Dorussen and Michael Taylor (eds.), *Economic Voting*, Routledge, London.

Narud, Hanne Marthe, and Henry Valen 2008, 'Coalition Membership and Electoral Performance', in Kaare Strøm, Wolfgang Müller and Torbjörn Bergman (eds.), *Cabinets and Coalition Bargaining: The Democratic Life Cycle in Western Europe*, Oxford University Press, Oxford, pp. 369–402.

National Business Review 2014, 'Peters jumps in poll', 18 September, http://www.nbr.co.nz/article/peters-jumps-poll-ck-162510.

National Party 2014, 'Will Labour's Capital Gains Tax (one of Five New Taxes) Punish Kiwi Families When Their Parents Pass Away? Let's Ask Them' [Facebook post], 4 September, https://www.facebook.com/NZNATS/photos/a.527149817300618.137166.183355881680015/952319578116971/.

National Party 2014a, 'National Will Make Every Prison a Fully Working Prison by 2017. This Will Give Prisoners the Opportunity to Learn New Skills and Take Responsibility for Their Lives. ntnl.org.nz/1Ax0kFX #Working4NZ' [Facebook post], 10 September, https://www.facebook.com/NZNATS/photos/a.527149817300618.137166.183355881680015/955988387750090/?type=1&permPage=1.

Nelson, Georgia 2014, 'Civilian Party promises to build wall around Hamilton', 16 September, Newstalk ZB, http://www.newstalkzb.co.nz/news/politics/civilian-party-promises-to-build-wall-around-hamilton/.

New Zealand Herald 2014, 'Judith Collins on Her Last Chance – Key', 19 August, http://www.nzherald.co.nz/nz/news/article.cfm?c_id=1&objectid=11311222.

New Zealand Herald 2014a, 'Key Announces Judith Collins' Resignation', 30 August, http://www.nzherald.co.nz/national/news/video.cfm?c_id=1503075&gal_cid=1503075&gallery_id=145153.

New Zealand Herald 2014b, 'Tariana Turia hits out at Labour', 20 April, http://www.nzherald.co.nz/nz/news/article.cfm?c_id=1&objectid=11241363.

New Zealand Herald 2014c, 'Editorial: ACT needs to come up with fresher ideas than flat tax', 26 February, http://www.nzherald.co.nz/nz/news/article.cfm?c_id=1&objectid=11209807.

New Zealand Herald 2014d, 'David Cunliffe's letter to supporters', 22 September, http://www.nzherald.co.nz/nz/news/article.cfm?c_id=1&objectid=11329235.

New Zealand Herald 2014e, 'David Cunliffe's full resignation statement', 27 September, http://www.nzherald.co.nz/nz/news/article.cfm?c_id=1&objectid=11332676.

New Zealand Herald 2014f, 'Labour open to Internet Mana deal', 5 June, http://www.nzherald.co.nz/nz/news/article.cfm?c_id=1&objectid=11267738.

New Zealand Herald 2015, 'Nailed it! Not . . . John Key admits: "I'm no handyman"', 10 March, http://www.nzherald.co.nz/nz/news/article.cfm?c_id=1&objectid=11414883.

Ng, Keith 2014, 'Sunlight Resistance', *On Point. Public Address*, 21 September, http://publicaddress.net/onpoint/sunlight-resistance/.

Nippert, Matt 2014, 'Harawira hitches ride into oblivion', *Sunday Star Times*, 21 September, http://www.stuff.co.nz/national/politics/10525465/Hone-Harawira-hitches-ride-into-oblivion.

Nippert, Matt 2014a, 'All the Financier's Men', *Sunday Star Times*, 31 August, http://www.stuff.co.nz/business/industries/10442831/All-the-financiers-men.

Nippert, Matt 2014b, 'Bloggers Targeted Business Journalist', *Stuff*, 1 September, http://www.stuff.co.nz/national/politics/10447644/Bloggers-targeted-business-journalist.

Nippert, Matt 2014c, 'Real Reason behind Judith Collins' Demise', *Sunday Star Times*, 31 August, http://www.stuff.co.nz/national/politics/10443223/Real-reason-behind-Judith-Collins-demise.

Nippert, Matt 2014d, 'Domcom brand "poisons" Mana', *Sunday Star Times*, 21 September, p. A5, http://www.stuff.co.nz/national/politics/10525483/Dotcom-brand-poisons-Mana.

Nissen, Wendyl 2014, 'Tuning out: Dirty Politics and the Blogs', *New Zealand Herald*, 16 September, http://www.nzherald.co.nz/nz/news/article.cfm?c_id=1&objectid=11325097.

Norquay, Kevin 2014, 'National secures three more years', *Stuff*, 21 September, http://www.stuff.co.nz/national/politics/10524781/National-secures-three-more-years.

O'Brien, Tova 2014, 'Labour MP told off for anti-Internet Mana website', *3News*, 4 August, http://www.3news.co.nz/politics/labour-mp-told-off-for-antiinternet-Mana-website-2014080417#axzz3T4Q3tudv.

O'Brien, Tova 2014a, 'Internet Mana leaders fall out over weed', *3News*, 8 September, http://www.3news.co.nz/nznews/internet-mana-leaders-fall-out-over-weed-2014090818.

O'Brien, Tova 2014b, 'Paying "club" gets access to National MPs', *3News*, 6 May, http://www.3news.co.nz/politics/paying-club-gets-access-to-national-mps-2014050616#axzz3Z9gue5Wc.

O'Brien, Tova 2014c, 'Dotcom labelled "thug" by Labour MP', *3News*, 8 August, http://www.3news.co.nz/politics/dotcom-labelled-a-thug-by-labour-mp-2014080818#axzz3blA6uwXZ.

O'Brien, Tova 2014d, 'Leaders won't rule out making Peters deputy PM', *3News*, 18 September, http://www.3news.co.nz/politics/leaders-wont-rule-out-making-peters-deputy-pm-2014091819#axzz3blA6uwXZ.

O'Brien, Tova 2014e, 'Winston Peters hits back over Wong "joke"', *3News*, 11 August, http://www.3news.co.nz/politics/winston-peters-hits-back-over-wong-joke-2014081115#axzz3iO3jQVg1.

O'Neill, Peter 2014, 'Editorial: Online post too much', *Timaru Herald*, 12 August, http://www.stuff.co.nz/timaru-herald/opinion/10372529/Editorial-Online-post-too-much.

One News 2013, 'Peter Dunne's bad week gets worse', 31 May, http://tvnz.co.nz/politics-news/peter-dunne-s-bad-week-gets-worse-5453039.

One News 2014, 'Labour dumps key policies', 22 January, http://www.scoop.co.nz/stories/HL1401/S00049/labour-dumps-tax-policies-for-upcoming-election.htm.

One News 2014a, '"Kill the PM" song not worth a response – Key', 26 August, http://tvnz.co.nz/vote-2014-news/kill-pm-song-not-worth-response-key-6064653.

One News 2014b, 'As it happened: *One News* Multi-Party Leaders' debate', 5 September, http://tvnz.co.nz/vote-2014-news/happened-one-multi-party-leaders-debate-6073724/video.

One News 2014c, 'Expletive-laden Harawira email highlights divisions', 8 September, http://tvnz.co.nz/vote-2014-news/expletive-laden-harawira-email-highlights-divisions-6075762.

One News 2014d, 'Judith Collins maintains innocence, quits Cabinet post', 30 August, http://tvnz.co.nz/vote-2014-news/judith-collins-maintains-innocence-quits-cabinet-post-6067680.

Otago Daily Times 2014, 'Judith Collins resigns as minister', 30 August, http://www.odt.co.nz/news/election-2014/314294/judith-collins-resign.

Owen, Lisa 2014, 'Debate: Grant Robertson and Steven Joyce on the wealth of the nation', *The Nation*, 1 August, http://www.3news.co.nz/tvshows/thenation/debate-grant-robertson-and-steven-joyce-on-the-wealth-of-the-nation-2014080211.

Owen, Lisa 2014a, 'Interview with David Cunliffe', *The Nation*, 21 September, http://www.3news.co.nz/tvshows/thenation/interview-labour-leader-david-cunliffe-2014092112.

Parliamentary Library 2015, 'The 2014 New Zealand General Election: Final Results and Voting Statistics, February', Parliamentary Library Research Paper, http://www.parliament.nz/en-nz/parl-support/research-papers/00PLLawRP2015011/final-results-2014-general-election.

Peacock, Colin 2014, 'Dirty Politics: Warnings for the Media?', *Mediawatch*, 31 August, http://www.radionz.co.nz/news/on-the-inside/253410/dirty-politics-warnings-for-the-media.

Pew Research Center n.d., 'Principles of Journalism', *Pew Research Center's Journalism Project*, http://www.people-press.org/1999/03/30/section-i-the-core-principles-of-journalism/.

Piketty, Thomas 2013–14, *Capitalism in the Twenty-first Century*, Harvard University Press, Cambridge, 2014 [an English translation of the French original, published in 2013].

Price, Steven 2013, 'Is Whale Oil a Journalist?', *Media Law Journal*, 1 December, http://www.medialawjournal.co.nz/?p=622.

Pullar-Strecker, Tom 2014, 'GCSB Clarifies "Project Speargun"', *Stuff*, 19 September, http://www.stuff.co.nz/technology/digital-living/61372504/gcsb-clarifies-project-speargun.

Quilliam, Rebecca 2014, 'Former TVNZ Executive's Work Reviewed,' *New Zealand Herald*, 18 February, http://www.nzherald.co.nz/nz/news/article.cfm?c_id=1&objectid=11204581.

Radio New Zealand 2014, 'Election Special', *Mediawatch*, 21 September, http://www.radionz.co.nz/audio/player/20150564.

Radio New Zealand 2014a, 'Prime Minister Stands by Minister and Staff', *Morning Report*, 18 August, http://www.radionz.co.nz/national/programmes/morningreport/audio/20146025/prime-minister-stands-by-minister-and-staff.

Radio New Zealand 2014b, 'Candidate warned over Shylock slur', 12 August, http://www.radionz.co.nz/news/political/251915/candidate-warned-over-shylock-slur.

Radio New Zealand 2014c, 'Cunliffe places Labour candidate on final warning', *Morning Report*, 12 August, http://www.radionz.co.nz/national/programmes/morningreport/audio/20145307/cunliffe-places-labour-candidate-on-final-warning.

Radio New Zealand 2014d, 'Craig delays ministerial ambition', 11 September, http://www.radionz.co.nz/news/political/254303/craig-delays-ministerial-ambition.

Radio New Zealand 2014e, 'Advert ruling against Conservatives', 19 September, http://www.radionz.co.nz/news/political/255018/advert-ruling-against-conservatives.

Radio New Zealand 2014f, 'United Future result "embarrassing"', 15 November, http://www.radionz.co.nz/news/political/259432/united-future-result-'embarrassing'.

Radio New Zealand 2014g, 'No regrets over Internet Mana alliance', 13 December, http://www.radionz.co.nz/news/political/261700/no-regrets-over-internet-mana-alliance.

Radio New Zealand 2014h, 'Key disappointed in Collins', 12 March, http://www.radionz.co.nz/news/political/238613/key-disappointed-in-collins.

Radio New Zealand 2014i, 'Cunliffe says no to Internet-Mana', 5 August, http://www.radionz.co.nz/news/political/251425/cunliffe-says-no-to-internet-mana.

Rapira, Laura O'Connell 2014, 'Things I have learned running RockEnrol', *Speaker, Public Address*, 18 September, http://publicaddress.net/speaker/things-i-have-learned-running-rockenrol/.

Renshon, Stanley 1996, *Psychological Assessment of Presidential Candidates*, NYU Press, New York.

Riga Theatre 2010, 'The Sound of Silence', play presented at the 2010 New Zealand Festival of the Arts; reviews at www.nzherald.co.nz/entertainment/news/article.cfm?c_id=1501119&objectid=10628240 and http://www.theatreview.org.nz/reviews/production.php?id=1469.

Roberts, Nigel S. and Stephen Levine 1996, 'Bias and Reliability: Political Perceptions of the New Zealand News Media', in Judy McGregor (ed.), *Dangerous Democracy? News Media Politics in New Zealand*, Dunmore Press, Palmerston North.

Rodrik, Dani 2011, *The Globalization Paradox*, Oxford University Press, Oxford.

Rose, Richard and Thomas T. Mackie 1983, 'Incumbency in Government: Liability or Asset?' in Hans Daalder and Peter Mair (eds.), *West European Party Systems*, Sage, London, pp. 115–137.

Ross, Karen and Tobias Bürger 2014, 'Face to Face(book): Social Media, Political Campaigning and the Unbearable Lightness of Being There', *Political Science* vol. 66, no. 1, pp. 46–62.

Roughan, John 2014, *John Key: Portrait of a Prime Minister*, Penguin, Auckland.

Roy Morgan 2015, 'NZ Government Confidence (2007–2015): New Zealand Heading in the "Right" or "Wrong" Direction?', http://www.roymorgan.com/morganpoll/new-zealand/nz-government-confidence.

Rutherford, Hamish 2014, 'PM Reveals Slater Texts', *Stuff*, 26 November, http://www.stuff.co.nz/national/politics/63570264/pm-reveals-slater-texts.

Rutherford, Hamish 2014a, 'Peters pledge could force one-or-other choice on Nats', *Dominion Post*, 30 July, p. A5.

Rutherford, Hamish 2014b, 'Harawira: No regrets over Dotcom alliance', *Stuff*, 5 October, http://www.stuff.co.nz/national/10581654/Harawira-No-regrets-over-Dotcom-alliance.

Rutherford, Hamish 2014c, 'More MPs but kingmaker job redundant', *Dominion Post*, 22 September, p. A2.

Rutherford, Hamish 2014d, 'Winston Peters disappointed with impotent role', *Stuff*, 21 September, http://www.stuff.co.nz/national/politics/10526603/Winston-Peters-disappointed-with-impotent-role.

Rutherford, Hamish 2014e, 'Peter Dunne keeps ministerial portfolios', *Stuff*, 29 September, http://www.stuff.co.nz/national/politics/10557042/Peter-Dunne-keeps-ministerial-portfolios.

Rutherford, Hamish and Kelly Dennett 2014, 'David Cunliffe: I'm sorry for being a man', *Stuff*, 4 July, http://www.stuff.co.nz/national/politics/10232457/David-Cunliffe-I-m-sorry-for-being-a-man.

Rutherford, Hamish and Vernon Small 2014, 'Peters lays down his rules for coalition', *Dominion Post*, 10 September, p. A2, http://www.stuff.co.nz/national/politics/10478793/Peters-lays-down-his-rules-for-coalition.

Rutherford, Hamish and Vernon Small 2014a, 'Greens coalition ideas farcical: Peters', *Stuff*, 15 September, http://www.stuff.co.nz/national/politics/10500792/Greens-coalition-ideas-farcical-Peters.

Ryan, Sophie 2014, 'Cunliffe: It's just "Winston being Winston"', *New Zealand Herald*, 30 July, http://www.nzherald.co.nz/nz/news/article.cfm?c_id=1&objectid=11301308.

Sabin, Brook 2014, 'Internet Mana launch ends in chaos', *3News*, 24 August, http://www.3news.co.nz/politics/internet-mana-launch-ends-in-chaos-2014082417#axzz3blA6uwXZ.

Satherly, Dan 2014, 'At a glance: Labour's leadership election process', *3News*, 20 October, http://www.3news.co.nz/nznews/at-a-glance-labours-leadership-election-process-2014102013#axzz3R92PgwJR

Savage, Jared 2014, 'Collins Resigns: Jared Savage and Fran O'Sullivan Respond', *New Zealand Herald*, 30 August, http://www.nzherald.co.nz/nz/news/article.cfm?c_id=1&objectid=11316711.

Savage, Jared 2014a, 'David Cunliffe wrote letter supporting Liu's residency bid', *New Zealand Herald*, 18 June, http://www.nzherald.co.nz/nz/news/article.cfm?c_id=1&objectid=11276510.

Savage, Jared 2014b, 'Maurice Williamson resigns as a minister', *New Zealand Herald*, 1 May, http://www.nzherald.co.nz/nz/news/article.cfm?c_id=1&objectid=11247424.

Savage, Jared 2014c, 'David Cunliffe wrote letter supporting Liu's residency bid', *New Zealand Herald*, 18 June, http://www.nzherald.co.nz/nz/news/article.cfm?c_id=1&objectid=11276510.

Seymour, David 2014, 'Meet David Seymour (ACT Epsom Candidate)', campaign video, 28 April, https://www.youtube.com/watch?v=hEkPoZSBXh0.

Sharples, Pita 2007, 'The Maori Party', in Stephen Levine and Nigel S. Roberts (eds.), *The Baubles of Office: The New Zealand General Election of 2005*, Victoria University Press, Wellington.

Slater, Cameron 2010, 'And They Wonder Why I Call Them Repeaters', *Whale Oil Beef Hooked*, 23 December, http://www.whaleoil.co.nz/tag/repeaters/page/2/.

Slater, Cameron 2014, 'Chaos & Mayhem Is Never Going to Stop', *Whale Oil Beef Hooked*, 30 November, http://www.whaleoil.co.nz/2014/11/chaos-mayhem-never-going-stop/.

Slater, Cameron 2014a, 'And Here Was Me Thinking Hager Would Just Bug Me', *Whale Oil Beef Hooked*, 1 September, http://www.whaleoil.co.nz/2014/09/thinking-hager-just-bug/.

Small, Vernon 2014, 'Cunliffe's worst day', *Dominion Post*, 5 March, http://www.stuff.co.nz/national/politics/9789728/Cunliffes-worst-day.

Small, Vernon 2014a, 'Māori Party: No Internet Party link', *Dominion Post*, 25 March, http://www.stuff.co.nz/national/politics/9865557/Maori-Party-No-Internet-Party-link.

Smallman, Elton and Aimee Gulliver 2014, 'Peters pushes away aggressive heckler', *Stuff*, 14 August, http://www.stuff.co.nz/national/politics/10383748/Peters-pushes-away-aggressive-heckler.

Sorrenson, Keith 2014, *Ko Te Whenua Te Utu/Land is the Price: Essays on Māori History, Land and Politics*, Auckland, Auckland University Press.

Southern Cross Cable Network 2014, 'Claims of Cable Access Total Nonsense', press release, 15 September, http://www.scoop.co.nz/stories/BU1409/S00529/claims-of-cable-access-total-nonsense.htm.

Stewart, Matt and Alex Fensome 2014, 'Moa-hunting Mallard hangs on in Hutt [South]', *Sunday Star Times*, 21 September, p. A6.

StopPress Team 2014, 'How the Internet Party Will Be Chasing Your Vote', *Idealog*, 20 June, http://idealog.co.nz/venture/2014/06/how-internet-party-will-be-chasing-your-vote.

Strangio, Paul, Paul t'Hart and James Walter (eds.) 2013, *Understanding Prime-Ministerial Performance: Comparative Perspectives*, Oxford University Press, Oxford.

Stuff 2014, 'Campaign Diary: Monday, Sept 15', http://www.stuff.co.nz/national/politics/10498175/Campaign-Diary-Monday-Sept-15.

Stuff 2014a, 'Labour keeps its coalition tight', 8 September, http://www.stuff.co.nz/national/politics/10471767/Labour-keeps-its-coalition-tight.

Stuff 2014b, 'New role for Flavell in National deal', 5 October, http://www.stuff.co.nz/national/politics/10581713/New-role-for-Flavell-in-National-deal.

Stuff 2015, 'John Banks acquitted by Court of Appeal on false return charge', http://www.stuff.co.nz/national/68668623/john-banks-acquitted-by-court-of-appeal-on-false-return-charges.

Sunday Star Times 2014, 'David Cunliffe's leadership on the line', 21 September, p. 1.

The Political Scientist 2014, 'A Tale of Two Tracks. Part I – A Two Track World', http://www.thepoliticalscientist.org/a-tale-of-two-tracks-part-i-a-two-track-world/.

The Treasury 2014, 'Holding on and Letting Go, Treasury briefing to the incoming minister', October.

Thompson, Alastair 2015, 'Reinventing News As A Public Right – A Public Conversation', 16 January, http://www.scoop.co.nz/stories/HL1501/S00058/reinventing-news-as-a-public-right-a-public-conversation.htm#7.

Tiso, Giovanni 2014, 'Of Journalism and Monsters', *Bat, Bean, Beam*, 18 August, http://bat-bean-beam.blogspot.co.nz/2014/08/of-journalism-and-monsters.html.

Tiso, Giovanni 2014a, 'Dirty Journalism', *Bat, Bean, Beam*, 27 October, http://bat-bean-beam.blogspot.co.nz/2014/10/dirty-journalism.html.

Trevett, Claire 2012, 'David Shearer calls vote for Labour leadership', *New Zealand Herald*, 19 November, http://www.nzherald.co.nz/nz/news/article.cfm?c_id=1&objectid=10848489.

Trevett, Claire 2014, 'Trumping dirty politics with integrity and decency', *New Zealand Herald*, 11 December, http://www.nzherald.co.nz/nz/news/article.cfm?c_id=1&objectid=11372252.

Trevett, Claire 2014a, 'Cunliffe May Boycott Leaders' Debate over Hosking', *New Zealand Herald*, 24 July, http://www.nzherald.co.nz/nz/news/article.cfm?c_id=1&objectid=11298450.

Trevett, Claire 2014b, 'Key close to getting boot from Helensville electorate', *New Zealand Herald*, 12 August, http://www.nzherald.co.nz/nz/news/article.cfm?c_id=1&objectid=11307437.

Trevett, Claire 2014c, 'Key would be "committed" to whole of third term', *New Zealand Herald*, 4 February, http://www.nzherald.co.nz/nz/news/article.cfm?c_id=1&objectid=11196520.

Trevett, Claire 2014d, 'Kingmaker Peters spells it out: No deal without a royal commission into *Dirty Politics*', *New Zealand Herald*, 3 September, http://www.nzherald.co.nz/nz/news/article.cfm?c_id=1&objectid=11318071.

Trevett, Claire 2014e, 'David Cunliffe's holiday regrets', *New Zealand Herald*, 22 July, http://www.nzherald.co.nz/nz/news/article.cfm?c_id=1&objectid=11297426.

Trevett, Claire 2014f, 'Prime Minister takes pot-shot at Greens', *New Zealand Herald*, 20 August, http://www.nzherald.co.nz/nz/news/article.cfm?c_id=1&objectid=11311779.

Trevett, Claire 2014g, 'Māori Party focused on rebuild', *New Zealand Herald*, 1 November, http://www.nzherald.co.nz/nz/news/article.cfm?c_id=1&objectid=11351508.

Trevett, Claire 2014h, 'Oh David –it's come down to a question of trust', *New Zealand Herald*, 19 June, http://www.nzherald.co.nz/nz/news/article.cfm?c_id=1&objectid=11277287.

Trevett, Claire 2014i, '"He has the vision to win the trust of New Zealanders" – Andrew Little elected Labour leader', *New Zealand Herald*, 18 November, http://www.nzherald.co.nz/nz/news/article.cfm?c_id=1&objectid=11360509.

Trevett, Claire 2014j, 'Cunliffe questions Key's role in Liu letter scandal', *New Zealand Herald*, 19 June, http://www.nzherald.co.nz/nz/news/article.cfm?c_id=1&objectid=11276826.

Trevett, Claire 2014k, 'Labour all but rules out Internet-Mana', *New Zealand Herald*, 5 July, http://www.nzherald.co.nz/nz/news/article.cfm?c_id=1&objectid=11288220.

Trevett, Claire and David Fisher 2014, 'Dotcom Email Is a Fake – Warner Bros', *New Zealand Herald*, 15 September, http://www.nzherald.co.nz/nz/news/article.cfm?c_id=1&objectid=11324988.

Turia, Tariana 2014, 'My Life in Parliament and Returning Home', speech to the Federation of Māori Authorities Annual Conference, War Memorial Hall, Whanganui, 26 September, http://maoriparty.org/panui/speech-federation-of-maori-authorities-annual-conference-tariana-turia/.

TVNZ 2014, 'Corin Dann's Full Interview with Journalist Glenn Greenwald', *Q+A*, 14 September, http://tvnz.co.nz/q-and-a-news/corin-dann-s-full-interview-journalist-glenn-greenwald-video-6080059.

TVNZ 2014a, 'Kim Dotcom Adamant John Key Lying', *One News*, http://tvnz.co.nz/national-news/kim-dotcom-adamant-john-key-lying-5221947.

TVNZ 2014b, 'Vote Compass', http://tvnz.co.nz/votecompass.

TVNZ 2014c, '"Blind panic" led to Judith Collins' resignation – journalist', 1 September, http://tvnz.co.nz/vote-2014-news/blind-panic-led-judith-collins-resignation-journalist-6068499.

Uberti, David 2014, 'How Political Campaigns Use Twitter to Shape Media Coverage', *Columbia Journalism Review*, 9 December, http://www.cjr.org/behind_the_news/how_political_campaigns_use_tw.php#sthash.TSIFRKgX.dpuf.

United Future 2015, 'United Future Facebook Page', https://www.facebook.com/UnitedFutureNZ.

Vallone, Robert P., Lee Ross and Mark R. Lepper 1985, 'The Hostile Media Phenomenon: Biased Perception and Perceptions of Media Bias in Coverage of the Beirut Massacre', *Journal of Personality And Social Psychology*, vol. 49, no. 3, pp. 577–85.

Vance, Andrea 2013, 'GCSB Acted Illegally on Kim Dotcom', *Stuff*, 29 August, http://www.stuff.co.nz/national/9103159/GCSB-acted-illegally-on-Kim-Dotcom.

Vance, Andrea 2014, 'The Snowden Files: What Did We Learn?', *Stuff*, 16 September, http://www.stuff.co.nz/national/politics/10503457/The-Snowden-files-What-did-we-learn.

Vance, Andrea 2014a, '"Moment of Truth" – Do Believe the Hype', *Stuff*, 16 September, http://www.stuff.co.nz/national/politics/opinion/10502898/Moment-of-truth-do-believe-the-hype.

Vance, Andrea 2014b, 'Labour Claims Hosking's Biased', *Stuff*, 24 July, http://www.stuff.co.nz/national/politics/10303335/Labour-claims-Hoskings-biased.

Vance, Andrea 2014c, 'How the Snowden Story Unfolded', *Stuff*, 17 September, http://www.stuff.co.nz/national/politics/10510250/How-the-Snowden-story-unfolded.

Vance, Andrea 2014d, 'Labour MPs could dump David Cunliffe', *Dominion Post*, 18 June, http://www.stuff.co.nz/national/politics/opinion/10173408/Labour-MPs-could-dump-David-Cunliffe.

Vance, Andrea 2014e, 'Labour cool on Internet-Mana deal', *Stuff*, 6 August, http://www.stuff.co.nz/national/politics/10353381/Labour-cool-on-Internet-Mana-deal.

Vance, Andrea 2014f, 'Knives out for Cunliffe', *Dominion Post*, 22 September, p. 1, http://www.stuff.co.nz/national/politics/opinion/10527227/Labour-leadership-contest-likely.

Vance, Andrea 2014g, 'Greens searching for answers', *Dominion Post*, 22 September, p. 2.

Vance, Andrea 2014h, 'John Key nixes deal with Greens', *Stuff*, 12 September, http://www.stuff.co.nz/national/politics/10492794/John-Key-nixes-deal-with-Greens.

Vance, Andrea, Stacey Kirk and Michael Fox 2014, 'Taurima Was Unfair to Me – Bennett', *Stuff*, 18 February, http://www.stuff.co.nz/national/politics/9734475/Taurima-was-unfair-to-me-Bennett.

Volden, Craig and Clifford Carrubba 2004, 'The Formation of Oversized Coalitions in Parliamentary Democracies', *American Journal of Political Science*, vol. 48, no. 3, pp. 521–537.

Vowles, Jack 2001, 'Voting Behaviour', in Raymond Miller (ed.), *New Zealand Government and Politics*, Oxford University Press, Auckland.

Vowles, Jack 2003, 'Voting Behaviour', in Raymond Miller (ed.), *New Zealand Government and Politics*, third edition, Oxford University Press, Melbourne.

Vowles, Jack 2012, *Report of the Electoral Commission on the Review of the MMP Voting System*, 29 October, Wellington.

Vowles, Jack 2014, 'Putting the 2011 Election in Its Place', in Jack Vowles (ed.), *The New Electoral Politics in New Zealand: The Significance of the 2011 Election*, Institute for Governance and Policy Studies, Wellington.

Vowles, Jack and Peter Aimer 2004, 'Conclusion', in Jack Vowles, Peter Aimer, Susan Banducci, Jeffrey Karp and Raymond Miller (eds.), *Voters' Veto: The 2002 Election in New Zealand and the Consolidation of Minority Government*, Auckland University Press, Auckland.

Wall, Tony 2014, '"We'll be back" vow big-spending Conservatives', *Sunday Star Times*, 21 September, p. 4, http://www.stuff.co.nz/national/politics/10525671/We-ll-be-back-big-spending-Conservatives.

Watkin, Tim 2014, 'What Collins' Resignation Means for Journalism & the Campaign', *Pundit*, 1 September, http://pundit.co.nz/content/what-collins-resignation-means-for-journalism-the-campaign.

Watkin, Tim 2014a, 'Affidavit of Timothy Marcus Watkin', Colin Graeme Craig v Mediaworks TV Limited, Auckland High Court CIV-2014-404-001972 [2014] NZHC 1875, 8 August.

Watkins, Tracy 2010, 'Budget GST Rise "Attack on the Poor"', *Dominion Post*, 20 May, http://www.stuff.co.nz/business/budget-2010/3716930/Budget-GST-rise-attack-on-the-poor.

Watkins, Tracy 2014, 'One step forward, two back for National', *Dominion Post*, 7 August, http://www.stuff.co.nz/national/politics/opinion/10356218/One-step-forward-two-back-for-National.

Watkins, Tracy 2014a, 'Dirty Tactics, or Just Politics at Play?', *Stuff*, 16 August, http://www.stuff.co.nz/dominion-post/comment/columnists/tracy-watkins/10389592/Dirty-tactics-or-just-politics-at-play.

Watkins, Tracy 2014b, 'I'm working my butt off – Cunliffe', *Dominion Post*, 21 July, p. A2, http://www.stuff.co.nz/national/politics/10289379/I-m-working-my-butt-off-Cunliffe.

Watkins, Tracy 2014c, 'Cunliffe "set himself up" – Key', *Stuff*, 20 June, http://www.stuff.co.nz/national/politics/10181027/Cunliffe-set-himself-up-Key.

Watkins, Tracy 2014d, 'Tight race ahead for Key and Cunliffe', *Stuff*, 19 September, http://www.stuff.co.nz/national/politics/polls/10516895/Tight-race-ahead-for-Key-and-Cunliffe.

Westen, Drew, Pavel S. Blagov, Keith Harenski, Clint Kilts and Stephan Hamann, 2006, 'Neural Bases of Motivated Reasoning: An FMRI Study of Emotional Constraints on Partisan Political Judgment in the 2004 U.S. Presidential Election', *Journal of Cognitive Neuroscience*, vol. 18, no. 11, pp. 1947–58.

Whyte, Jamie 2014, 'ACT is holding the balance of power', campaign speech, Newmarket, 14 September, http://www.scoop.co.nz/stories/PO1409/S00316/act-is-holding-the-balance-of-power.htm.

Williams, Melissa 2015, *Panguru and the City: Kāinga Tahi, Kāinga Rua*, Bridget Williams Books, Wellington.

Wills, Kris 2014, '5 Questions – Te Tai Hauāuru Answers', *Wanganui Chronicle*, 13 September, http://www.nzherald.co.nz/wanganui-chronicle/news/article.cfm?c_id=1503426&objectid=11324089.

Wilson, Chris 2014, 'Infographic: Obama Accepts Rare Outside Into Golf Game', *Time*, 3 January, http://swampland.time.com/2014/01/03/obama-golfs-with-new-zealand-prime-minister/.

Wilson, Simon 2014, 'Doubling Down', *Metro*, 1 September, http://www.metromag.co.nz/editors-blog/doubling-down/.

Winter, David 2003, 'Personality and Political Behavior', in David O. Sears, Leonie Huddy and Robert Jervis (eds.), *Oxford Handbook of Political Psychology*, Oxford University Press, Oxford, pp. 110–45.

Wolf, Martin 2014, 'Strip private banks of their power to create money', *Financial Times*, 24 April, http://www.ft.com/cms/s/0/7f000b18-ca44-11e3-bb92-00144feabdc0.html#axzz3h2VkXigH.

Wong, Simon 2014, 'Leaders: Too Many Distractions in Campaign', *3News*, 17 September, http://www.3news.co.nz/politics/leaders-too-many-distractions-in-campaign-2014091720#axzz3S4Lp7BPf.

Wong, Simon 2014a, 'Video: John Key talks Nicky Hager's *Dirty Politics*', *3News*, 14 August, http://www.3news.co.nz/politics/video-john-key-talks-nicky-hagers-dirty-politics-2014081414.

Wong, Simon 2014b, 'Slater Gets Temporary Injunction against Hacker', *3News*, 5 September, http://www.3news.co.nz/politics/slater-gets-temporary-injunction-against-hacker-2014090517#axzz3S4Lp7BPf.

Wong, Simon 2014c, 'Commission bans "Planet Key" song', *3News*, 12 August, http://www.3news.co.nz/politics/commission-bans-planet-key-song-2014081218#axzz3blA6uwXZ.

Wong, Simon 2014d, 'Harré resigns as Internet Party leader', *3News*, 15 December, http://www.3news.co.nz/nznews/harre-resigns-as-internet-party-leader-2014121512#axzz3cGelYAJ0.

Woodward, W. E. 1945, *Tom Paine: America's Godfather 1737–1809*, Dutton and Company, New York.

Worthy, Trevor H. 2015, 'Moa', in *Te Ara*, the New Zealand Ministry for Culture and Heritage, online *Encyclopedia of New Zealand*, http://www.teara.govt.nz/en/moa.

Young, Audrey 2014, 'Moment of Truth Gifts Team Key a Late Bounce in Polls', *New Zealand Herald*, 19 September, http://www.nzherald.co.nz/nz/news/article.cfm?c_id=1&objectid=11327321.

Young, Audrey 2014a, 'Peters sets out New Zealand First's priorities', *New Zealand Herald*, 10 September, http://www.nzherald.co.nz/nz/news/article.cfm?c_id=1&objectid=11321714.

Young, Audrey 2014b, 'National MP Claudette Hauiti calls it quits', *New Zealand Herald*, 22 July, http://www.nzherald.co.nz/nz/news/article.cfm?c_id=1&objectid=11297254.

Young, Audrey 2014c, 'Williamson's "significant error of judgment"', *New Zealand Herald*, 1 May, http://www.nzherald.co.nz/nz/news/article.cfm?c_id=1&objectid=11247618.

Young, Audrey 2014d, 'Labour rebuffs Greens plans to get closer', *New Zealand Herald*, 9 April, http://www.nzherald.co.nz/nz/news/article.cfm?c_id=1&objectid=11235338.

Young, Audrey 2014e, 'Peters takes Greens to task', *New Zealand Herald*, 11 April, http://www.nzherald.co.nz/nz/news/article.cfm?c_id=1&objectid=11236078.

Young, Audrey 2014f, 'Deals with National on the fast track', *New Zealand Herald*, 24 September, http://www.nzherald.co.nz/nz/news/article.cfm?c_id=1&objectid=11330243.

2014 CONFIDENCE AND SUPPLY AGREEMENT WITH ACT NEW ZEALAND

ACT New Zealand agrees to provide confidence and supply for the term of this Parliament to a National-led Government in return for National's agreement to the policy programme and other matters set out in this document.

The agreement between ACT and National builds on the stable and constructive relationship developed between the two parties over the past six years and will continue to be based on good faith and no surprises.

Consultation arrangements

The Government will consult with ACT including on:

- the broad outline of the legislative programme
- key legislative measures
- major policy issues
- broad budget parameters; and
- policy issues and legislative measures to which ACT is likely to be particularly sensitive.

Consultation will occur in a timely fashion to ensure ACT views can be incorporated into final decision-making. Formal consultation will be managed between the Prime Minister's Office and the Office of David Seymour.

Other co-operation will include:

- access to relevant Ministers
- regular meetings between the Prime Minister and David Seymour.
- advance notification to the other party of significant announcements by either the Government or ACT, and
- briefings by Ministers and officials on significant issues and issues that are likely to be politically sensitive before any public announcement.

Policy programme

National and ACT have worked together constructively over the past two parliamentary terms to provide stable government and to implement policies to promote a strong economy.

In this parliamentary term, ACT has a number of priorities to progress with the government – making further progress on the development of partnership schools; reducing the regulatory burden on businesses and consumers; and on reform of the Resource Management Act, among the key ones, as follows:

1. Partnership Schools/Kura Hourua

National and ACT agree to further develop the model and expand the trial of Partnership Schools/Kura Hourua, for the purpose of improving educational outcomes for disadvantaged students. This will include maintaining the momentum and continuity of the initiative by strengthening and enhancing the application and governance processes in order to foster high quality applications and high-performing schools.

2. Regulatory Reform

National and ACT agree with the OECD that excessive and poor-quality regulation is holding New Zealand back. The two parties will continue to work together on reducing the regulatory burden.

3. Resource Management Act reform

National and ACT agree that priority should be given to reform of the Resource Management Act, in the interests of promoting investment, jobs and prosperity as well as environmental protection.

National agrees to work with ACT on these and other policy areas as may be identified from time to time in good faith.

With respect to National's legislative agenda, ministerial offices will work with the office of David Seymour on matters to come before the House. ACT will consider its position on each Bill in good faith and advise the office of the Prime Minister and the Government Whips.

Executive position

David Seymour will be appointed to the positions of Parliamentary Under Secretary to the Minister of Education and Parliamentary Under Secretary to the Minister for Regulatory Reform, with each of these roles reflecting the policy priorities and objectives set out in the Agreement.

David Seymour will be nominated by National to be a member of the Finance and Expenditure Select Committee and will be appointed a member of the Cabinet Appointments and Honours Committee. He will also attend other Cabinet committees as appropriate.

Ministerial questions

National and ACT agree that National will consider and not unreasonably decline to allocate some of their questions plus supplementary questions to ACT, upon request from David Seymour.

Speaking slots

National and ACT agree that from time to time and on a case-by-case basis, National will consider giving David Seymour a full ten minute speaking slot in the House on readings and in the general debate. In addition, National will consider and not unreasonably decline giving David Seymour a five minute 'split' speaking slot on readings on bills before the House.

Proxy vote casting

National and ACT agree that National will cast proxy votes on behalf of David Seymour at his request when the need arises for him to be absent from the House.

Confidentiality

It is agreed that where briefings are provided to ACT, or where ACT is involved in consultative arrangements with regard to legislation, policy or budgetary matters, all such discussions shall be confidential unless otherwise agreed.

In the event that Government papers are provided to ACT in the course of consultation or briefings they shall be treated as confidential and shall not be released, or the information used for any public purpose, without the express agreement of the relevant Minister.

In the event that Cabinet or Cabinet committee papers are provided to ACT for the purposes of consultation they shall be provided to a designated person within the Office of David Seymour, who will take responsibility for ensuring they are accorded the appropriate degree of confidentiality.

Collective responsibility

David Seymour agrees to be bound by collective responsibility in relation to his responsibilities as a Parliamentary Under Secretary. When he speaks about issues within his portfolio responsibilities he will speak for the Government, representing the Government's position in relation to those responsibilities. When he speaks about matters outside his responsibilities, however, he may speak as an ACT MP, or as a Member of Parliament. He will support the Government's position in all matters that are the subject of confidence and supply votes.

Where there has been full participation in the development of a policy initiative outside of any portfolio responsibility held by David Seymour, and that participation has led to an agreed position, it is expected that all parties to this agreement will publicly support the process and the outcome.

Cabinet Manual

David Seymour agrees to be bound by the Cabinet Manual in the exercise of his responsibilities as a Parliamentary Under Secretary and, in particular, agrees to be bound by the provisions in the Cabinet Manual on the conduct, public duty, and personal interests of Ministers.

Procedural motions

ACT agrees that it will support the Government on procedural motions in the House and in Select Committees, unless ACT has previously advised that such support is not forthcoming. The Government agrees that it will operate a no-surprises policy in terms of procedural motions it intends to put before the House or a Select Committee.

Legislative programme

Support for particular measures which do not relate to confidence or supply will be negotiated on a case-by-case basis.

Dated: 29 September 2014

Rt Hon John Key   David Seymour
National Leader   ACT Parliamentary Leader

Source: http://www.parliament.nz/resource/en-nz/00PlibMPPNationall1/0ff3caff dcd840e9f98094f393a3bbb08b769eb1

2014 CONFIDENCE AND SUPPLY AGREEMENT WITH UNITED FUTURE NEW ZEALAND

United Future agrees to provide confidence and supply support for the term of this Parliament to a National-led government in return for National's agreement to the matters set out in this document.

The agreement between United Future and National builds on the stable and constructive relationship developed between the two parties over the past six years and will continue to be based on good faith and no surprises.

Consultation arrangements

The Government will consult with United Future including on:

- the broad outline of the legislative programme
- key legislative measures
- major policy issues;
- broad budget parameters; and
- policy issues and legislative measures to which United Future is likely to be particularly sensitive.

Consultation will occur in a timely fashion to ensure United Future views can be incorporated into final decision-making.

Formal consultation will be managed between the Prime Minister's Office and the Office of the Leader of United Future.

Other co-operation will include:

- access to relevant Ministers
- regular meetings between the Prime Minister and the United Future Leader
- advance notification to the other party of significant announcements by either the Government or United Future, and
- briefings by Ministers and officials on significant issues and issues that are likely to be politically sensitive before any public announcement.

Policy programme

National and United Future have worked together constructively over the past two parliamentary terms to provide stable government and to implement policies to promote a strong economy.

In this parliamentary term, United Future has a number of priorities to progress with the government – the next iteration of the National Medicines Strategy – *Medicines New Zealand* – including the enhanced role of Pharmacists in patient medicines management and primary care; improving water quality in our lakes, rivers and streams; giving recreational fishers more opportunities as acknowledge in National's recently announced recreational fishing reserves policy; and re-affirming the use of public-private partnerships for major roading projects where appropriate; among the key ones.

National agrees to work with United Future on these and other policy areas as may be identified from time to time in good faith.

With respect to National's legislative agenda, ministerial offices will work with the office of the United Future Leader on matters to come before the House. United Future will consider its position on each Bill in good faith and on a case-by-case basis and advise the Office of the Prime Minister and the Government Whips.

Executive Position

Hon Peter Dunne will be appointed to the positions of Minister of Internal Affairs, Associate Minister of Health and Associate Minister of Conservation. Mr Dunne will be a Minister outside Cabinet.

Mr Dunne will be appointed a member of the Cabinet Appointments and Honours Committee, Cabinet Social Policy Committee, and the Cabinet Committee on State Sector Reform and Expenditure Control. He will also attend other Cabinet Committees as appropriate.

Ministerial questions

National and United Future agree that National will allocate on a case-by-case basis question opportunities for Hon Peter Dunne to use in the House.

Speaking slots

National and United Future agree that from time to time on a case-by-case basis Hon Peter Dunne will be allocated a National speaking slot in the House on legislation and other general debates.

Confidentiality

It is agreed that where briefings are provided to United Future, or where United Future is involved in consultative arrangements with regard to legislation, policy or budgetary matters, all such discussions shall be confidential unless otherwise agreed.

In the event that government papers are provided to United Future in the course of consultation or briefings they shall be treated as confidential and shall not be released, or the information used for any public purpose, without the express agreement of the relevant Minister.

In the event that Cabinet or Cabinet committee papers are provided to United Future for the purposes of consultation they shall be provided to a designated person within the Office of the United Future Leader, who will take responsibility for ensuring they are accorded the appropriate degree of confidentiality.

Collective responsibility

Hon Peter Dunne agrees to be bound by collective responsibility in relation to his portfolios. When he speaks about issues within his portfolio responsibilities he will speak for the Government, representing the Government's position in relation to those responsibilities. When he speaks about matters outside his portfolio responsibilities, however, he may speak as Leader of United Future, or as the Member of Parliament for Ōhāriu.

He will support the Government's position in all matters that are the subject of confidence and supply votes.

Where there has been full participation in the development of a policy initiative outside of any portfolio responsibility held by Hon Peter Dunne, and that participation has led to an agreed position, it is expected that all parties to this agreement will publicly support the process and the outcome.

Cabinet Manual

Hon Peter Dunne agrees to be bound by the Cabinet Manual in the exercise of his Ministerial responsibilities and, in particular, agrees to be bound by the provisions in the Cabinet Manual on the conduct, public duty, and personal interests of Ministers.

Procedural Motions

United Future agrees that it will support the Government on procedural motions in the House and in Select Committees, unless United Future has previously advised that such support is not forthcoming. The Government agrees that it will operate a no-surprises policy in terms of procedural motions it intends to put before the House or a Select Committee.

Dated: 29 September 2014

Rt Hon John Key   Hon Peter Dunne MP
National Leader   United Future Leader

Source: http://www.parliament.nz/resource/en-nz/00PlibMPPNational1/75f0b0e 24b9bc9ac953c6b7365fdfcd28b3d62f5

2014 RELATIONSHIP ACCORD AND CONFIDENCE AND SUPPLY AGREEMENT WITH THE MĀORI PARTY

'Te Tatau ki te Paerangi' – A doorway to our horizons

The Māori Party agrees to provide confidence and supply through positive votes of support for the term of this Parliament to a National-led Government in return for National's agreement to the matters set out in this document.

The agreement between the Māori Party and National builds on the stable and constructive relationship developed between the two parties over the past six years and will continue to be based on good faith and no surprises.

Consultation arrangements

The Government will consult with the Māori Party including on:

- the broad outline of the legislative programme
- key legislative measures
- major policy issues
- broad budget parameters; and
- policy issues and legislative measures to which the Māori Party is likely to be particularly sensitive.

Consultation will occur in a timely fashion to ensure the Māori Party views can be incorporated into final decision-making.

Formal consultation will be managed between the Prime Minister's Office and the Office of the Co-leaders of the Māori Party.

Other co-operation will include:

- access to relevant Ministers
- regular meetings between the Prime Minister and Māori Party Co-leaders

- advance notification to the other party of significant announcements by either the Government or the Māori Party, and
- briefings by Ministers and officials on significant issues and issues that are likely to be politically sensitive before any public announcement.

Policy programme

National and the Māori Party have worked together constructively over the past two parliamentary terms to provide stable government.

Throughout the six years, the Māori Party has continued to be a strong, independent voice for Māori and has voted against government legislation when it has believed that to be in the best interests of Māori.

But by being "at the table", the Māori Party has gained significant policy wins for its constituents.

In this parliamentary term the Māori Party wishes to continue to pursue its policy priorities with the government – ongoing investment in Whānau Ora; the continuation of the work by the Ministerial Committee on Poverty; a focus on Māori economic and regional development; encouraging greater Māori participation in the electoral process, among the key ones. These priorities will guide the work of Te Puni Kōkiri and be reflected in the Statement of Intent to be agreed between the Minister and Chief Executive.

National agrees to work with the Māori Party on these and other policy areas as may be identified from time to time in good faith.

With respect to National's legislative agenda, Ministerial offices will work with the Māori Party Co-Leader's Office on matters to come before the House. The Māori Party will consider its position on each Bill in good faith and advise the relevant Minister.

Executive position

Te Ururoa Flavell will be appointed to the positions of Minister for Māori Development and Minister for Whānau Ora, and Associate Minister for Economic Development.

Te Ururoa Flavell will be appointed a member of the Cabinet Appointments and Honours Committee, the Cabinet Committee on Treaty of Waitangi Negotiations, the Cabinet Committee on Social Policy and the Cabinet Economic Growth and Infrastructure Committee. He will also attend other Cabinet committees as appropriate.

Ministerial questions

National and the Māori Party agree that National will allocate on a case-by-case basis question opportunities for the Māori Party to use in the House.

Speaking slots

National and the Māori Party agree that from time to time on a case-by-case basis the Māori Party will be allocated a National speaking slot in the House on legislation and other general debates.

Confidentiality

It is agreed that where briefings are provided to the Māori Party, or where the Māori Party is involved in consultative arrangements with regard to legislation, policy or budgetary matters, all such discussions shall be confidential unless otherwise agreed.

In the event that Government papers are provided to the Māori Party in the course of consultation or briefings they shall be treated as confidential and shall not be released, or the information used for any public purpose, without the express agreement of the relevant Minister.

In the event that Cabinet or Cabinet committee papers are provided to the Māori Party for the purposes of consultation they shall be provided to a designated person within the Office of Te Ururoa Flavell, who will take responsibility for ensuring they are accorded the appropriate degree of confidentiality.

Collective responsibility

Te Ururoa Flavell agrees to be bound by collective responsibility in relation to his portfolios. When he speaks about issues within his portfolio responsibilities he will speak for the Government, representing the Government's position in relation to those responsibilities. When he speaks about matters outside his portfolio responsibilities, however, he may speak as a Māori Party Co-leader, or as a Member of Parliament. He will support the Government's position in all matters that are the subject of confidence and supply votes.

Where there has been full participation in the development of a policy initiative outside of any portfolio responsibility held by Te Ururoa Flavell, and that participation has led to an agreed position, it is expected that all parties to this agreement will publicly support the process and the outcome.

Cabinet Manual

Te Ururoa Flavell agrees to be bound by the Cabinet Manual in the exercise of his responsibilities as a Minister and, in particular, agrees to be bound by the provisions in the Cabinet Manual on the conduct, public duty, and personal interests of Ministers.

Procedural motions

The Māori Party agrees it will support the Government on procedural motions in the House and in Select Committees, unless the Māori Party has previously advised that such support is not forthcoming. The Government agrees that it will operate a no-surprises policy in terms of procedural motions it intends to put before the House or a Select Committee.

Legislative programme

Support for particular measures, which do not relate to confidence or supply, will be negotiated on a case-by-case basis.

Engagement with Māori

The two parties commit to an engagement strategy with whānau, hapū and iwi, Māori organisations and business to share at a local level progress being achieved for Māori across priority policy areas.

When engaging with iwi and Māori organisations, the Government will keep the Māori Party informed and involved where appropriate.

Dated: 5 October 2014

| Rt Hon John Key | Hon Tariana Turia | Te Ururoa Flavell |
| National Party Leader | Māori Party Co-Leader | Māori Party Co-Leader |

Source: http://www.parliament.nz/resource/en-nz/00PlibMPPNational1/15a58cb e14e78257349a8224381ca515dfefea7e

MPs IN THE 51st PARLIAMENT

National

Amy Adams	(Selwyn)
Kanwaljit Singh Bakshi	(list)
* Todd Barclay	(Clutha-Southland)
Maggie Barry	(North Shore)
* Andrew Bayly	(Hunua)
David Bennett	(Hamilton East)
Paula Bennett	(Upper Harbour)
* Chris Bishop	(list)
Chester Borrows	(Whanganui)
Simon Bridges	(Tauranga)
Gerry Brownlee	(Ilam)
David Carter	(list)
Jonathan Coleman	(Northcote)
Judith Collins	(Papakura)
Jacqui Dean	(Waitaki)
* Matt Doocey	(Waimakariri)
* Sarah Dowie	(Invercargill)
Bill English	(list)
Christopher Finlayson	(list)
Craig Foss	(Tukituki)
Paul Foster-Bell	(list)
Paul Goldsmith	(list)
Jo Goodhew	(Rangitata)
Tim Groser	(list)
Nathan Guy	(Ōtaki)
Joanne Hayes	(list)
* Brett Hudson	(list)
Steven Joyce	(list)
Nikki Kaye	(Auckland Central)
John Key	(Helensville)

* Nuk Korako	(list)
* Barbara Kuriger	(Taranaki-King Country)
Melissa Lee	(list)
Peseta Sam Lotu-Iiga	(Maungakiekie)
Tim Macindoe	(Hamilton West)
Todd McClay	(Rotorua)
Murray McCully	(East Coast Bays)
Ian McKelvie	(Rangitīkei)
Mark Mitchell	(Rodney)
* Todd Muller	(Bay of Plenty)
* Jono Naylor	(list)
Alfred Ngaro	(list)
Simon O'Connor	(Tāmaki)
Hekia Parata	(list)
* Parmjeet Parmar	(list)
* Shane Reti	(Whangarei)
Jami-Lee Ross	(Botany)
*** Mike Sabin	(Northland)
* Alastair Scott	(Wairarapa)
Scott Simpson	(Coromandel)
Nick Smith	(Nelson)
* Stuart Smith	(Kaikōura)
Lindsay Tisch	(Waikato)
Anne Tolley	(East Coast)
Louise Upston	(Taupō)
Nicky Wagner	(Christchurch Central)
Maurice Williamson	(Pakuranga)
Michael Woodhouse	(list)
Jian Yang	(list)
Jonathan Young	(New Plymouth)

Labour

Jacinda Ardern	(list)
David Clark	(Dunedin North)
Clayton Cosgrove	(list)
David Cunliffe	(New Lynn)
Clare Curran	(Dunedin South)

** Kelvin Davis	(Te Tai Tokerau)
Ruth Dyson	(Port Hills)
Kris Faafoi	(Mana)
Phil Goff	(Mt Roskill)
* Peeni Henare	(Tāmaki Makaurau)
Chris Hipkins	(Rimutaka)
Annette King	(Rongotai)
Iain Lees-Galloway	(Palmerston North)
Andrew Little	(list)
Nanaia Mahuta	(Hauraki-Waikato)
Trevor Mallard	(Hutt South)
Sue Moroney	(list)
** Stuart Nash	(Napier)
Damien O'Connor	(West Coast-Tasman)
David Parker	(list)
Grant Robertson	(Wellington Central)
* Adrian Rurawhe	(Te Tai Hauāuru)
* Jenny Salesa	(Manukau East)
** Carmel Sepuloni	(Kelston)
David Shearer	(Mt Albert)
Su'a William Sio	(Māngere)
Rino Tirikatene	(Te Tai Tonga)
Phil Twyford	(Te Atatū)
Louisa Wall	(Manurewa)
Meka Whaitiri	(Ikaroa-Rāwhiti)
Poto Williams	(Christchurch East)
Megan Woods	(Wigram)

Green

Steffan Browning	(list)
David Clendon	(list)
Catherine Delahunty	(list)
Julie Anne Genter	(list)
Kennedy Graham	(list)
Kevin Hague	(list)
Gareth Hughes	(list)
Jan Logie	(list)

Mojo Mathers	(list)
Russel Norman	(list)
Denise Roche	(list)
Eugenie Sage	(list)
* James Shaw	(list)
Metiria Turei	(list)

New Zealand First

* Darroch Ball	(list)
* Mahesh Bindra	(list)
** Ron Mark	(list)
Tracey Martin	(list)
* Clayton Mitchell	(list)
Denis O'Rourke	(list)
** Pita Paraone	(list)
Winston Peters	(list)
Richard Prosser	(list)
Barbara Stewart	(list)
* Fletcher Tabuteau	(list)

Māori Party

Te Ururoa Flavell	(Waiariki)
* Marama Fox	(list)

ACT

* David Seymour	(Epsom)

United Future

Peter Dunne	(Ōhāriu)

* a new member of Parliament
** previously a member of Parliament, but not in the 2011–14 Parliament
*** Mike Sabin resigned from Parliament on 30 January 2015. He was succeeded by Winston Peters, elected in a by-election held on 28 March 2015. Ria Bond replaced Winston Peters as a New Zealand First list MP (on 24 April 2015).
Source: New Zealand Parliament; MPs elected in 2014 general election (6 October 2014) http://www.parliament.nz/en-NZ/MPP/MPs/MPs/

THE GOVERNMENT*

Ministers in the Cabinet

1	John Key	Prime Minister
		Minister for National Security and Intelligence
		Minister of Tourism
		Minister responsible for Ministerial Services
2	Bill English	Deputy Prime Minister
		Minister of Finance
		Minister responsible for HNZC[†]
3	Gerry Brownlee	Minister for Canterbury Earthquake Recovery
		Minister of Defence
		Leader of the House
		Minister responsible for the Earthquake Commission
4	Steven Joyce	Minister for Economic Development
		Minister for Regulatory Reform
		Minister of Science and Innovation
		Minister for Tertiary Education, Skills and Employment
		Minister responsible for Novopay
		Associate Minister of Finance
5	Paula Bennett	Minister of Local Government
		Minister for Social Housing
		Minister of State Services
		Associate Minister of Finance
		Associate Minister of Tourism
6	Jonathan Coleman	Minister of Health
		Minister for Sport and Recreation

7	Amy Adams	Minister of Justice
		Minister for Courts
		Minister of Broadcasting
		Minister for Communications
8	Christopher Finlayson	Attorney-General
		Minister for Treaty of Waitangi Negotiations
		Minister in charge of the NZSIS[†]
		Minister responsible for the GCSB[**]
		Associate Minister for Māori Development
9	Simon Bridges	Minister of Energy and Resources
		Minister of Transport
		Deputy Leader of the House
		Associate Minister for Climate Change Issues
		Associate Minister of Justice
10	Hekia Parata	Minister of Education
11	Anne Tolley	Minister for Social Development
12	Nick Smith	Minister for the Environment
		Minister for Building and Housing
13	Murray McCully	Minister of Foreign Affairs
		Associate Minister for Sport and Recreation
14	Nathan Guy	Minister for Primary Industries
		Minister for Racing
15	Nikki Kaye	Minister for ACC[††]
		Minister of Civil Defence
		Minister for Youth
		Associate Minister of Education
16	Tim Groser	Minister of Trade
		Minister for Climate Change Issues
17	Michael Woodhouse	Minister of Immigration
		Minister of Police
		Minister for Workplace Relations and Safety

18	Todd McClay	Minister of Revenue
		Minister for State Owned Enterprises
		Associate Minister of Foreign Affairs
		Associate Minister of Trade
19	Peseta Sam Lotu-Iiga	Minister of Corrections
		Minister for Ethnic Communities
		Minister for Pacific Peoples
		Associate Minister of Health
20	Maggie Barry	Minister for Arts, Culture and Heritage
		Minister of Conservation
		Minister for Senior Citizens

Ministers outside Cabinet

21	Craig Foss	Minister for Small Business
		Minister of Statistics
		Minister of Veterans' Affairs
		Associate Minister of Immigration
		Associate Minister of Transport
22	Jo Goodhew	Minister for the Community and Voluntary Sector
		Minister for Food Safety
		Associate Minister for Primary Industries
		Associate Minister for Social Development
23	Nicky Wagner	Minister of Customs
		Minister for Disability Issues
		Associate Minister for Canterbury Earthquake Recovery
		Associate Minister of Conservation
24	Louise Upston	Minister for Land Information
		Minister for Women
		Associate Minister of Local Government
		Associate Minister for Tertiary Education, Skills and Employment

| 25 | Paul Goldsmith | Minister of Commerce and Consumer Affairs |
| | | Associate Minister for ACC[††] |

Ministers outside Cabinet from parties with confidence and supply agreements

Peter Dunne	Minister of Internal Affairs
	Associate Minister of Conservation
	Associate Minister of Health
Te Ururoa Flavell	Minister for Māori Development
	Minister for Whānau Ora
	Associate Minister for Economic Development

Parliamentary Under-Secretary (from a party with a confidence and supply agreement)

| David Seymour | Parliamentary Under-Secretary to the Minister of Education |
| | Minister for Regulatory Reform |

[*] As at 8 October 2014
[†] Housing New Zealand Corporation
[†] New Zealand Security Intelligence Service
[**] Government Communications Security Bureau
[††] Accident Compensation Corporation

Source: Cabinet Office, Ministerial List; http://www.dpmc.govt.nz/cabinet/ ministers/ministerial-list

Therese Arseneau received her DPhil from the University of Oxford which she attended as a Commonwealth Scholar. She has been a lecturer at New Zealand and Canadian universities since 1988 and currently is a senior research fellow in the school of political science and communication at the University of Canterbury. Originally from Canada, she provided a distinctive perspective on New Zealand's politics through her appearances as a television commentator at the 2005, 2008 and 2011 elections. Her chapter 'The Defining Features of the 2005 Election: A "Glass Ceiling" and "Constitutional Innovation"' appeared in *The Baubles of Office: The New Zealand General Election of 2005*, and she contributed a further chapter, '2008: National's winning strategy', to *Key to Victory: The New Zealand General Election of 2008*. She was co-author of '"Kicking the tyres" on MMP: the results of the referendum reviewed' in *Kicking the Tyres: The New Zealand General Election and Referendum of 2011*. She has been an expert advisor to the New Zealand Electoral Commission both prior to the 2011 electoral referendum and subsequently, in connection with the post-referendum review. In 2011 she was a recipient of the University of Canterbury Teaching Award for excellence in teaching.

Tim Barnett is General Secretary of the New Zealand Labour Party. He was a Member of Parliament from 1996 to 2008, representing the Christchurch Central electorate, and serving as Senior Government Whip following the 2005 election until his retirement from Parliament in 2008. He was appointed Global Programmes Manager for the World AIDS Campaign in February 2009 and was based in South Africa until his return to New Zealand in July 2012 to take up his position with the Labour Party. His article 'Moral Leadership from the Back Benches', providing an analysis of what backbench MPs are capable of accomplishing (based on his own experience with two landmark pieces of legislation, the Prostitution Reform Act 2003 and the Civil Union Act 2004), was published in a special issue of *Political Science*, 'Leadership in New Zealand' (volume 56, December 2004), now available online from the SAGE website.

Matthew Beveridge is a graduate student at Massey University and creator of the *Social Media & the 2014 General Election* blog. His Master's thesis topic is the use of Twitter by political parties and candidates during the 2014 New Zealand general election.

David Carter is Speaker of the New Zealand House of Representatives. He was elected to that position in January 2013 and was re-elected following the 2014 election. He has been a National Party Member of Parliament since 1994 and has served in various ministerial roles, first as Minister for Senior Citizens in the National-led government of Prime Minister Jenny Shipley, and subsequently as Minister for Biosecurity, Minister of Forestry and Minister of Agriculture (2008–11), Minister for Primary Industries (2011–13) and Minister for Local Government (2012–13) during the National-led government of Prime Minister John Key. His foreword to this book is an edited version of his introductory remarks at the opening of the December 2014 post-election conference held in the Legislative Council Chamber in New Zealand's Parliament Buildings.

Stephen Church has a PhD in political science from the University of Canterbury, his doctoral dissertation winning a Wallace Award from the New Zealand Electoral Commission for its contribution to the understanding of party and electoral systems. As a research fellow at Victoria University of Wellington he co-edited (and contributed to) two of the books in this series of election studies, *Left Turn: The New Zealand General Election of 1999* and *New Zealand Votes: The General Election of 2002*. He has since served in a number of advisory roles in Parliament, including most recently as senior ministerial advisor to Simon Power until the minister's retirement from Parliament in November 2011, and is currently working as a freelance consultant. His chapter on post-2011 government formation – 'The post-election government: formation, "FOMOs" and "frenemies"' – was published in *Kicking the Tyres: The New Zealand General Election and Electoral Referendum of 2011*.

Jane Clifton is a political columnist for *The Listener* and for Wellington's *Dominion Post* newspaper. Her witty and insightful observations of New Zealand's parliamentary personalities led in 2005 to publication of her first book, *Political Animals: Confessions of a Parliamentary Zoologist*. In similar spirit she contributed a chapter entitled 'More Political Animals', reflecting on the personalities involved in New Zealand's 2005 election campaign, to *The Baubles of Office: The New Zealand General Election of 2005*. In August 2011 she offered her thoughts on New Zealand's politicians as orators at the 'political rhetoric' conference opened by the Speaker, Dr the Rt Hon Lockwood Smith, at Parliament's Legislative Council Chamber. Her chapter, 'The media in 2011: complicity in an inane campaign', was published in *Kicking the Tyres: The New Zealand General Election and Electoral Referendum of 2011*.

Peter Dunne, leader and co-founder of the United Future Party and Member of Parliament for Ōhāriu, was first elected to Parliament in 1984 and, with eleven successive election victories, is one of the longest-serving Members in the history of the New Zealand House of Representatives. He first served as a minister in a Labour government and subsequently in both Labour- and National-led governments. He was appointed Minister of Revenue and Associate Minister of Health following the 2008 election. He was reappointed to these positions (as well as Associate Minister of Conservation) following the 2011 election. He is Minister of Internal Affairs, Associate Minister of Health and Associate Minister of Conservation in the government formed following the 2014 election. He has contributed to two previous books in this series, writing on United Future's 2005 election campaign (in *The Baubles of Office: The New Zealand General Election of 2005*) and on the party's 2011 campaign (in *Kicking the Tyres: The New Zealand General Election and Electoral Referendum of 2011*).

Te Ururoa Flavell was chosen co-leader of the Māori Party on 13 July 2013. He was first elected to Parliament in 2005 and has now won four consecutive elections as the MP for Waiariki. He is Minister for Māori Development, Minister for Whānau Ora, and Associate Minister for Economic Development in the government formed following the 2014 election. Trained as a teacher, he held a number of roles in the education sector, including school principal, and CEO of Te Whare Wānanga o Awanuiārangi (Whakatāne). He has also been a consultant to several government agencies prior to his election to Parliament.

Morgan Godfery studied law and political science at Victoria University of Wellington. He has appeared on New Zealand television and in other media as a commentator on various aspects of Māori politics, both during and subsequent to both the 2011 and 2014 elections. He contributed a chapter on 'The fragmentation of Māori politics' to *Kicking the Tyres: The New Zealand General Election and Electoral Referendum of 2011* and is a columnist for *Overland Literary Journal* in Australia.

Corin Higgs is a political science graduate from Victoria University of Wellington, where he was awarded several prizes for his academic achievements. In 2014 he completed his Master's thesis on New Zealand's Consumers Price Index. In 2011 he assisted Television New Zealand's election coverage, assembling its in-house guide to the election – the parties, the candidates, the issues and the electorates. Prior to the 2014 election he was a researcher at the New Zealand Parliament and he is presently a political consultant. His contributions to *Kicking the Tyres: The New Zealand General Election and Electoral Referendum of 2011* were two-fold: he wrote the chapter '"Show me the tea": media narratives, television punditry and the 2011 election campaign', and compiled the contents of the DVD which accompanied the book.

Colin James is among New Zealand's most experienced political journalists. He has edited and written numerous books, including *The Quiet Revolution: Turbulence and Transition in Contemporary New Zealand* and *New Territory: The Transformation of New Zealand, 1984–92*, as well as three on New Zealand elections. He contributed chapters to post-election books on the 1987, 1990 and 1993 elections and to the six previous MMP election books in this series: 'Policies, Issues and Manifestos' (*From Campaign to Coalition*, 1997); 'Assessing the Issues' (*Left Turn*, 2000); 'Two Million Voters in Search of a Rationale' (*New Zealand Votes*, 2003); 'A Contest of Values or a Contest of Wills? Factors and Issues in the 2005 Election' (*The Baubles of Office*, 2007); '2008: The last baby-boomer election' (*Key to Victory*, 2010); and 'On a wing and a smile: political transition in National's business-as-usual re-election' (*Kicking the Tyres*, 2012). In 2008 he was awarded an honorary doctorate from Victoria University of Wellington.

Jon Johansson is a senior lecturer in political science and international relations at Victoria University of Wellington. In 2011 he contributed an introduction to a new edition of Professor Leslie Lipson's classic study of New Zealand government and politics, *The Politics of Equality: New Zealand's Adventures in Democracy*, first published in 1948, and was instrumental in bringing the book back into print. Dr Johansson's *The Politics of Possibility: Leadership in Changing Times* – a study of cycles of political leadership in New Zealand politics, including a focus on challenges and opportunities facing John Key and his government – was published in August 2009, and he is also the author of *Two Titans: Muldoon, Lange and Leadership*, which was published in 2005, as well as editor of a special issue on 'Political Leadership in New Zealand' for *Political Science*. He has contributed to four previous books in this series: 'Leadership and the Campaign', in *New Zealand Votes: The New Zealand General Election of 2002*; 'Brash, Owera and the Politics of Race' in *The Baubles of Office: The New Zealand General Election of 2005*; '2008: Leadership during transition' in *Key to Victory: The New Zealand General Election of 2008*; and 'Leadership and ambivalence: words, deeds and the 2011 election' in *Kicking the Tyres: The New Zealand General Election and Electoral Referendum of 2011* (which he co-edited). In 2014 his book *US Leadership in Political Time and Space: Pathfinders, Patriots, and Existential Heroes* was published by Palgrave Macmillan.

Steven Joyce was first elected to Parliament in 2008 and was immediately appointed to Cabinet, serving as Minister of Transport and Minister for Communications and Information Technology (as well as Associate Minister of Finance and Associate Minister for Infrastructure). He was re-elected in 2011 and was reappointed to Cabinet (ranked fourth) with several new ministerial responsibilities. Ranked fourth following the 2014 election, his ministerial portfolios are listed in Appendix 5. He led the 2003 constitutional changes for the National Party; was the party's campaign director at the 2005, 2008, 2011 and 2014 elections; and contributed chapters on National's campaigns to three previous books in this series of election studies: *The Baubles of Office: The New Zealand General Election of 2005*; *Key to Victory: The New Zealand General Election of 2008*; and *Kicking the Tyres: The New Zealand General Election and Electoral Referendum of 2011*.

Nicola Kean is a producer of the New Zealand politics and current affairs programme, *The Nation*, broadcast on TV3. She is a BA (Honours) graduate in political science at Victoria University of Wellington, where she won awards as the political science and international relations programme's top student at three stages of her academic career. Winner of a Fulbright Graduate Award, in 2011 she received a Master of Science degree from Columbia University's Graduate School of Journalism. She contributed a chapter on 'The campaign in cyberspace' in *Key to Victory: The New Zealand General Election of 2008*.

John Key is in his third term as New Zealand's Prime Minister. He became Leader of the New Zealand National Party in November 2006, having been elected a Member of Parliament for the Helensville electorate at the July 2002 general election, and he became Prime Minister after the 2008 election. He worked as a foreign exchange dealer prior to service in Parliament, including positions at Merrill Lynch as head of Asian foreign exchange and, subsequently, global head of foreign exchange. His chapter in this book was presented as the keynote speech at the 2014 post-election conference held in December 2014 in the Legislative Council Chamber in New Zealand's Parliament Buildings.

Stephen Levine is a professor of political science at Victoria University of Wellington. He is founder of VUW's parliamentary internship programme and has written extensively about New Zealand's politics, elections and international relations. He has co-edited (and contributed to) books about each of New Zealand's elections under MMP and was director of the New Zealand Political Change Project (1995–2003), examining the impact of MMP on New Zealand's government and politics. In 2009 he was recognised in the Queen's Birthday Honours List for 'services to education and the Jewish community' and appointed an Officer of the New Zealand Order of Merit. He served as co-editor of the New Zealand Ministry of Culture and Heritage's theme issue, 'Government and Nation', launched by the Governor-General in June 2012 as part of New Zealand's national online encyclopedia, *Te Ara*.

Andrew Little was elected Leader of the New Zealand Labour Party in November 2014 following the 2014 general election. He was first elected a Member of Parliament at the 2011 election. Prior to parliamentary service he was national secretary of the Engineering, Printing and Manufacturing Union and he served as president of the New Zealand Labour Party from 2009 to 2011.

Kate McMillan is a senior lecturer in Political Science at Victoria University of Wellington. One of her areas of specialisation is the news media's political role in New Zealand. She is co-editor of *Politics and the Media* (Pearson Education, 2013) and author of the 'Politics and the Media in New Zealand' entry in the Ministry for Culture and Heritage's 'Government and Nation' theme issue of *Te Ara,* the online encyclopaedia (2012). She has also lectured and published on radio's role in New Zealand politics, on women's representation and participation in the news media, and on matters relating to immigration and citizenship. Between 2010 and 2015 she was co-editor of *Political Science*, New Zealand's scholarly journal of political science and international relations, published by SAGE. Her previous contribution to this series, 'Winning the Metadebate: New Zealand's 2005 Televised Leaders' Debates in Comparative Perspective', was published in *The Baubles of Office: The New Zealand General Election of 2005.*

Stephen Mills is Executive Director of UMR Research, an Australasian issue management market research company founded in 1987. UMR has worked on scores of political campaigns in Australasia and Southeast Asia. Stephen Mills has personally worked on over 50 election campaigns in Australia and New Zealand, including as lead researcher for the Australian Labor Party in Queensland in its unexpected victory in February 2015 over the state's Liberal National Party government. He has written numerous op-ed features drawing attention to the political implications of UMR survey findings. Prior to joining UMR he served as a senior political advisor to Prime Minister David Lange and, following Lange's resignation, to Deputy Prime Minister Helen Clark.

Russel Norman first entered Parliament in 2008. He became co-leader of the Green Party in June 2006 (following the death of the party's co-leader Rod Donald MP). In January 2015 he announced that he would be retiring from the co-leadership position, as of May 2015. His chapter 'The Greens – The Campaign and its Challenges', written when he was the Green Party's campaign director, was published in *The Baubles of Office: The New Zealand General Election of 2005.*

Winston Peters, leader and co-founder of the New Zealand First Party, was first elected to Parliament in 1978. He has served as a minister under both National and Labour prime ministers. Following the first MMP election (in 1996) he became Deputy Prime Minister (and Treasurer) as part of a National-led government. After the 2005 election he was appointed Minister of Foreign Affairs, holding the position (as the first Māori to do so) until the Labour-led government was defeated at the November 2008 election. He was re-elected to Parliament in 2011 and 2014, and on 28 March 2015 he won a by-election victory to become MP for Northland. He is co-author of the chapter on New Zealand First's 2011 campaign, published in *Kicking the Tyres: The New Zealand General Election and Electoral Referendum of 2011*.

Nigel S. Roberts was a professor of political science at Victoria University of Wellington until his retirement from the university in 2010. An experienced observer of New Zealand elections, he was frequently seen on New Zealand television as an election night commentator (from 1987 through 2008) and prior to that he was an election night commentator for Radio New Zealand (from 1975 to 1984). He has written extensively on New Zealand politics and elections, and co-edited books about New Zealand's first five elections under MMP (1996–2008). He has won four Wallace Awards from New Zealand's Electoral Commission for his 'contribution to public understanding of electoral matters'. In 2010 he was recognised in the Queen's Birthday Honours List for 'services to education' and appointed an Officer of the New Zealand Order of Merit. He served as co-editor of the New Zealand Ministry of Culture and Heritage's theme issue, 'Government and Nation', launched in June 2012 as part of New Zealand's national online encyclopedia, *Te Ara*. He was an expert advisor to the New Zealand Electoral Commission prior to the 2011 electoral referendum and subsequently, in connection with the post-referendum review. In 2013 he was honoured by Victoria University of Wellington through appointment as emeritus professor of political science.

Rob Salmond is owner of Polity, an analytics and communications firm based in Wellington. He was assistant professor of political science at the University of Michigan from 2007 to 2012 and has also lectured in comparative politics in Victoria University's political science and international relations programme. He has held positions in the Ministry of Foreign Affairs and Trade, the Office of the Prime Minister (2007, under Prime Minister Helen Clark) and in Parliament (as political director for Labour leader David Shearer, 2013). He has contributed to every post-election book in this series since 2002, writing on a wide range of topics, including candidate selection (2002), blogs (2005), YouTube (2008), opinion polls and prediction markets (2008 and 2011), and New Zealand's experience with MMP (2005). His first book, published in 2011, is *The New New Zealand Tax System*, and he has contributed studies on legislative and electoral politics to various academic journals, including *Legislative Studies Quarterly*, *The Journal of Legislative Studies*, *Gender & Politics*, *Political Science* and *PS: Political Science and Politics*.

David Seymour is Leader of the ACT Party. Elected to Parliament in September 2014, he represents the Epsom electorate. A new MP and party leader, he was appointed to the government led by Prime Minister John Key, serving as

Parliamentary Under-Secretary to the Minister of Education and to the Minister for Regulatory Reform. Prior to his election to Parliament he was a policy analyst for a Canadian public policy think tank, the Frontier Centre for Public Policy, and for the Manning Foundation. By training David is an electrical engineer, one of only two engineers in Parliament.

Chris Slane regularly provides political cartoons for *The Listener* and provided the cartoon imagery (front cover and spine) for the previous book in this series, *Kicking the Tyres: The New Zealand General Election and Electoral Referendum of 2011*. In 2015 he was named 'Cartoonist of the Year' at New Zealand's Canon Media Awards.

David Talbot served as Campaign Manager for the New Zealand Labour Party during the 2014 general election. He studied Law and Philosophy at the University of Otago and stood as the Clutha-Southland candidate for Labour in 2005 (against incumbent MP and former National Party leader Bill English). Following the election he took up a position as an organiser with the Labour Party Head Office in Wellington, remaining there for several years before taking up a position in Parliament working in communications for Labour leaders Phil Goff and David Shearer. Subsequently he worked in London as Campaigns Director for the UK's version of the people-powered campaign organisation Moveon.org, known in Britain as 38 Degrees – the angle at which a human-triggered avalanche is most likely to occur. He is presently a Research Director at UMR Research.

93, 120, 132, 138–139, 155; preferred Prime
Minister, 271, 303; *see also* research
Port Hills electorate, 329
post-election conference: John Key's speech at, 17,
26, 117–122; leaders at, 17–19; Rt Hon David
Carter's introduction to, 11–12, 24
post-election period: ACT in, 65–66;
Conservative Party in, 64–65; government
formation in, 104–108; Green Party in,
63–64; Internet Mana Party in, 67–68; John
Key in, 69; Labour party in, 61–63; Māori
Party in, 66–67; National Party in, 61, 104;
new MPs' speeches, 69; New Zealand First
in, 64; opposition formation in, 104; United
Future in, 66
Power, Simon, 98
Prebble, Richard, 107n9, 169
prison work, National Party policy regarding,
290–291
privacy and global politics, 74
privatisation: 1984 election and, 71; National
Party policy regarding, 89, 100, 328; New
Zealand First policy regarding, 43
property sales to foreign buyers, 75, 83, 90
'Putting people first' (Labour pamphlet), 40

Rangitata electorate: controversy in, 38–39;
results, 54
Rankin, Christine, 65
Rātana movement, 81, 262
'Rawshark' leaks, 197–198, 210, 212, 218–219
referendums held and proposed: flag, 102,
327–329; MMP, 88, 108, 327; state-owned
assets, 100–101, 150, 328
regulation, National Party policy regarding,
82–83, 89
research: ACT Party strategy and, 169; Labour
Party strategy and, 135–136, 138–139, 144,
246; Māori Party strategy and, 161; National
Party strategy and, 123; survey findings,
264–286; 'Vote Compass', 194–195; *see also*
polls
results, 50–55, 264–286; 2011 and 2014 party
vote comparison, 50, 52, 306, 311–312; ACT
Party, 52, 55–56, 80–81, 264, 310–314;
Budget's influence on, 268–270; Conservative
Party, 52, 57–58, 88, 95, 264, 311–314;
economy and, 268–271; Green Party, 52, 58–
59, 85, 88–89, 92–93, 147, 264, 269, 310–314;
Internet Mana Party, 52, 59, 264, 310–314;

Labour Party, 52, 58, 84, 88–89, 92, 134, 142,
264, 266–271, 272–274, 304–310; Mana
Party, 52, 310–314; Māori Party, 52, 59–60,
264; National Party, 52, 60–61, 88, 264,
266–274, 304–310; New Zealand First, 52, 60,
88–89, 153, 156, 264; political blocs, 281–282,
301; preferred Prime Minister, 271; public
mood, 266–267; survey findings, 264–286;
United Future, 52, 56, 81, 264, 310–314
retirement age, 134, 155
Rich, Katherine, 219, 227
Robertson, Grant, 54, 63, 84–85, 91n3, 205–206
'RockEnrol', 195
Roughan, John, 92n4, 200–201
Rowling, Bill, 43n13, 63, 91
Rurawhe, Adrian, 257–260
Russia, 73
Ryall, Tony, 53n25, 76, 83

Sabin, Mike, 61, 109n10, 157n2
Salesa, Jenny, 143
Savage, Michael Joseph, 92n4, 325
security: GCSB, 139, 215; National Party policy
regarding, 83
Security Council membership: ACT Party
opposition to, 47; winning of, 102
Security Intelligence Service, 83, 95, 150, 201,
217, 223n5, 231, 235, 277–278
Seeds of Distrust (book), 275
'selfies', John Key's use of, 196–197
Selwyn electorate: controversy in, 38–39; results,
54, 329
Sepuloni, Carmel, 53, 85, 143, 308n3
Serious Fraud Office, 95, 198, 218–219, 223n5,
224
Seymour, David, 45, 55, 56, 65–66, 68, 81, 111,
119, 317; campaign, reflection on, 168–174;
confidence and supply agreement and,
377–380; as Parliamentary Under Secretary,
61, 378, 396; *see also* ACT Party; Epsom
electorate
Sharples, Pita, 19, 59, 93, 119, 142, 167, 259, 327
Shaw, James, 64, 68, 86
Shearer, David, 17, 29, 58, 62, 78, 92, 211, 271,
303
Shipley, Jenny, 92n4, 96, 324–325
'Shylock' controversy, 38
Slater, Cameron: 'Chaos and Mayhem', 214;
corporate lobbyists and, 218, 227, 230;
defamation, 220; John Key and, 83, 230–231;

The DVD which accompanies *Moments of Truth* includes a diverse assortment of items – many of them referred to in various chapters – from the 2014 New Zealand election campaign. The DVD begins with the broadcast campaign statements of political parties, large and small. Party commercials come next, followed by footage of the leaders' debates. A selection of photographs of parties' and candidates' campaign hoardings follows as the next segment. Supplementing the book's chapters in the fifth section is a montage of items chronicling the election year, including the 'dirty politics' controversy and the 'moment of truth' event, election round-ups from commentators Patrick Gower and Brook Sabin, election night statements from the Prime Minister and other party leaders, and Labour leader David Cunliffe's post-election resignation statement. The DVD's final section includes election documents, with political party policy statements and a post-election report from New Zealand's Electoral Commission. Overall, the DVD provides a remarkable resource, enormously informative, communicating much of the flavour of an unusual and lively election campaign.

The DVD is divided into six sections:

1. Party statements.

2. Commercials.

3. Debates.

4. Campaign Hoardings.

5. Campaign Footage.

6. Election Documents.